Contents

1. Number Revisited   1

2. Algebra 1   24

3. Sets   40

4. Factors   53

5. Bills – Interest – Income Tax   63

6. Perimeter – Area – Volume   83

7. Statistics 1: Collecting Data   107

8. Probability   119

9. Statistics 2: Measures of Average and Spread   141

10. Geometry 1: Triangles and Quadrilaterals   162

11. Time and Speed   183

12. Simultaneous Equations   192

13. Quadratic Equations   201

14. Coordinate Geometry: The Line   208

15. Statistics 3: Presenting Data   233

16. Indices – Scientific Notation – Reciprocals   259

17. Circles and Cylinders   274

18. Geometry 2: Triangles and Circles   289

19. Patterns and Sequences ✓   308

20. Algebra 2: Inequalities – Algebraic Fractions   331

21. Functions   347

22. Graphing Functions   359

23. Trigonometry   374

24. Drawing and Interpreting Real-life Graphs   394

25. Geometry 3: Transformations – Constructions   410

Answers   430

Project Maths

2015 ONWARDS

Text & Tests 2

Junior Certificate Ordinary Level Maths
Strands 1–5

O. D. Morris · Paul Cooke · Paul Behan

The Celtic Press

Acknowledgements
I would like to express my deep gratitude to Aidan Raleigh and Declan Muldoon for
their invaluable advice at all stages of the production of this book.

First published in 2012 by
The Celtic Press
Ground Floor – Block B
Liffey Valley Office Campus
Dublin 22

This reprint: January 2018

ISBN: 978-1-907705-26-7

Design: Identikit Design
Layout and artwork: Tech-Set Limited, Gateshead

Preface

Text & Tests 2 – Junior Certificate Ordinary Level was compiled and written as a two-year course in mathematics for students starting second-year in second-level schools. It follows on from **Text & Tests 1 – Common Introductory Course** which students will have used in first-year. It contains **all five strands** of the **Project Maths Syllabus** for Junior Cycle. The book reflects the overall approach to the teaching of mathematics as envisaged in *Project Maths*. It encourages not only the development of the students' mathematical knowledge and skills but also the understanding needed for continuing their learning of mathematics.

The greater emphasis on the understanding of maths is achieved through the use of well-structured questions and diagrams which lead the student to appreciate the connection and relationship between algebra and graphs. The large selection of real-life problems and graphs will help students appreciate that maths is part of their everyday lives.

The book contains a wide variety of problems, from the basic to the advanced, to cater for a range of student abilities and interests. Every effort has been made to contextualise problems so that students can see everyday uses and practical applications of the mathematics they are studying.

The motivating and stimulating full-colour design, together with the large number of well-constructed diagrams, should help the student's understanding of the topic being studied. At the beginning of each chapter, there is a list of *Key Words* that students are expected to know and understand when the chapter is completed. Each chapter concludes with a blue-coloured *Test Yourself* section which provides comprehensive consolidation and revision.

A large selection of **digital resources** as well as the **e-Book** will be available online to teachers using this book.

O.D. Morris
Paul Cooke
Paul Behan
July 2012

Number Revisited

Key words

factor **highest common factor (HCF)** **multiple** **lowest common multiple (LCM)**
prime number **integer** **proper fraction** **improper fraction** **mixed number**
equivalent fractions **decimal** **percentage** **ratio** **proportion**

Section 1.1 Natural numbers

The **natural numbers** are the counting numbers 1, 2, 3, 4, 5, 6, …
Since there is no largest number, we say that the set is **infinite**.

The natural numbers are represented on the number line by dots :

The **factors** of a natural number are all the whole natural numbers which divide into it, leaving no remainder.

The factors of 12 are 1, 2, 3, 4, 6 and 12.

The **HCF (highest common factor)** of two or more natural numbers is the largest factor that is common to all of them.

Example 1

Find the HCF of 24 and 40.

The factors of 24 are: 1, 2, 3, 4, 6, 8, 12, 24.
The factors of 40 are: 1, 2, 4, 5, 8, 10, 20, 40.
The HCF of 24 and 40 is 8.

Multiples

The **multiples** of a number are obtained by multiplying it by 1, 2, 3, 4, … .
The multiples of 8 are 8, 16, 24, 32, 40, 48, …
The multiples of 10 are 10, 20, 30, 40, 50, 60, …

As seen above, the **lowest common multiple (LCM)** of 8 and 10 is 40.
The lowest common multiple of any two numbers is the **smallest** multiple which is common to both of them.

Prime numbers

A **prime number** is a natural number which has only two factors, itself and 1.
The first seven prime numbers are: 2, 3, 5, 7, 11, 13, 17, …

Note: The number 4, for example, is not prime as it has three factors, 1, 2 and 4.

Example 2

Express 72 as a product of its prime factors.

2	72
2	36
2	18
3	9
3	3
	1

72 expressed as a product of its prime factor is

$2 \times 2 \times 2 \times 3 \times 3$.

This can be written as $2^3 \times 3^2$.

Exercise 1.1

1. State whether each of these numbers is a natural number:
   (i) 6   (ii) -4 (iii) $3\frac{1}{2}$ (iv) 0.5   (v) 0   (vi) 23

2. Write the first six multiples of 5.

3. (i) Write the first eight multiples of 6.
   (ii) Write the first eight multiples of 7.
   (iii) What is the lowest common multiple of 6 and 7?

4. Write down all the factors of each of these numbers:
   (i) 28   (ii) 30   (iii) 45   (iv) 60   (v) 72.

5. Find the highest common factor (HCF) of
   (i) 12 and 18   (ii) 24 and 30   (iii) 36 and 64   (iv) 20, 24 and 36.

6. Write down the three multiples of 6 that are between 50 and 70.

7. (i) Write down the first ten prime numbers.
   (ii) Explain why there is only one even prime number.

8. Which of these numbers are prime?

    (i) 13   (ii) 21   (iii) 23   (iv) 31   (v) 39   (vi) 53

9. Write each of these numbers as a product of its prime factors :

    (i) 24   (ii) 36   (iii) 42   (iv) 66   (v) 100

10. Write three two-digit prime numbers which, when their digits are reversed, are also prime. (Exclude 11.)

11. Find two prime numbers with a sum of 46 and a difference of 12.

12. The lowest common multiple of two numbers is 24.
    What could these numbers be?

13. Find three numbers whose lowest common multiple is 36.

14. Three bells chime at intervals of 4, 5 and 6 seconds respectively.
    If they all chime at the same instant, how long before they all chime together again?

15. | P | Q | R | S | is a four-digit number.

    Find the number given the following clues :
    Clue 1 :   All the digits are different.
    Clue 2 :   The product of the digits R and S equals digit P.
    Clue 3 :   Digit Q is one more than P.
    Clue 4 :   The sum of all the digits is 18.
    Clue 5 :   The four-digit number is divisible by 11.

Section 1.2 Integers and order of operations

The set of natural numbers, zero and negative whole numbers together form the set of integers, i.e.,

$$\ldots, -5, -4, -3, -2, -1, 0, 1, 2, 3, 4, 5, \ldots$$

We use the letter Z to represent integers.

When we show the set of integers on the number line, it will look like this :

Adding integers

1. When the signs are the same, add the numbers and retain the sign.

2. When the signs are different, retain the sign of the numerically bigger number and take the smaller number from the bigger number.

Examples :   (i) $3 + 8 - 3 - 4 = 11 - 7 = 4$

(ii) $-3 + 7 - 9 + 2 = 7 + 2 - 3 - 9$
$$= 9 - 12 = -3$$

(iii) $-6 + 13 = 7$

Multiplying and dividing integers

The rules for multiplying and dividing integers are highlighted on the right.

When multiplying or dividing integers,
> like signs give plus
> unlike signs give minus

Example 1

Write each of these as a single integer:

(i) $6 \times (-4)$ (ii) $-3 \times (-10)$ (iii) $\dfrac{-9 \times (-8)}{-12}$

(i) $6 \times (-4) = -24$ (ii) $-3 \times (-10) = 30$ (iii) $\dfrac{-9 \times (-8)}{-12} = \dfrac{72}{-12}$
$$= -6$$

Order of operations

When a calculation involves more than one operation, we need a set of rules to help us perform the operations in the correct order.

BIMDAS represents the order of operations that enables us to do the calculation correctly.

If there are **brackets** in a calculation, do the calculation inside them first.

When a calculation involves brackets as well as other operations, this is the correct order to work out the answers.

First	Second	Third	Fourth
( )	$\square^2$ or $\boxed{\sqrt{}}$	$\times$ or $\div$	$+$ or $-$

B – brackets
I – indices (powers)
M – multiplication
D – division
A – addition
S – subtraction

Example 2

Evaluate: $6 \times (2 + 7) - 2 \times 7$.

$$6 \times (2 + 7) - 2 \times 7 = 6 \times (9) - 14$$
$$= 54 - 14 = 40$$

Note: If a calculation involves a combination of multiplications and divisions, work across the line from left to right.

Exercise 1.2

1. Write each list of temperatures in order, lowest first:
   (i) $-4°C$, $3°C$, $10°C$, $-7°C$, $0°C$,
   (ii) $7.5°C$, $-5°C$, $6°C$, $-4.5°C$, $-1°C$.

2. Work out the finishing temperature in each of these:
   (i) Start at $2°C$, fall 6 degrees. (ii) Start at $-5°C$, fall 4 degrees.
   (iii) Start at $-10°C$, rise 8 degrees. (iv) Start at $2°C$, fall 12 degrees.

3. Work out each of these:
   (i) $8 - 2 - 1$ (ii) $5 - 2 - 4$ (iii) $-10 + 3 - 2$ (iv) $3 - 4 - 7$
   (v) $-3 + 10 - 9$ (vi) $-5 - 4 - 10$ (vii) $3 - 14 + 9$ (viii) $-2 - 5 + 11$

4. Work out the answers and write them in order, lowest first:
   The letters will spell the name of a car.

R	U	A	S	B	U
$12 - 7$	$-4 - 2$	$-2 + 5$	$-5 - 4$	$6 - 8$	$10 - 4$

5. From the numbers in the loop,
find two numbers which add up to
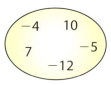
   (i) 3   (ii) −5   (iii) −16   (iv) 5.

6. Write down the answer to each of these :
   (i) $4 \times (-3)$ (ii) -3×6 (iii) $-2 \times (-3)$ (iv) -4×10
   (v) $6 \times (-20)$ (vi) $7 \times (-8)$ (vii) $2 \times 3 \times (-4)$ (viii) $-2 \times (-4) \times (-6)$

7. Copy and complete these :
   (i) $? \times (-6) = -12$ (ii) $4 \times ? = -20$ (iii) $8 \times ? = -24$
  (iv) $-6 \times ? = 42$ (v) $-7 \times ? = -56$ (vi) $? \times (-6) = -30$

8. Find the value of each of these :
   (i) $-14 \div 2$ (ii) $-28 \div (-7)$ (iii) $36 \div -4$ (iv) $-72 \div (-8)$

9. Work out the answers to the questions below.
Use the code to change them to letters.
Re-arrange the letters to spell some animals.

A	B	C	E	G	H	I	M	O	P	R	S	T	W
−12	−24	−28	−36	24	30	−18	48	20	−20	36	28	−60	−48

  (i) 4×-5 (ii) -6×4 (iii) 12×4
        3×10 9×-2 6×-6
     -6×6 3×-8 2×14
        4×7 -10×6 5×6
     -9×4 -2×6 2×18
                         4×9 -3×4
                                       15×-4

10. Evaluate each of the following :
   (i) $14 \div 2 + 3 \times 4$ (ii) $60 \div 3 \div 4 + 2$ (iii) $(16 + 4) \div 5 \times 3$
  (iv) $5 \times (4 - 3) + 9$ (v) $6 \times (2 + 7) - 2 \times 7$ (vi) $5 + 7 - 3 \times 2$
  (vii) $3 \times 15 - 6 \times 5$ (viii) $18 \div 2 \times 10 - (7 \times 8)$ (ix) $6 \times 9 + 4$

11. Insert brackets where necessary to make the following equations true :
   (i) $6 + 8 - 1 = 13$ (ii) $54 \div 6 + 3 + 2 = 8$
  (iii) $6 + 34 \div 2 + 3 \div 2 = 13$ (iv) $42 \div 5 + 2 \times 5 = 30$
  (v) $15 + 4 \times 5 - 5 = 15$ (vi) $81 \div 9 \div 2 + 1 = 3$

12. State whether each of the following is true or false :

(i) $16 \div (3 + 1) \times 3 + 6 = 36$ (ii) $(2 + 3 \times 5) - (3 + 16 \div 4) = 18$

(iii) $5 \times 10 + 3 \times 8 \div 4 = 56$ (iv) $44 \div 4 + 7 \times 2 - 3 = 5$

13. Insert the symbols $\times, \div, +, -$ to make the following equations true :

(i) $(2 \boxed{} 8) \boxed{} 5 = 2$ (ii) $(14 \boxed{} 5) \boxed{} 9 = 81$ (iii) $6 \boxed{} (8 \boxed{} 3) = 30$

(iv) $(21 \boxed{} 5) \boxed{} 2 = 13$ (v) $12 \boxed{} 8 \boxed{} 5 = 9$ (vi) $40 \boxed{} (14 \boxed{} 7) = 38$

14. Simplify each of the following :

(i) $\dfrac{53 - 21}{9 - 5}$ (ii) $\dfrac{3 \times 8 + 6}{6}$ (iii) $\dfrac{57}{7 - (2 \times 3)}$ (iv) $\dfrac{(3 + 8) - 5}{3 + (8 - 5)}$

15. (i) Choose three numbers from this set to make the highest product :

$\boxed{} \times \boxed{} \times \boxed{}$

(ii) Choose three numbers from the set to make the lowest product.

16. In this puzzle find the four numbers from this set which fit the clues.

3	4	1	6	2
-3	-4	-1	-6	-2

Clue 1   The product of the numbers in the top row is -12.
Clue 2   The sum of numbers in the left-hand column is -3.
Clue 3   The numbers in the right-hand column are multiplies of 2.
Clue 4   The sum of the numbers in the bottom row is 1.

Section 1.3 **Fractions**

A **fraction** consists of two whole numbers
– a **numerator** and a **denominator**
– separated by a bar symbol, as shown

$\dfrac{4}{5}$ $\leftarrow$ numerator
$\phantom{\dfrac{4}{5}}$ $\leftarrow$ denominator

Types of fractions

$\frac{4}{5}$ is a **proper fraction**   … as the numerator is less than the denominator

$\frac{7}{6}$ is an **improper fraction**   … as the numerator is greater than the denominator

$2\frac{3}{4}$ is a **mixed number**   … as it is really $2 + \frac{3}{4}$

$\frac{1}{2}, \frac{3}{6}$ are **equivalent fractions**   … as both fractions represent equal portions

Adding and subtracting fractions

To add (or subtract) two fractions, we convert them to two fractions with the same denominator, and then add (or subtract) the new numerators.

Example 1

Find   (i) $\frac{5}{6} + \frac{3}{4}$ (ii) $1\frac{4}{5} - 1\frac{1}{3}$

(i) $\frac{5}{6} + \frac{3}{4} = \frac{10}{12} + \frac{9}{12} = \frac{19}{12} = 1\frac{7}{12}$ … the LCM of 6 and 4 is 12

(ii) $1\frac{4}{5} - 1\frac{1}{3} = \frac{9}{5} - \frac{4}{3} = \frac{27}{15} - \frac{20}{15} = \frac{7}{15}$

Multiplying and dividing fractions

To multiply two fractions, multiply the numerators together and multiply the denominators together, and then simplify.

Examples: (i) $\frac{2}{3} \times \frac{1}{4} = \frac{2}{12} = \frac{1}{6}$

(ii) $4\frac{2}{3} \times 1\frac{1}{2} = \frac{14}{3} \times \frac{3}{2} = \frac{42}{6} = 7$

Note: An alternative method for working out (i) and (ii) is as follows:

(i) $\dfrac{\overset{1}{\cancel{2}}}{3} \times \dfrac{1}{\underset{2}{\cancel{4}}} = \dfrac{1}{6}$ (ii) $4\frac{2}{3} \times 1\frac{1}{2} = \dfrac{\overset{7}{\cancel{14}}}{\underset{1}{\cancel{3}}} \times \dfrac{\overset{1}{\cancel{3}}}{\underset{1}{\cancel{2}}} = \dfrac{7 \times 1}{1} = 7$

To **divide** by a fraction, multiply by its reciprocal.

> The reciprocal of $\frac{2}{3}$ is $\frac{3}{2}$.

Examples: (i) $2 \div \frac{3}{4} = \frac{2}{1} \times \frac{4}{3} = \frac{8}{3} = 2\frac{2}{3}$

(ii) $2\frac{1}{3} \div \frac{2}{3} = \dfrac{7}{\underset{1}{\cancel{3}}} \times \dfrac{\overset{1}{\cancel{3}}}{2} = \dfrac{7 \times 1}{1 \times 2} = \dfrac{7}{2} = 3\frac{1}{2}$

Example 2

If $\frac{7}{8}$ of a number is 56, find the number.

$\frac{7}{8}$ of the number $= 63$

$\frac{1}{8} = \frac{63}{7} = 9$ ... ÷ by 7

$\frac{8}{8} = 9 \times 8 = 72$

∴ the number is 72

Exercise 1.3

1. Copy and complete each statement:

(i) $\frac{1}{2} = \frac{\square}{10}$ (ii) $\frac{1}{4} = \frac{\square}{12}$ (iii) $\frac{2}{5} = \frac{\square}{20}$ (i) $\frac{2}{3} = \frac{4}{\square}$

2. Write these fractions in their simplest form:

(i) $\frac{4}{8}$ (ii) $\frac{10}{15}$ (iii) $\frac{21}{28}$ (iv) $\frac{15}{25}$ (v) $\frac{15}{21}$

3. Convert these mixed numbers to improper fractions:

(i) $1\frac{2}{3}$ (ii) $2\frac{5}{8}$ (iii) $3\frac{3}{4}$ (iv) $5\frac{3}{5}$ (v) $7\frac{5}{8}$

4. Convert these improper fractions to mixed numbers, simplifying where possible:

(i) $\frac{8}{5}$ ii) $\frac{23}{4}$ (iii) $\frac{16}{7}$ (iv) $\frac{26}{8}$ (v) $\frac{39}{6}$

5. Which of these fractions is the largest? $\frac{17}{4}$ $\frac{13}{10}$ $\frac{18}{5}$ $\frac{9}{2}$

6. Arrange these fractions in order of size, smallest first.

$\frac{11}{4}$ $\frac{15}{5}$ $\frac{17}{10}$ $\frac{10}{3}$ $\frac{8}{7}$

7. Add each of these, giving your answer in its lowest terms:

(i) $\frac{4}{7} + \frac{2}{7}$ (ii) $\frac{2}{9} + \frac{4}{9}$ (iii) $\frac{8}{15} - \frac{2}{15}$ (iv) $\frac{13}{24} - \frac{7}{24}$

8. Find the lowest common denominator for each pair of fractions:

(i) $\frac{5}{6}$ and $\frac{2}{3}$ (ii) $\frac{3}{4}$ and $\frac{5}{6}$ (iii) $\frac{1}{6}$ and $\frac{4}{9}$ (iv) $\frac{7}{12}$ and $\frac{3}{8}$

9. Work out each of these, simplifying your answers where possible :

(i) $\frac{1}{5} + \frac{7}{10}$ (ii) $\frac{3}{8} + \frac{1}{4}$ (iii) $\frac{5}{12} + \frac{1}{6}$ (iv) $\frac{3}{4} + \frac{2}{3}$

(v) $\frac{1}{6} + \frac{5}{9}$ (vi) $\frac{2}{5} + \frac{2}{3}$ (vii) $\frac{6}{7} + \frac{1}{4}$ (viii) $\frac{4}{9} + \frac{5}{12}$

10. Work out each of these. Express each answer in its simplest form :

(i) $\frac{11}{12} - \frac{5}{6}$ (ii) $\frac{4}{5} - \frac{3}{8}$ (iii) $\frac{5}{6} - \frac{3}{5}$ (iv) $\frac{6}{7} - \frac{4}{21}$

11. Arrange these fractions in order, starting with the smallest each time :

(i) $\frac{1}{2}$ $\frac{1}{4}$ $\frac{2}{5}$ $\frac{1}{10}$ $\frac{3}{5}$ (ii) $\frac{5}{8}$ $\frac{3}{4}$ $\frac{5}{6}$ $\frac{2}{3}$ $\frac{7}{12}$ $\frac{17}{24}$

12. Simplify each of these :

(i) $2\frac{2}{3} + 1\frac{1}{4}$ (ii) $2\frac{4}{5} + 1\frac{1}{2}$ (iii) $5\frac{1}{2} + \frac{7}{10}$ (iv) $2\frac{5}{6} + 1\frac{3}{4}$

(v) $2\frac{4}{5} - 1\frac{1}{2}$ (vi) $2\frac{2}{3} - \frac{3}{5}$ (vii) $1\frac{3}{8} - \frac{3}{4}$ (viii) $5\frac{5}{6} - 3\frac{2}{3}$

13. Work these out, simplifying your answer where possible :

(i) $\frac{5}{6} \times \frac{3}{4}$ (ii) $\frac{4}{7} \times \frac{1}{2}$ (iii) $\frac{2}{3} \times \frac{9}{14}$ (iv) $\frac{5}{6} \times \frac{2}{15}$

14. Simplify each of these :

(i) $\frac{2}{7} \times 14$ (ii) $\frac{5}{7} \times 35$ (iii) $1\frac{1}{9} \times 18$ (iv) $\frac{7}{12} \times 36$

15. Work out each of these :

(i) $2\frac{1}{4} \times \frac{2}{3}$ (ii) $2\frac{1}{2} \times 1\frac{5}{7}$ (iii) $1\frac{2}{3} \times \frac{6}{11}$ (iv) $3\frac{2}{3} \times 2\frac{1}{4}$

16. Simplify each of these :

(i) $\frac{5}{6} \div \frac{2}{3}$ (ii) $\frac{7}{12} \div \frac{1}{6}$ (iii) $\frac{9}{10} \div \frac{3}{4}$ (iv) $\frac{7}{10} \div \frac{4}{5}$

(v) $3\frac{1}{2} \div \frac{3}{4}$ (vi) $10 \div 1\frac{2}{3}$ (vii) $4\frac{1}{2} \div 3$ (viii) $\frac{6}{7} \div 1\frac{2}{3}$

17. Work out each of these :

(i) $1\frac{1}{8} \div 2\frac{1}{4}$ (ii) $8\frac{1}{4} \div 1\frac{3}{8}$ (iii) $3\frac{1}{8} \div 3\frac{3}{4}$ (iv) $4\frac{2}{3} \div 1\frac{7}{9}$

18. Which is the larger in each pair? Show your working.

(i) $\frac{2}{3}$ of 81 or $\frac{11}{12}$ of 60 (ii) $\frac{3}{4}$ of 24 or $\frac{2}{3}$ of 27.

19. (i) Match each calculation to a diagram.

(ii) Work out the result of each calculation.

20. Work out each answer and use the code to change it to a letter. Then rearrange the letters to spell a city.

S	G	R	I	O	A	D	P	W	L	E	M
$\frac{1}{12}$	$\frac{1}{10}$	$\frac{1}{9}$	$\frac{1}{8}$	$\frac{1}{6}$	$\frac{3}{16}$	$\frac{1}{5}$	$\frac{1}{4}$	$\frac{3}{8}$	$\frac{1}{2}$	$\frac{2}{5}$	$\frac{3}{4}$

$\frac{1}{2}$ of $\frac{3}{4}$ $\frac{1}{2}$ of $\frac{1}{5}$ $\frac{1}{3}$ of $1\frac{1}{2}$ $\frac{1}{8}$ of $\frac{2}{3}$ $\frac{1}{4} \times \frac{2}{3}$ $\frac{1}{4} \times \frac{3}{4}$ $\frac{1}{5} \times \frac{1}{2}$

21. Jan uses $\frac{1}{4}$ litre of milk to make a milkshake.

Which calculation gives how much milk she would need to make 10 milkshakes?

A $\frac{1}{4} + 10$ **B** $10 - \frac{1}{4}$ **C** $\frac{1}{4} \times 10$ **D** $\frac{1}{4} \div 10$

22. A year-group of 72 students was asked how they travelled to school one morning. $\frac{1}{4}$ of the year-group travelled by bicycle, $\frac{2}{9}$ by bus, $\frac{1}{3}$ on foot, and the rest by car. How many of the students travelled by car?

23. Alec's dog eats $\frac{2}{3}$ of a tin of *Butch* each day.

What is the least number of tins Alec needs to buy to feed his dog for 7 days?

24. (i) If $\frac{3}{4}$ of a number is 36, find the number.

(ii) The difference between $\frac{1}{3}$ and $\frac{1}{2}$ of a number is 14; find this number.

25. A bottle contains $1\frac{1}{2}$ litres of detergent.

Each load of washing needs $\frac{1}{20}$ of a litre.

How many loads of washing can be done using one bottle?

26. In a bag of 28 coloured counters, $\frac{1}{4}$ are red, $\frac{2}{7}$ are blue and the rest are yellow. How many of the counters are yellow?

27. Adam spent $\frac{5}{9}$ of his money. If he had €36 left, how much had he at first?

28. Which of these two rectangles has the greatest length?
Express the difference between the lengths as a fraction of a metre.

(i)

Area
$2\frac{3}{4}$ m² $1\frac{4}{7}$ m

(ii)

Area
$4\frac{2}{3}$ m² $3\frac{1}{3}$ m

29. Jane has a chocolate bar.
Jane eats $\frac{1}{3}$ of it and a friend eats $\frac{1}{4}$ of the bar.
The remaining chocolate is shared between Jane's two brothers.
What fraction of the bar does each brother get?

30. What is the largest and smallest answer that you
can make using two of the numbers from the box?
You can either multiply or divide the numbers.

$$\frac{3}{5} \qquad 1\frac{3}{4}$$
$$\frac{1}{10} \qquad 3\frac{5}{6}$$
$$\frac{1}{8} \qquad 2\frac{2}{3}$$

Section 1.4 Decimals and percentages

The number $1\frac{3}{10}$ may also be written as the decimal 1.3.

A decimal point in a number separates the whole number part from the fractional part.

The decimal $4.85 = 4 + \frac{8}{10} + \frac{5}{100}$

$$= 4 + \frac{80}{100} + \frac{5}{100} = 4\frac{85}{100}$$

Here are some more decimals converted to fractions:

(i) $0.4 = \dfrac{0.4 \times 10}{10} = \dfrac{4}{10} = \dfrac{2}{5}$

(ii) $0.65 = \dfrac{0.65 \times 100}{100} = \dfrac{65}{100}^{13}_{\ 20} = \dfrac{13}{20}$

(iii) $0.125 = \dfrac{0.125 \times 1000}{1000} = \dfrac{125}{1000} = \dfrac{1}{8}$

Adding and subtracting decimals

When adding or subtracting decimals, line up the decimal points directly beneath one another.

$$38.42$$
$$+ \ 6.08$$
$$\overline{44.50} = 44.5$$

$$15.06$$
$$-3.465$$
$$\overline{11.595}$$

Fractions to decimals

If the denominator of a fraction contains 10, 100, 1000 …, it can easily be converted to a decimal.

(i) $\frac{7}{10} = 0.7$ (ii) $\frac{67}{100} = 0.67$ (iii) $\frac{135}{1000} = 0.135$

To convert a fraction such as $\frac{3}{8}$ to a decimal, we divide 3 by 8 as shown.

$$8 \overline{)3.000}$$
$$0.375$$

∴ $\frac{3}{8} = 0.375$

 When using a calculator to convert $\frac{3}{8}$ as a decimal,

Key in $3 \boxed{\div} 8 \boxed{=}$. The answer is 0.375.

Multiplying and dividing decimals

To **multiply** 23.24 by 1.2, we first multiply 2324 by 12

$$2324$$
$$\times \quad 12$$
$$\overline{27888}$$

Count the total number of digits to the right of the decimal point in the question.
This number is 3.
Therefore, there will also be three digits after the decimal point in your answer.

Thus $23.24 \times 1.2 = 27.888$

When **dividing** a number by a decimal, change the denominator into a whole number as follows :

(i) $\dfrac{28}{0.4} = \dfrac{28 \times 10}{0.4 \times 10} = \dfrac{280}{4} = 70$

(ii) $\dfrac{115.2}{0.09} = \dfrac{115.2 \times 100}{0.09 \times 100} = \dfrac{11\,520}{9} = 1280$

Percentages

Percent means 'out of every hundred'.

$$\frac{20}{100} = 20\% \qquad \frac{80}{100} = 80\% \qquad \frac{35}{100} = 35\% \qquad \frac{6}{100} = 6\%$$

To convert a **fraction to a percentage**, multiply the fraction by 100 and add the % symbol.

(i) $\frac{1}{5} = \frac{1}{5} \times \frac{100}{1}\% = 20\%$

(ii) $\frac{3}{4} = \frac{3}{4} \times \frac{100}{1}\% = \frac{300}{4}\% = 75\%$

The diagram below shows the close relationship between decimals and percentages:

0.1 is equivalent to 10%

Example 1

(i) Express 0.46 as a percentage.

(ii) Express $\frac{11}{20}$ as a percentage.

(i) $0.46 = \frac{46}{100} = 46\%$

(ii) $\frac{11}{20} = \frac{11}{20} \times \frac{100}{1}\% = \frac{1100}{20}\% = \frac{110}{2}\% = 55\%$

Here are some useful conversion facts you should know, as they are used very frequently.

> To change a fraction or decimal to a percentage, multiply by 100 and add the % sign.

Percentage	Decimal	Fraction
1%	0.01	$\frac{1}{100}$
5%	0.05	$\frac{1}{20}$
10%	0.1	$\frac{1}{10}$
$12\frac{1}{2}\%$	0.125	$\frac{1}{8}$
20%	0.2	$\frac{1}{5}$
25%	0.25	$\frac{1}{4}$
$33\frac{1}{3}\%$	0.333 ...	$\frac{1}{3}$
50%	0.5	$\frac{1}{2}$
75%	0.75	$\frac{3}{4}$
100%	1	1

Exercise 1.4

(Do not use a calculator for this exercise.)

1. Express each of these decimals as a fraction in its simplest form :
  (i) 0.8   (ii) 0.25   (iii) 0.75   (iv) 0.35   (v) 0.05

2. Express each of these fractions as a decimal :
  (i) $\frac{7}{10}$ (ii) $\frac{65}{100}$ (iii) $\frac{87}{100}$ (iv) $\frac{5}{100}$ (v) $\frac{35}{1000}$

3. Write down the answer to each of these :
  (i) 1.6×10 (ii) 1.34×100 (iii) 1.04×100 (iv) 0.2×100

4. Work out each of these :
  (i) $74 \div 10$ (ii) $345 \div 100$ (iii) $1.5 \div 100$ (iv) $184 \div 1000$

5. Work out each of these :
  (i) $\frac{1.8}{2}$ (ii) $\frac{3.6}{0.6}$ (iii) $\frac{2.16}{0.3}$ (iv) $\frac{61.5}{5}$ (v) $\frac{8.15}{0.5}$

6. Given that $12.7 \times 7.5 = 95.25$, without doing any further multiplication, write down the answer to each of these :
  (i) 1.27×7.5 (ii) 0.127×7.5 (iii) 12.7×0.075

7. Work out each of these :
  (i) 20×0.6 (ii) 0.3×90 (iii) 0.04×30 (iv) 0.6×500
  (v) 0.3×400 (vi) 0.2×15 (vii) 0.3×0.7 (viii) 2.1×0.4

8. What decimal number does each arrow point to?

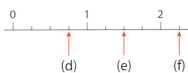

9. Change each of these percentages to a fraction in its simplest form :
  (i) 60%   (ii) 25%   (iii) 75%   (iv) 65%   (v) $12\frac{1}{2}$%

10. Work these out :
  (i) 20% of 70   (ii) 30% of 80   (iii) 75% of 36   (iv) 40% of 60

11. This pie chart shows how 120 first-year pupils travel to school.
  (i) How many children walk to school?
  (ii) How many come by car?
  (iii) How many come by bus?
  (iv) How many cycle?

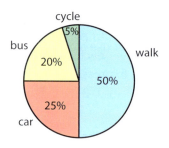

12. Work out each of these:
  (i) Increase 60 by 25%
  (ii) Increase 140 by 15%
  (iii) Decrease 75 by 20%
  (iv) Decrease 240 by $12\frac{1}{2}$%

13. Find four matching pairs that give the same answer.

10% of 40	20% of 50	50% of 6	5% of 80

30% of 10	30% of 50	25% of 40	75% of 20

14. (i) What fraction of this shape is shaded?
  (ii) What percentage of the shape is shaded?
  (iii) Copy the shape and shade in more squares so that $\frac{4}{5}$ of the shape is shaded.

15. (i) Write 15% as a decimal.
  (ii) Write $\frac{2}{5}$ as a decimal.
  (iii) Use your answers to (i) and (ii) to help you write these in order, smallest first:

  0.2   15%   0.09 $\frac{2}{5}$

16. Write each of these lists in order of size, smallest first.
  (i) 0.3   28% $\frac{1}{4}$ 0.18
  (ii) 8%   0.6 $\frac{7}{10}$ 0.55
  (iii) 78% $\frac{3}{4}$ 0.09   0.8
  (iv) $\frac{1}{2}$ 48%   0.4   0.19

17. Copy and complete this table.

Percentage	Fraction	Decimal
21%	$\frac{21}{100}$	
	$\frac{57}{100}$	
		0.41
9%		
	$\frac{3}{100}$	
		0.08

18. Ronan's test scores are given in the table.

(i) Copy and complete the table by working out Ronan's percentage score for each subject.

Subject	Score	Percentage
English	$\frac{70}{80}$	
Maths	$\frac{34}{40}$	
Geography	$\frac{28}{35}$	
Business	$\frac{54}{60}$	
Science	$\frac{56}{64}$	

(ii) In which subject did Ronan achieve his best result?

19. Dermot's garden is a rectangle measuring 15 metres by 5 metres.

(i) What is the total area of the garden?

(ii) The lawn takes up 55% of the garden. What is the area of the lawn?

(iii) A flower bed is a rectangle measuring 3 m by 2 m.
What percentage of the garden is this?

20. House prices increased by 4% in June.
In November it was reported that house prices had fallen by 4%.
A house was valued at €240 000 in May.
Work out the value of this house in December.

Section 1.5 Revision of ratio

1. Ratio

We use ratio to compare two or more quantities.
In the given figure, the ratio of green squares to yellow squares is 8:4.
The ratio 8:4 can be simplified by dividing each term by 4.
Thus, 8:4 = 2:1.
2:1 is called the **simplest form** of the ratio.

To express the ratio 15 minutes : $1\frac{1}{2}$ hours as a ratio without units, we express both parts in the same units.
Thus, 15 minutes : $1\frac{1}{2}$ hours = 15 minutes : 90 minutes = 1:6.
A ratio is normally expressed in whole numbers.
The ratio $\frac{1}{2}:\frac{3}{4}$ can be expressed in whole numbers by multiplying each term by 4, the LCM of 2 and 4.
Thus, $\frac{1}{2}:\frac{3}{4} = \frac{4}{2}:\frac{3}{4} \times \frac{4}{1} = 2:3$.

Example 1

Divide €720 between Alan and Beth in the ratio 5 : 4.

We divide €720 into nine parts, since 5 + 4 = 9.
€720 ÷ 9 = €80
Alan gets 5 parts and Beth gets 4 parts.
Alan's share = €80 × 5 = €400;   Beth's share = €80 × 4 = €320.

2. Proportion

While ratios compare one part to another part, proportion compares a part to the total.
The proportion of the given circle that is shaded red is $\frac{2}{6}$ or $\frac{1}{3}$.
Proportion is generally expressed as a fraction, decimal or percentage.

If 1 litre of petrol cost €1.60, 2 litres cost €3.20 and 3 litres cost €4.80.
Here the costs of 1 litre, 2 litres and 3 litres are in **direct proportion**.

Example 2

A car travels 78 km on 9 litres of petrol.
 (i) How far is it likely to travel on 21 litres of petrol?
 (ii) How many litres would be required for a journey of 390 km?

 (i) Here we are looking for **distance**, so we keep distance last.
    9 litres do 78 km

    1 litre does $\frac{78}{9}$ km

    21 litres do $\left(\frac{78}{9} \times \frac{21}{1}\right)$ km = 182 km.

 (ii) Here we are looking for **litres**, so we keep litres last.
    78 km require 9 litres

    1 km requires $\frac{9}{78}$ litres

    390 km require $\left(\frac{9}{78} \times \frac{390}{1}\right)$ litres = 45 litres

    ∴   A 390 km journey would require 45 litres.

Exercise 1.5

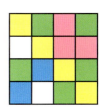

1. For this pattern of coloured squares, write down these ratios:
- (i)   green : yellow
- (ii) pink : white
- (iii) blue : green
- (iv) white : yellow.

Now write down as a fraction in its simplest form
- (v)   the proportion of the whole figure that is coloured blue
- (vi) the proportion of the whole figure that is coloured yellow
- (vii) the percentage of the whole figure that is coloured white.

2. Give each of these ratios in its simplest form:
- (i) $3 : 6$
- (ii) $4 : 12$
- (iii) $20 : 25$
- (iv) $16 : 28$
- (v) $60 : 48$
- (vi) $30 : 75$
- (vii) $35 : 63$
- (viii) $24 : 36$

3. Fill in the missing numbers so that the ratios are equivalent:
- (i) $1 : 3 = 3 : \boxed{}$
- (ii) $3 : 5 = 9 : \boxed{}$
- (iii) $2 : \boxed{} = 6 : 18$
- (iv) $\boxed{} : 7 = 4 : 14$
- (v) $12 : \boxed{} = 36 : 9$
- (vi) $7 : 3 = \boxed{} : 12$

4. Express these ratios in their simplest terms:
- (i)   15 mins : 1 hour
- (ii) 3 days : 2 weeks
- (iii) 30c : €1.50.

5. Express the following ratios as whole numbers:
- (i) $\frac{1}{2} : 2$
- (ii) $\frac{3}{4} : 1\frac{1}{2}$
- (iii) $\frac{1}{2} : \frac{1}{3}$
- (iv) $\frac{3}{4} : \frac{7}{8}$

6. The line below is divided into ten equal parts.

Find the ratios:
- (i) $\dfrac{|AB|}{|AE|}$
- (ii) $\dfrac{|AB|}{|BC|}$
- (iii) $\dfrac{|AE|}{|AB|}$
- (iv) $\dfrac{|CD|}{|CB|}$

Now write down which point divides $|AD|$
- (v) in the ratio $5 : 3$
- (vi) in the ratio $1 : 7$.

7. Express these ratios in their simplest form:
- (i)   length of rectangle A to length of rectangle B
- (ii) width of rectangle A to width of rectangle B
- (iii) area of rectangle A to area of rectangle B.

8. A pink-coloured paint is made by mixing red and white in the ratio of 1 : 5.
If the red and white paints were mixed in the ratio 1 : 8, would the paint be lighter or darker than the original?

9. A school consists of boys and girls in the ratio 4 : 3.
If there are 560 students in the school, find how many boys and girls are in the school.

10. Two brothers, Tom and Gerry, are to divide €1890 between them in the ratio 5 : 4. How much does each receive?

11. Divide €200 in the ratio 2 : 3 : 5.

12. Sand and cement are mixed together in the ratio 4 : 1.
If there are 375 kg in the mixture, how many kg of cement are in it?

13. A sum of money is divided between A and B in the ratio 3 : 2.
If A receives €840, find the sum of money.

14. This is a recipe for pastry to make 16 mince pies.
    (i) To make 24 mince pies what weight would you need of
        (a) flour (b) sugar (c) butter?
    (ii) How many egg yolks would you need for 40 mince pies?
    (iii) If a quantity of pastry contained 135 g of brown sugar, how many mince pies could be made?

Pastry for Mince Pies
(makes 16 pies)

500 g wholeweat flour
180 g brown sugar
240 g of butter (chopped)
4 egg yolks
2–3 drops of vanilla

15. If nine copies of a book cost €165.60, find the cost of four copies.

16. A car travels 40 km in 30 minutes. How far would it travel in
    (i) 10 minutes (ii) 45 minutes (iii) $2\frac{1}{2}$ hours?
    How long would it take to do a journey of 100 km?

17. A car travels 144 km on 16 litres of fuel.
    (i) How far will it travel on 1 litre?
    (ii) How far will it travel on 14 litres?
    (iii) How many litres of fuel would be needed for a journey of 90 km?

18. Adam is 12 years old and Emer is 8 years old.
€5400 is divided between them in the ratio of their ages.
How much does each receive?

In eight years time, another €5400 will be divided between them in the ratio of their ages at that time. How much will they each receive then?

19. Three quarters of the pupils in a class are boys and the rest are girls.
What is the ratio of boys to girls in the class?

20. A square has the same area as a rectangle.
The sides of the rectangle are in the ratio 9 : 4.
The perimeter of the rectangle is 130 cm.
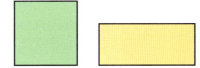
   (i)   Calculate the lengths of the sides of the rectangle.
  (ii)   Calculate the area of the rectangle.
 (iii)   Calculate the side length of the square.
 (iv)   Write down the ratio of the perimeters of the two shapes in the form perimeter of square : perimeter of rectangle.
         Give your answer in its simplest form.

Test yourself 1

1. (a) (i) Find the lowest common multiple of 8 and 12.
(ii) Find the highest common factor of 12 and 30.

(b) (i) Copy this shape and shade 20% of it.

(ii) Arrange these fractions in order, starting with the largest:
$$\frac{3}{4} \quad \frac{4}{5} \quad \frac{7}{10} \quad \frac{3}{5} \quad \frac{9}{10} \quad \frac{13}{20}$$

(c) A prize fund is divided between A, B and C in the ratio $4:3:2$ respectively. If C's share is €1224, find the total fund.

2. (a) Put these in three matching groups.

$\frac{4}{5}$ 80%   0.8   40% $\frac{4}{10}$
$\frac{3}{4}$ $\frac{2}{5}$ 75%   0.75

(b) State whether each of the following is TRUE or FALSE:
(i) $(16 + 3 \times 2) \div 11 - 1 = 1$
(ii) $15 \times 3 \div (6 + 3) + 1 = 6$
(iii) $100 \div 25 \times (6 + 2) = 26$
If the result is false, give the correct answer.

(c) Find the value of each expression when $n = -4$.
Use the code to change to letters.
Rearrange the letters to make a European country.

$4n + 2 \qquad 3n + 10 \qquad 2n \qquad n - 2$
$-6 - n \qquad n - 1 \qquad n + 2$

A	B	C	E	G
-2	-14	-12	-9	-26

I	L	M	N	U
-8	-5	1	-6	-11

3. (a) A recipe uses 12 onions to make $1\frac{1}{2}$ litres of chutney.
(i) How much chutney can be made with 48 onions?
(ii) How many onions are needed for $4\frac{1}{2}$ litres of chutney?

(b) Write each list in order, starting with the smallest:
(i) $\frac{1}{2} \quad \frac{1}{4} \quad \frac{2}{5} \quad \frac{3}{10} \quad \frac{3}{5}$
(ii) 60% $\frac{3}{4}$ $\frac{1}{2}$ $\frac{4}{5}$ 0.65 $\frac{2}{3}$

(c)

Which point divides the line [AK] in the ratio:
(i) $9:1$ (ii) $7:3$ (iii) $3:7$ (iv) $4:1$ (v) $1:4$?

4. (a) This is a recipe for 4 servings.
How much of each ingredient would
be needed for 10 servings?

> **Pancakes**
> 3 cups of flour
> 2 tsp baking powder
> $\frac{1}{4}$ litre of milk

  (b) Work out these percentages:
   (i) 40c as a percentage of €5.
   (ii) 18 minutes as a percentage of 4 hours.

  (c) In a town, the ratio of adults to children is 2 : 5.
If there are 2400 adults in the town, find its population.

5. (a) Which pair is the larger? Show your working.

$\frac{3}{4}$ of 32   or $\frac{2}{3}$ of 36

  (b) (i) A woman walks 9 km in 2 hours.
If she walks at the same pace, how far can she walk in 5 hours?

   (ii) An expedition company has lists of suggested meals.
This is a list of food for one meal for five people.

> 20 veggie sausages
> 750 g rice
> 5 litres of water

   Make a list of food they would need for seven people.

  (c) For each pair of equations below, write down which is the correct equation,
(a) or (b):
   (i) (a) $16 \div 4 + 4 = 8$ (b) $16 \div (4 + 4) = 8$
   (ii) (a) $(13 + 8) \div (3 + 4) = 3$ (b) $13 + 8 \div 3 + 4 = 3$
   (iii) (a) $81 \div 9 + 1 = 9$ (b) $81 \div 9 + 1 = 10$

  (b) A rectangle is divided into four triangles, as shown.
Find the ratio of

   smallest triangle : largest triangle.

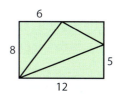

2 Algebra 1

Key words

expression   term   variable   coefficient   constant   like terms
brackets   index   indices   evaluating   linear equations
algebraic division

Section 2.1 Dealing with algebraic expressions

$2x^2 + 3x - 4$ is called an **expression**.

It consists of three **terms**.

The terms are separated by a plus $(+)$ or a minus $(-)$ sign.

The letter x is called a **variable**.

A **coefficient** is a number before a variable.

In $2x^2$, the coefficient is 2; in $3x$, the coefficient is 3.

The term -4 is known as a **constant**; it does not change.

In the expression $2x^2 + 5x - 2 + 3x + 4x^2$,

    $2x^2$ and $4x^2$ are called **like terms**;
    $5x$ and $3x$ are also like terms.

The expression $2x^2 + 5x - 2 + 3x + 4x^2$ may be simplified by combining the like terms as follows:

$$2x^2 + 5x - 2 + 3x + 4x^2$$
$$= 2x^2 + 4x^2 + 5x + 3x - 2$$
$$= 6x^2 + 8x - 2$$

Like terms only may be added or subtracted.

Example 1

Simplify   (i) $4a + 6b + 6 - 2a + b - 3$ (ii) $2x^2 - 3x - 7 - x^2 - 5x + 3$

(i) $4a + 6b + 6 - 2a + b - 3$
    $= 4a - 2a + 6b + b + 6 - 3$
    $= 2a + 7b + 3$

(ii) $2x^2 - 3x - 7 - x^2 - 5x + 3$
    $= 2x^2 - x^2 - 3x - 5x - 7 + 3$
    $= x^2 - 8x - 4$

Exercise 2.1

Simplify each of the following expressions by adding like terms:

1. $5x + 3x + 2x$

2. $4a + 5a - 2a$

3. $2a + 3b + 3a + 5b$

4. $2x + 3y + 4x - y$

5. $12a + b + 3a + 5b$

6. $3x + 2y + 3 + 4x + 3y + 1$

7. $5x - 4 + 2x + 8$

8. $7x - 4 - 3x + 7$

9. $6a + b + 3 + 2a + 2b - 1$

10. $3x + 4 + 2x - 6 + x + 3$

11. $3a - b + 4a + 5b - 2a$

12. $2ab + 4 + 3ab - 2$

13. $2p + 3q - r + p - 4q + 2r$

14. $5k + 3 - 4k + 6 + k - 4$

15. $2ab + c + 5ab - 4c$

16. $3xy + 2z + xy + 9z$

17. $6ab + 2cd - ab + 3cd$

18. $6x - xy + 5x - 7xy$

19. $10 + 13a - 7a + 2a$

20. $3x^2 + 2x + 7x^2 - x$

21. $10t + 2w - 11t - 6w$

22. $7 + 4h - 10h - 16$

23. $5m^2 + 7m + 3 - 2m^2 - 5m$

24. $6a^2 + 9a - 1 + 5a^2 - 10a$

25. $9a^2 + 6a^2 - a^2 - 10a - a$

26. $5ab - 4bc + 2ab + 3bc$

27. Write down a simplified expression for the perimeter of each shape:

(i) (ii) (iii)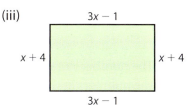

28. The number in each box is found by adding the numbers in the two boxes under it. Find the missing expressions a, b, c, d, e, f and g. Write each expression in its simplest form.

29. Work out an expression for each length marked **?**.

(i) ◄——— 4p ———►◄— 2 —►

◄——————— ? ———————►

(ii) ◄——— 6p + 2 ———►◄—— ? ——►

◄————————— 6p + 5 —————————►

(iii) ◄——x + 4——►◄—— ? ——►

◄———— 3x + 4 ————►

(iv) ◄——— 5x + 4 ———►◄—— ? ——►

◄————————— 10x + 8 —————————►

30. Here are six cards with expressions written on them:

(i) | 2x | (ii) | x − 5 | (iii) | 7 − x | (iv) | 3x + 1 | (v) | x + 3 | (vi) | 4 − 2x |

   (i) Which two cards total $4x + 4$?
  (ii) Which two cards total $x + 5$?
 (iii) Which two cards total 4?
 (iv) Which two cards total 10?
  (v) Which three cards total 12?
 (vi) Which three cards total $3x + 11$?
(vii) What is the total of all of the expressions on the cards?

31. Write out each of these with the question marks filled in:
  (i) $2a − \mathbf{?} + b + 2a = 4a − 2b$
 (ii) $2w + x − \mathbf{?} + 3x = 4x − 3w$
(iii) $3k − \mathbf{?} − j − k = 2k − 5j$
(iv) $10 − 2k + \mathbf{?} − k − 8j − \mathbf{?} = 6 − \mathbf{?} − 5j$

32. Work out an expression
for the missing length.

◄——— 2d + 10 ———►◄—— ? ——►

◄———— 12 − 3d ————►

33. The number in each box is found by adding
the numbers in the two boxes under it.
Find the missing expressions a, b and c.

34. $2x^2 + 3xy − 4x + 6$ is an expression.
  (i) Name two variables in this expression.
 (ii) What is the coefficient of x in the expression?
(iii) How many variables are in the expression?
(iv) Which term contains two variables?
(iv) What is the constant in the expression?

Section 2.2 Removing brackets

To write $3x \times 4y$ as a single term, we multiply the coefficients 3 and 4 and then multiply the variables x and y.

Thus, $3x \times 4y = 3 \times 4 \times x \times y = 12xy$.

Similarly, (i) $3a \times 6b = 18ab$ (ii) $-3p \times 4q = -12pq$.

In your study of algebra so far, you will have learned how to remove brackets as follows:

$a(b + c) = ab + ac$ Here each term inside the bracket is multiplied by a.

Similarly, (i) $5(2x + 6) = 10x + 30$
(ii) $-4(5a - 2) = -20a + 8$
(iii) $-(6x - 4) = -6x + 4$
(iv) $-(-9a + 6) = 9a - 6$.

> If there is a minus outside the brackets, the sign of each term inside the brackets is changed when the brackets are removed.

Multiplication involving indices

As 5×5 can be written as 5^2, similarly $x \times x$ is written as x^2.

Also, $a \times a \times a = a^3$

and $a^2 \times a^2 = a \times a \times a \times a = a^4$

$a^2 \times a^3 = a \times a \times a \times a \times a = a^5$

$3x(2x^2 - x + 4) = 6x^3 - 3x^2 + 12x$.

> When multiplying powers of the same number, add the indices.

Multiplying two expressions

Here is a reminder of how to multiply two expressions, each containing two terms:

$$(2x + 3)(3x - 5) = 2x(3x - 5) + 3(3x - 5)$$
$$= 6x^2 - 10x + 9x - 15$$
$$= 6x^2 - x - 15$$

Example 1

Remove the brackets and simplify:

$(2x - 3)(3x + 4)$

$$(2x - 3)(3x + 4) = 2x(3x + 4) - 3(3x + 4)$$
$$= 6x^2 + 8x - 9x - 12$$
$$= 6x^2 - x - 12$$

Exercise 2.2

1. Express each of the following as a single term by removing the multiplication sign:

(i) $3 \times 4a$ (ii) $3x \times 7$ (iii) $8 \times 2m$ (iv) $12a \times 4$

(v) $3m \times 2m$ (vi) $2p \times 3q$ (vii) $k \times 6k$ (viii) $3a \times 2b$

2. Simplify each of these:

(i) $ab \times a$ (ii) $2ab \times b$ (iii) $3ab \times 2ab$ (iv) $5cd \times 2de$

(v) $2b \times 3a$ (vi) $9a \times 2bc$ (vii) $a \times b \times c$ (viii) $2x \times 3y \times 2x$

3. Simplify these products:

(i) $(-3x) \times 5$ (ii) $7 \times (-2m)$ (iii) $(-4) \times (-3a)$

(iv) $9m \times (-3)$ (v) $(-5) \times (-6k)$ (vi) $(-7a) \times (-2)$

(vii) $(-a) \times 2b$ (viii) $(-p) \times (-q)$ (ix) $5n \times (-2m)$

(x) $(-6t) \times (-w)$ (xi) $(-8x) \times 7y$ (xii) $10m \times (-3m)$

Remove the brackets and simplify each of these:

4. $3(2x - 1) + 5(x + 2)$ **5.** $2(x - 4) + 3(2x + 5)$

6. $5(3x - 2) - 2(x - 1)$ **7.** $3(3x + 2) - 4(2x + 1)$

8. $6(2x - 3) + 2(3x - 1)$ **9.** $5(x - 2) - (2x + 4)$

10. $3(2a - 7) - 5(a - 4)$ **11.** $2(3a - 4) - (5a - 3)$

12. $2(x^2 - 3x + 1) + 2(x^2 + x - 4)$ **13.** $5(x^2 - x - 4) - 2(2x^2 - 3x + 2)$

Find the product of each of these:

14. $(2x + 1)(x + 3)$ **15.** $(2x + 3)(x + 4)$ **16.** $(x + 5)(2x + 1)$

17. $(3x + 2)(x - 4)$ **18.** $(x + 3)(2x - 3)$ **19.** $(2x - 2)(x + 4)$

20. $(2x - 3)(x + 1)$ **21.** $(x - 3)(x - 2)$ **22.** $(2x - 3)(x - 2)$

23. $(4x - 5)(x + 3)$ **24.** $(2x + 1)(x - 6)$ **25.** $(3x + 2)(x - 5)$

26. $(x - 5)(2x - 3)$ **27.** $(5x - 2)(2x + 3)$ **28.** $(2x - 1)(x + 4)$

29. $(2x - 2y)(x - 3y)$ **30.** $(3x - y)(4x + 3y)$ **31.** $(4x - 5y)(x + y)$

32. $(x + 4)^2$ **33.** $(2x + 3)^2$ **34.** $(2x - 1)^2$

35. Find an expression, in its simplest form, for

(i) the perimeter of this rectangle

(ii) the area of the rectangle.

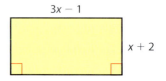

$3x - 1$

$x + 2$

Section 2.3 Evaluating expressions

When $x = 3$, the value of $2x + 5$ is $2(3) + 5 = 6 + 5 = 11$.

When $x = 2$, the value of $3x^2 - 6x$ is $3(2)^2 - 6(2) = 3(4) - 12 = 12 - 12 = 0$.

Example 1

If $a = 2$, $b = 3$ and $c = -4$, find the value of

(i) $a + b$ (ii) $2a - b$ (iii) $3a^2 - 2c$ (iv) $2c^2 - 4ab$

$$\begin{aligned} \text{(i)} \quad a + b &= 2 + 3 \\ &= 5 \end{aligned} \qquad\qquad \begin{aligned} \text{(ii)} \quad 2a - b &= 2(2) - 3 \\ &= 4 - 3 = 1 \end{aligned}$$

$$\begin{aligned} \text{(iii)} \quad 3a^2 - 2c &= 3(2)^2 - 2(-4) \\ &= 3(4) + 8 \\ &= 12 + 8 = 20 \end{aligned} \qquad \begin{aligned} \text{(iv)} \quad 2c^2 - 4ab &= 2(-4)^2 - 4(2)(3) \\ &= 2(16) - 4(6) \\ &= 32 - 24 = 8 \end{aligned}$$

Remember

When evaluating an expression,

(i) multiply and divide before you add or subtract

(ii) any number multiplied by zero is zero, e.g. $6 \times 0 = 0$.

Exercise 2.3

1. If $x = 3$ and $y = 2$, find the value of each of these:

(i) $5x$ (ii) $4x - 3$ (iii) $x + 2y$ (iv) $2x - y$

2. If $a = 4$ and $b = 2$, find the value of each of these:

(i) $2a + b$ (ii) $a + 2b$ (iii) $b - 3a$ (iv) $3a - 2b$

3. If $x = 2$, $y = 3$ and $z = -1$, evaluate each of these:

(i) $x + 2y$ (ii) $3x + z$ (iii) $2y + 3z$ (iv) $4x + 5z$

4. Work out the value of each of these when $a = -3$:

(i) $a + 8$ (ii) $6a$ (iii) $7 - a$ (iv) $3a - 5$

5. Work out the value of each of these when $x = 2$:

(i) $x^2 + 5$ (ii) $2x^2 - 3$ (iii) $x^2 + 2x$ (iv) $3x^2 - 4x + 2$

6. If $a = 4$ and $b = -3$, evaluate each of these:

(i) $2a + b$ (ii) $a - 4b$ (iii) $2a^2 - b$ (iv) $b^2 - 2a$

(v) $2(a + b)$ (vi) $3(a^2 + 3b)$ (vii) $2b^2 - a$ (viii) $b^2 - 2b + a$

7. If $x = 4$, find the value of each of these:

(i) $2x^2 - 3$ (ii) $\dfrac{x^2 + 4}{x + 1}$ (iii) $\dfrac{3x - 2}{9 - x}$ (iv) $\dfrac{2x^2 - 2}{2x + 2}$

8.

A	B	C	E	G	H	I	M	O	P	R	S	T	U	W
−2	−5	8	3	−3	0	−6	2	−6	−1	5	1	−4	6	−9

Work out the value of the expressions in each list below.
Change the numbers to letters using the code above.
Rearrange the letters to spell an animal.

(a)
> $p + 4$ when $p = -5$
> $r - 1$ when $r = 9$
> $t - 11$ when $t = 2$

(b)
> $2 - p$ when $p = -1$
> $3q + 8$ when $q = -2$
> $15 + 3r$ when $r = -3$
> $2d + 4$ when $d = -4$
> $9 + 5e$ when $e = -2$

(c)
> $-1 - u$ when $u = -8$
> $6 + v$ when $v = -3$
> $15 + 4w$ when $w = -2$
> $\frac{1}{2}x + 4$ when $x = -6$
> $1 + \frac{1}{2}y$ when $y = -4$

9. If $a = 4, b = 2$ and $c = 1$, find the value of each of these:

(i) $a(b + c)$ (ii) ab (iii) $3bc$ (iv) $2ab - 3c$
(v) $2abc$ (vi) $a^2 - bc$ (vii) $2b^2 - a$ (viii) $2ab - 5c$

Section 2.4 Solving linear equations

The three scales below will help you recall the steps involved in solving an equation.
Here we need to solve the equation $3x + 2 = 14$.

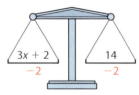
Take 2 from both sides

Divide both sides by 3

$x = 4$ is the solution

The scales above illustrate that solving an equation requires us to change the equation
into a simpler one. This is done by adding, subtracting, multiplying or dividing **both
sides** of the equation by the **same number**.

Example 1

Solve the equation $3x - 5 = 16$.

$$3x - 5 = 16$$
$$3x - 5 + \mathbf{5} = 16 + \mathbf{5} \quad \text{... add 5 to both sides}$$
$$3x = 21$$
$$x = 7 \quad \text{... divide both sides by 3}$$

Example 2

Solve the equation $3(2x - 6) = 2(2x + 1)$.

$$3(2x - 6) = 2(2x + 1)$$
$$6x - 18 = 4x + 2 \quad \text{... remove the brackets}$$
$$6x - \mathbf{4x} - 18 = 4x + 2 - \mathbf{4x} \quad \text{... take } 4x \text{ from each side}$$
$$2x - 18 = 2$$
$$2x - 18 + \mathbf{18} = 2 + \mathbf{18} \quad \text{... add 18 to each side}$$
$$2x = 20$$
$$x = 10 \quad \text{... divide each side by 2}$$

Exercise 2.4

1. Each symbol stands for a number. Find its value.

   (i) $\blacktriangleleft + 1 = 7$ (ii) $\blacksquare - 2 = 12$ (iii) $\bigstar \times 3 = 21$ (iv) $5 + \blacktriangleright = 14$

   (v) $8 - \blacklozenge = 3$ (vi) $4 \times \clubsuit = 32$ (vii) $\bullet \div 3 = 11$ (viii) $\ast + \ast = 30$

2. Write down the missing numbers to make these equations true:

   (i) $\square + 8 = 15$ (ii) $12 - \square = 8$ (iii) $\square \times 3 = 30$

   (iv) $\square \times 6 + 2 = 26$ (v) $27 \div \square + 1 = 10$ (vi) $7 + 5 + \dfrac{\square}{2} = 15$

3. Solve each of these equations:

   (i) $2x = 8$ (ii) $3x = 27$ (iii) $5x = 35$ (iv) $6x = 42$ (v) $9x = 63$

Solve these equations:

4. $x - 2 = 5$ 5. $x - 7 = 9$ 6. $x + 5 = 12$

7. $2x - 1 = 7$ 8. $3x - 1 = 8$ 9. $3x - 5 = 16$

10. $4x + 2 = 26$ 11. $2x + 5 = 13$ 12. $5x - 3 = 22$

13. $3x - 2 = x + 4$ **14.** $3x + 3 = 2x + 7$ **15.** $4x - 2 = 3x - 1$

16. $6x - 2 = 4x + 10$ **17.** $7x + 10 = 4x - 2$ **18.** $7x - 12 = 4x$

Remove the brackets and then solve the following equations:

19. $4(2x - 3) = 36$

20. $5x + 5 = 2(2x + 5)$

21. $3(2x + 1) = 2x + 11$

22. $5(2x - 1) = 8x + 7$

23. $5(x - 2) = 4(x - 1)$

24. $5(x - 5) = 3(x + 1)$

25. $4(x + 5) = 2(x + 1)$

26. $4(3x + 6) = 3(5x - 2)$

27. $3(2x + 1) = 2x + 11$

28. $3(x - 2) = 5x - 12$

29. $3(x - 9) - 3 = x - 2$

30. $2(5 + x) - 12 = 4$

31. $4(2x - 3) = 2(3x - 5)$

32. $3(5x - 2) = 4(3x + 6)$

33. $3(x + 3) - 7 = 5(x - 4) + 18$

34. $4(x - 2) - 6 = 6 - (x + 5)$

35. Work out the value of x for each strip:

(i)

(ii)

36. Work out what x stands for in each of these:

(i)

(ii)

37. The perimeter of the given triangle is 36 cm.
Form an equation and solve it to find the value of x.

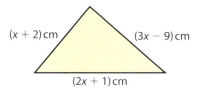

38. Solve each of these equations:
   (i) $3(a + 2) - 2(a + 1) = 6$
   (iii) $5(n + 4) - 3(n - 2) = 30$
   (ii) $5(m + 3) - 4(m + 2) = 10$
   (iv) $6(a + 2) - 4(a - 1) = 20$

Section 2.5 Writing and solving equations

The ability to change a problem expressed in words into a mathematical equation and then to solve it is very important in mathematics.

The following example will show how equations can be formed from word problems.

Example 1

When 3 is taken from five times a certain number, the result is the same as adding 6 to twice the number. Find the number.

Let x be the required number.

Equation:

$$5x - 3 = 2x + 6$$
$$5x - 3 + 3 = 2x + 6 + 3 \quad \text{... add 3 to each side}$$
$$5x = 2x + 9$$
$$5x - 2x = 2x + 9 - 2x \quad \text{... take 2x from each side}$$
$$3x = 9$$
$$x = 3$$

The required number is 3.

Exercise 2.5

1. Write an equation for each of the following and solve it.
   Let x be the unknown number in each case.

   (i) I think of a number.
        When I multiply it by 3 and then add 2, the answer is 17.
        What is the number?

   (ii) I think of a number.
         When I multiply it by 4 and then add 1, the answer is 13.
         What is the number?

   (iii) I think of a number.
          When I multiply the number by 3 and then subtract 4, the answer is the same as twice the number.
          What is the number?

   (iv) I think of a number.
         When I add 2 to the number and multiply my answer by 4, the result is 20.
         What is the number?

2. If I multiply a number by 4 and then add 3, the result is the same as adding 8 to three times the number.
   Form an equation in x and solve it to find the number.

3. I think of a number, multiply it by 8, and then subtract 2.
   I get the same result as when I multiply this number by 2 and add 10.
   What is this number?

4. A number is multiplied by 3 and 5 is then added.
   If the result is 17, find the number.

5. When 3 is added to a number and the result is doubled, the result is 24.
   Write an equation in x and solve it to find the number.

6. 9 is subtracted from a certain number and the result is multiplied by 4.
   If the answer is 24, what is the number?

7. One number is 4 bigger than another number.
   If x is the smaller number, what is the larger one?
   When twice the smaller number is added to the larger, the result is 16.
   Find the two numbers.

8. One number is 5 greater than another number.
   If the smaller number is added to twice the larger number, the answer is 28.
   Find the two numbers.

9. (i) Find an expression for the perimeter of this triangle.
   (ii) What value of x gives a perimeter of 55?

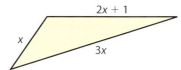

10. If we subtract 4 from a number and then multiply the result by 5, the answer is 15.
    Find the number.

11. (i) Find an expression, in terms of x, for the perimeter of this rectangle.
    Give your answer in its simplest form.
    (ii) The perimeter of the rectangle is 44 cm.
    Write down an equation and solve it to find the value of x.

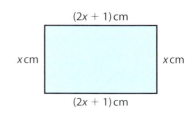

12. (i) Write an expression for the sum of the angles marked in this triangle.
    Give your answer in its simplest form.
    (ii) The angles of a triangle add up to 180°.
    Write down an equation in x and use it to find the value of x.

13. In a furniture store, a chair costs €x and a stool costs €10 less than a chair.
If 2 stools and 3 chairs cost €230, find the cost of a chair and the cost of a stool.

14. In this diagram, the number in each
box is found by adding the two numbers
above it.
Find the value of x.

15. The given figure is a square.
Form an equation in x and solve it.
Hence, find the length of the side
of the square.

$(3x - 7)$ cm

$(x + 5)$ cm

16. Emer is 4 years older than Leah.
If twice the sum of their ages is 48 years, how old is Leah?

17. 166 people live in an apartment block and of these,
x are women.
There are 8 fewer men than women, and there are 30
more children than women.
How many women live in the block?

18. A triangle and rectangle are shown below:

Find the value of x which
(i) gives a triangle with a perimeter of 63
(ii) gives a triangle and rectangle with equal perimeters
(iii) makes the rectangle into a square.

Section 2.6 **Algebraic division**

We have already learned how to multiply two algebraic expressions such as $(x + 4)(x + 3)$.

In this section, we will learn how to divide an expression such as $x^2 + x - 12$ by $(x + 4)$ by using a method very similar to long division in arithmetic.
The work is laid out as follows:

$$
\begin{array}{r}
x - 3 \\
x + 4\overline{)x^2 + x - 12} \\
\underline{x^2 + 4x} \\
-3x - 12 \\
\underline{-3x - 12}
\end{array}
$$

... divide x into x^2

... multiply $(x + 4)$ by x

... subtract and then divide x into $-3x$

... multiply $(x + 4)$ by -3 and then subtract

The answer is $x - 3$.

Example 1

Divide $2x^2 - 5x + 3$ by $x - 1$.

$$
\begin{array}{r}
2x - 3 \\
x - 1\overline{)2x^2 - 5x + 3} \\
2x^2 - 2x \\
-3x + 3 \\
-3x + 3
\end{array}
$$

... divide $2x^2$ by x to get $2x$

... multiply $(x + 4)$ by x

... subtract and then divide x into $-3x$

... multiply $(x + 4)$ by -3 and then subtract

The answer is $2x - 3$.

Exercise 2.6

Divide each of the following:

1. $x^2 + 5x + 6 \div x + 3$

2. $x^2 + 8x + 15 \div x + 5$

3. $x^2 + 9x + 14 \div x + 2$

4. $2x^2 + 9x + 4 \div x + 4$

5. $6x^2 + 5x + 1 \div 2x + 1$

6. $2x^2 + x - 10 \div 2x + 5$

7. $6x^2 - 10x - 4 \div 3x + 1$

8. $2x^2 - 7x - 4 \div x - 4$

9. $3x^2 - 22x + 7 \div 3x - 1$

10. $6x^2 + 11x - 35 \div 2x + 7$

11. $10x^2 - 7x - 12 \div 2x - 3$

12. $15x^2 - 26x + 8 \div 5x - 2$

Test yourself 2

1. (a) Simplify each of these expressions:

    (i) $4x + 5 - 2(x + 1)$ (ii) $6(y + 4) - 2(y + 3)$ (iii) $4(3 + k) - 2(k - 5)$

  (b) Find the value of each of these when $x = 3$ and $y = -2$:

    (i) $2x + y$ (ii) xy (iii) $x + 3y$ (iv) $2x^2 + y^2$

  (c) (i) By forming an equation work out what x stands for.

     (ii) What is the length of the plank?

2. (a) Simplify each of these:

    (i) $3x + 4 + 5x - 1$ (ii) $5x - 3 - 2x + 4 + 3x - 6$

  (b)

A $17 + (a + b)$ B $20 - (b + c)$ C $20 - (a + c)$

    When $a = 3$, $b = 4$ and $c = 5$, which of the expressions above is the biggest?

  (c) Solve each of these equations:

    (i) $9x + 10 = 5x - 2$ (ii) $2(5 + x) - 14 = 4$

3. (a) If $x = 3$ and $y = -2$, find the value of

    (i) $4x$ (ii) $2x + y$ (iii) $2x - 3y$ (iv) $2(x + y)$

  (b) Look at these rods:

    Write an expression for each length marked **?**

    (i)   (ii)

          ?   **?**

    $2g + 5$ $10 - g$ $t + 5$ $7 - 2t$

  (c) If I add 3 to a number and multiply the result by 4, the answer is 48.

    Write an equation in x and solve it to find the number.

4. (a) Remove the brackets and simplify each of these:

    (i) $3(2x - 6) + 2(x - 2)$ (ii) $3x(x + 4) - 2x(x - 3)$

  (b)

A $2a + 12$ B $3(a + 2)$ C $\dfrac{a}{2} + 8$

D $2(a - 4)$ E $\dfrac{a + 10}{2}$ F $\dfrac{a}{2} - 1$

    (i) Work out the value of each expression when $a = 20$.

    (ii) Which expression has the value 0 when $a = 4$?

    (iii) Which expression has the smallest value when $a = 10$?

    (iv) Which two expressions have the same value when $a = 6$?

5. (a)   Simplify each of these:
   (i) $6a + 3b - 2a + b$ (ii) $6p - 2q + 4 - 4p + 3q - 2$

(b)   What expression does the question mark (**?**) stand for in each of these shapes?

(c)   In the given triangle, the two marked sides are equal in length.
   Find the value of x.
   Now find the total length of the three sides.

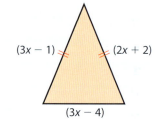

6. (a)   In a magic square, each row, column and diagonal add up to the same number.
   Show that this is a magic square when $a = 7, b = 2$ and $c = 3$.

$a - b$	$a + b - c$	$a + c$
$a + b + c$	a	$a - b - c$
$a - c$	$a - b + c$	$a + b$

(b)   Which of the expressions in the boxes has the highest value when $x = 5$?
   Which of the expressions has the lowest value when $x = 5$?

| $2 - 4x^2$ | $10(x + 3)$ | $2(10 - x)$ |

| $\dfrac{x^2}{2}$ | $\dfrac{25}{x - 4}$ |

(c)   *Temporary Work* hires out workers to companies.
   For each worker you hire, they charge a fee of €a and then €b per hour worked.
   (i) For a lorry driver, the fee is €30 and the hourly rate €15.
      How much would it cost to hire a lorry driver for 8 hours?
   (ii) A worker works for 6 hours.

      If T is the total hire fee for the worker in euro, write down a formula connecting T, a and b.

Rainy-day Challenge

Make a photocopy of this page to avoid writing on the book.

Simplify each part and put the letter for that part in the box above the correct answer.

The sequence of letters should answer this question.

Why didn't the boy drink his milk after his bath?

F $10x + 7x$

B $2p \times 9$

T $6m - 10m$

H $12k - 6l + 2k$

N $15y \div (-3y)$

H $-12k + 10k$

E $(-18ab) \div 9b$

H $3x - 7x$

A $16mn \div 8$

H $8x \times 3xy$

D $8pq + 7pq - 3p$

O $13k \times 2k \div k^2$

I $-m + n + m - n$

K $(-2x) \times 5x \times (-3)$

E $(-6m) \times (-6m)$

H $6m - 5m$

M $20b \div b$

I $(-3) \times 6q$

O $8t \times 7t$

A $5x^2 + 2x - 3x^2$

A $9a - 7a - a$

F $ab \times ac$

I $-3m + 10m$

M $(-6a) \times (-3b)$

R $14m^2 \div (-7m)$

N $4m \times 2n \times 5$

R $3m^2 + m^2 - 6m^2$

F $3a \times 4b \times 5c$

L $24ab \div 6a \times 2b$

L $5ab + (6a \times 2b)$

E $3a + 2a + 6a$

R $2a \times a$

E $(-40n) \div (-10)$

T $36pq \div 9q$

D $7m - (-3m)$

T $9a \times 7b$

S $2x \times \frac{1}{2}x$

K $9p - 2q - 7p$

O $7m - 3m + 2n$

G $5ab + 7ba$

R $16x \div 4x \times 2x$

T $3x + 7y - 2y + x$

I $100bc \div 20b$

O $6y^2 + 7y - 8y^2 + 2y$

N $(32x^2 \div 4x) - 7x$

a | a^2bc | $-4m$ | $-2a$ | $-2m^2$ | $10m$ | $-2m$ | $-18q$ | x | $30x^2$ | $7m$ | -5 | $12ab$ | $-4x$ | 0 | x^2 | $18p$ | $2mn$ | $4p$ | m | $-2k$ | $11a$

$14k - 6l$ | $2x^2 + 2x$ | $15pq - 3p$ | $40mn$ | $-2y^2 + 9y$ | $2a^2$ | $56t^2$ | $4m + 2n$ | $18ab$ | $8b^2$ | $36m^2$ | $60abc$ | $4x + 5y$ | $17x$ | 26 | $8x$ | $63ab$ | $24x^2y$ | $4n$ | 20 | $5c$ | $17ab$ | $2p - 2q$

3 Sets

Key words

equal sets   union   intersection   subset   universal set
complement of a set   cardinal number (#)   set difference
commutative property

Section 3.1 Revision of sets terminology

In this section we will revise the sets operations that you will have met in first-year.

1. Equal sets

Two sets are **equal** if they contain exactly the same elements.

If $A = \{2, 4, 6, 8\}$ and $B = \{4, 6, 8, 2\}$, then **$A = B$**.

2. Union of two sets ($A \cup B$)

The **union** of two sets A and B is found by putting together in a new set all the elements of A and B without repeating an element. It is written **$A \cup B$**.

If $A = \{1, 2, 3, 4\}$ and $B = \{3, 4, 5, 6\}$,
then $A \cup B = \{1, 2, 3, 4, 5, 6\}$.

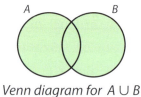

Venn diagram for $A \cup B$

3. Intersection of two sets ($A \cap B$)

The **intersection** of two sets A and B is the set of elements that are in both A and B.

It is written **$A \cap B$**.

In the given Venn diagram, $A \cap B$ is shaded.

Venn diagram for $A \cap B$

If $A = \{1, 3, 5, 7, 9, 11\}$ and $B = \{6, 7, 8, 9, 10, 11, 12\}$, then $A \cap B = \{7, 9, 11\}$.

4. Subsets ($B \subset A$)

Set B is a **subset** of set A if all the elements of B are contained in A.

It is written **$B \subset A$**.

If $A = \{1, 2, 3, 4, 5\}$ and $B = \{3, 5\}$, then $B \subset A$.

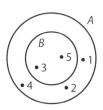

5. The universal set (*U*)

The set from which all other sets being considered are taken is called the **universal set**.

It is denoted by the capital letter *U* and is represented by a rectangle.

6. The complement of a set (*A'*)

The complement of a set *A* is the set of elements in the universal set *U* which are not in *A*.

It is written as **A'** and is illustrated by the shaded area in the given Venn diagram.

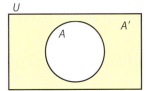

Example 1

Use the given Venn diagram to list the elements of each of these sets:

  (i) *A*   (ii) $A \cup B$ (iii) *A'*

(iv) $A \cap B$ (v) $(A \cap B)'$.

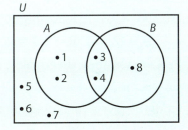

(i) $A = \{1, 2, 3, 4\}$

(ii) $A \cup B = \{1, 2, 3, 4\} \cup \{3, 4, 8\} = \{1, 2, 3, 4, 8\}$

(iii) $A' = \{5, 6, 7, 8\}$

(iv) $A \cap B = \{1, 2, 3, 4\} \cap \{3, 4, 8\} = \{3, 4\}$

(v) $(A \cap B)' = \{1, 2, 5, 6, 7, 8\}$

---

7. The cardinal number of a set (#)

The number of elements in a set is called the **cardinal number** of the set.

The symbol **#** is used to denote the cardinal number.

From the given Venn diagram,

  $\#A = 6$ $\#B = 6$

  $\#(A \cap B) = 2$ $\#(A \cup B) = 10$.

Exercise 3.1

1. What is the diagram on the right called?
   Now list the elements of A.
   What is #A?

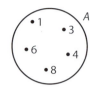

2. On the right, set X is represented by a Venn diagram. Say if each of the following is true or false:

   (i) $d \in X$ (ii) $g \in X$
   (iii) $e \in X$ (iv) $f \in X$.

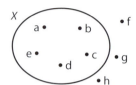

3. What do the symbols $\in$ and $\notin$ stand for?

   $A = \{1, 2, 3, 4\}$ $B = \{a, b, c, d\}$ $C = \{x, y, z\}$

   Copy and insert the correct symbol $\in$ or $\notin$ in each of the following:

   (i) $3 \ldots A$ (ii) $2 \ldots B$ (ii) $c \ldots B$ (iv) $d \ldots C$ (v) $z \ldots C$.

4. Which two of the following sets are equal?

   $A = \{2, 3, 4, 6\}$ $B = \{6, 4, 3, 1\}$ $C = \{6, 3, 4, 2\}$.

   Explain why they are equal.

5. From the given Venn diagram, list the elements of each of these sets:

   (i) A (ii) B
   (iii) $A \cap B$ (iv) $A \cup B$.

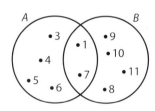

6. $A = \{1, 2, 3, 4, 5, 6\}$ $B = \{4, 5, 6, 7, 8\}$ $C = \{7, 8, 9, 10\}$
   List the elements of each of these sets:

   (i) $A \cap B$ (i) $B \cup C$ (i) $B \cap C$ (i) $A \cap C$.

7. From the Venn diagram on the right, write down

   (i) #A   (ii) #B
   (iii) $\#(A \cap B)$ (iv) $\#(A \cup B)$.

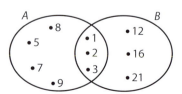

8. Given $U = \{1, 2, 3, 4, 5, 6, 7, 8, 9\}$
     $A = \{1, 3, 5, 7\}$
     $B = \{5, 6, 7, 8\}$.

   Copy the Venn diagram on the right
   and illustrate the given information
   on it.

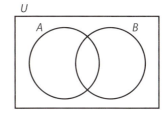

9. From the given Venn diagram,
   list the elements of

   (i) P (ii) Q
   (iii) $P \cap Q$ (iv) $P \cup Q$.

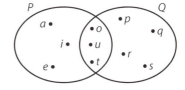

10. From the given Venn diagram,
    list the elements of each of these
    sets:

    (i) U (ii) A (iii) A'.

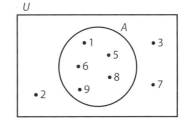

11. Use the given Venn diagram to
    list the elements of each of these
    sets:

    (i) A (ii) B (iii) A'
    (iii) B' (iv) $A \cup B$ (vi) $(A \cup B)'$.

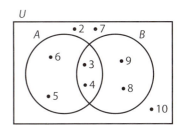

12. In the given Venn diagram, each dot
    represents an element.
    Write down

    (i) $\#A$ (ii) $\#B$ (iii) $\#U$
    (iv) $\#(A \cup B)$ (v) $\#(A \cap B)$ (vi) $\#(A \cup B)'$.

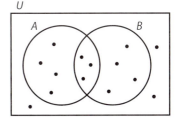

13. If $U = \{1, 2, 3, 4, 5, 6, 7, 8, 9, 10\}$
      $A = \{1, 3, 5, 7\}$
      $B = \{3, 4, 5, 6\}$, list the elements of

    (i) A' (ii) B' (iii) $A \cup B$ (vi) $(A \cup B)'$.

14. Given $U = \{1, 2, 3, \ldots, 12\}$
$A = \{1, 2, 3, 4, 5, 6\}$
$B = \{3, 5, 7, 9, 11\}$.

Make a copy of the given Venn diagram
and fill in the information provided.

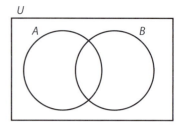

15. Using the Venn diagram on the right,
say if each of the following is true or
false:

(i) $7 \in (A \cup B)$ (ii) $3 \in B$
(iii) $6 \in (A \cap B)$ (iv) $9 \in A'$
(v) $9 \in U$ (vi) $8 \in (A \cup B)$.

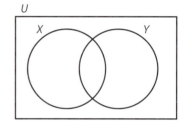

16. Given $U = \{a, b, c, d, e, f, g\}$
$X = \{a, b, c, d\}$
$Y = \{b, e, f\}$.
(i) Place the letters a, b, c, d, e, f, g in
the Venn diagram on the right.
(iii) List the elements of X'.
(v) What is $\#(X \cup Y)'$?

17. What do the symbols $\subset$ and $\not\subset$ stand for?
Now state which of the two symbols should be inserted in the space provided in
each of the following to make the statement true:

(i) $\{a, b\} \ldots \{a, b, c, d\}$ (ii) $\{2, 3\} \ldots \{2, 3, 4, 5\}$
(iii) $\{1\} \ldots \{2, 4, 6, 8\}$ (iv) $\{d, e, f\} \ldots \{a, b, c, d, e\}$

Section 3.2 Set difference

In this section we introduce a new term called **set difference**.

To illustrate set difference, we take two sets A and B, where

$A = \{1, 2, 3, 4, 5, 6\}$ and $B = \{4, 6, 8, 10\}$.

If we remove from set A all the elements which are in set B, we have **A less B**.

'A less B' is denoted by **$A \backslash B$**.

$\therefore$ $A \backslash B = \{1, 2, 3, 5\}$

Set difference $A \backslash B$ is the set of elements of A which are not in B.

Set difference can be illustrated by Venn diagrams as follows:

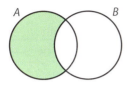

Shaded area is $A \backslash B$

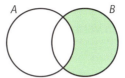

Shaded area is $B \backslash A$

Example 1

If $A = \{a, b, c, d, e, f, g\}$ and $B = \{e, f, g, h, i\}$, find

(i) $A \backslash B$ (ii) $B \backslash A$ (iii) $(A \cup B) \backslash (A \cap B)$

(i) $A \backslash B$ is the set of elements of A which are not in B.
   $\therefore$ $A \backslash B = \{a, b, c, d\}$

(ii) $B \backslash A = \{h, i\}$

(iii) $A \cup B = \{a, b, c, d, e, f, g, h, i\}$ and $A \cap B = \{e, f, g\}$
   $\therefore$ $(A \cup B) \backslash (A \cap B) = \{a, b, c, d, h, i\}$

The commutative property

It is obvious that $3 + 4 = 4 + 3$ and that $3 \times 4 = 4 \times 3$.

This illustrates that addition and multiplication are **commutative**.

By this we mean that we can change the order in which two numbers are added (or multiplied) without changing the result.

However, since $6 - 2 \neq 2 - 6$, we can say that subtraction is not commutative.

Also division is not commutative as $12 \div 6 \neq 6 \div 12$.

If $A = \{2, 3, 4, 5\}$ and $B = \{4, 5, 6, 7\}$,
then $A \cup B = B \cup A = \{2, 3, 4, 5, 6, 7\}$.
Also, $A \cap B = B \cap A = \{4, 5\}$.

> The union of sets and the intersection of sets are commutative.

Taking the sets A and B above, we have

(i) $A \backslash B = \{2, 3\}$ (ii) $B \backslash A = \{6, 7\}$

This illustrates that $A \backslash B \neq B \backslash A$ and so set difference is not commutative.

Remember   Set difference is not commutative.

Exercise 3.2

1. $A = \{1, 2, 3, 4, 5, 6, 7, 8\}$, $B = \{3, 6, 9, 10\}$ and $C = \{2, 4, 6, 8\}$.
List the elements of the following sets.
    (i) $A \backslash B$ (ii) $B \backslash C$ (iii) $A \backslash C$ (iv) $C \backslash A$

2. From the given Venn diagram, list the elements of
    (i) $A \backslash B$
    (ii) $B \backslash A$
    (iii) $U \backslash A$
    (iv) $U \backslash (A \cap B)$

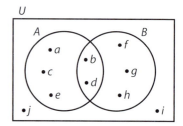

3. Based on the given Venn diagram, say if each of the
following is true or false:
    (i) $3 \in A \backslash B$ (ii) $7 \in B \backslash A$
    (iii) $\#(B \backslash A) = 3$ (iv) $\#U = 12$
    (v) $\#(A \cap B) = 2$ (vi) $6 \in U \backslash A$
    (vii) $\#(U \backslash A) = 6$ (viii) $\#(U \backslash B) = 8$

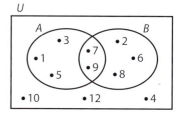

4. Given $X = \{2, 4, 6, 8, 10, 12\}$ and $Y = \{3, 6, 9, 12, 15\}$.
Find   (i) $X \backslash Y$ (ii) $Y \backslash X$.
Is $X \backslash Y = Y \backslash X$? What has your result shown?

5. Given $A = \{4, 5, 6, 8, 10, 12\}$ $B = \{1, 2, 3, 4, 5, 6\}$
          $C = \{2, 4, 10, 14\}$ $D = \{0, 5, 10, 15\}$

List the elements of the following sets:
    (i) $A \backslash C$ (ii) $B \backslash D$ (iii) $D \backslash A$
    (iv) $A \backslash (B \cap C)$ (v) $B \backslash (C \cup D)$ (vi) $(A \cup B) \backslash (A \cap B)$

6. $U = \{a, b, c, d, e, f, g, h, i\}$, $A = \{d, f, g, e, i\}$ and $B = \{b, e, h, i\}$.
Draw a Venn diagram to illustrate these sets.
Use the Venn diagram to write down
    (i) $\#(A \backslash B)$ (ii) $\#(U \backslash A)$ (iii) $\#[U \backslash (A \cup B)]$ (iv) $\#[U \backslash (A \cap B)]$

7. Make two copies of this Venn diagram.
    (i) On the first, shade in $P \backslash Q$.
    (ii) On the second, shade in $Q \backslash P$.

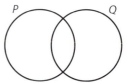

8. Based on the given Venn diagram, say whether each of the following is true or false:

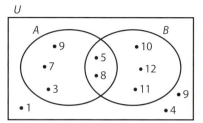

  (i) $A \backslash B = \{9, 7, 3\}$ (ii) $\#(B \backslash A) = 3$

 (iii) $\#(U \backslash A) = 6$ (iv) $\#(A \cup B) = 6$

  (v) $\#[U \backslash (A \cap B)] = 9$ (vi) $(A \cap B) \subset U$.

Section 3.3 Using Venn diagrams to solve problems ——

Venn diagrams are very useful when solving problems involving two or more sets. In these problems we are interested in the **number** of elements in the set rather than the elements themselves.

Consider the given Venn diagram.

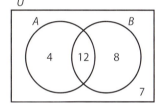

U represents a class of students.
A represents those who study Art.
B represents those who study Biology.

The numbers in each of the four regions are shown.

12 study **both** Art and Biology.
 4 study Art **only**.
 8 study Biology only.
 7 study neither of these subjects.

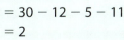

In a class of 30 pupils, 17 study German, 16 study Spanish and 5 study both German and Spanish.

Represent this information on a Venn diagram.

Use the Venn diagram to write down the number of pupils who study

  (i) German only   (ii) Spanish only   (iii) neither German nor Spanish.

We use the given information to fill in the Venn diagram.

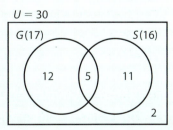

First place 5 in the set $G \cap S$ ... 5 study both German and Spanish

  (i) German only $= 17 - 5 = 12$

 (ii) Spanish only $= 16 - 5 = 11$

(iii) Neither $= 30 - 12 - 5 - 11$

           $= 2$

Example 2

All of the 30 students in a class have either a mobile phone, or an iPad or both.
If 22 students have a mobile phone and 15 have an iPad, how many students have

(i) both items   (ii) a mobile phone only   (iii) an iPad only?

In the Venn diagram,
M = mobile phone and P = iPad.

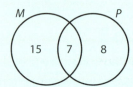

Since $22 + 14 = 37$, which is more than the
30 in the class, there is an 'overlap' of 7.
Therefore, 7 have both a mobile phone and
an iPad.
Now, we fill in the three regions shown:

  (i) 7 students have both items
 (ii) 15 students have a mobile phone only ... $22 - 7 = 15$
(iii) 8 students have an iPad only. ... $15 - 7 = 8$

Exercise 3.3

1. In the given Venn diagram,

   U is the set of pupils in the class
   B is the set of pupils who play basketball
   F is the set of pupils who play football.

   (i)   How many pupils play both games?
   (ii) How many pupils are there in the class?
   (iii) How many pupils play football only?
   (iv) How many pupils play neither of the two games?

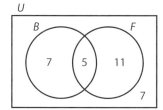

2. 30 pupils were asked which of the television
   programmes P and Q they watch. Some of
   the information obtained is represented
   in the Venn diagram shown.

   (i)   How many pupils watched programme P?
   (ii) How many pupils watched programme Q only?
   (iii) How many pupils watched both programmes?
   (iv) How many watched neither?

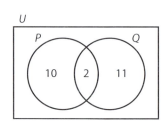

3. In the given Venn diagram,
   U is the set of teenagers in a Youth Club.
   P is the set of teenagers who use PlayStation.
   X is the set of teenagers who use Xbox.

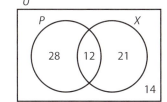

   (i)   How many teenagers use PlayStation?
   (ii) How many teenagers use Xbox?
   (iii) How many teenagers use PlayStation only?
   (iv) How many teenagers use neither of these games?

4. In a class of 30 students,
   12 study Biology (*B*), 16 study
   French (*F*), and 5 study both subjects.
   Copy the Venn diagram and represent
   the given information on it.

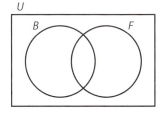

   (i)   Write down the number of students who study
         Biology but not French.
   (ii) How many students study neither of these two subjects?
   (iii) How many students study only one of these subjects?

5. Copy the Venn diagram shown and fill
   in the number of elements in each region,
   given that
   #(*A*) = 10, #(*B*) = 16 and #(*A* ∩ *B*) = 4.

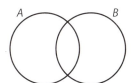

6. The Venn diagram shows two intersecting
   sets *A* and *B* and the number of elements
   in each region.
   Find   (i)   #*A*   (ii) #*B*
             (iii) #(*A* ∩ *B*)   (iv) #(*A* ∪ *B*).

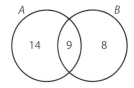

7. Copy the given Venn diagram and fill in
   the four regions, given that

   #*U* = 42, #*A* = 21, #*B* = 18, and #(*A* ∩ *B*) = 6.

   Now write down

   (i) #(*A* ∪ *B*)   (ii) #*B*′   (iii) #(*A* ∪ *B*)′.

8. In a survey of 40 households, 22 had a dog and 16 had a cat.
   If 8 households had both a cat and a dog, represent this information on a Venn
   diagram and write down how many households had neither.

9. In the given Venn diagram,

U = the students in Class 2L,

H = the students in 2L who study
Home Economics,

G = the students in 2L who study
German.

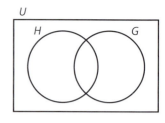

If 20 students study Home Economics, 12 study German, 8 study both these
subjects, and 9 study neither, show this information on a copy of the Venn diagram.

  (i)   How many students are there in the class?

 (ii)   How many students study Home Economics but not German?

(iii)   How many students study just one of these subjects?

10. Copy the Venn diagram shown and fill
in the three regions given that
$\#A = 12$, $\#B = 14$ and $\#(A \cup B) = 22$.

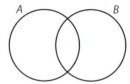

Write down   (i) $\#(A \cap B)$ (ii) $\#(B \backslash A)$.

11. In a class of 32 girls, 16 play hockey and 12 play tennis.
If 10 girls play neither of these sports, represent this information on a Venn diagram.
Use the Venn diagram to write down

  (i)   the number of girls who play both sports

 (ii)   the number of girls who play hockey but not tennis

(iii)   the number of girls who play at least one of these sports.

12. In a survey of 80 people, 56 had watched RTE1 on the previous night and 34 had
watched TV3.
If 22 people had watched neither of these stations, how many people had watched
both?

13. Copy the Venn diagram and fill in the
number of elements in each region
given that
$\#A = 21$, $\#B = 16$, $\#(A \cup B) = 30$ and
$\#U = 43$.

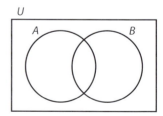

Find   (i) $\#(A \cap B)$ (ii) $\#(B \backslash A)$ (iii) $\#(A \cup B)'$.

Test yourself 3

1. (a) Based on the given Venn diagram,
write down the elements
of these sets:

    (i) A (ii) $A\backslash B$

    (iii) A' (iv) $\#(A \cup B)'$.

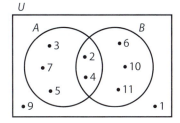

  (b) In the given diagram, each dot
represents an element.
Now write down

    (i) $\#A$ (ii) $\#(A \cup B)$

    (iii) $\#U$ (iv) $\#(A \cap B)'$.

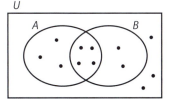

2. (a) From the given Venn diagram, list the
elements of each of these sets:

    (i) P (ii) Q

    (iii) $P \cup Q$ (iv) $P\backslash Q$.

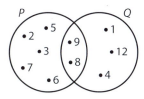

  (b) U is the set of pupils in a class.
T is the set of pupils who play tennis.
H is the set of pupils who play hurling.

    (i) How many pupils are there in the class?

    (ii) How many pupils play tennis?

    (iii) How many pupils play both games?

    (iv) How many pupils play neither of the two games?

    (v) How many pupils play one game only?

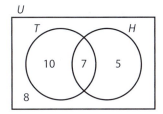

3. (a) Given $A = \{1, 2, 3, 4\}, B = \{4, 5, 6\}$ and $C = \{1, 4, 8\}$.
Write down the element(s) of these sets:

    (i) $A \cap B$ (ii) $A\backslash C$ (iii) $A \cup C$ (ii) $(A \cup C)\backslash B$.

  (b) In the Venn diagram on the right, which **one**
of the following statements is true?

    (i) $6 \in (A\backslash B)$

    (ii) $\#A = 2$

    (iii) $\#(A \cup B) = 2$

    (iv) $\#(A \cup B)' = 2$.

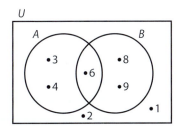

4. (a) From the given Venn diagram, list the elements of each of these sets:

(i) X (ii) Y (iii) U

(iv) $X \cap Y$ (v) X' (vi) $(X \cup Y)'$.

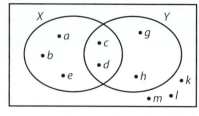

(b) Forty students took a mathematics examination consisting of two parts. Thirty students passed in Part 1 and twenty eight students passed in Part 2. If twenty four students passed in both parts, how many students passed in neither part?

5. (a) Examine the given Venn diagram and list the elements of these sets:

(i) B (ii) $A \cup B$

(iii) $A \backslash B$ (iv) A'.

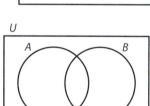

(b) Copy the Venn diagram on the right and fill in the four regions, given that $\#U = 40$, $\#A = 19$, $\#B = 16$ and $\#(A \cap B) = 7$.

Now write down

(i) $\#(A \cup B)$ (ii) $\#(A \backslash B)$ (iii) $\#(A \cup B)'$

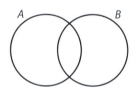

6. (a) In the given Venn diagram,

$A \cup B = \{4, 9, 12, 15, 18, 20\}$.

Copy this Venn diagram.
In the set A, put numbers divisible by 2.
In set B, put numbers divisible by 3.
Now use the Venn diagram to write down the numbers divisible by both 2 and 3.

(b) In a survey, 100 people were asked if they had been on a sun holiday or on a skiing holiday the previous year.
60 had been on a sun holiday, 15 had been on a skiing holiday and 30 had been on neither.
Copy the given Venn diagram and insert the appropriate numbers in the brackets.

Factors

Key words

factor   highest common factor   grouping terms   difference of two squares
quadratic expressions

Section 4.1 Factorising with common factors

Since $9 \times 5 = 45$, we say that 9 and 5 are **factors** of 45.
15 and 3 are also factors of 45.

The factors of 24 are 1, 2, 3, 4, 6, 8, $\boxed{12}$, 24.
The factors of 36 are 1, 2, 3, 4, 6, 9, $\boxed{12}$, 18, 36.
The **highest common factor** is 12.

Here are two algebraic terms: $6xy$ and $12x$.
The highest common factor of the numbers is 6.
The highest common factor of the variables is x.
So the highest common factor of the two terms is $6 \times x$, i.e. $6x$.

Similarly, the highest common factors of

(i) $3a$ and $6a^2 = 3a$ (ii) $6x^2 - 12xy = 6x$
(iii) $5a^2b - 15ab = 5ab$ (iv) $4x^2 + 16xy^2 = 4x$

Take the expression $5x + 10$.
$$5x + 10 = 5(x + 2)$$
5 and $(x + 2)$ are called the factors of $5x + 10$.

To factorise an algebraic expression:

> Find the highest common factor and write it outside the brackets.
> Divide each term by this factor and write the results inside the brackets.
> Check your result by expanding the brackets.

Here are some expressions that have been factorised:

(i) $x^2 + 7x = x(x + 7)$ (ii) $3x^2 - 9x = 3x(x - 3)$
(iii) $3xy - 12x = 3x(y - 4)$ (iv) $12x^2y^2 - 6xy = 6xy(2xy - 1)$

Exercise 4.1

1. Write down the highest common factor of each of these:

   (i) 9 and 12   (ii) 12 and 18   (iii) 14 and 21   (iv) 21 and 35

2. Write down the highest common factor of each of these:

   (i) $4x$ and $12x$ (ii) $3n$ and $9n$ (iii) $10x$ and $15x$

   (iv) $3a^2$ and $6a$ (v) $3xy$ and $12x^2$ (vi) $2a^2b$ and $6ab$

Copy and complete numbers (**3–16**).

3. $4x + 8 = 4($ $)$

4. $6a + 12b = 6($ $)$

5. $7x + 14y = 7($ $)$

6. $22a + 33b = 11($ $)$

7. $12x - 24y = 12($ $)$

8. $ab + bc = b($ $)$

9. $2ax + 4ay = 2a($ $)$

10. $x^2 + x = x($ $)$

11. $5x^2 - 10x = 5x($ $)$

12. $3a^2 + 6a = 3a($ $)$

13. $4x^2 - 12x = 4x($ $)$

14. $6ab - 12bc = 6b($ $)$

15. $7x^2y - 14xy = 7xy($ $)$

16. $6x^2y - 15x^2 = 3x^2($ $)$

Factorise each of the following:

17. $4x + 16$

18. $6x + 18y$

19. $10a - 40b$

20. $ab + ay$

21. $3ab + 3bc$

22. $2xy - 2xz$

23. $7xy + 14xz$

24. $5ab - 15bc$

25. $6ax - 12ay$

26. $x^2 + 4x$

27. $3x^2 + 9x$

28. $5x^2 + 10x$

29. $6a^2 - 12a$

30. $7a^2 - 21a$

31. $10x^2 + 40x$

32. $25x^2 - 15x$

33. $7x^2 - 28x$

34. $12x^2 + 18x$

35. $15x^2 + 25xy$

36. $3x^2 - 6x^2y$

37. $x^3 + x^2 + x$

38. $3ab^2 - 6ab$

39. $12xy - 24x^2y$

40. $15x^3 - 35x^2$

41.

E	H	P	S	O	A	I	L	G	R	T	U	N
5	$2a$	$3a$	$2b$	$7b$	a^2	ab	$3b^2$	$a+b$	$a-5b$	$2a-b$	$ab+1$	$2a+3b$

Fully factorise each expression below as the product of two factors.
Use the code above to find a letter for each factor.
Rearrange each set of letters to spell a bird.

(i) $3a^2 - 15ab$	$2a^3 - a^2b$	$7ab - 35b^2$
(ii) $4a^2 - 2ab$	$2a^2b + 2a$	$2ab - 10b^2$
(iii) $7ab + 7b^2$	$5a - 25b$	$2ab^2 + 2b$
(iv) $4ab - 2b^2$	$3b^2a + 3b^3$	$a^3 - 5a^2b$	$2a^2b + 3ab^2$

Section 4.2 **Factorising by grouping terms**

Some four-termed expressions do not have an overall common factor, but can be factorised by pairing the four terms.

For example,

$$ab + ac + bd + dc$$

$$= a(b + c) + d(b + c) \qquad \text{... factorising each pair separately}$$

$$= (b + c)(a + d) \qquad \text{... removing common factor } (b + c)$$

Example 1

Find the factors of   (i) $2ab + 2ac + 3bx + 3cx$

(ii) $3ax - bx - 3ay + by$

(i) $2ab + 2ac + 3bx + 3cx = 2a(b + c) + 3x(b + c)$

$$= (b + c)(2a + 3x)$$

(ii) $3ax - bx - 3ay + by = x(3a - b) - y(3a - b)$

$$= (3a - b)(x - y)$$

Note: **1.** $-(x + y)$ is the same as $-1(x + y)$
So if you have $x(x + y) - (x + y)$, the factors are
$(x + y)(x - 1)$

2. Be careful when dealing with negative terms.
For example,   (i) $-3ax - 6ay = -3a(x + 2y)$
(ii) $-5x^2 + 10xy = -5x(x - 2y)$

Example 2

Factorise $6x^2 + 2a - 3ax - 4x$.

Regroup: $6x^2 - 3ax + 2a - 4x$

$3x(2x - a) + 2(a - 2x)$

$= 3x(2x - a) - 2(2x - a)$

$= (2x - a)(3x - 2)$

$\therefore\ 6x^2 + 2a - 3ax - 4x = (2x - a)(3x - 2)$

> Here we initially had no common factor, so we changed $+2(a - 2x)$ to $-2(2x - a)$. $(2x - a)$ is now a common factor.

Exercise 4.2

Write down the factors of each of the following:

1. $a(x + 4) + b(x + 4)$

2. $x(2a + 3) + 4(2a + 3)$

3. $x(y + z) + y(y + z)$

4. $a(b + 2c) + 3(b + 2c)$

5. $a(x - 6) + 3(x - 6)$

6. $2a(x + y) - 3b(x + y)$

7. $3x(2x - 3) + (2x - 3)$

8. $2a(3b - c) - (3b - c)$

Find the factors of each of the following expressions:

9. $ax + ay + bx + by$

10. $ab + bc + ad + cd$

11. $ac + bc + 3a + 3b$

12. $mp + np + mq + nq$

13. $2ab + 2bc + 3ad + 3cd$

14. $7ax - 7bx + 3a - 3b$

15. $ac - bc + 2a - 2b$

16. $ac - bc + 2ad - 2bd$

17. $2ax + 3ay + 2bx + 3by$

18. $4x - 4y + ax - ay$

19. $3a - 3b + ax - bx$

20. $ax - 2a + 4x - 8$

21. $2ab - bc + 2ad - cd$

22. $2ax - ay + 2bx - by$

23. $x^2 + ax + bx + ab$

24. $a^2 - 2ab + ac - 2bc$

25. $4ay + xy - 4az - xz$

26. $3mx - am + 3nx - an$

27. $x^2 - xy + xz - yz$

28. $2x - 2y - cx + cy$

29. $3x + 3y - bx - by$

30. $5a + 5b - ac - bc$

31. $x^2 - 2x + xy - 2y$

32. $a^2 - 3a + ab - 3b$

33. $ax - a - bx + b$

34. $ay - 2by - az + 2bz$

35. $x(2a - 3b) + 2a - 3b$

36. $a(x + 2y) - x - 2y$

37. $ab - bc + ac - b^2$

38. $ab - 2cd - bc + 2ad$

39. $3a - 3b + ab - 9$

40. $3ax - 4by + 2bx - 6ay$

Section 4.3 Difference of two squares

Numbers such as 1, 4, 9, 16, 25, … are called **perfect squares** as they are obtained by multiplying some whole number by itself, e.g. $4 = 2^2, 9 = 3^2, …$

Similarly, in algebra, $4x^2 = (2x)^2$ and $9y^2 = (3y)^2$.

Expressions such as $10^2 - 4^2$, $x^2 - y^2$ and $4x^2 - 9$ are known as the **difference of two squares**.

When you multiply $(x + y)(x - y)$, you get $\boldsymbol{x^2 - y^2}$.
Thus, the factors of $x^2 - y^2$ are $(x + y)(x - y)$.

$$x^2 - y^2 = (x + y)(x - y)$$

In words: $(\text{first})^2 - (\text{second})^2 = (\text{first} + \text{second})(\text{first} - \text{second})$

Example 1

Factorise (i) $x^2 - 9$ (ii) $x^2 - 4y^2$ (iii) $9a^2 - 25b^2$

(i) $x^2 - 9 = (x)^2 - (3)^2 = (x + 3)(x - 3)$

(ii) $x^2 - 4y^2 = (x)^2 - (2y)^2 = (x + 2y)(x - 2y)$

(iii) $9a^2 - 25b^2 = (3a)^2 - (5b)^2 = (3a + 5b)(3a - 5b)$

Example 2

Use the difference of two squares to evaluate $51^2 - 49^2$.

$51^2 - 49^2 = (51 + 49)(51 - 49)$ … $a^2 - b^2 = (a + b)(a - b)$
$\qquad\qquad = (100)(2)$
$\qquad\qquad = 200$

Exercise 4.3

Factorise each of the following:

1. $x^2 - 4$ **2.** $x^2 - 16$ **3.** $y^2 - 36$ **4.** $y^2 - 100$

5. $x^2 - y^2$ **6.** $x^2 - 16y^2$ **7.** $a^2 - 9b^2$ **8.** $4x^2 - y^2$

9. $9a^2 - 1$ **10.** $4x^2 - 9$ **11.** $9x^2 - 100$ **12.** $100x^2 - 1$

13. $4a^2 - 25b^2$ **14.** $36x^2 - 49y^2$ **15.** $1 - 36x^2$ **16.** $1 - 100a^2$

17. $49 - 81x^2$ **18.** $64 - 81y^2$ **19.** $64x^2 - 25y^2$ **20.** $x^2y^2 - 1$

21. By first taking out the highest common factor, factorise fully each of the following.
(The first one is done for you.)
   (i) $3a^2 - 12b^2 = 3(a^2 - 4b^2) = 3(a + 2b)(a - 2b)$
   (ii) $5c^2 - 5d^2$ (iii) $3a^2 - 27b^2$ (iv) $3x^2 - 75y^2$ (v) $12a^2 - 27$

Use factors to find the value of each of these:

22. $27^2 - 3^2$ **23.** $41^2 - 39^2$ **24.** $101^2 - 99^2$ **25.** $55^2 - 54^2$

26. $62^2 - 52^2$ **27.** $76^2 - 24^2$ **28.** $190^2 - 10^2$ **29.** $293^2 - 7^2$

Section 4.4 **Factorising quadratic expressions**

An expression of the form $ax^2 + bx + c$ – where a, b and c are numbers – is called a
quadratic expression since the highest power of x is 2.

Since $(x + 5)(x + 2) = x^2 + 7x + 10$, we say that $(x + 5)$ and $(x + 2)$ are the factors
of $x^2 + 7x + 10$.

outside terms

In the product $(x + 5)(x + 2) = x^2 + 7x + 10$,

inside terms

> An expression in the form
> $ax^2 + bx + c$ is generally
> called a quadratic trinomial
> as it contains 3 terms.

(i) x^2 is obtained from the product $x \times x$
(ii) 10 is the product of 5 and 2, the two number
      terms
(iii) $7x$ is obtained by adding the product of the outside
      terms to the product of the inside terms,
      i.e. $2x + 5x = 7x$.

We factorise a quadratic expression by 'trial and error' to find numbers such that the
product of the outside terms, added to the product of the inside terms, gives the middle
term.

Here are the factors of $x^2 + 7x + 12$:

outside terms

$(x + 4)(x + 3)$

inside terms

$3x + 4x = 7x$

$3 \times 4 = 12$

Example 1

Factorise $x^2 + 8x + 15$.

The factors of $x^2 + 8x + 15$ will take the form $(x + ?)(x + ?)$
We are looking for the factors of 15 whose sum is 8.
These factors are 3 and 5.
$\therefore$ the factors are $(x + 3)(x + 5)$.

Note: To verify that your factors are correct, use the middle-term check as follows:

outside terms

$(x + 3)(x + 5)$ i.e. $5x + 3x = 8x$ … correct

inside terms

Third term positive, middle term negative

If the third term of a quadratic expression is positive and the middle term is negative,
e.g. $x^2 - 8x + 15$, then the factors will take the form

$(x - ?)(x - ?)$

Example 2

Find the factors of $x^2 - 11x + 28$.

The factors of 28 which add up to -11 are -7 and -4.
$\therefore$ the factors are $(x - 7)(x - 4)$.

$-4x$

Verification: $(x - 7)(x - 4)$ i.e. $-4x - 7x = -11x$.

$-7x$

Exercise 4.4

Find the factors of each of the following:

1. $x^2 + 3x + 2$
2. $x^2 + 4x + 4$
3. $x^2 + 8x + 7$

4. $x^2 + 5x + 6$
5. $x^2 + 8x + 12$
6. $x^2 + 9x + 14$

7. $a^2 + 7a + 12$
8. $x^2 + 4x + 3$
9. $a^2 + 6a + 8$

10. $a^2 + 9a + 18$
11. $a^2 + 10a + 16$
12 $a^2 + 10a + 24$

13. $x^2 + 11x + 24$
14. $x^2 + 12x + 20$
15. $x^2 + 12x + 27$

16. $x^2 + 13x + 22$
17. $x^2 + 13x + 30$
18. $x^2 + 11x + 30$

19. $x^2 + 14x + 33$
20. $x^2 + 15x + 36$
21. $x^2 + 15x + 44$

22. $x^2 + 9x + 20$
23. $x^2 + 18x + 17$
24. $x^2 + 18x + 32$

25. $x^2 - 4x + 3$
26. $x^2 - 5x + 6$
27. $x^2 - 6x + 8$

28. $x^2 - 5x + 4$
29. $x^2 - 7x + 12$
30. $x^2 - 7x + 10$

31. $x^2 - 9x + 14$
32. $x^2 - 11x + 24$
33. $x^2 - 8x + 15$

34. $x^2 - 9x + 18$
35. $x^2 - 9x + 20$
36. $x^2 - 12x + 20$

37. $x^2 - 12x + 35$
38. $x^2 - 10x + 24$
39. $x^2 - 14x + 24$

40. $x^2 - 12x + 27$
41. $x^2 - 11x + 30$
42. $x^2 - 13x + 30$

43. $x^2 - 17x + 30$
44. $x^2 - 13x + 36$
45. $x^2 - 15x + 36$

46. $x^2 - 14x + 45$
47. $x^2 - 14x + 40$
48. $x^2 - 13x + 40$

Section 4.5 Quadratic expressions – Third term negative

Take the expression $x^2 - 2x - 8$.

Here the final term is negative.

When the final term is negative, the factors will be of the form

$(x + ?)(x - ?) \ldots$ [or $(x - ?)(x + ?)$].

In this case, the factors are $(x + 2)(x - 4)$.

$$\overset{-4x}{}$$

Check: $(x + 2)(x - 4)$ $\ldots -4x + 2x = -2x \ldots$ correct
$$\underset{2x}{}$$

Exercise 4.5

Factorise each of the following:

1. $x^2 - x - 2$ **2.** $x^2 - 2x - 3$ **3.** $x^2 - 3x - 4$

4. $x^2 + 2x - 3$ **5.** $x^2 - x - 12$ **6.** $x^2 + x - 12$

7. $x^2 - 4x - 12$ **8.** $x^2 - 3x - 10$ **9.** $x^2 - 9x - 10$

10. $x^2 - 5x - 14$ **11.** $x^2 - 2x - 15$ **12** $x^2 + 7x - 18$

13. $x^2 + 3x - 18$ **14.** $x^2 + 4x - 21$ **15.** $x^2 - 2x - 24$

16. $x^2 + 5x - 24$ **17.** $x^2 - 10x - 24$ **18.** $x^2 - x - 30$

19. $x^2 + 7x - 30$ **20.** $x^2 - 13x - 30$ **21.** $x^2 + 3x - 28$

22. $x^2 - 12x - 28$ **23.** $x^2 + 5x - 36$ **24.** $x^2 - 9x - 36$

25. $x^2 + 6x - 40$ **26.** $x^2 - 3x - 40$ **27.** $x^2 - 18x - 40$

28. $x^2 - 4x - 45$ **29.** $x^2 + 6x - 16$ **30.** $x^2 - 8x - 48$

Factorise each of the following which contain examples of the three types we have met so far:

31. $x^2 + 9x + 14$ **32.** $x^2 - 12x + 27$ **33.** $x^2 + 2x - 24$

34. $x^2 - 8x + 7$ **35.** $x^2 - 9x + 14$ **36.** $x^2 - 4x - 32$

37. $x^2 + 14x + 24$ **38.** $x^2 + x - 42$ **39.** $x^2 + 5x - 50$

40. $x^2 - 11x + 28$ **41.** $x^2 - 4x - 60$ **42** $x^2 - 17x + 60$

Test yourself 4

1. (a) Copy and complete each of the following:

(i) $9x^2 + 36x = 9x($ $)$ (ii) $5ab + 15bc = 5b($ $)$

(iii) $6ax - 12ay = 6a($ $)$ (iv) $6x^3 - 18xy = 6x($ $)$

(b) Factorise each of these:

(i) $7a + 7b + xa + xb$ (ii) $a^2 - 5ab + ac - 5bc$

(c) Factorise each of these:

(i) $x^2 - 16x + 55$ (ii) $16x^2 - 121$

2. (a) Find the missing expressions in these statements:

(i) $3p^2 - 6p = 3p($ $)$ (ii) $20n^2 + 5n = 5n($ $)$

(iii) $9x^2 - 3x = 3x($ $)$ (iv) $5d^2 - 15d = 5d($ $)$

(b) Copy and complete each of these:

(i) $(n + 3)($ $) = n^2 + 4n + 3$ (ii) $(n + 4)($ $) = n^2 + 8n + 16$

(iii) $(n - 2)($ $) = n^2 + 4n - 12$ (iv) $(n - 3)($ $) = n^2 - 11n + 24$

(c) (i) Factorise $144 - 9b^2$.

(ii) Use the difference of two squares to evaluate $53^2 - 47^2$.

3. (a) Complete the following:

(i) $2xy - 6yz = 2y($ $)$ (ii) $3x^2y - 9xyz = 3xy($ $)$

(b) Factorise each of these:

(i) $6ax - 3bx + 2ay - by$ (ii) $x^2 - 15x + 54$

(c) (i) Factorise $36x^2 - 1$.

(ii) Use factors to find the value of $93^2 - 87^2$.

4. (a) Factorise each of these:

(i) $8a + 12b - 16c$ (ii) $6x^2 - 18x$

(b) Factorise the following:

(i) $5x + xy + y^2 + 5y$ (ii) $x^2 - 13x + 22$

(c) (i) Factorise $16 - a^2b^2$.

(ii) Find the factor that is common to $x^2 - x - 20$ and $x^2 - 25$.

Bills – Interest – Income Tax

chapter 5

Key words

VAT profit and loss cost price selling price principal rate per annum
amount annual interest compound interest income tax tax credit
gross tax tax payable standard rate take-home pay currency exchange

Section 5.1 Household bills

In this section we will deal with various household bills such as electricity, gas and telephone bills. We will also deal with the cost of postage, holidays and insurance as well as car hire and mobile phone charges.

Example 1

Calculate the electricity bill from the information given opposite:

Standing charge:	€23.80
Number of units used:	1025
Cost per unit:	23 cent
VAT on total bill at 10%.	

1025 units @ 23c per unit	= 1025 × 23c	
	= €235.75	
Standing charge	= 23.80	
Total	= €259.55	
VAT @ 10%	= 25.96	[€259.55 ÷ 10 = €25.96]
Total (including VAT)	= €285.51	

Exercise 5.1

1. Find the total of this garage bill:

7 litres of oil at €8.30 per litre	=
20 litres of petrol at €1.65 per litre	=
4 brake pads at €35.40 each	=
3 hours labour at €21 per hour	=
4 tyres at €74.80 each	= _____

Total: €

2. Find the total amount of this bill, including VAT:

9 litres of paint @ €10.50 a litre =

3 brushes at €8.30 each =

6 rolls of wallpaper at €14.25 each =

3 packets of paste at €6.90 each =

10 sheets of sandpaper at 95c each = _____

= €

VAT at 20% =

Total: = €

3. Find the total of this bill from a garden centre:

7 rose bushes at €9.30 each =

5 shrubs at €14.40 each =

$4\frac{1}{2}$ dozen bulbs at €8.40 per dozen =

2 spades at €35.50 each =

800 grams of grass-seed at €4.80 per 100 g =

12 kg of fertiliser at €4.55 per kg = _____

VAT at $12\frac{1}{2}$% =

Total = €

4. A plumber goes to a builders' providers and buys the following items:

30 metres of copper piping at €6.80 a metre

12 taps at €28.30 each

16 copper fittings at €7.30 each

5 radiators at €184 each

Find the amount he has to pay if he is given a discount of 20%.

5. An electricity bill shows the following:

Meter Readings	
Present Reading	**Previous Reading**
87642	86971

(i) How many units were used?

(ii) Each unit costs 21c. Find the total cost of the units used.

6. A householder's electricity bill is charged in the following way:
- ❯ A standing charge of €26.80
- ❯ 1256 units at 23c per unit
- ❯ VAT at 10% on the total bill.

Find the total amount of the electricity bill.

7. Mrs Heaton received a bill of €130.80 for the electricity she used in a two-month period. The bill included a standing charge of €25.20. If each unit of electricity cost 22 cent, find how many units were used.

8. An electricity bill contains the following information:

Present meter reading: 38429 units
Previous meter reading: 36738 units
Standing charge €18.40

Find the total amount of the bill, including the standing charge, if each unit of electricity costs 23 cent.

9. A supplier charges for electricity supplied in the following way:

Day rate: 24c per unit   *Night rate*: 10.5c per unit

Calculate the electricity bill for each of the following users based on the unit rates given above:

Name	No. of units used at *day rate*	No. of units used at *night rate*	Standing Charge
D. Maher	420	130	€28.90
G. O'Gorman	560	370	€25.60

10. A refrigerator uses 1.2 units of electricity a day (24 hours).
What does it cost to operate a refrigerator for a year (365 days) if each unit of electricity costs 15c?

11. Rachel's gas meter was read on 1 March.
The reading was | 1 | 7 | 4 | 2 |

92 days later, the meter was read again.
The reading was | 1 | 9 | 5 | 6 |

Calculate the total gas bill that Rachel will have to pay for the 92 days from 1 March, using the charges given on the right.

QAQ GAS SUPPLIES

CHARGES:
Standing charge, 28c per day
Gas used: 84c per unit

12. A householder is charged for the gas that he uses in the following way:
Standing charge: €26.30.
Reducing rate for therms used:
    0–20 therms: €1.40 per therm
    21–40 therms: €1.26 per therm
    over 40 therms: €1.06 per therm.
Calculate the householder's bill for a period in which he uses 54 therms.

13. The table on the right gives the postage rates for parcels to any part of Ireland. Find the total cost of sending the following parcels.

Weight not over	Cost
1 kg	€6.50
3 kg	€9.80
5 kg	€12.60
10 kg	€17.60

   (i) 2 parcels weighing 3.4 kg each
  (ii) 4 parcels weighing 1.6 kg each
 (iii) 1 parcel weighing 7.1 kg
 (iv) 2 parcels weighing 4.8 kg each.

14. John hired this car for 8 days and drove 850 kilometres. How much did the hire of the car cost him?

SPEEDY'S CAR HIRE

€70 per day & 40c per kilometre

15. Alan earns €12.80 per hour for working a basic week of 38 hours.
Overtime is paid at 'time and a half'.
The table below shows the hours Alan worked last week.

Day	Monday	Tuesday	Wednesday	Thursday	Friday
Hours	10	8	7	9	12

   (i) How many hours overtime did he work last week?
  (ii) Calculate his total pay for last week.
 (iii) If Alan earned €582.40 in a particular week, how many hours overtime did he work that week?

16. The charges for Olivia's bill-pay phone per month are as follows.

        Fixed charge: €15
        Call charges: First 50 minutes free
                        Additional minutes, 18 cent per minute
        Text messages: First 100 text messages free
                        Additional text messages, 14 cent each.

During June, Olivia used 120 minutes call-time and sent 128 text messages.
   (i) Calculate the total charge for all her phone calls.
  (ii) Find the total amount of her bill for the month.

17. *Eircom* charges 15c for each metered unit used. If each local telephone call uses 1 unit every 3 minutes (or part thereof) during peak time, calculate the cost of each of these local calls made at peak time:

	Starting time	Finishing time
(i)	9.07 a.m.	9.12 a.m.
(ii)	12.49 p.m.	1.04 p.m.
(iii)	11.54 a.m.	12.16 p.m.

18. A telephone call to Australia is charged in the following way:

€5.40 for the first 3 minutes, and

€1.75 for each minute (or part of minute) over 3 minutes

Find the cost of a call to Australia which lasts $8\frac{1}{2}$ minutes.

19. The table below gives the cost per adult for a two-week holiday in a hotel, apartment or villa:

Accommodation	May	June	July	August
Hotel Loredo	€1120	€1280	€1390	€1470
Vista Apartments	€760	€850	€930	€1020
Centra Villas	€830	€900	€970	€1080
Children under 16 years of age: Half price				

Find the total cost of each of the following holidays:
(i) two adults in *Hotel Loredo* for 2 weeks in July
(ii) four adults in *Centra Villas* for 2 weeks in August
(iii) two adults and two children aged 8 years and 12 years in *Vista Apartments* for 2 weeks in May
(iv) two adults and three children aged 10, 11 and 17 years in *Hotel Loredo* for 2 weeks in August

20. The table below gives the premiums for insuring buildings and contents as quoted by the *Coverall Insurance Company*.

	Buildings per €1000	Contents per €1000
Area 1	€2.80	€7.40
Area 2	€3.20	€8.50
Area 3	€3.60	€10.25
Area 4	€3.84	€11.10

Based on the table above, calculate the premium for insuring each of the following:
(i) a house worth €320,000 in Area 3
(ii) a house worth €260,000 with contents worth €25,000 in Area 4
(iii) a house worth €220,000 with contents worth €42,000 in Area 1
(iv) a house worth €180,000 with contents worth €32,000 in Area 2.

An insurance company charges €5.40 per €1000 value to insure a premises against fire. If the owner of a premises pays €1404 to the insurance company, find the value of this premises.

Section 5.2 Applying percentages ────────────────

When dealing with problems involving percentages, it is very important to be able to convert a percentage to a decimal.

When a percentage is expressed as a decimal, the electronic calculator is particularly useful for finding the required percentage.

Some examples are highlighted below:

To find 4%, multiply by 0.04.   To find 104%, multiply by 1.04.
To find $6\frac{1}{2}$%, multiply by 0.065.   To find $106\frac{1}{2}$%, multiply by 1.065.
To find 12%, multiply by 0.12.   To find 112%, multiply by 1.12.
To find 87%, multiply by 0.87.   To find 187%, multiply by 1.87.

1. Value-added tax (VAT)

Value-added tax or **VAT** is a government tax which is added to many of the things that we buy. In most shops, the marked price of an item includes VAT and so we do not have to calculate it.

Sometimes, the prices of more expensive items such as television sets, commercial vehicles and furniture are given without VAT. In these cases, the shopkeeper calculates the VAT amount and adds it to the price of the item.

If an article is priced at €280 plus VAT at 23%, the full price can be worked out as follows:

1% of €280 = €2.80

23% of €280 = €2.80 × 23 = €64.40

∴   the full price = €280 + €64.40
                                = €344.40

 Using a calculator:
100% + 23% = 123%
To find 123%, we multiply by 1.23
Full price = €280 × 1.23
                    = €344.40

Example 1

The rate of VAT on bicycles is 23%.

  (i)   Find the selling price of a bicycle priced at €360 + VAT.

  (ii) Another bicycle is advertised at €615 which includes VAT. Find the price of this bicycle before VAT was added.

(i) 23% of €360 = €360 × 0.23 = €82.80

∴ the selling price of the bicycle = €360 + €82.80

= €442.80

Or

Adding 23% gives 123%

123% of €360 = €360 × 1.23 = €442.80 ... as above.

(ii) €615 represents 123% of the price before VAT is added.

$$123\% = €615$$

$$1\% = €\frac{615}{123}$$

$$100\% = €\frac{615}{123} \times \frac{100}{1}$$

$$100\% = €500$$

∴ the price of the bicycle before VAT was added was €500.

2. Percentage profit or loss

When dealing with percentage profit or loss, we base this percentage on the **cost price**, unless otherwise stated.

$$\text{Percentage profit} = \frac{\text{Profit}}{\text{Cost price}} \times \frac{100}{1}\%; \quad \text{Percentage loss} = \frac{\text{Loss}}{\text{Cost price}} \times \frac{100}{1}\%$$

Example 3

(i) A hardware store buys lawnmowers for €480 and sells them for €576. Calculate the percentage profit the store makes on the lawnmowers.

(ii) By selling washing machines for €650, an electrical store makes a profit of 25%. What did the store pay for these washing machines?

(i) Profit = €576 − €480 = €96

$$\text{Percentage profit} = \frac{\text{Profit}}{\text{Cost Price}} \times \frac{100}{1}\%$$

$$= \frac{96}{480} \times \frac{100}{1} = 20\%$$

The percentage profit = 20%.

(ii) €650 represents 125% of the cost price ... 25% profit margin.

∴   125% = €650

1% = €$\frac{650}{125}$

100% = €$\frac{650}{125} \times \frac{100}{1}$

= €520

∴   the store paid €520 for the washing machines.

Exercise 5.2

1. Express each of the percentages as decimals:
  (i) 6%　　(ii) 8%　　(iii) $7\frac{1}{2}$%　　(iv) $9\frac{1}{2}$%　　(v) 10%
  (vi) 13%　(vii) $12\frac{1}{2}$%　(viii) 106%　(ix) 112%　(x) 84%

2. (i) Increase 200 by 10%.
   (ii) Increase 120 by 20%.
   (iii) Increase 250 by 4%.
   (iv) Decrease 120 by 15%.

3. (i) Find 80% of 400.　　　　(ii) Find 5% of 360.
   (iii) Find 185% of 600.　　　(iv) Find $12\frac{1}{2}$% of 120.

4. Find the selling price of each of the following:
   (i) An iPad costing €650 + VAT at 23%.
   (ii) A games console costing €120 + VAT at 21%.
   (iii) A set of tyres costing €300 + VAT at $13\frac{1}{2}$%.
   (iv) A patio furniture set costing €1200 + VAT at 15%.

5. A meal for 4 people cost €110 + VAT at 9%.
   Find the cost of the meal after VAT is added.

6. An hotel bill amounts to €220 after VAT at 10% is added.
   Find the amount of the bill before VAT is added.

7. The selling price of a television set is €984.
   If this includes VAT at 23%, find the price before VAT is added.

8. An electricity bill amounts to €135 after VAT at $12\frac{1}{2}$% is added.
   Find the amount of the bill before VAT is added.

9. Write out the amounts that should go in the highlighted boxes marked A to G.

Cost price	Profit or loss	Selling price
€176	€8.80 profit	A
€460	€92 loss	B
€1.80	€0.63 profit	C
D	€5000 loss	€25 000
E	€4.20 profit	€42
F	€2560 loss	€8000
€3680	G	€4800

10. A greengrocer buys oranges for 80c and sells them for €1.
Find his percentage profit.

11. Jack bought a painting for €600 and sold it for €660. Find
   (i) his profit   (ii) his percentage profit.

12. A menswear store buys jackets for €320 and sells them for €400.
Find the percentage profit the store makes.

13. A jeweller bought an engagement ring for €1200 and sold it at a profit of 15%.
Find the sale price of the ring.

14. By selling television sets for €720, a store makes a profit of 20%.
   (i) What did the store pay for the television sets?
   (ii) If the store sold the television sets for €690, what percentage profit would it make?
   (iii) If the store sold the television sets for €570, what percentage loss would it make?

15. A shop owner marks everything up by 30%.
If she sells an article for €78, find both the cost price and the profit on the article.

16. A garden centre buys azaleas for €11.50 and sells them for €14.95.
Calculate the percentage profit it makes.

17. In a sale, the marked prices are reduced by 30%.
   (i) Calculate the sale price of a jacket if the marked price is €350.
   (ii) Find the marked price of a dress if the sale price is €168.

18. By selling a laptop for €1150, a store makes a profit of 25%.
   (i) What did the store pay for the laptop?
   (ii) At what price should the laptop be sold to make a profit of 20%?

19. When an item is sold for €176, the profit is 10% on the cost price. When the selling price is increased to €192, calculate the percentage profit on the cost price.

20. A greengrocer buys 30 boxes of strawberries at €5.25 each and sells 28 of them at a profit of 30%. If the remaining two boxes are unsaleable, find his percentage profit on the deal.

21. By selling a jacket for €416, a store makes a profit of 30%.
    (i) Find the cost price of the jacket.
    (ii) If the selling price of the jacket is reduced by 10% in a sale, calculate the percentage profit the store now has on the cost price.

Section 5.3 Annual interest

If we invest money in a bank, building society or credit union, we are paid for the use of this money.

The money we receive is called **interest**.

The sum of money we invest is called the **principal**.

If we are paid 6% interest, we receive €6 each year for every €100 we invest.

The percentage interest that we receive is called the **rate**.

If you invest €100 for 1 year at 8%, you will receive €8 interest.

You will then have €108 in your account at the end of the year.

The sum of money you have in your account at the end of any year is called the **amount**.

> Amount = Principal + Interest

Examine the following where the rate of interest is 5%:

| €100 earns €5 in 1 year | €400 earns €20 in 1 year | €400 earns €40 in 2 years |

Example 1

Find the interest on €600 for 3 years at 4% per annum.

€100 earns €4 in 1 year
€600 earns €24 in 1 year
€600 earns €72 in 3 years

> Per annum is per year.

The electronic calculator is very useful when finding the percentage of a number.

To find 8% of €600, we multiply €600 by 0.08 to get €48.

To find $5\frac{1}{2}$% of €300, we multiply €300 by 0.055 to get €16.50.

To find 4%, multiply by 0.04.   To find 104% multiply by 1.04.

Example 2

€350 is invested for 1 year at 6% per annum.
Find the amount at the end of the first year.

$$\begin{aligned}
\text{Amount} &= 106\% \text{ of } €350 \\
&= €350 \times 1.06 \\
&= €371
\end{aligned}$$

Exercise 5.3

1. Without using a calculator, write down,

    (i) 6% of €100

    (iii) 4% of €200

    (v) 3% of €600

    (ii) 8% of €100

    (iv) 7% of €300

    (vi) 12% of €700.

2. Use your calculator to find

    (i) 4% of €600

    (iii) 9% of €950

    (v) 10% of €680

    (ii) 7% of €750

    (iv) 11% of €1200

    (vi) 13% of €6250.

3. Use your calculator to find

    (i) $4\frac{1}{2}$% of €600

    (iii) $7\frac{1}{2}$% of €1380

    (v) $14\frac{1}{2}$% of €1400

    (ii) $8\frac{1}{2}$% of €1500

    (iv) $12\frac{1}{2}$% of €2400

    (vi) $3\frac{1}{2}$% of €840.

4. Use your calculator to find

    (i) 108% of €300

    (iii) 104% of €1600

    (v) 115% of €1050

    (ii) 106% of €900

    (iv) 112% of €1750

    (vi) 110% of €680.

5. Copy and complete the following to find the interest on €800 for 2 years at 6%:

€100 earns €6 after 1 year

€800 earns ☐ after 1 year

€800 earns ☐ after 2 years.

6. Find the interest earned on each of the following:

    (i) €300 after 1 year at 3%
            (ii) €700 after 1 year at 6%

    (iii) €1200 after 1 year at 8%
        (iv) €1400 after 1 year at $4\frac{1}{2}$%

    (v) €600 after 1 year at $2\frac{1}{2}$%
        (vi) €2000 after 1 year at $6\frac{1}{2}$%.

7. Work out the interest earned on each of these:

    (i) €200 for 2 years at 4%
           (ii) €500 for 2 years at 6%

    (iii) €900 for 3 years at 5%
       (iv) €700 for 3 years at 7%.

8. Find the interest earned on each of the following:

    (i) €700 for 2 years at 8%
           (ii) €400 for 3 years at $2\frac{1}{2}$%

    (iii) €1200 for 3 years at 4%
       (iv) €1500 for 2 years at $4\frac{1}{2}$%.

9. Find the amount (interest plus principal) for each of these:

    (i) €600 after 2 years at 7%
          (ii) €1500 after 2 years at $8\frac{1}{2}$%

    (iii) €1250 after 3 years at 10%
      (iv) €1800 after 2 years at $12\frac{1}{2}$%.

10. (i) A sum of money was invested for 2 years at 5% per annum. If the interest earned was €30, find the sum invested.

     (ii) €400 was invested for x years at 6% per annum. If the interest earned was €48, find the value of x.

Section 5.4   Compound interest

Jack invested €500 in a credit union at 6% per annum.

His interest for the first year was €30.

At the end of the first year, he then had €530 in his account.

For the second year, €530 earned interest at 6%.

$$6\% \text{ of } €530 = €530 \times 0.06$$
$$= €31.80$$

Notice that the interest for the second year is greater than the interest for the first year.

This happened because the interest for the first year itself earned interest during the second year.

∴   the amount at the end of the second year is

     €530 + €31.80   = €561.80

This kind of interest is called **compound interest**.

The basic method for calculating compound interest is illustrated in the following example.

Example 1

€1200 is invested for 3 years at 4% per annum compound interest.
What will the investment amount to?

Principal for the first year	= €1200
Interest for the first year	= 4% of €1200
	= 1200 × 0.04 = €48
Principal for the second year	= €1200 + €48 = €1284
Interest for the second year	= 4% of €1248
	= 1248 × 0.04 = €49.92
Principal for the third year	= €1248 + €49.92 = €1297.92
Interest for the third year	= 4% of €1297.92
	= 1297.92 × 0.04
	= 51.9168 = €51.92
∴ Amount at end of third year	= €1297.92 + €51.92
	= €1349.84

Exercise 5.4

Find the compound interest on each of the following.

Give your answers correct to the nearest cent, where necessary.

1. €400 for 2 years at 6%

2. €800 for 2 years at 8%

3. €900 for 2 years at 5%

4. €1000 for 2 years at 9%

5. €700 for 2 years at 4%

6. €850 for 2 years at 10%

7. €800 for 3 years at 5%

8. €1200 for 2 years at 12%

9. €700 for 2 years at 11%

10. €1800 for 3 years at 4%

11. Find, correct to the nearest euro, the compound interest on €840 for 2 years at 7% per annum.

12. Find what €1200 will amount to if invested for two years at 12% per annum compound interest.

13. A woman invests €1500 in a building society for three years at 5% per annum compound interest. How much has she in the society at the end of the three years?

14. €1400 was invested for two years at compound interest.

The rate of interest for the first year was 8% and the rate for the second year was 10%.

Calculate the amount at the end of the two years.

15. A farmer borrowed €12 000 from a bank at 9% per annum compound interest. What did he owe the bank at the end of three years?

Section 5.5 Income tax

Most wage and salary earners pay a portion of their wages or income to the state.

The money is deducted from their wages by their employers and passed on to the Revenue Commissioners.

Money paid to the state in this way is called **income tax**.

Workers pay income tax on **all** their income at one of two rates.

These rates are called the **Standard Rate** and the **Higher Rate**.

The Standard Rate is generally around 20% and the Higher Rate is around 40%.

In this chapter we will deal only with the standard rate.

At the beginning of the year every worker gets a **tax credit** certificate.

This gives the amount of money that a person can deduct from his **gross tax** every week or month. The employer subtracts the tax credit from the gross tax to get the **tax payable**.

> Tax payable = gross tax − tax credit

A worker earns €800 a week and has a tax credit of €70.

The standard rate of income tax is 20%.

His income tax is calculated as follows:

$$\text{Gross tax} = 20\% \text{ of } €800$$
$$= €800 \times 0.2 = €160$$
$$\text{Tax payable} = \text{gross tax} - \text{tax credit}$$
$$= €160 - €70$$
$$= €90$$

The worker pays €90 in income tax each week.

His **take-home pay** is €800 − €90 = €710.

Example 1

A printer has a weekly wage of €860.
He pays income tax on all his wage at the standard rate of 21%.
If he has a tax credit of €66 a week, find how much income tax he pays.

$$\text{Gross tax} = 21\% \text{ of } €860$$
$$= €860 \times 0.21 = €180.60$$
$$\text{Tax payable} = \text{gross tax} - \text{tax credit}$$
$$= €180.60 - €66$$
$$= €114.60$$

The printer pays €114.60 income tax each week.

Exercise 5.5

1. Aaron's weekly wage is €800.
His tax credit is €90 a week.
He pays income tax at the rate of 20%.
Copy and complete the table on the right
to find Aaron's take-home pay.

Gross pay	€800
Tax @ 20%	……
Tax credit	€90
Tax payable	……
Take-home pay	……

2. Helen's gross pay for the year is €34 800.
Her tax credit is €2585.
She pays income tax at the rate of 22%.
Copy and complete the table on the right.

Gross pay	
Tax @ 22%	
Tax credit	
Tax payable	
Take-home pay	

3. Copy and complete the following:

Weekly wage = €600
Tax @ 20% on all income = €600 × 0.2 = €…
Tax credits = €42
Tax payable = €… − €42 = €….

4. Leah has a weekly wage of €770.
Her weekly tax credit is €72 and the standard rate of tax is 25%.
How much income tax does she pay each week?

5. Conor has a monthly wage of €3200.
His monthly tax credit is €280 and the standard rate of tax is 22%.
Find how much income tax he pays each month.

6. Elaine has a weekly wage of €920.
   Her weekly tax credit is €84 and the standard rate of tax is 24%.
   How much income tax does she pay each week?

7. Jill has an annual salary of €42 000.
   Her annual tax credit is €3600 and the standard rate of tax is 22%.
   How much income tax does she pay for the year?

8. A carpenter has a weekly wage of €1050.
   His weekly tax credit is €78 and the standard rate of income tax is 24%.
   (i) Calculate how much income tax he pays each week.
   (ii) What is his net pay (i.e. take-home pay) for the week?

9. Emma is paid €10.40 per hour for a 35-hour working week.
   For each hour over 35 hours, she is paid $1\frac{1}{2}$ times the normal hourly rate.
   Her tax credit for the week is €68 and the standard rate of tax is 26%.
   If in a particular week she worked 45 hours, find
   (i) her gross wage for the week
   (ii) the amount of income tax she pays
   (iii) her take-home pay for the week.

10. John White is a factory manager and he earns €54 000 a year.
    His yearly tax credit is €4300 and the standard rate of income tax is 24%.
    He also makes a pension contribution of 6% of his salary.
    (i) Find his pension contribution for the year.
    (ii) How much income tax does he pay for the year?
    (iii) Find his net pay after income tax and pension contribution have been deducted.

Section 5.6 **Currency transactions**

When we visit a country that does not use the euro, we generally change our euro into the currency of that country.

In Britain, their money is pounds sterling (£).

In the USA, money is in US dollars (US$).

If you visit a foreign exchange counter, you will generally see displayed the amounts of other currencies that you will receive for €1. An example of such a table is shown on the right.

€1 =	
Sterling	0.85
US dollar	1.40
Japanese yen	110
Swiss franc	1.3

When working out how much of one currency you should get in exchange for another, always put the currency you **require** on the **right-hand side**.

> ## Example 1
>
> If €1 = $1.4 and €1 = 110 yen, find
> (i) how many dollars you would get for €400
> (ii) how many euro you would get for 5000 yen.
>
> (i) €1 = $1.4
>   ∴   €400 = $1.4 × 400
>   = $560
>
> (ii) 110 yen = €1
>   1 yen = €$\frac{1}{110}$
>   5000 yen = 5000 × $\frac{1}{110}$ = $\frac{5000}{110}$ = €45.4545
>   = €45.45
>   ∴   5000 yen = €45.45
>
> > You require dollars; have dollars on the right.

Exercise 5.6

1. If €1 = $1.45 and €1 = 115 yen,
  (i) how many dollars would you get for €300
  (ii) how many yen would you get for €750?

2. If €1 = 1.3 US dollars, find
  (i) how many dollars you would get for €450
  (ii) how many euro you would get for 800 dollars.

3. If €1 = 120 yen, find
  (i) how many yen you would receive for €900
  (ii) how many euro you would receive for 9000 yen.

4. Given that €1 = £0.80 sterling, find
  (i) how many pounds sterling you would get for €1200
  (ii) how many euro you would get for £600.

5. On a visit to Switzerland, a person bought a leather jacket
  for 560 Swiss francs.
  If €1 = 1.4 Swiss francs, find the cost of the jacket in euro.

6. If €1 = 1.4 Canadian dollars,
  (i) how many Canadian dollars would you get for €3500?
  (ii) how many euro would you get for 5600 Canadian dollars?

7. If €1 = $1.4 and €1 = £0.85 sterling,
    (i) find in euro the cost of a camera which is priced in New York at $350
    (ii) find in euro the cost of a watch in London priced at £360.

8. If €1 = 9.2 Swedish krona, find
    (i) how much in Swedish krona would you get for €750?
    (ii) how much in euro you would get for 1500 krona?

9. A Swiss visitor exchanged 4200 Swiss francs for euro at a bureau de change.
The rate of exchange was €1 = 1.45 Swiss francs.
Find, correct to the nearest euro, what the visitor received if the bureau charged
1% commission.

10. If €1 = 9.5 South African rand, find
    (i) the price in euro of a car in South Africa with a marked price of 64 000 rand
    (ii) the cost in rand of a flight from Dublin to Cape Town if the quoted price is €840.
        Give your answer to part (i) correct to the nearest euro.

Test yourself 5

1. (a) Karen is arranging a picnic lunch for 8 people.
        She spends €36.20 on sandwiches, €8.40 on crisps and €15.40 on drinks.
        (i) What is the total cost of the picnic?
        (ii) The 8 people agree to share the total cost equally.
            How much does each person pay?

    (b) Caroline buys a painting for €800 and sells it for €1040.
        What is her percentage profit?

2. (a) Pam wants to buy a *Hooper* washing machine.
        Hooper washing machines are sold in three different shops.

Washing Power	Whytes	Clean Up
$\frac{1}{4}$ OFF usual price of €660	20% OFF usual price of €640	€410 plus VAT at $17\frac{1}{2}$%

        (i) Work out the cost of the washing machine in the *Washing Power* shop.
        (ii) Work out the cost of the washing machine in the *Whytes* shop.
        (iii) Work out the cost of the washing machine in the *Clean Up* shop.

(b) A householder's electricity bill is charged in the following way:

> A standing charge of €23.40
> 1256 units at 22c per unit
> VAT at 10% on the total bill.

Find the total amount of the electricity bill.

3. (a) Find the gross wage of each of the following workers if they all receive *time and a half* after 40 hours work:

(i) A van driver who works 45 hours at €15.40 per hour
(ii) A plumber who works 48 hours at €18 per hour

(b) Mrs Moore received a bill for €176.24 for the electricity used during a two-month period. This included a fixed charge of €22.40. If each unit of electricity cost 24c, find how many units of electricity she used.

4. (a) Here is the menu at the *Red Robin Cafe*.

(i) Jack bought 3 burgers, 3 french fries and 2 soft drinks.
How much did he pay?
(ii) Jill bought 3 cheeseburgers and 3 soft drinks.
What change did she get out of €30?

The Red Robin Cafe	
Burger	€4.20
Cheese burger	€5.10
French fries	€2.70
Soft drinks	€1.95

(b) Barry has a weekly wage of €620. He has a tax credit of €34 and he pays income tax on all his wages at the standard rate of 22%.
Find how much income tax he pays each week.

5. (a) A gas company charges the following *reducing rate* for the gas used by domestic consumers:

First 585 kWh per two months	12c per kWh
Next 585 kWh per two months	8c per kWh
All other gas each two months	6c per kWh

In a two-month period, Mrs O'Leary used 1476 kWh of gas.
If the standing charge on her bill was €45.20, calculate the amount of her bill after VAT at 15% was added.
Give your answer correct to the nearest euro.

(b) Find the compound interest earned on €900 for 2 years at 6% per annum.

6. (a) A car may be rented by either of the following methods:

A: €85 per day with no extra charges
B: €35 per day and 60c for each km travelled.

A man wanted to rent a car for 2 weeks and travel 1200 km. Find
   (i) how much he would pay by each method
   (ii) how much he would save by taking the cheaper method.

(b) If €1 = 40 Thai baht, find
   (i) how many baht can be exchanged for €1800
   (ii) how much 2200 baht are worth in euro.

7. (a) In a two-month period, the McCabes used 980 units of electricity.
Each unit of electricity cost 21c and the standing charge was €21.30.
Find the total amount of their bill when VAT at $12\frac{1}{2}\%$ was added on.

(b) €4500 was invested for 2 years at compound interest.
The rate for the first year was 8% and for the second year 6%.
Find the total interest earned.

8. (a) Find the percentage increase in each of these:
   (i) From €25 to €28.50   (ii) From 2 metres to 2.14 metres.

(b) Jean has an annual income of €42 000.
Her tax credit for the year is €3200.
She pays income tax at the rate of 24%.
   (i) Find how much income tax she pays in the year.
   (ii) Find her take-home pay for the year.

9. (a) Every percentage increase or decrease corresponds to a multiplier.
Match these percentage changes to their multipliers.

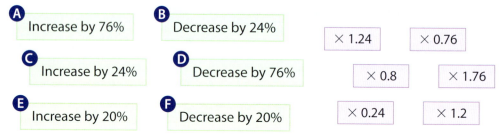

(b) To hire a car, a person has to pay €390 per week, plus 22 cent for each
kilometre travelled.
   (i) Find the cost of hiring the car for 2 weeks if 960 km were travelled.
   (ii) A tourist hired a car for two weeks and paid €1275.
        How many kilometres did she travel?

(c) On a flight a certain weight of luggage is carried free, but there is a charge
of €10 per kilogram for any additional luggage above this weight. Lucy's
luggage, which weighs a total of 50 kg, is overweight and she is charged €150.
If Eva's luggage weighs a total of 30 kg, what will she have to pay?
   A €0   B €30   C €50   D €90   E €100

Perimeter – Area – Volume

Key words

perimeter   square   rectangle   triangle   parallelogram
perpendicular height   rectangular solid   volume   cube   surface area
net   capacity   litre   scale drawing

Section 6.1 Review of perimeter and area

In your *Common Introductory Course* you found the perimeter and area of squares, rectangles and triangles.

The box below summarises what you learned.

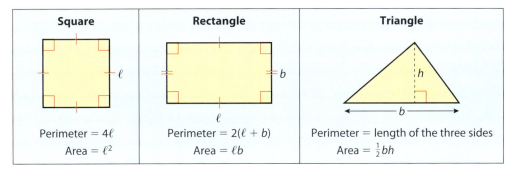

Square	Rectangle	Triangle
Perimeter = 4ℓ Area = ℓ^2	Perimeter = $2(\ell + b)$ Area = ℓb	Perimeter = length of the three sides Area = $\frac{1}{2}bh$

Here are three triangles which all have different shapes.

In each triangle, the base (*b*) and perpendicular height (*h*) are shown.

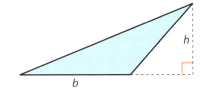

For each triangle, the area $= \frac{1}{2}bh$.

Example 1

Find the area of the shaded region of this figure.

Shaded area = area of rectangle − area of triangle
$$= (20 \times 16) - \left(\tfrac{1}{2} \times 12 \times 9\right)$$
$$= 320 - 54$$
$$= 266 \text{ cm}^2$$

Example 2

The area of the given triangle is 56 cm².
Find the perpendicular height, h.

$$\text{Area} = \tfrac{1}{2} \times 14 \times h \quad \dots \text{base} = 14 \text{ cm}$$
$$\therefore \quad \tfrac{1}{2} \times 14 \times h = 56$$
$$7h = 56$$
$$h = 8 \text{ cm}$$

Exercise 6.1

1. Work out the perimeter of each of these rectangles:

(i)

9 cm

14 cm

(ii)

8 cm

13 cm

(iii)

17 cm

11 cm

2. Find the area of each of the rectangles in Question **1.** above.

3. Find   (i) the perimeter
          (ii) the area
of the given figure

3 cm

2 cm

3 cm

10 cm

4. Work out the area of each of these floors.

(i)

(ii)

5. Find the areas of the following triangles:

(i)

(ii)

(iii)

6. Find the areas of the following triangles:

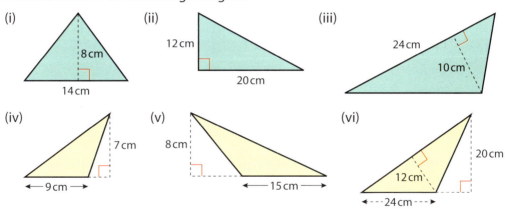

7. Find the areas of the following shapes which are composed of rectangles and triangles.

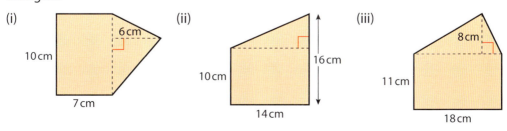

8. Calculate the area of each of the coloured figures shown below:

9. Find the area of the border in each of these rectangles:

10. Find the length of the missing side in each of these rectangles; the area is given in each case:

11. Find the length of the side of each square shown below:

12. Find the height h, in centimetres, of each of these triangles:

13. Find the length of the line segment marked *x* in each of these triangles:

(i)

Area = 90 cm²

(ii)

Area = 112 cm²

(iii)
Area = 120 cm²

14. Work out the perimeter of each of these shapes, where all the angles are right angles:

(i)

(ii)

(iii)
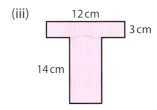

(You have sufficient dimensions to find these perimeters.)

15. Triangle *B* is double the area of triangle *A*.
The height of both triangles is 6 cm.

  (i) Find the area of triangle *A*.
  (ii) Find the area of triangle *B*.
  (iii) Work out the value of *x*.

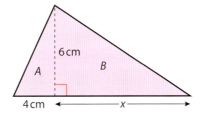

16. Find the area of the shaded portion of the diagram on the right.

Hence find the area of the unshaded part.

17. Find the area of the shaded part of each triangle:

(i)

(ii)

(iii)

87

18. This is an abstract painting in which white rectangles are painted over a coloured background. Each white rectangle measures 15 cm by 24 cm and the painting is 102 cm by 60 cm.

   (i) Find the area of the white paint showing.

  (ii) Find the area of the coloured paint showing.

 (iii) If the rectangles are evenly spaced, both across the painting as well as from top-to-bottom, find the widths of the coloured parts of the painting.

Section 6.2   Area of a parallelogram

A parallelogram is a figure in which the opposite sides are both equal in length and parallel.

By cutting the parallelogram on the left above along the dotted line and then placing the blue triangle at the other end, a rectangle is formed.

Area of rectangle $= 6\,\text{cm} \times 3\,\text{cm} = 18\,\text{cm}^2$

$\therefore$ area of parallelogram is also $18\,\text{cm}^2$, i.e., 6 cm by 3 cm

Area of parallelogram is
   base $\times$ perpendicular height.

Area $= b \times h$

Area of this parallelogram

    = base × perpendicular height

    = 12 cm × 8 cm

    = 96 cm²

Exercise 6.2

1. Find the area of each of these parallelograms:

(i)   (ii)   (iii)

2. Work out the area of each of these parallelograms:

(i)   (ii)   (iii)

3. Write down the value of h in each of these parallelograms:

(i)   (ii)   (iii)

Area = 30 cm²   Area = 63 cm²   Area = 27 cm²

4. Select the correct measurements to find the area of each of these parallelograms:

(i)   (ii)   (iii)

5. Calculate the missing length in each parallelogram:

(i)

7 cm

?

Area = 35 cm²

(ii)

?

12 cm

Area = 78 cm²

(iii)

?

9 cm

Area = 108 cm²

6. Work out the area of the white parallelogram inside the given rectangle.

Hence find the area of the shaded region of the figure.

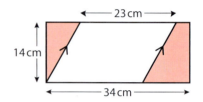

23 cm

14 cm

34 cm

7. (i) Work out the area of each of the parallelograms below.

(ii) Use the area you found to calculate the missing measurement in each figure.

(a)

2 cm

4 cm

3 cm

?

(b)

3 cm

2 cm

?

2.4 cm

(c)

3 cm

2.4 cm

1.8 cm

?

Section 6.3 **Rectangular solids**

The figure on the right is a **rectangular solid** (or **cuboid**).

The space occupied by this solid is called its **volume**.

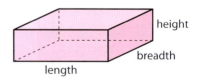

height

breadth

length

The solid on the right is called a **cube** because its length, breadth and height are all equal.

Its volume is **1 cm³**, pronounced **one cubic centimetre**.

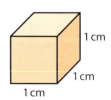

1 cm

1 cm

1 cm

The figure on the right is made up of three layers of cubes.
In each layer there are 24 cubes.
In the three layers there are 72 cubes altogether.
From this we can see that the volume is found by multiplying the length by the breadth by the height.

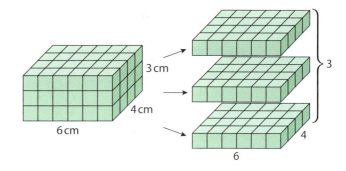

$$\text{Volume} = 6\,\text{cm} \times 4\,\text{cm} \times 3\,\text{cm} = 72\,\text{cm}^3$$

> **Volume of rectangular solid = length × breadth × height**

Surface area of rectangular solid

The given solid shows three faces A, B and C.
The three faces that we cannot see are also A, B and C.

Area of A = 5 cm × 4 cm = 20 cm²
Area of B = 3 cm × 4 cm = 12 cm²
Area of C = 5 cm × 3 cm = 15 cm²

$\therefore$ Surface area of solid = (2 × 20 cm²) + (2 × 12 cm²) + (2 × 15 cm²)
= 40 cm² + 24 cm² + 30 cm² = 94 cm²

Surface area of rectangular solid

> The surface area of a rectangular solid of length ℓ, breadth b and height h is
> $$2\ell b + 2\ell h + 2bh$$

Volume and surface area of a cube

> Volume $= \ell \times \ell \times \ell = \ell^3$
> Surface area $= 6\ell^2$

Example 1

Find (i) the volume (ii) the surface area
of the given rectangular solid.

(i) Volume = $\ell \times b \times h$

$= 11 \text{ cm} \times 7 \text{ cm} \times 8 \text{ cm} = 616 \text{ cm}^3$

(ii) Surface area = $2\ell b + 2\ell h + 2bh$

$= 2(11 \text{ cm} \times 7 \text{cm}) + 2(11 \text{ cm} \times 8 \text{ cm}) + 2(7 \text{ cm} \times 8 \text{ cm})$

$= 154 \text{ cm}^2 + 176 \text{ cm}^2 + 112 \text{ cm}^2 = 442 \text{ cm}^2$

Example 2

The volume of the rectangular box shown is
2156 cm³.
Find the length of the side marked x.

Volume = length × breadth × height

$\therefore$ 2156 cm³ = 22 cm × x × 7 cm

2156 cm³ = $154x$ cm³

$154x = 2156$

$x = \dfrac{2156}{154} = 14$

The side marked x is 14 cm.

Nets of solids

If the figure on the left above was folded along the dotted lines, it would form the cube
shown on the right.
The figure on the left is called the **net** of the solid.

On the left below is the net of a closed rectangular box.
It has a base, a top and four sides.
On the right below is the net of an open rectangular box.
It has a base, four sides, but no top.

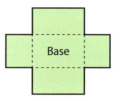

A net for a cube was shown on the previous page.
Here are two more nets for a cube.

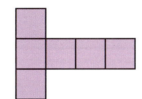

There are 11 different nets for a cube.

Example 3

By drawing a net of this closed rectangular box, find its total surface area.

The net for the box is shown below.

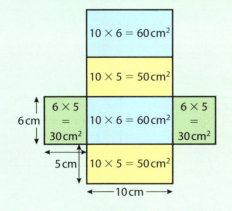

Total surface area

$= 60 + 60 + 50 + 50 + 30 + 30$

$= 280 \text{ cm}^2$

Example 4

This is the net of an open box.
If this net is folded along the dotted lines to
make a box, find

  (i) the volume of the box

  (ii) the surface area of the outside of the box.

  (i) This is the box that is formed from the net.

      Volume $= 14 \times 8 \times 3$

           $= 336\,\text{cm}^3$

  (ii) Surface area $= 2(14 \times 3) + 2(8 \times 3) + (14 \times 8)$ ... no top on box

                   $= 84 + 48 + 112 = 244\,\text{cm}^2$

Capacity – The Litre

The capacity of a container is the amount of liquid it can hold.
The most commonly-used metric measure of capacity is the **litre**.
A cube with edge of length 10 cm contains 1 litre.

    $\therefore$ $1000\,\text{cm}^3 = 1$ litre

Remember   To convert cubic centimetres (cm^3) to litres, divide by 1000.

Exercise 6.3

1. Find the volume of each of these rectangular solids:

(i)   (ii)   (iii)

2. Find the surface area of each of the solids in Question **1.** above.

3. Find (a) the volume (b) the surface area of these solid cuboids:

(i)
16 cm
←18 cm→
8 cm

(ii)
24 cm
←20 cm→
16 cm

(iii)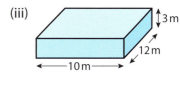
3 m
12 m
←10 m→

4. Find the surface area of each of these solids:

(i)
6 cm
4 cm
10 cm

(ii)
7 cm
4 cm
19 cm

(iii)
15 cm
9 cm
10 cm

5. The diagram shows a rectangular box partly filled with cubes of side 1 cm.
How many more of these cubes are required to fill the box?

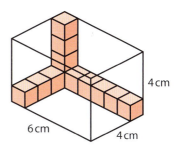
4 cm
6 cm
4 cm

6. Each of the solid shapes below can be broken into two or more rectangular solids. The dotted lines indicate how the figures may be divided.
Now find the total volume of each of these shapes:

(i)
6 cm
5 cm
5 cm
14 cm
9 cm

(ii)
6 cm
3 cm
2 cm
4 cm
4 cm
8 cm
14 cm

(iii)
10 cm
4 cm
7 cm
9 cm
7 cm
4 cm

7. Five cubes of side 2 cm are joined to make the solid shown.
Which of the following is the surface area of the solid?

(i) 68 cm² (ii) 72 cm² (iii) 20 cm² (iv) 88 cm²

8. Find (i) the volume and (ii) the surface area of the given cube.

5 cm

9. The volume of each of the following rectangular solids is given. Find the length of the side marked with a letter.

(i)

3 cm

a 8 cm

Volume = 120 cm³

(ii)

b

6 m   10 m

Volume = 420 m³

(iii)

8 cm

c

14 cm

Volume = 2240 cm³

10. The volume of a cube is 64 cm³.
Find (i) the length of the side of the cube
      (ii) the surface area of the cube.

11. The surface area of this cube is 150 cm².
Find (i) the length of the side of the cube
      (ii) the volume of the cube.

12. The figure on the right shows a stack of cubes of side 3 cm.
  (i) How many cubes are there in the stack?
  (ii) Find the volume of the stack.

13. Hannah is packing packets of soap powder into a box, as shown.
  (i) How many will fit along one 30 cm side?
  (ii) How many packets will there be in the bottom layer when the box is full?
  (iii) How many layers will there be when the box is full?
  (iv) How many packets of soap powder will fit in the box altogether?

30 cm   24 cm   28 cm

4 cm   SOAP POWDER   SOAP POWDER

5 cm   6 cm

14. A hotel buys washing powder in boxes which are
20 cm long, 12 cm wide and 16 cm high.

   (i) Calculate the volume of powder in the box.

The hotel puts the powder into smaller boxes
which are cubes of side 4 cm.

  (ii) How many smaller boxes can be filled from
one of the large boxes?

15. A box has dimensions 10 cm by 8 cm by 6 cm.
Dice like these are to be packed into this box.
What is the largest number of dice the box will hold?

16. If 1 litre $= 1000$ cm^3, find the capacity of these rectangular containers in litres.

(i)

(ii)

(iii)

17. A square sheet of metal has a side of length 30 cm.
Four identical squares of side 4 cm are cut away
from the corners, as shown.
The remaining shape is folded to form a box.

   (i) Is the box an open or closed box?
  (ii) Find the volume of the box.
 (iii) Find the outer surface area of the box.

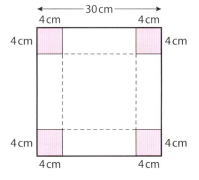

18. This is the net of a rectangular box.
When it is folded to make a box,

   (i) write down the dimensions of the base.
  (ii) what is the height of the box?
 (iii) calculate the volume of the box.
 (iv) calculate the external surface area of
the box.

19. This is the net of a cube. The length of each side is 4 cm.

    (i) Find the volume of the cube.

    (ii) Find the surface area of the cube.

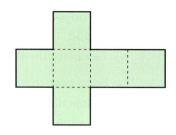

20. The net shown is folded to make a rectangular box.
The pink rectangle will be the base of the box.

    (i) Write down the height of the box.

    (ii) Is the box open or closed?

    (iii) Find the volume of the box.

    (iv) Work out the surface area of the box.

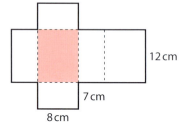

21. The diagram shows a net of a cube with a different
letter on each face. When the cube is assembled,
which letter is opposite the letter:

    (i) A   (ii) E   (iii) D?

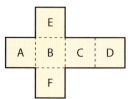

22. When the given net is formed into a cube, which
letter is opposite the letter:

    (i) A   (ii) E   (iii) D?

23. This is the net of a rectangular box.
Draw a rough sketch of the assembled box and
then calculate

    (i) the volume of the box,

    (ii) the surface area of the box.

24. Shown on the right is the net of a dice.
Make a copy of this net and label the faces from 1 to 6
so that when it is folded to form a dice, the numbers on
the opposite faces add up to 7.

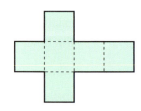

25. The dimensions of a closed rectangular box
are shown on the right.
Draw an accurate sketch of the net for this box.

3 cm

2 cm

4 cm

Section 6.4 **Scale drawing**

The height of the cat in this drawing is 4 cm.
We are told that the **scale** is 1 : 10.
This means that the real cat is 10 times as tall as the
cat shown in the drawing.
The height of the 'real cat' is 4 cm × 10 = 40 cm.
The picture shown is an example of a scaled drawing.

In everyday life, people such as architects and
engineers make scale drawings of buildings and bridges.
Builders must then be able to read and understand
them so that the structures can be built properly.

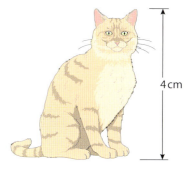

4 cm

Scale = 1 : 10

❯ Scale drawings have the same shapes as the objects that they represent but they are
   of different sizes.

❯ The scale of a drawing is length of drawing : real length.
   A scale of 1 : 100 means that the real size is 100 times the size of the drawing.

❯ The scale determines the size of the drawing.
   A 1 : 10 scale drawing of an object would be bigger than a 1 : 100 scale drawing of
   the same object.

Here is a scale drawing of a clock.

The scale is 1 : 6.

The drawing is 5 cm by 5 cm.

The actual length of the clock is 5 cm × 6
                                          = 30 cm.

Accordingly, the actual dimensions of the clock
are 30 cm by 30 cm.

Scale 1 : 6

Example 1

Part of a house plan drawn to a scale of 1 : 100 is shown. Bedroom 1 is a square of sides 5 cm.

(i)   Find the actual length of this bedroom in metres.

(ii) Measure the width of bedroom 2 on the plan and hence write down its width in metres.

(iii) The kitchen in the house is 6.5 metres by 4.8 metres. What are the dimensions of the kitchen in the plan?

bedroom 2

bedroom 1

(i)   On the plan, 1 cm = 100 cm   ... 1:100 scale
            ∴   5 cm = 500 cm
                      = 5 metres
      The length of bedroom 1 is 5 metres.

(ii) The width of bedroom 2 is 3 cm.
            3 cm = (3 × 100) cm in real width
                  = 300 cm = 3 metres
      The width of bedroom 2 is 3 metres.

(iii) The kitchen is 6.5 m by 4.8 m or 650 cm by 480 cm.
      Since the scale is 1 : 100, we divide both 650 cm and 480 cm by 100 to find the dimensions in the plan.
      Dimensions in the plan $= \dfrac{650}{100}$ cm by $\dfrac{480}{100}$ cm
                      $= 6.5$ cm by 4.8 cm

Example 2

The scale on a map is 1 : 100 000.

(i)   Find the distance in kilometres between two towns which are 7 cm apart on the map.

(ii) Two train stations are 25 km apart.
      How many centimetres apart are they on the map?

(i) Scale = 1 : 100 000

∴   1 cm = 100 000 cm

7 cm = 700 000 cm

$$= \frac{700\,000}{100} \text{ metres} = 7000 \text{ m} = 7 \text{ km}$$

The towns are 7 km apart.

(ii) $25 \text{ km} = \frac{25}{100\,000}$ km on the map

$$= \frac{25 \times 1000}{100\,000} \text{ metres}$$

$$= \frac{25}{100} \text{ m} = 0.25 \text{ m} = 25 \text{ cm}$$

The train stations are 25 cm apart on the map.

Exercise 6.4

1. The scale on a building plan is 1 : 50.
Find the actual length if the length of the line on the plan is:

(i) 3 cm   (ii) 7 cm   (iii) 18 cm   (iv) 6.5 cm   (v) 12.8 cm

2. The scale on a map is 1 cm = 10 km.

(i) Find the distance between two towns if they are 8 cm apart on the map.

(ii) If two train stations are 60 km apart, how far are they apart on the map?

3. Find the actual lengths of the following lines on a building plan for which the scale is given:

(i) 2 cm – scale is 1 : 300   (ii) 6 cm – scale is 1 : 400

(iii) 8 cm – scale is 1 : 500   (iv) 7.5 mm – scale is 1 : 1000

4. Use the scales given to find the actual heights of the animals below:

1 : 30   1 : 90   1 : 45

4 cm

4 cm

3 cm

5. This is the scale drawing of a lorry.
The scale is 1 : 100.
Measure the length of this drawing
and hence write down the actual
length of the lorry.
Find also the maximum height of the
lorry.

Scale 1:100

6. A walking map has a scale of 1 : 20 000.
   (i) Find the actual distance for each of these scaled distances:
      (a) 2 cm   (b) 5 cm   (c) 8.5 cm   (d) 12.5 cm

   (ii) Find the distances on the map for these actual distances:
      (a) 10 km   (b) 4 km   (c) 40 km   (d) 27 km

7. A map has a scale of 1 : 500 000.
   (i) The distance between two service stations
       on the map is 3.4 cm.
       What is the actual distance?
   (ii) The next emergency phone is 22 km away.
       How many centimetres would this be on the map?

8. From the drawing,
by measurement
and calculation, find:
   (i) the maximum
       length of the bus
   (ii) the maximum
       height of the bus.

Scale = 1 : 80

9. A surveyor needs to draw an accurate
plan of this awkwardly-shaped field.
The scale he will use is 1 cm = 10 m.
   (i) What lengths will these lines have on the plan?
      (a) [AB]   (b) [BC]
   (ii) Construct an accurate scale drawing of this
       field using the given scale.

10. The scale on a map is 5 cm to 2 km. Express this in the form 1 : *n*.
Now find the distance, in cm, on the map between two towns, A and B, which are in
reality 30 km apart.

11. A girl made this scale drawing to calculate the height, |AB|, of a triangular wall.

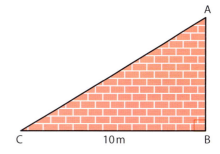

   (i) Measure the distance |CB| on the scale drawing and calculate the scale of the drawing.
   (ii) By measurement and calculation, find the real height |AB|.
   (iii) Find the area of this triangular wall.

12. (i) A 1:50 scale model of a yacht is to be built.
            If the yacht is 25 metres long, how long will the model yacht be?
         (ii) A scale drawing is to be made of a car.
            If the car is 6.25 m long, and the model is to be 25 cm long, what should the scale be?
            Give your answer in the form 1:?.

Test yourself 6

1. (a) Find the area of the figure shown on the right.

    (b) Find (i) the volume
             (ii) the total surface area
    of the given rectangular solid.

2. (a) Find the area of the shaded region of the given figure.

    (b) The volume of the given solid is 1080 cm^3. Find the height h of the solid.

    (c) The area of the given triangle is 49 cm^2. Find the perpendicular height h.

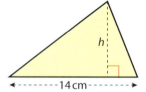

3. (a) Find the total length of ribbon used to tie a box as illustrated. 15 cm extra is required for the knot and bow.

(b) A rectangular petrol tank has dimensions as shown on the right.

(i) Find the volume of the tank in cm³.

(ii) How many litres of petrol would fit in the tank?

(c) Here is the net of a cube.
Which face would be opposite face 1 when folded?

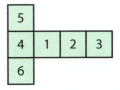

4. (a) Denise has a rectangular garden that measures 10 m by 13 m.

Her garden has a lawn, a square patio of side length 5 m and a vegetable patch that is 4 m by 1.5 m.

What is the area of the lawn?

(b) Find the volume of the figure shown on the right.

(c) To find the area of the given parallelogram, only two of the given measurements are necessary.
By selecting the correct two, find its area.

5. (a) In the given diagram, equal lengths are marked.
  (i) Find the area of △ABE.
  (ii) Find the area of △ACD.
  (iii) Hence find the area of BCDE.

(b) Here is the net of a rectangular box.
  The shaded rectangle is the base of the box.
  (i) What is the height of the box?
  (ii) Find the volume of the box.
  (iii) Find the surface area of the box.

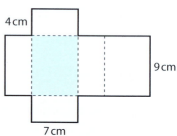

6. (a) The diagram on the right shows a room 5 m
  long and 4 m wide.
  A carpet is placed in the room so that there
  is a uniform border $\frac{1}{2}$ m in width left all round.

  Find (i) the area of the carpet in m²
     (ii) the area of the border in m²
     (iii) the cost of the carpet if 1 m² costs €80
     (iv) the cost of staining the border at €14 per m².

(b) A map has a scale of 1 : 25 000.
  (i) What is the actual distance if the scaled distance is 4 cm?
  (ii) What is the scaled distance if the actual distance is 3.5 km?

7. (a) The volume of the stack of cubes shown in 216 cm³.
  (i) Find the volume of one cube.
  (ii) Find the length of the edge of each cube.

(b) Peter is finding the height of a telegraph pole.
  He has a tripod 0.9 m high.
  He puts the tripod 5.5 m from the pole and
  measures the angle of elevation as 40°.
  (i) Draw an accurate scale diagram using
     a scale of 2 cm to 1 m.
  (ii) Use your diagram to find the height of
     the pole, correct to 1 decimal place.
  (iii) Peter says that 2 cm on his diagram is 100 cm in reality.
     Explain how to write this scale as a ratio.

Key words

data	raw data	numerical data	discrete data
continuous data	categorical data	nominal	ordinal
primary data	secondary data	sample	simple random sample
population	questionnaire	bias	representative

Section 7.1 Types of data

In this section, we revisit some of the words and definitions you encountered in your study of data in first-year.

Data is another name for the facts and pieces of information that we collect.
Data that is not in an organised form is called **raw data**.
Data can be divided into two broad categories, namely **categorical data** and **numerical data**.

Categorical data

Data which fits into a group or category is called **categorical data**.
It is generally described using words such as colour, favourite sport or country of birth.

Categorical data such as
> colours of cars
> male or female
> true/false
> favourite books,   is generally called **nominal data**.

Categorical data in which the categories have an obvious order such as first division, second division, third division, etc., is called **ordinal data**.

Here are some more examples of ordinal data:
> type of car (luxury, executive, family, economy, …)
> examination grades (A, B, C, D, …)
> opinion scales (strongly agree, agree, don't know, disagree, strongly disagree).

Numerical data

Data which can be counted or measured is called **numerical data** because the answer is a number.

Numerical data can be either **discrete** or **continuous**.

<table>
<tr><td>

Discrete data

Data which can take only certain individual values is called **discrete data**.

Here are some examples of **discrete data**:

> The numbers of goals scored by football teams on a Saturday
> The numbers of desks in the classrooms of the school
> The marks achieved in a test.

</td><td>

Continuous data

Continuous data is measured on some scale and can take any value on that scale.

Here are some examples of **continuous data**:

> The heights of students in your class
> The speeds of cars passing a certain point on a road
> The time taken to complete a 100-metre sprint

</td></tr>
</table>

Here is a summary of data types:

Example 1

For each of the following, write down whether it is numerical or categorical data:
  (i)   the number of goals scored in a hockey match
  (ii) the temperature in an oven
  (iii) people's hair colours
  (iv) countries where cars were manufactured
  (v)   star ratings of the quality of hotels
  (vi) time taken for athletes to run 400 metres.

  (i)   numerical   (ii) numerical   (iii) categorical
  (iv) categorical   (v)   categorical   (vi) numerical

Exercise 7.1

1. State whether each of the following is numerical or categorical data:
- (i) The number of cars sold by a certain garage last month
- (ii) The favourite soccer teams of pupils in your class
- (iii) The continent of birth of people who came to Ireland in the past year
- (iv) The number of horses in a race
- (v) The time taken by the winning horse to complete the race
- (vi) The blood-types of the teachers in your school
- (vii) The types of trees in a wood
- (viii) The length of time taken to complete a sudoku puzzle.

2. State whether each of the following pieces of numerical data is discrete or continuous:
- (i) The number of animals in the zoo
- (ii) The time taken to run a marathon
- (iii) The score on a dice
- (iv) Patients' body temperatures
- (v) The number of homes in a postal district with internet access
- (vi) The area of a football pitch.

3.
- (i) Is the breed of this dog categorical or numerical data?
- (ii) The dog weighs 23 kg.
  Is this discrete or continuous data?
- (iii) The dog has 4 legs, is 4 years old and eats 4 *munchies* for his lunch.
  State whether each 4 is discrete or continuous.

4. Each of the following is categorical data.
State whether each is nominal or ordinal.
- (i) The types of animals on a large farm
- (ii) The credit ratings of countries (Triple A, …)
- (iii) The divisions in a football league
- (iv) The countries visited while supporting the Irish soccer team
- (v) The subjects available to study in fifth-year
- (vi) The categories of medals that can be won at the Olympic Games
- (vii) The grades I can get in my Junior Certificate examinations.

5. Eight candidates were interviewed for a job.
Based on the results of the interview, they were placed in order from 1 to 8.
Use two words to describe the data contained in each statement.

Section 7.2 **Collecting data**

Data is collected for a variety of reasons and from a variety of sources.

> Companies do market research to find out what customers like or dislike about their products and to see whether or not they would like new products.

> The government carries out a census of every person in the country every five years. The information gathered is used by other people and organisations for further planning.

Data can be collected by any of these methods:

> Doing a survey by means of a questionnaire and recording what people say

> Carrying out an experiment which may involve the use of technology such as a computer or data logger

> Using sources such as reference books, websites, databases, newspapers and historical records.

Before you collect data, you need to have a clear aim in mind. You then need to decide what sort of data to collect and the most suitable and efficient method of collecting it.

The data you collect can be divided into two broad categories, namely, **primary data** and **secondary data**.

Primary data	**Secondary data**
Data that is collected by an organisation or individual that is going to use it is called **primary data**.	Data which is already available or has been collected by someone else for a different purpose is called **secondary data**.

Surveys

Primary data is generally collected by means of a **survey**.
The main survey methods are:

> personal interviews in which people are asked questions; this is generally done by means of a **questionnaire**.

> telephone surveys; here the interview is conducted by phone

> **observation**; this involves monitoring behaviour

> **experiments**; these are particularly useful for collecting scientific data; drug companies carry out expeirments to test the benefits and the side-effects of new drugs.

Questionnaires

A **questionnaire** is a set of questions designed to obtain data from individuals.

People who answer questionnaires are called **respondents**.

There are two ways in which the questions can be asked.

> An interviewer asks the questions and fills in the questionnaire

> People are given a questionnaire and asked to fill in the responses themselves.

When you are composing questions for a questionnaire,

> be clear what you want to find out and what data you need

> ask short, concise questions

> start with simple questions to encourage the person who is giving the responses

> provide response boxes where possible: Yes ☐   No ☐

> avoid leading questions such as

　　　'Don't you agree that there is too much sport on television?'

　or　'Do you think that professional footballers are overpaid?'

> avoid personal questions such as those which involve name, exact age or weight.

Avoiding bias

When you are collecting data, you need to make sure that your survey or experiment is **fair** and avoids **bias**. If bias exists, the data collected might be unrepresentative.

Here are some questions which should be avoided because they suggest a particular answer or because they may cause embarrassment or shame.

Have you ever stolen money from your parents?

Yes ☐   No ☐

Few students are likely to answer this question honestly if they have already stolen.

Do you agree that the Minister for Finance should resign because of the poor state of the economy?

Yes ☐   No ☐

The wording of this question suggests that the right answer is 'yes'. It is a leading question and therefore likely to be **biased**.

Exercise 7.2

1. State whether each of the following is an example of primary data or secondary data:
   (i) Conor tossed a coin 100 times and recorded the result to investigate if the coin was fair.
   (ii) Brenda counted the number of SUVs that passed the school gate between 9 a.m. and 10 a.m..
   (iii) Shane used the internet to check the number of medals Ireland won in boxing in the last four Olympic Games.
   (iv) Emer checked the Central Statistics Office website to check the number of people on the Live Register for each of the last twenty four months.

2. A brewery wants to produce a new type of beer.
   Suggest how they might use both primary and secondary data to do market research.

3. Niamh wants to find out how often adults go to the cinema.
   She uses this question on a questionnaire.

   'How many times do you go to the cinema?'

   ☐   ☐   ☐
   Not very often   Sometimes   A lot

   (i) Write down **two** things wrong with this question.
   (ii) Design a better question for her questionnaire to find out how often adults go to the cinema.
       You should include some response boxes.

4. Eamonn is trying to find out what people think of the *FFG Political Party*.
   He is trying to decide between these two questions for his questionnaire.
   Which question should he use? Explain your answer.
   (i) How do you rate the *FFG Party's* economic policies?
       Strongly   Don't   Strongly
       agree ☐   Agree ☐   know ☐   Disagree ☐   disagree ☐
   (ii) Do you agree that the *FFG Party* has the best economic policies?
       Yes ☐   No ☐

5. Explain what is wrong with each of the following survey questions.
Suggest a better alternative for each question.
  (i) What age are you?
 (ii) Would you describe yourself as being well-educated?
(iii) Normal people like animals.
      Do you like animals?
 (iv) Would you agree that top actors are paid too much?
  (v) Have you ever taken illegal drugs?
 (vi) Where exactly do you live?
(vii) In view of the huge numbers of road accidents outside this school, do you
      think the speed limit should be reduced?

6. Aidan wants to find out what students think about the library service at his college.
Part of the questionnaire he has written is shown.

> **Q1.** What is your full name? ....
>
> **Q2.** How many times a week do you go to the library?
>   ☐ Often   ☐ Sometimes   ☐ Never

  (i) Why should Q1 not be asked?
 (ii) What is wrong with the choices offered in Q2?

7. This question was included in a questionnaire.

> How old are you?   Young ☐   Middle-aged ☐   Elderly ☐

  (i) What is wrong with the question and responses?
 (ii) Rewrite the question and responses in a better way.

8. Valerie is the manager of a supermarket.
She wants to find out how often people shop at her supermarket.
She will use a questionnaire.

Design a suitable question for Valerie to use on her questionnaire.
You must include some response boxes.

9. Give a reason why questions A and B below should be re-worded before being
included in a questionnaire.
Rewrite each one showing exactly how you would present it in a questionnaire.
Question A: Do you live in a working-class or middle-class area?
Question B: The new supermarket seems to be a great success. Do you agree?

Section 7.3 Sampling

If you were asked to investigate the claim,

'Rugby players in Ireland are taller than Gaelic football players',

do you measure the heights of all rugby players and all Gaelic football players in the country?

This would be an enormous task as there are thousands of players in these categories.

In this study, we use the word **population** to describe **all** the rugby and Gaelic footballers in the country.

When a population is too large for a study, we collect data from some members of the population only. In statistics, this group is called a **sample**. The purpose of a sample is to collect data from some of the population and use it to draw conclusions about the whole population.

Bias

The sample you select for your study is very important. If the sample is not properly selected, the results may be **biased**. If **bias** exists, the results will be distorted and so will not be properly representative of the population as a whole.

The **size** of a sample is also important. If the sample is too small, the results may not be very reliable. If the sample is too large, the data may take a long time to collect and analyse.

Simple random sample

One of the ways to avoid bias in a survey is to take a **simple random sample** (or more commonly called a **random sample**).

In a random sample, every member of the population being considered has an equal chance of being selected. Random samples need to be carefully chosen.

Methods for choosing a **simple random sample** could involve giving each member of the population a number and then selecting the numbers for the sample in one of these ways:

> putting the numbers into a hat and then selecting however many you need for the sample

> using a random number table

> using a random number generator on your calculator or computer.

Electronic calculators are very useful for generating random numbers.

If you want to generate 3-digit numbers, press [SHIFT], and then press [Ran #].

Now press [=] and disregard the decimal point.

If the number displayed is 0.107, write 107.

Press [=] repeatedly to get more random numbers.

Exercise 7.3

1. A school has 820 students and an investigation concerning the school uniform is being conducted.
   40 students from the school are randomly selected to complete the survey on their school uniform. In this situation,
   (i) what is the population size
   (ii) what is the size of the sample?

2. Melanie wants to find out how often people go to the cinema.
   She gives a questionnaire to all the women leaving a cinema.

   Her sample is biased.
   Give **two** possible reasons why.

3. Amy wants to find out how often people play sport.
   She went to a local sports shop and questioned the people she met.
   Explain why this sample is likely to be biased.

4. Dara wants to find out how people get to work each day.
   Which of the following is the most appropriate group to question?
   A: Every fourth person at a bus stop.
   B: A group of people at lunch break.
   C: People arriving late for work.

5. Jennifer wants to investigate if people want longer prison sentences for criminals.
   Which of the following is the most appropriate group to question?
   A: Members of the gardaí.
   B: People at a football match.
   C: People who have been in prison.
   Explain your answer.

6. Amanda wants to choose a sample of 500 adults from the town where she lives.
She considers these methods of choosing her sample:

Method 1:   Choose people shopping in the town centre on Saturday mornings.
Method 2:   Choose names at random from the electoral register.
Method 3:   Choose people living in the streets near her house.

Which method is most likely to produce an unbiased sample?
Give a reason for your answer.

7. Comment on any possible bias in the following situations:
  (i)   Sixth-year students only are interviewed about changes to the school uniform.
  (ii) Motorists stopped in peak-hour traffic are interviewed about traffic problems.
  (iii) Real estate agents are interviewed about the prices of houses.
  (iv) A 'who will you vote for?' survey at an expensive city restaurant.

8. A research company is canvassing peoples'
opinions on whether smoking should be
banned in all public places.

They canvass people standing outside
buildings in the city during office hours.
Explain why the data collected is likely to
be biased.

9. Use the ⸢Ran #⸣ key on your calculator to choose a sample of 8 pupils from a
year-group of 100.

10. Which of the following samples are likely to be representative samples?
For those that are not representative, give a reason why they are not.
  Ⓐ Survey task: To test the effectiveness of a new drug for migraines.
      Sample: Chosen by giving the drug to all patients, of just one doctor,
                      who suffer from migraines.
  Ⓑ Survey task: To survey opinion about fresh bread baked in a local
                      supermarket.
      Sample: Chosen by interviewing every 20th shopper at the supermarket
                      checkout on a Saturday
  Ⓒ Survey task: To survey the voting intentions of residents of a particular
                      constituency in the coming election.
      Sample: A random sample of people at the local train station between
                      7 a.m. and 9 a.m. are surveyed.

Test yourself 7

1. State whether each of the following sets of data is numerical or categorical:
   (i) Favourite type of apple.
   (ii) The head-count at a small protest rally.
   (iii) The weights of three-year-old children.
   (iv) The brands of dog-food on sale in a supermarket.
   (v) County of birth.
   (vi) The amount of rainfall in each month of the year.

2. State whether each of the following numerical data is discrete or continuous:
   (i) The number of vehicles passing through an intersection each hour.
   (ii) Times taken for athletes to run 100 m.
   (iii) The boiling points of a variety of liquids found in your school's science lab.
   (iv) The stopping distances of cars doing 80 km/hr.
   (v) The number of matches in a selection of match boxes.
   (vi) Star-ratings of the quality of hotels.

3. Each of the following types of data is categorical.
   State whether or not each is ordinal data.
   (i) The county of birth of a group of 200 adults.
   (ii) The five divisions in a basketball league.
   (iii) The classification of houses from 1-bedroomed to 6-bedroomed.
   (iv) Any favourite type of music.
   (v) The grading of public beaches during the bathing season.

4. State whether each of the following is primary data or secondary data:
   (i) Counting the number of hatchback cars passing the school gate.
   (ii) Looking at records to see how many people passed through Shannon Airport each day in June one year.
   (iii) Examining tourist brochures to find the average weekly snowfall at a skiing resort.
   (iv) Checking *Wikipedia* to see how many gold medals each country won at the London Olympics.

5. (a) Which of the two questions and responses below are the more suitable for inclusion in a questionnaire?
   Give a reason for your selection.

(i)

Do you agree that having a lovely, warm,
relaxing bath at night helps you go to sleep?

Yes ☐   No ☐

(ii)

Does a warm bath at night help you go to sleep?

Yes ☐   No ☐   Not sure ☐

(b)   To gather information about the
public's opinion on whether
money should be spent upgrading
the local library, a questionnaire
form is placed in the library for
members of the public to fill out.
Explain why this sample is likely
to be biased.

6. (a)   Explain what is wrong with each of the following survey questions and suggest
better alternatives.
   (i)   How many phones are there in your home?
  (ii)   What type of car do you own?
 (iii)   What is your email address?

(b)   A county engineer is carrying out a traffic survey.
He is trying to find out how busy a particular road is.
Each day, he counts the number of cars passing a particular point between
2 p.m. and 3 p.m..
He uses this information to write a report.
State why his sample is likely to be biased.

7. What is wrong with the following examples of collecting information?
   (i)   I phoned 1000 people and discovered that 92 per cent of people have a
telephone.
  (ii)   I interviewed 100 people who came out of *Zac's Discount* and found that
63 per cent of people use *Zac's Toothpaste*.
 (iii)   I asked 50 people to answer Yes or No to the question "Have you stopped
insulting your neighbours?", and found that 80 per cent of people have
stopped insulting their neighbours

Probability

Section 8.1 Listing outcomes

Here is a spinner with 8 sectors.
It has 8 different numbers and 3 different colours.
If the spinner is spun, you may get any of the numbers
1, 2, 3, 4, 5, 6, 7 or 8.
These are called **outcomes**.
If we are interested in colours only, then the possible
outcomes are green, blue and yellow.

For the spinner above, we **listed** all the **possible outcomes** for numbers and for colours.

We will now consider the outcomes when this spinner is spun and a coin is tossed.

Here is the list of the possible outcomes:

1H, 2H, 3H, 4H, 5H, 6H, 7H, 8H, 1T, 2T, 3T, 4T, 5T, 6T, 7T, 8T,

where H stands for head and T stands for tail.
Notice that there are **16** possible outcomes.

The number of outcomes can be found much more easily by multiplying **8** (number of
outcomes for the spinner) and **2** (number of outcomes for the coin), i.e. 8 × 2 = 16.

The preceding example illustrates the
Fundamental Principle of Counting
which is given on the right.

> If one event has **m** possible outcomes
> and a second event has **n** possible
> outcomes, the two events have **m** × **n**
> possible outcomes.

Two-way tables

When the two spinners on the right
are spun, the possible outcomes can
be shown in an organised way by
means of a **two-way table**, as
shown below.

Numbers

	3	4	5	6
R	3R	4R	5R	6R
B	3B	4B	5B	6B
G	3G	4G	5G	6G

Colours

Number of possible outcomes is

$4 \times 3 = 12$

The **Fundamental Principle of Counting** can be extended to any number of events.

If a businessman has to choose a shirt, a tie and a jacket from 5 shirts, 3 ties and 4 jackets,
he has

$5 \times 3 \times 4$ choices $= 60$ choices

Exercise 8.1

1. An 'early-bird' menu consists of 3 starters and 4 main courses.
   How many different 2-course meals can you have?

2. Two coins are tossed.
   List all the possible outcomes using H for head and T for tail.

3. This spinner is spun and the dice is thrown.

   (i)   How many different outcomes of colour
         and number can you have?
   (ii) How many of these outcomes will have
         the colour yellow?
   (iii) How many of the outcomes will have the number 3?

4. A code consists of one of the letters A, B, C or D followed by a digit from 1 to 9.
   How many different codes are possible?

5. A lunch menu consists of 3 starters, 4 main courses and 2 desserts.
   How many different 3-course meals can a person have?

6. A car manufacturer produces different types of cars as follows:
   > the model can be Saloon, Estate or Hatchback
   > the colours can be silver, black or red
   > the style can be Standard, Deluxe or Premium.

   How many different choices of car does a buyer have?

7. A game consists of spinning the given spinner and throwing a dice.

   (i) If the outcome of the game is a letter and a number, how many different outcomes are possible?

   (ii) If the game consists of a colour and a number, how many different outcomes are possible?

8. A pupil must choose one subject out of each of the following subject groups:

   ❯ Group A has 3 modern language subjects

   ❯ Group B has 2 science subjects

   ❯ Group C has 2 business subjects.

   How many different subject selections are possible?

9. A restaurant advertises its lunch menu using the sign shown on the right.

   (i) The menu has a choice of five starters and nine main courses.
   How many items must appear on the dessert menu to justify the claim of 180 different lunches?

   (ii) On a particular day, one of the starters and one of the main courses were not available.
   How many different three-course lunches was it possible to have on that day?

> **Lunch Menu**
>
> **3 courses for €18**
>
> Choose from our range of starters, main courses and desserts.
> 180 different lunches to choose from.

Section 8.2 **Chance and the probability scale**

You will already be familiar with words such as

Impossible   Unlikely   Even chance   Likely   Certain

to describe the **chance** or **probability** of something happening.

If we want to be more specific, we use numbers to describe how likely something is to happen.

An event which is **certain to happen** has a **probability of 1**.

An event which **cannot happen** has a **probability of 0**.

All other probabilities will be a number greater than 0 and less than 1.

The more likely an event is to happen, the closer the probability is to 1.

The line shown below is called a **probability scale**.

There is an **even chance** that the next person you meet on the street will be a male.

It is **certain** that the sun will rise in Ireland tomorrow.

It is **impossible** to get 7 when a normal dice is rolled.

Exercise 8.2

1. Which of these labels best describes the likelihood of each of the events below occurring?

| Impossible | Unlikely | Even Chance | Likely | Certain |

   (i)   A coin will show 'tails' when you toss it.
   (ii) You are more than ten years old.
   (iii) The sun will not set in Ireland tomorrow.
   (iv) You will win an Olympic medal.
   (v)   The next person you meet on the street will be Irish.
   (vi) You will get an even number when an ordinary dice is thrown.
   (vii) You will get less than 5 winning numbers when playing the *Euromillions* some Friday.
   (viii) It will snow later today.
   (ix) I draw a red card from a standard pack of playing cards.
   (x)   You will get homework tonight.

2. For each of the events given below, choose one of these words:

   impossible   **unlikely**   **even chance**   **likely**   **certain**

   (i) A dice is to be thrown.
        Event 1:   A 6 will be thrown.
        Event 2:   A number less than 4 will be thrown.
        Event 3:   A number greater than 3 will be thrown.
        Event 4:   A zero will be thrown.
        Event 5:   A natural number less than 7 will be thrown.

   (ii) One card is to be chosen at random from these five.
        Event 1:   The card will be a *heart*.
        Event 2:   The card will be less than 8.
        Event 3:   The card will be a *diamond*.
        Event 4:   The card will be a 2.
        Event 5:   The card will not be a 3.

3. Here are four
spinners with
different colours:

  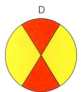

A   B   C   D

All the spinners
are spun.

  (i) Which spinner has an even chance of showing blue?

 (ii) Which spinner has an even chance of showing red?

(iii) Which spinner has the least chance of showing yellow?

(iv) Which spinner has one chance in three of showing yellow?

 (v) Which spinner has one chance in four of showing red?

(vi) Which spinner has the greatest chance of showing red?

4. Order each of the events below from least likely to most likely:

  (i) A dice is to be thrown.

     (a) The number showing will be even.

     (b) The number showing will be larger than 4.

     (c) The number showing will be less than 6.

 (ii) One card is to be chosen at random from these six.

     (a) The card will be a 2.

     (b) The card will be a 7.

     (c) The card will be greater than a 3.

5. The jar shown contains red, blue and green marbles.
When a marble is taken from the bag, the chances of
obtaining each of the three colours are shown on the
probability scale below.

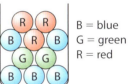

B = blue
G = green
R = red

Link each colour to either (a), (b) or (c).

6.

Purple   Red Blue

In a game, Todd spins an arrow.
The arrow stops in one of sixteen equal sectors of a circle.
Each sector of the circle is coloured.
The probability scale above shows how likely it is for the
arrow to stop on any one colour.
How many sectors are

 (i) coloured red   (ii) coloured blue   (iii) coloured purple?

Section 8.3 Probability and equally likely outcomes

Before you can start a certain game, you must throw a dice and get a six.

The act of throwing a dice is called a **trial**.

The numbers 1, 2, 3, 4, 5 and 6 are all the possible **outcomes** of the trial.

The list of all possible outcomes is called a **sample space**.

The desired result is called an **event**.

If you require an even number when throwing a dice, then the **events** or **successful outcomes** are the numbers 2, 4 and 6.

> The result we want is called an event.

Equally likely outcomes

Two events are **equally likely** if they each have the same chance of happening.

The chance of getting a red with this spinner is the same as the chance of getting a blue. Getting a red and getting a blue are **equally likely**.

The chances of getting a red or getting a blue with this spinner are **not** equally likely. The probability of getting a red when this spinner is spun is one chance in four.

We write this as Probability (red) $= \frac{1}{4}$.
This is shortened to P(red) $= \frac{1}{4}$.

The outcome we want may also be called a **favourable outcome**.

> A favourable outcome is an outcome that you want.

> For **equally likely outcomes**, the probability of event E occurring is given by
>
> $$P(E) = \frac{\text{Number of favourable outcomes}}{\text{Number of possible outcomes}}$$

For the spinner on the right,

P(green) $= \frac{1}{5}$, because 1 of the 5 sections is green

P(yellow) $= \frac{2}{5}$, because 2 of the 5 sections are yellow.

Example 1

Below is a number of lettered tiles.

| P | A | R | A | L | L | E | L | O | G | R | A | M |

One of these tiles is selected at random.
Work out the probability of getting:

  (i) an A   (ii) an L   (iii) an O
(iv) an A or an L   (v) an A or an O   (vi) an L or an O.

  (i) There are 3 tiles lettered A out of the 13 tiles.

$$P(A) = \frac{\text{number of As}}{\text{total number}} = \frac{3}{13}$$

 (ii) $P(L) = \dfrac{\text{number of Ls}}{\text{total number}} = \dfrac{3}{13}$

(iii) $P(O) = \dfrac{1}{13}$

(iv) $P(A \text{ or } L) = \dfrac{\text{number of As} + \text{Ls}}{\text{total number}} = \dfrac{6}{13}$

 (v) $P(A \text{ or } O) = \dfrac{4}{13}$ (vi) $P(L \text{ or } O) = \dfrac{4}{13}$

Exercise 8.3

1. (i) State the sample space for each of these spinners:

  (a)   (b)   (c)

 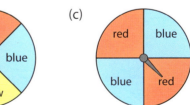

 (ii) For each of the spinners, write down the probability that the pointer ends on red.

2. What is the probability of getting a 6 on each of these spinners?

  (i)   (ii)   (iii)

What is the probability of getting a 2 or a 6 on spinner (iii)?

3. A fair dice is rolled.
What is the probability of getting

   (i) a 5   (ii) a 1 or a 2
  (iii) 4 or more   (iv) an odd number
  (v) less than 3   (vi) a prime number?

4. Here is a selection of shapes.

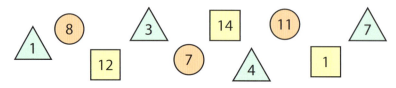

One of these shapes is chosen at random.
Work out the probability that the shape will be:

  (i) a square   (ii) a triangle   (iii) a square or a triangle
(iv) an odd number   (v) a 2-digit number   (vi) a green odd number.

5. A letter is chosen at random from the word *PROBABILITY*.
Write down the probability that it will be

  (i) *A*   (ii) *B*   (iii) *I*   (iv) a vowel   (v) a *B* or an *I*.

6. For each of the following unbiased spinners, find the probability that the outcome
of one spin will be a four.

  (i)   (ii)   (iii)

7. A dart board has 36 sectors, labelled 1 to 36.
Determine the probability that a dart thrown
at the board hits:

  (i) a multiple of 4
  (ii) a number between 6 and 9 inclusive
  (iii) a number greater than 20
  (iv) 9
  (v) a multiple of 13
  (vi) an odd number that is a multiple of 3.

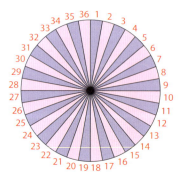

8. A standard pack of cards has 4 suits: hearts (♥), diamonds (♦), clubs (♣) and spades (♠).

   There are 13 cards in each suit and 52 cards altogether.

   The first of these cards is called an **Ace**. The last three cards are the *picture* or *court* cards: the **Jack**, the **Queen** and the **King**.

   From the 13 cards shown above, one card is to be chosen at random.
   What is the probability that the card chosen will be:

   (i) the 7 (ii) the Ace (iii) a picture card
   (iv) a heart (v) a spade (vi) either a 9 or a 10?

9. From a standard pack of 52 cards, a card is chosen at random.
   What is the probability that the card will be:

   (i) a diamond (ii) a red card (iii) a black card
   (iv) a 3 (v) a picture card (vi) either an Ace or a King?

10. A box contains twelve green marbles, six blue marbles and eight white marbles.
    A marble is selected by a blind-folded person.
    What is the probability that the marble selected is:

    (i) green or white (ii) blue or white
    (iii) not green (iv) orange?

11. A square dart board is divided into sixteen smaller squares. Fourteen of the squares are painted as shown.

    (i) What colour(s) should the two remaining squares be painted so that the probability of landing on red is $\frac{3}{8}$ and it is impossible to land on black?
    (ii) What colour(s) should the two remaining squares be painted so that the probability of landing on red is twice the probability of landing on blue?

red	yellow	red	blue
white	red	white	blue
red	blue	white	red
white	yellow	?	?

12. What is the probability that the pointer of these spinners lands in the blue section?

    (i)   (ii)   (iii)   (iv)

13. Design a spinner for which the probability of the pointer landing on the blue section is:

   (i) half   (ii) less than half

   (iii) three times as likely as on red.

14. Assuming that a person is equally likely to be born on any day of the week or in any month of the year, what is the probability that a randomly-chosen person has his/her birthday

   (i) on a Tuesday   (ii) on a Saturday or Sunday

   (iii) in January or February   (iv) in a month ending in y?

15. A bag contains five red discs with the numbers 1 to 5 painted on them and seven blue discs painted with the numbers 1 to 7. If a disc is chosen at random, what is the probability of choosing

   (i) a red disc   (ii) a disc numbered 3

   (iii) a disc numbered 6   (iv) the blue disc numbered 1

   (v) an even-numbered disc   (vi) an odd-numbered disc?

Explain why the probabilities in (v) and (vi) sum to 1.

16. In a pre-election poll of 400 people, 120 supported the A party, 140 supported the B party and the rest were undecided. If a person is selected at random from this group, what is the probability that they:

   (i) support the A party   (ii) support the B party

   (iii) support a party   (iv) are undecided?

17. At the end of a Summer Camp, 50 boys and girls were asked to name their favourite game at the camp. The results are given in the table below:

	Tennis	Basketball	Volleyball
Girls	15	10	5
Boys	6	12	2

If a person was selected at random from the group of 50, calculate the probability that the person

   (i) was a boy

   (ii) was a girl who named tennis as her favourite game

   (iii) named basketball as her/his favourite game.

If a girl was selected, find the probability that she had named volleyball as her favourite game.

18. Of 100 tickets sold in a raffle, Luke bought 10, Heather bought 5 and Alan bought 1.
A ticket was chosen at random to determine who won the only prize.
What is the probability that the prize was won by:
  (i) Alan
  (ii) Luke
  (iii) Heather
  (iv) none of these three people?

How many of the 100 tickets would I need to buy for the probability of my winning to be:
  (v) $\frac{3}{10}$
  (vi) 0.2
  (vii) 25%
  (viii) 100%?

19. There are 8 counters in a box.
The probability of taking a green counter out of the box is $\frac{1}{2}$.
A green counter is taken out of the box and put to one side.
Gerry now takes a counter at random from the box.
What is the probability it is green?

20. A game is played by picking a card, without looking, from a pack of 52 playing cards.
The table shows the results of picking various cards.

If Eileen picks a card, what is the probability that she will
  (i) lose money
  (ii) win money
  (iii) neither win nor lose
  (iv) not lose money?

Card	Result
Ace	Win €2
K, Q or J	Win 50c
6, 7, 8, 9, 10	Break even
2, 3, 4, 5	Lose 50c

Section 8.4 Two events – Use of sample spaces

When a dice is thrown and a coin is tossed, the set of possible outcomes is as follows:

{H1, H2, H3, H4, H5, H6, T1, T2, T3, T4, T5, T6}.

This set of possible outcomes is called a **sample space**.

Using the sample space above, we can write down the probability of getting a head and a 6, for example.

  $P(H, 6) = \frac{1}{12}$ ... 12 possible outcomes

The probability of a head and an even number can be found by counting the required outcomes.
These are H2, H4 and H6.

∴ $P(H \text{ and even number}) = \frac{3}{12} = \frac{1}{4}$

An experiment such as throwing two dice has a large number of possible outcomes, so we need to set out the sample space in an organised way, as shown in the following example.

Example 1

If two dice are thrown and the scores are added, set out a sample space giving all the possible outcomes. Now find the probability that
   (i)   the total is exactly 7
   (ii) the total is 4 or less
   (iii) the total is 11 or more
   (iv) the total is a multiple of 5.

The sample space is set out on the right.
There are 36 outcomes.

Total = 4 or less (red)

	1	2	3	4	5	6
1	2	3	4	5	6	7
2	3	4	5	6	7	8
3	4	5	6	7	8	9
4	5	6	7	8	9	10
5	6	7	8	9	10	11
6	7	8	9	10	11	12

Total = 7 (green)

   (i)   There are 6 totals of 7.
      $\Rightarrow \quad P(7) = \frac{6}{36} = \frac{1}{6}$

   (ii) There are 6 totals of 4 or less.
      $\Rightarrow \quad P(4 \text{ or less}) = \frac{6}{36} = \frac{1}{6}$

   (iii) There are 3 totals of 11 or more.
      $\Rightarrow \quad P(11 \text{ or more}) = \frac{3}{36} = \frac{1}{12}$

   (iv) The multiples of 5 are 5 and 10.
      There are 7 totals of 5 or 10.
      $\Rightarrow \quad P(\text{multiple of 5}) = \frac{7}{36}$

Exercise 8.4

1. These are the possible outcomes when a coin is tossed twice:

   HH, HT, TH, TT

   Write down the probability of getting
      (i)   2 tails
      (ii) 2 heads
      (iii) a head and a tail.

2. When these two spinners are spun and the scores are added, you get the results shown on the right.

Number on 1st spinner

	1	2	3	4
1	2	3	4	5
2	3	4	5	6
3	4	5	6	7
4	5	6	7	8

Number on 2nd spinner

Use the table to write down the following probabilities:
   (i)   the total score is 6
   (ii) the total score is an odd number
   (iii) the total score is 7 or more
   (iv) the total score is 2 or 3.

3. A fair three-sided spinner has sections labelled 2, 4 and 6.

The spinner is spun once and a fair six-sided dice is rolled once.

The number that the spinner lands on is added to the number that the dice shows. This gives the score.

Copy and complete the table to show all possible scores.

Use the table to write down the probability that the score is

  (i) 4   (ii) 5

(iii) 7   (iv) 9 or more

 (v) 5 or less   (vi) a multiple of 4

		Dice					
	+	1	2	3	4	5	6
Spinner	2	3					
	4						
	6						12

4. Karl has two fair spinners, numbered as shown. He spins them and finds the **product** of the two scores.

  (i) Copy and complete the grid to show all possible outcomes (products) of the two spins.

 (ii) What is the probability that the product is

    (a) 12

    (b) greater than 10

    (c) a multiple of 3?

5. The ace, king, queen and jack of clubs and the ace, king, queen and jack of diamonds are put into two separate piles. The sample space diagram shows all the possible outcomes when a card is taken from each pile.

Write down the probability that

  (i) both cards will be kings

 (ii) one card will be a club

(iii) only one of the cards will be a queen

(iv) the cards will make a matching pair

 (v) at least one of the cards will be a queen

(vi) neither card will be a jack.

6. Three fair coins are tossed.
Make out a sample space for all
the possible outcomes.

Now write down the probability
that the outcome will be

  (i) three heads   (ii) two heads and one tail (in any order)

 (iii) no heads   (iv) at least one head.

7. Two dice are thrown and the scores obtained
are added. The resulting outcomes are
shown in the given sample space.
Find the probability that the sum of
the two numbers is

  (i) 9   (ii) 10

 (iii) 3 or less   (iv) 10 or 11.

8. Chloe is playing a word game and chooses
both a vowel and a consonant at random
from her letters.

  (i) Show all the possible choices she can make on a sample space diagram.

 (ii) What is the probability of choosing A and R?

 (iii) What is the probability of choosing I and L?

 (iv) Work out the probability of choosing I and not choosing L.

9. Bag A contains 2 red beads and 1 white bead.
Bag B contains 2 white beads and 1 red bead.
A bead is drawn at random from each bag.

Copy and complete the table to show all
the possible pairs of colours.

		Bag A		
		R	R	W
Bag B	W	RW		
	W			
	R			

  (i) Find the probability that both beads
are red.

 (ii) Find the probability that the two beads
are the same colour.

 (iii) Find the probability that the pair of beads will be different in colour.

10. A red car (R), a blue car (B) and a green car (G) are parked on a narrow driveway,
one behind the other.

  (i) List all the possible orders in which the three cars could be parked.

The cars are parked on the driveway at random.

 (ii) What is the probability that the blue car is the first on the driveway?

Section 8.5 **Estimating probability from experiments**

Activity

Toss a fair coin ten times and record the results.
The results might look something like this.

Here there are 6 heads and 4 tails.

Now toss a coin 50 times and record the results.

Now toss the coin another 50 times and again record the results.

It could help if you found a few friends to do the same experiment, that is, tossing a coin 50 times.

If you were to combine all the results you would very likely end up with a table like the one shown below.

The first column is the number of times the coin was tossed.

The second column is the number of heads obtained.

The third column is the number in the second column divided by the number in the first column.

Number of tosses	Number of heads	Heads ÷ tosses
10	6	0.6
20	11	0.55
100	53	0.53
200	108	0.54
400	194	0.485
500	242	0.484
1000	490	0.49

As the numbers of tosses increase, the values of the number of heads divided by the number of tosses get closer to 0.5, i.e. $\frac{1}{2}$.

The value of the number of heads divided by the number of tosses is called the **experimental probability**.

It gives an **estimate** of the *true probability*.

As the number of trials or experiments increases, the value of the experimental probability gets closer to the true or theoretical probability.

Doing an experiment

Suppose I wanted to estimate the probability of a drawing pin landing 'point upwards' when dropped onto a hard surface.

Is it **equally likely** that the point lands upwards or downwards?

Since we are not sure that each event is equally likely, we cannot calculate the exact probability of the event happening.

But we can get an **estimate of the probability** by doing an **experiment**.

To find an estimate of the probability that a drawing pin lands 'point upwards', we could toss the pin 500 times and record the number of times it finishes 'point upwards'.

If the drawing pin landed 'point upwards' 350 times in 500 tosses, we could then write down an **estimate** of the probability.

$$\text{Probability (point upwards)} = \frac{\text{Number of 'point upwards'}}{\text{Total number of tosses}}$$
$$= \frac{350}{500} = \frac{35}{50} = \frac{7}{10}$$

In general, if we need a more accurate estimate of the probability of some event happening, we increase the number of trials or experiments conducted.

Example 1

The table below shows the results in Division One of a football league.

Home wins	Away wins	Draws
24	10	6

Use the data in this table to estimate the probability of getting the following results in a randomly selected match taking place in the next round of fixtures.
(i) a home win   (ii) an away win   (iii) a draw

(i) There were 24 home wins out of 40 matches.

Estimated probability of home win $= \dfrac{24}{40} = \dfrac{6}{10} = \dfrac{3}{5}$

(ii) Estimated probability of away win $= \dfrac{10}{40} = \dfrac{1}{4}$

(iii) Estimated probability of a draw $= \dfrac{6}{40} = \dfrac{3}{20}$

Exercise 8.5

1. Shane tosses a fair coin six times. He gets a head four times. Shane says that if he tosses it another six times, he will get four heads again. Explain why Shane could be wrong. If the coin is tossed 100 times, how many heads should Shane expect?

2. (i) If a fair dice is thrown, what is the probability of getting a six?
   Now throw the dice 10 times and record the number of sixes you get.
   (ii) Use your answer to find an estimate of the probability of getting a six.
   Now throw the dice 50 times and record the number of sixes you get.
   (iii) Again, use your answer to find an estimate of the probability of getting a six.
   (iv) Is the experimental probability of getting a six closer to $\frac{1}{6}$ in (ii) or (iii)?

3. Jane and Nicky both did the 'dropping a drawing pin' experiment.
   Here are their results.

   Jane
Trials	20
'Point up'	10

   Nicky
Trials	100
'Point up'	75

   Another drawing pin is dropped.
   (i) For Jane, what is the probability of getting 'point up'?
   (ii) For Nicky, what is the probability of getting 'point up'?
   (iii) Whose result is likely to be more reliable? Explain your answer.

4. 50 cars are observed passing the school gate.
   15 of these cars are red.
   Use these results to estimate the probability that the next car to pass the school gate will be red.

5. Eric is a goalkeeper. His manager records the number of shots he saves.

	Tally	Frequency
Saves	ЖЖ ЖЖ ЖЖ ЖЖ ЖЖ IIII	29
Doesn't save	ЖЖ ЖЖ ЖЖ I	16

   Estimate the probability that Eric saves the next shot.
   Give your answer as a decimal, correct to one decimal place.

6. Ciara surveyed the colours of vehicles passing her home. Here are her results.

Colour	Red	Black	Silver	Green	White	Other
Frequency	6	10	24	4	12	8

   Calculate an estimate of the probability that the next vehicle to pass will be silver.

7. Eoin is carrying out the experiment 'dropping a spoon'.
   He records whether the spoon lands up or down.

Up
Down

   (i) Copy and complete this table of Eoin's results.

Number of drops	5	10	20	25	50	100
Number of times landed up	3	7	11	15	32	63
Probability	0.6	0.7				

   (ii) What do you think would be a reasonable estimate for the probability
   of this spoon landing up?
   Give your answer as a decimal, correct to 1 decimal place.

8. A fair six-sided dice has its faces painted either red (R),
   blue (B) or white (W).
   The dice is thrown 36 times.

   Here are the results.

   B B R W B W B R W
   B R W R B B W W B
   W B B R W B W W B
   B B R B B W R W B

   Copy and complete the table below for these results.

Outcome	Tally	Frequency
Red		
White		
Blue		
Total		36

   (i) Use these results to estimate the probability that the next throw will be
   red.
   (ii) Estimate the probability that the next throw will be white.
   (iii) Based on these results, how many faces do you think are painted blue?

9. A biased dice is cast 1000 times and the results recorded.

   Biased means
   not fair.

Number on dice	1	2	3	4	5	6
Frequency	60	196	84	148	162	350

   Use the results to estimate the probability of obtaining a six when the dice is cast
   again. Give your answer as a decimal.

10. Sean collected the results of 40 *Rovers* home games.
Estimate the probability that in their next home game:

Won	18
Lost	10
Drawn	12

  (i) they will win
 (ii) they will lose.

For *Rover's* next 40 home games, the results were as follows:
Using all 80 results, estimate the probability of *Rovers*

Won	24
Lost	10
Drawn	6

(iii) winning their next home game
 (iv) drawing their next home game.

Would you expect these probabilities to be more accurate than those based on the first 40 matches? Why?

11. Bill is interested in the colour of cars.
He records the colours of 100 cars entering a car park.
The table below shows his results.

Colour	Red	Silver	Black	Yellow	White
Frequency	24	16	30	10	20

Use Bill's results to estimate the probability that the colour of the next car to enter the car park is:
  (i) red
 (ii) yellow
(iii) not white

12. The results from 40 spins of a numbered spinner are:

2   1   4   3   2   1   3   4   5   2   1   2   2   3   2   1   2   4   5   2
1   5   3   4   2   3   3   3   2   4   2   3   4   2   1   5   3   3   5   3

Make out a frequency table to show this data.
Use the table to estimate the probability of getting a 2 with the next spin.

13. A bag contained coloured beads. Darren randomly selects a bead and then replaces it. He does this 60 times. Here are the results.

Colour	White	Green	Blue
Frequency	10	30	20

Estimate the probability that on his next draw he will select
  (i) a white bead
 (ii) a green bead
(iii) a white bead or a blue bead.

14. Kathy is recording in which direction cars go when they reach a T-junction in the road near her school.

She writes right (R) or left (L) for each car. Here are her results in order.

```
R  R  L  R  L  R  R  L  L  L  R  R  R  L  L  R  L
R  L  R  L  R  L  L  R  R  R  R  R  L  L  R  L  R
L  R  R  R  L  R  R  L  R  R  R  L  L  R  R  R
```

Estimate the probability of the next car turning right after the following numbers of results (write each answer as a decimal);

(i)   after the first 10 cars have passed

(ii) after 20 cars have passed

(iii) after 50 cars have passed.

Kathy's local council have also carried out a survey at this junction. They observed over 1000 cars and estimated that the probability of a car turning right is 0.62.

(iv) Do you think Kathy's results agree with this?

(v)   Whose estimate do you think is more accurate, Kathy's or the council's? Explain your answer.

15. In an experiment Tom drops 12 drawing pins onto a hard floor. He does the experiment 10 times and counts how many pins land 'point up' each time. His results were

Number of the 12 drawing pins that landed 'point up'									
3	5	6	2	4	7	3	3	4	5

(i) Use Tom's data to work out the probability that a *single* drawing pin will land 'point up'.

(ii) Tom continues the experiment until he has dropped the 12 drawing pins 100 times. About how many drawing pins in total would you expect to land 'point up'?

16. Rachel, Barry and Leanore each rolled a different dice 360 times.
The results are shown in the given table. Only one of the dice was fair.
Whose was it? Explain your answer.

Number	Rachel	Barry	Leanore
1	27	58	141
2	69	62	52
3	78	63	56
4	43	57	53
5	76	56	53
6	67	64	5

Test yourself 8

1. (a) A bag contains 50 marbles: 20 are red, 12 are pink and 18 are black.
   What is the probability that a marble selected at random is:

   (i) red   (ii) pink   (iii) not black?

   (b) The first 100 vehicles to pass a checkpoint gave the results in the table. If these figures truly represent the traffic at any time passing this checkpoint, determine the probability that the next vehicle will be:

Type of vehicle	Frequency
Cars	70
Trucks	15
Motorcycles	10
Buses	5

        (i) a car   (ii) a motorcycle

        (iii) a bus   (iv) *not* a car

        (v) *not* a car or truck

   (c) Raffle tickets are numbered 1 to 300. Lucy buys five tickets and gets the numbers 8, 9, 10, 11 and 12. Robbie buys five tickets and gets the numbers 18, 29, 182, 207, 234. One ticket is chosen at random.
   Is Lucy or Robbie more likely to have the winning number?
   Explain your answer.

2. (a)

         A   B   C

   For which of these spinners is the probability of spinning a 3 equal to:

   (i) 20%   (ii) 25%   (iii) $\frac{1}{3}$?

   (b) Silvia has cards numbered 1, 2, 3, 4 and 5. She puts several cards in a bag. She takes out a card at random, records the number on the card, and then replaces it in the bag.

   The table shows her results.

Number on card	1	2	3	4	5
Tally	⅏ I	III	II	⅏ III	⅏
Frequency					

   Copy the table and complete the last row.

   (i) How many times did Silvia take a card out of the bag?

   (ii) Which number did she take out most often?

   (iii) Estimate the probability that the next card Silvia picks has the number 2 on it.

(c) Tom has a four-sided dice.
He rolls the dice 100 times.
The table shows the outcomes.
Is the dice fair? Explain your answer.

Outcome	1	2	3	4
Frequency	18	44	19	19

3. (a) A bag contains two red counters, three blue counters and three green counters.
A counter is taken out of the bag at random.
Find, as a fraction, the probabilities of these outcomes:
  (i) a red counter
  (ii) a blue counter
  (iii) a green counter
  (iv) either a red or a blue counter.
Add together your answers for (i), (ii) and (iii).
Explain your result.

(b) An ordinary pack of playing cards is shuffled well and a card is drawn out.
Determine the probability that it is:
  (i) a red card
  (ii) the ace of spades
  (iii) a number less than ten and greater than four
  (iv) a black picture card
  (v) an ace
  (vi) a number between four and ten inclusive.

(c) One ball is selected at random from the bag shown and
then replaced. This procedure is done 400 times.
How many times would you expect to select:
  (i) a blue ball
  (ii) a red ball?

4. (a) In an experiment a gardener plants 40 daffodil bulbs of which 36 grew to
produce flowers. Use these results to estimate the probability that his next
daffodil bulb will grow to produce a flower.

(b) Ava spins a coin and rolls a dice.
Some of the possible outcomes
are shown in the table.

Copy and complete the table.
  (i) What is the total number
     of outcomes?
  (ii) What is the probability of
     getting a head and a 5?
  (iii) What is the probability of getting a tail and a number less than 4?
  (iv) What is the probability of getting a 2?

Dice

Coin	1	2	3	4	5	6
H	H, 1	H, 2				
T				T, 4		T, 6

(c) The probability that a biased dice will land '3 up' is 0.4.
Mark rolls the biased dice 200 times.
Work out an estimate for the number of times that the dice will land '3 up'.

Statistics 2: Measures of Average and Spread

Key words

average   mode   median   mean   range   outlier   variability
frequency table

Section 9.1 Averages

When we collect data such as the numbers of hours our classmates spend watching television each week or the ages of people living in an apartment block, one of the first things we would like to find is an **average**.

When we look for an average, we are trying to find a **single** or **typical value** that will represent the **many values** we have collected.

The idea of an average is extremely useful because it enables us to compare one set of data with another by comparing just two values – their averages.
The most commonly-used averages in statistics are the **mode**, the **median** and the **mean**.
In this section we will deal with the first two of these, the mode and the median.

1. The mode

The mode is the value that occurs most often in the data. The mode is particularly relevant when one value appears much more often than the other values. The mode is often called the **modal value**.

Example 1

Find the mode of each data set:
 (i) 7, 9, 8, 7, 12, 10, 7, 11, 8
 (ii) red, blue, yellow, blue, green, yellow, blue, red, blue, yellow, red, blue

 (i) The mode is 7 because it appears more often than any other value.
 (ii) In the data set there are
      3 reds,   5 blues,   3 yellows,   1 green
      The mode is blue as it occurs most often.

---

2. The median

To find the median of a list of numbers, put the numbers in order of size, starting with the smallest. The median is the middle number.

> **Example 1**
>
> Find the median of each of these arrays of numbers:
> (i) 2, 5, 3, 4, 5, 8, 7, 9, 6
> (ii) 12, 15, 13, 9, 7, 15
>
> (i) We rewrite the numbers in order of size.
>   2, 3, 4, 5, 5, 6, 7, 8, 9
>   The middle number is 5, so 5 is the median.
> (ii) Again, we rewrite the numbers in order of size
>   7, 9, 12, 13, 15, 15
>   Here there are 6 numbers, so there are two middle numbers,
>   12 and 13.
>   The median is $\frac{1}{2}(12 + 13)$
> $$= \frac{1}{2}(25) = 12\frac{1}{2}$$
>
> **Note:** When there is an even number of numbers, the median is
> $\frac{1}{2}$ [Sum of the two middle numbers]

Exercise 9.1

1. Find the mode of each of these sets:
   (i) 7, 8, 3, 7, 5, 6, 3, 7, 2
   (ii) 15, 12, 16, 19, 12, 14, 16, 12
   (iii) 5.6, 5.4, 5.7, 5.5, 5.7, 5.6, 5.7
   (iv) bus, car, bus, walk, car, bus, cycle, car, bus, bus, walk, cycle, car, walk, bus

2. Write down the mode for each set of data:
   (i) 10, 1000, 100, 1000, 10, 10, 1000, 10, 1000, 100, 10
   (ii) sun, snow, sun, fog, rain, snow, fog, rain, sun, cloud, sun, rain
   (iii) $\frac{1}{2}, \frac{1}{4}, \frac{3}{4}, \frac{1}{4}, 1, \frac{1}{4}, \frac{3}{4}, 1, 0, \frac{1}{4}, 0, \frac{1}{4}, \frac{3}{4}, \frac{1}{2}, 1, \frac{1}{4}, \frac{1}{2}$

3. The mode of these numbers is 5. Find the value of *.
   2, 3, 7, 5, 2, 6, *, 5, 3

4. The girls in one class were asked how much
time they spend on homework each week.
The results are shown in this bar chart.

  (i) How many girls spend 3 hours
       on homework?
  (ii) What is the modal number
       of hours?

5. Explain why there is no single mode in the following set of data:

   2, 1, 3, 4, 6, 4, 1, 3, 0, 2, 6, 0

6. Joan did a survey to find the shoe sizes of pupils in her class.
The bar chart illustrates her data.

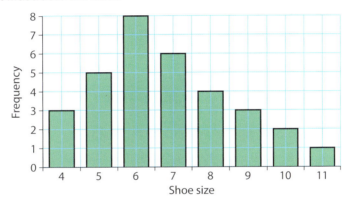

  (i)   How many pupils are there in Joan's class?
  (ii) What is the modal shoe size?
  (iii) Can you tell from the bar chart which shoe sizes are the boys and which are the
        girls in her class?
  (iv) Joan then decided to draw a bar chart to show the shoe sizes of the boys and the
        girls separately. Do you think that the mode for the boys and the mode for the
        girls will be the same as the mode for the whole class? Explain your answer.

7. What is the median height of this group of friends?

180 cm   163 cm   151 cm   180 cm   175 cm   171 cm   158 cm

8. Find the median of each set of numbers:
   (i)   3, 4, 6, 6, 7, 8, 9
   (ii) 12, 12, 13, 14, 14, 15, 15, 16, 17
   (iii) 3.2, 3.5, 3.5, 3.6, 3.6, 3.7, 3.8

9. Rewrite each of the following sets of data in order of size and then write down the median of each set.
   (i)   6, 8, 3, 9, 8, 5, 7, 2, 8
   (ii) 24, 23, 19, 27, 26, 20, 25, 23, 25
   (iii) 3.5, 3, 3.7, 3.7, 3.9, 3.5, 3.6, 3.8, 3.9

10. By finding half the sum of the two middle numbers, write down the median of this set of data:

   7, 10, 9, 13, 12, 9, 11, 14

11. Find the median of each of these sets of data:
   (i)   9, 12, 4, 8, 7, 5, 3, 10
   (ii) 23, 15, 19, 34, 16, 26, 18, 27
   (iii) €10, €5, €8, €5.50, €4, €7.50, €6, €9

12. Work out (i) the mode (ii) the median for this data set.

   5, 7, 9, 9, 8, 7, 9, 10, 12, 11, 9, 9, 5

13. In this set of data, the mode is 9.

   7, 4, 3, 3, 12, 9, x, 10, 9

   (i) Find the value of x.

   (ii) What is the median of the set?

14. The bar chart on the right shows the test scores of a group of pupils.

   (i)   What is the modal test score?
   (ii) How many pupils were in the group?
   (iii) List all the scores in order of size.
         The first four are listed for you.
               6, 6, 6, 7, ...
         Now write down the median test score.

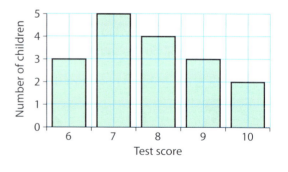

Section 9.2 **The mean**

The **mean** of the numbers

   4, 5, 7, 9, 10

> $$\text{Mean} = \frac{\text{Sum of the numbers}}{\text{Number of numbers}}$$

is the sum of these numbers divided by the number of numbers.

$$\therefore \quad \text{Mean} = \frac{4 + 5 + 7 + 9 + 10}{5}$$

$$= \frac{35}{5} = 7$$

In everyday language the word 'average' is generally used instead of 'mean'.
The mean is a very important value in statistics as it takes into account all the values in the set of data.

Example 1

In five basketball matches Joan scored 16 points, 10 points, 22 points, 18 points and 24 points. Calculate her mean score for the five matches.

$$\text{Mean} = \frac{16 + 10 + 22 + 18 + 24}{5} = \frac{90}{5} = 18$$

If the mean of three numbers is 9, it follows that the sum of the three numbers is 27, since $27 \div 3 = 9$.

Example 2

The mean of four numbers is 7.
When a fifth number is added, the mean of the five numbers is 9.
Find the fifth number.

If the mean of four numbers is 7, then the sum of the four numbers is
4×7, i.e. 28.
The mean of five numbers $= 9 \Rightarrow$ sum of the five numbers $= 45$ ... $5 \times 9 = 45$
$\therefore$ the fifth number $= 45 - 28$
$$= 17$$

Extreme values

Here are the marks scored by six pupils in a maths test:

   26, 35, 34, 46, 52, 95

The mean mark is $\dfrac{26 + 35 + 34 + 46 + 52 + 95}{6} = \dfrac{288}{6} = 48$

Notice that four out of the six students are below the mean mark.
This is caused by one mark, i.e. 95, which is much higher than all the other marks.

Such a mark is generally known as an **outlier** or **extreme value**. When an outlier exists, the mean may not fully represent the set of data given. This happens, in particular, when the number of data items is small.

Exercise 9.2

1. Find the mean of each of these sets of data.
   (i)   2, 4, 5, 6, 8
   (ii) 3, 7, 8, 10, 11, 15
   (iii) 14, 17, 21, 13, 6, 13
   (iv) 1, 0, 5, 7, 17, 12

2. Ava's marks in six subjects were 47, 68, 62, 76, 59 and 54.
   Find her mean mark.

3. A snooker player scored 208 points in 8 visits to the table.
   What was his average number of points per visit?

4. Five girls had these sums of money:
   €3.80, €8.30, €2.40, €5.70 and €11.30.
   Work out the mean sum of money.

5. Find the mean of the numbers 6, 8, 9, 10, 12.
   If a sixth number, zero, is added to these five numbers, find the mean of the six numbers.

6. The mean of four numbers is 9.
   Find the sum of the four numbers.

7. The mean of three numbers is 8.
   (i) What is the sum of the three numbers?
   (ii) If two of the numbers are 6 and 7, find the third number.

8. The mean of four numbers is 9.
   (i) What is the sum of the four numbers?
   (ii) If three of the numbers are 6, 11 and 14, find the fourth.

9. The mean of four numbers is 7. Three of the numbers are 3, 5 and 9.
   Find the fourth number.

10. The three sides of this triangle have a
mean length of 10 cm.
Find the length of the side [AC].

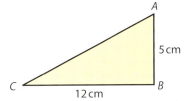

11. The mean of three numbers is 8. When a fourth number is added, the mean becomes 9.
Find the fourth number.

12. In the first three frames of a snooker match, a player got a mean score of 27 points.
In the fourth frame he scored 19 points. Find his mean score for the four frames.

13. The mean of three numbers is 10. The numbers 6 and 4 are added to these
numbers. Now find the mean of the five numbers.

14. The mean of seven numbers is 12.
One of the numbers is removed.
Find its value if
   (i)   the mean of the remaining numbers is reduced to 11
   (ii) the mean of the remaining numbers is unchanged
   (iii) the mean of the remaining numbers is increased to 14.

15. The average (mean) price of five packets of biscuits is €1.80.
The prices of two of the packets are €2.10 and €1.71.
The other three packets are all the same price.
Find this price.

16. Find the mean of these numbers:
         1, 4, 7, 8, 10
Now increase each number by 4.
Find the mean of these new numbers.
Now complete this sentence:
'When you increase each number in a set by 4, the mean is increased by …'

17. Find the mean of the numbers 1, 4, 7, 8, 10.
Multiply each number by 5.
Now find the mean of these numbers.
What have you discovered?

18. A darts player had an average score of 26 in six consecutive throws.
Calculate his total score for the six throws.
After his next throw, his average for the seven throws was 24.
Find his score for the seventh throw.

19. Write down five numbers so that:
the mean is 7
the median is 6
the mode is 4.

20. The table shows the marks which ten students obtained in Mathematics, English, and Science in their first-year examinations.

Student	Ava	Barry	Cliona	Derek	Emma	Finn	Gerry	Helen	Ian	Jack
Mathematics	45	56	47	77	82	39	78	32	92	62
English	54	55	59	69	66	49	60	56	88	44
Science	62	58	48	41	80	56	72	40	81	52

  (i) Calculate the mean mark for Mathematics.
 (ii) Calculate the mean mark for English.
(iii) Calculate the mean mark for Science.
(iv) Which student obtained a mark closest to the mean in Science?
 (v) How many students were above the mean mark in Mathematics?

Section 9.3 The range – variability

The **range** for a set of data is the highest value
of the set minus the lowest value.
For the data   3, 7, 9, 15, 21, 28
           Range $= 28 - 3$
                   $= 25$

> The range is largest value minus smallest value.

The range shows how **spread out** a set of data is.
It is very useful when comparing two sets of data.

The marks, out of 20, scored by Ava and Sean in 6 spelling tests are given below:

          Ava: 12, 10, 18, 14, 8, 10

          Sean: 12, 10, 16, 13, 11, 10

For **Ava:**   Mean $= \frac{72}{6} = 12$;   Range $= 18 - 8 = 10$
For **Sean:**   Mean $= \frac{72}{6} = 12$;   Range $= 16 - 10 = 6$

Notice that the mean mark for both is the same but Sean's marks have a smaller range. Since Sean's marks are less spread out, it shows that Sean's results are more **consistent** than Ava's.

This spread-out nature of Ava's marks compared to Sean's marks illustrates the **variability** of data and how important it can be when comparing two data sets.

The **range** is generally used as a measure of variability as it is easy to find and easy to understand.

Comparing data

To compare two sets of data, we use the **range** and one of the averages we have studied – the **mean**, the **mode** or the **median**.

In the example above comparing Ava's and Sean's marks, we used the range and the mean.

Exercise 9.3

1. Find the range for each of the following sets of data:
   (i)   3, 7, 6, 8, 12, 6, 14
   (ii) 18, 27, 36, 19, 21, 42, 20
   (iii) €8, €7, €16, €14, €23, €15

2. A golfer's scores in 6 rounds of golf were:

   75, 84, 92, 79, 85, 77

   (i) Find her mean score for the 6 rounds.
   (ii) What was the range of her scores?

3. Which of these two sets of data has the bigger range?
   (i) 23, 36, 42, 29, 34, 27
   (ii) 81, 74, 92, 77, 85, 89

4. Find the range for each of these sets of data:
   (i) 1.7, 2.3, 0.6, 0.8, 2.1, 1.9, 2.4
   (ii) 6, −1, 0, 3, −2, 4, −3, 1

5. Ann's marks in six maths tests were

   54, 82, 65, 72, 38, 66.

   John's marks in the same six tests were

   58, 62, 51, 66, 71, 64.

   (i) Find the range of marks for Ann and for John.
        Use your results to find which of the two had the more consistent marks.
   (ii) Which of the two had the higher mean mark?

6. In a golf competition between two clubs, the captain had to choose between Emer and Anna to play in the first round. In the previous eight rounds their scores were as follows:

Emer: 80, 73, 72, 88, 86, 90, 75, 92
Anna: 88, 84, 79, 85, 76, 85, 87, 80

(i)   Calculate the mean score for each golfer.
(ii) Find the range of scores for each golfer.
(iii) Which golfer would you choose to play in the competition?
     Explain your answer. (**Note:** In golf, the lower the score, the better.)

7. This table gives the times spent on facebook by six girls on two nights.

(i)   What is the modal time spent on facebook over both nights?
(ii) What is the modal time spent on Wednesday?
(iii) What is the range of the times spent on Wednesday?
(iv) What is the range of the times spent per night over the two days?

Time spent on facebook

Wednesday	Thursday
50 min	60 min
45 min	45 min
50 min	30 min
50 min	45 min
30 min	90 min
45 min	75 min

8. Here are the points scored by the Leinster and Munster rugby teams over six consecutive matches.

Leinster: 23, 14, 35, 18, 28, 34   **Munster:**   22, 25, 19, 27, 31, 26

(i)   Find the mean number of points for each team.
(ii) Find the range of scores for each team.
(iii) If you were coaching another team, which of these two teams would you like to play against? Explain your answer.

9. Sinead has five cards. The five cards have a mean of 7 and a range of 4.
What are the missing numbers?

10. The range of nine numbers on a card is 60.
One number is covered by a piece of blu-tack.
What could that number be?

[There are two possible answers.]

11. There were seven people sleeping in a tent.
The mean age of the people was 20 and
the range of their ages was 7.
Write each statement below, and then write
next to it whether it is *True*, *Possible* or *False*.

  (i)   The oldest person in the tent was 7 years older than the youngest.

 (ii)   The youngest person in the tent was 18 years old.

(iii)   Every person in the tent was 20 years old.

12. There were ten children on a coach journey. The mean age of the children was 11
and the range of their ages was 4. Write each statement below and then write next
to it whether it is *True*, *Possible* or *False*.

  (i)   The youngest child was 9 years old.

 (ii)   Nine of the children were 11 years old.

(iii)   All the children were at least 10 years old.

13. Derek has five cards, each of which has a positive
whole number printed on it.
Three of the cards have the number 8 written on them.
Without knowing the numbers on the other two cards, is it possible to find the value of

  (i)   the median   (ii)   the mode   (iii)   the mean?

If the mean of the five cards is 8, give two numbers that could be on the other two cards.
Now give two different numbers that could be on the cards.
What are the numbers on these two cards if their range is 12 and the mean of the
five cards is still 8?

Section 9.4 Which average to use

The three averages – the **mean**, the **mode**, and the **median** – are all useful, but
depending on the data, one may be more suitable than the other two.

We try to select the 'average' that is most representative of a set of data.

If you use the wrong average, your results may lead to an
incorrect conclusion.

Here are the times taken by six people to solve a puzzle:

     12 sec, 15 sec, 11 sec, 16 sec, 18 sec, 60 sec.

The mean time $= \dfrac{12 + 15 + 11 + 16 + 18 + 60}{6}$

$\qquad\qquad = \dfrac{132}{6} = 22$ seconds

The median time: 11, 12, $\boxed{15, 16,}$ 18, 60

$= \frac{1}{2}(15 + 16)$

$= 15.5$ seconds

Which of these two averages is the more suitable?

The mean time is 22 seconds.

Five of the six people take a shorter time than this mean (due to the outlier, 60).

The median, 15.5 seconds, is more typical of the data set and so the median is the more suitable average in this case.

Example 1

Here are the marks obtained by a group of 10 students in a geography test.

6, 7, 83, 84, 85, 86, 86, 87, 88, 89

Find   (i) the mean   (ii) the median.

State which of these averages best represents the data?

(i) Mean $= \dfrac{6 + 7 + 83 + 84 + 85 + 86 + 86 + 87 + 88 + 89}{10}$

          $= \dfrac{701}{10}$

          $= 70.1$

(ii) The median $= \dfrac{85 + 86}{2} = 85.5$

In the data, eight out of the ten marks are in the eighties.

Since the mean is only 70.1, the median is a more suitable average.

The **mode** is most useful when one value appears much more often than any other.

However, if the data is too spread out the mode may not be suitable.

Consider this set of data: 12, 3, 7, 3, 14, 15, 18, 20.

Here the mode is 3, but it is not very representative of all the other numbers in the set because it is the lowest value.

In this case the mode is not a suitable average.

Now consider these colours of dresses in a shop window:

blue, red, green, blue, black, silver, red, blue, white, black, blue, silver, red, blue

Here the mode is blue as it occurs more frequently than any other colour.

> For **categorical data**, such as the colours of dresses listed above, the **mode** is the **only** average that can be used.

Exercise 9.4

1. The numbers of computers in eight classrooms are

   3, 15, 1, 2, 1, 30, 2, 1.

   (i) What is the median number of computers?
   (ii) What is the modal number of computers?
   (iii) Why would the mean not be a sensible average for this data?

2. The teacher in charge of an outdoor pursuits centre has 10 pairs of boots.
   The sizes of the boots are as follows:

   4, 7, 5, 5, 3, 10, 8, 5, 5, 8

   The teacher calculates the median, the mode, the mean and the range.

   (i) Which of them will tell her how spread out the boot sizes are?
   (ii) Find the (a) mean (b) mode (c) median.
   (iii) Which of the three averages best represents the data?

3. For the set of numbers below, find the mean and the median.

   1, 3, 3, 3, 4, 6, 99

   Which average best describes the set of numbers?

4. Sixteen teenagers were asked to state their favourite colour.
   These are the results:

   blue, green, purple, black, purple, pink, white, blue, yellow, pink, black, green, orange, green, black, black

   State clearly, with reasons, which is the best average to use for the favourite colour of the teenagers.

   Why can you not find the mean of the favourite colours?

5. Jack and Daniel are backpacking in Australia and have recorded these daily temperatures for a week.

Day	1	2	3	4	5	6	7
Midday temperature (°C)	32	30	30	28	33	31	30

   (i) Find the mean midday temperature.
   (ii) Give a reason why the mean is appropriate for this data.

6. (i) Find the mean of this set of numbers:

   37, 26, 37, 18, 18, 20, 26, 18, 37, 37, 18

   (ii) Why is the mode a bad choice of average in this case?

7. In March, Rachel and Dave sold five different types of jacket in their clothes shop and in the amounts shown.

Jacket	Leather	Suede	Denim	PVC	Cotton
Amount sold	45	17	64	28	52

 (i) Find the modal type of jacket sold.

 (ii) Why is the mode appropriate for this data?

8. Customers at a roller-skating rink can hire skates.
 The first seven customers on Monday morning take the following skate sizes.

   7, 5, 6, 9, 8, 10, 5

 (i) For the seven customers, find
    (a) the median skate size   (b) the modal skate size.

 (ii) The manager is going to buy some new skates.
    He knows the median and modal skate size for 700 customers.
    Which of the values would be the more useful to him?
    Explain your answer.

9.

 The weights, in kilograms, of a boat crew are

   96, 86, 94, 96, 91, 95, 90, 96, 43.

 (i) Calculate
    (a) their median weight
    (b) the range of their weights
    (c) their mean weight.

 (ii) Which of the two averages, mean or median, best typifies the data above?
    Give a reason for your answer.

Section 9.5 **Frequency tables**

The number of children in each of 50 families in a certain district was recorded in the following way:

1, 3, 4, 3, 2, 2, 4, 2, 6, 7, 6, 2, 4, 5, 5, 4, 3, 4, 3, 2, 1, 6, 2, 5, 1,
4, 4, 4, 3, 5, 3, 6, 2, 4, 5, 7, 2, 4, 3, 5, 5, 3, 3, 4, 1, 2, 5, 3, 4, 4

This list would be much more useful and easier to read if it was presented in the form of a table, as shown below.

Number of children per family	1	2	3	4	5	6	7
Number of families	4	9	10	13	8	4	2

The table above is called a **frequency table** or **frequency distribution**.

This table shows the number of families (i.e. the *frequency*) with 1 child, 2 children and so on.

For example, there are 13 families with 4 children per family.

Mean and Mode of a Frequency Distribution

The frequency table below shows the numbers of children aged from 2 to 7 living on a certain road.

Age	2	3	4	5	6	7
Number of children	1	3	5	10	8	3

From the table it can be seen that the **mode** or **modal age** is 5 as it occurs more often than any other age.

To find the **mean** age of the children from the table, we perform these operations:

> 1. Find the sum of all the ages of the children.
> 2. Find the total number of children.
> 3. Divide the sum of the ages by the number of children.

1. To find the sum of the ages, we multiply each age by the number of children of that age and add up the results.

   Sum of ages $= (1 \times 2) + (3 \times 3) + (5 \times 4) + (10 \times 5) + (8 \times 6) + (3 \times 7)$
   $$= 2 + 9 + 20 + 50 + 48 + 21$$
   $$= 150$$

2. The number of children is $1 + 3 + 5 + 10 + 8 + 3 = 30$.

3. The mean age $= \dfrac{\text{Sum of all the ages}}{\text{Number of children}} = \dfrac{150}{30} = 5$

   $\therefore$ the mean $= 5$

Example 1

A road-check on 30 motor vehicles yielded the following record of the number of occupants each carried:

2, 1, 3, 4, 5, 3, 2, 1, 2, 3, 1, 1, 2, 4, 6, 5, 4, 2, 2, 1, 1, 2, 4, 6, 5, 2, 6, 2, 5, 3

Make out a frequency table for the above data and hence find the mean and mode of the distribution.

Number of occupants per vehicle	1	2	3	4	5	6
Number of vehicles	6	9	4	4	4	3

$$\text{Mean} = \frac{(6 \times 1) + (9 \times 2) + (4 \times 3) + (4 \times 4) + (4 \times 5) + (3 \times 6)}{6 + 9 + 4 + 4 + 4 + 3}$$

$$= \frac{90}{30} = 3$$

Mode = 2, as 2 occurs with the greatest frequency.

Exercise 9.5

1. Thirty students in a class were given a test which was marked out of 10. The results of the test are shown below:

   4, 6, 7, 5, 9, 8, 6, 4, 3, 5, 6, 9, 8, 7, 6, 10, 1, 3, 6, 7, 9, 8, 5, 3, 2, 4, 7, 9, 10, 5

   Copy and complete this frequency table:

Marks per student	1	2	3	4	5	6	7	8	9	10
Number of students			3							

   From the table, write down the number of students who got
   (i) 5 marks   (ii) 8 marks   (iii) 10 marks.
   What mark was got most frequently?

2. The following frequency table shows the number of people per car passing a certain point on the road in a five-minute period.

Number of people per car	1	2	3	4	5	6
Number of cars	8	12	7	6	2	1

   Use the frequency table to answer these questions:
   (i) How many cars had three people in them?
   (ii) How many cars had only 1 person in them?
   (iii) How many cars had 5 people or more in them?
   (iv) How many cars were in the survey?
   (v) What percentage of the cars had 2 people in them?

3. A factory produces 50 television sets per day.

Tests at the end of one Tuesday gave rise to the following data:

Number of faults per set	0	1	2	3	4	5	6
Number of sets	1	8	12	11	9	5	4

  (i)   How many sets had no fault?
 (ii)   How many sets had 6 faults?
(iii)   What was the modal number of faults?
 (iv)   What was the total number of faults recorded in all the sets?
  (v)   Find the mean number of faults per set.

4. The table below shows the numbers of goals scored in a number of matches on a Sunday morning.

Goals scored	1	2	3	4	5	6
Number of matches	14	16	8	8	6	8

  (i)   In how many matches were 6 goals scored?
 (ii)   What was the modal number of goals scored?
(iii)   What was the total number of goals scored?
 (iv)   Find the mean number of goals scored.
  (v)   Work out the greatest number of matches which could have ended in a draw.

5. Find the mean of the given frequency distribution.

Number	1	2	3	4	5	6
Frequency	9	9	6	4	7	3

This distribution has two modes. What are they?

6. The following table gives the numbers of children aged one to six years living on a certain road:

Age in years	1	2	3	4	5	6
Number of children	14	16	8	8	6	8

  (i)   Find the total number of children aged 1 to 6 living on the road.
 (ii)   How many of these children are aged 2 years or less?
(iii)   What percentage of these children are aged 3 years or more?
 (iv)   What is the mode of the distribution?
  (v)   Calculate the mean of the distribution.

7. A road-check on 50 motor vehicles yielded the following record of the number of occupants in each:

> 3, 2, 1, 5, 2, 1, 2, 3, 4, 6, 2, 4, 5, 6, 2, 1, 2, 3, 4, 3, 2, 1, 1, 4, 1,
> 3, 2, 1, 4, 3, 2, 1, 2, 3, 1, 4, 2, 3, 4, 1, 2, 1, 4, 5, 1, 2, 3, 2, 4, 2

  (i)   Construct a frequency table to illustrate the data.
  (ii) What is the modal number of occupants per car?
  (iii) What percentage of the cars had 5 occupants or more?

8. A group of 50 people were asked to count the number of coins they had in their pockets. The results are shown in the following frequency table.

Number of coins	0	1	2	3	4	5	6
Number of people	2	8	9	13	8	7	3

Calculate the mean number of coins per person.

9. The following frequency table shows the number of goals scored in 60 football matches.

Goals scored	1	2	3	4	5	6
Number of matches	15	14	9	6	10	6

  (i)   Find the mean number of goals scored per match.
  (ii) What was the modal number of goals scored?
  (iii) In what percentage of the matches were 3 or 4 goals scored?
  (iv) Find the greatest number of matches which could have ended in a draw.

10. The marks of 36 students in third-year are given below:

> 31 49 52 79 40 29 66 71 73 19 51 47 81 67 40 52 20 84
> 65 73 60 54 60 59 25 89 21 91 84 77 18 37 55 41 72 38

Copy and complete the grouped frequency table below:

Marks	1–20	21–40	41–60	61–80	81–100
Number of students					

  (i)   How many students scored between 21 and 60 inclusive?
  (ii) What is the modal class?
  (iii) Which class had the second largest number of students?
  (iv) Name one disadvantage of a grouped frequency table.

Test yourself 9

1. (a)   A rugby team played 10 games.
      Here are the numbers of points the team
      scored.

      12 22 14 11 7 18 22 14 36 14

      (i)   Write down the mode.
      (ii) Work out the range.
      (iii) Work out the mean.
      (iv) Work out the median.

   (b)   Paul got these marks in three tests: 72, 80 and 82
      He had one more test to sit.
      He wanted an average of 80 for the four tests.
      What mark must he get in the fourth test?

2. (a)   (i)   The number of safety matches in ten different boxes were as follows.

            48   47   47   50   46   50   49   49   47   51

         Find the modal number of matches in a box.
      (ii) The mean of three numbers is 8. Two of the numbers are 8 and 10.
         Find the third number.

   (b)   The table shows the scores achieved by 20 students who played a game.

Score	0	1	2	3	4	5
Frequency	3	5	6	2	3	1

   Calculate the mean score for the 20 students.

3. (a)   Find the mean, median and mode of this set of numbers:

            1, 1, 2, 3, 3, 3, 4, 6, 40

      Which of these averages best represents this data?
      Comment on your answer.

   (b)   Here are five number cards.

      (i)   Show how you could choose three of these cards so that the mean of the
         three numbers is bigger than the median.
      (ii) Now pick another three cards to make the median bigger than the mean.
      (iii) Finally, choose three cards where the mean and the median are equal.

4. The bar graph shows a survey on the number of children per family.

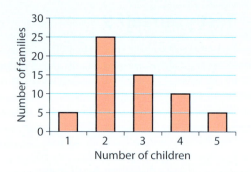

(a) How many families participated in the survey?

(b) How many children were there altogether?

(c) Calculate the mean number of children per family.

(d) If 1 more family of 4 children were to participate in the survey, how would the mean be affected?

5. (a) Last April, a certain garage sold five different types of cars.
The numbers sold were:

Car	Prestige	Sports	Ordinary	Coupe	4 × 4
Number sold	12	8	23	2	5

(i) Find the modal type of car sold.
(ii) Why is the mode appropriate for this data?

(b) (i) Find three numbers with a range of 6, a median of 8 and a mean of 8.
(ii) Find three numbers with a mode of 4, a median of 4 and a mean of 5.
(iii) Three people have a mean age of 25.
The range of the ages is 8 years and the median is 27.
How old is each person?

6. (a) There are 10 houses in Barrack Street.
On Monday, the numbers of letters delivered to the houses are:

　　　0　2　5　3　34　4　0　1　0　2

Calculate the mean, mode and median of the number of letters.
Which of the three averages best reflects the data?

(b) The mean number of lollies in a bag should be 35. The quality control person took a sample of ten bags to check that this was the case.
In the first nine bags there were 35, 42, 31, 43, 36, 33, 32, 31, 35.
(i) What was the total number of lollies in the first nine bags?
(ii) What was the mean number of lollies in the first nine bags?
(iii) How many lollies must be in the tenth bag so that the mean number of lollies for the ten bags is 35?

7. (a) Here are some sets of numbers. Add on another number to each set to obtain the median given on the right.

(i) 1, 8, 5, 2:   median 5 ← Hint: you need to make 5 the middle number.

(ii) 8, 4, 5, 3, 8, 4, 2, 9:   median 4

(iii) 7, 4, 3, 6, 2, 6, 8, 4:   median 5

(b) On the first five days of his holiday, David drove an average of 256 kilometres per day and on the next three days he drove an average of 172 kilometres per day.

(i) What is the total distance that David drove in the first five days?

(ii) What is the total distance that David drove in the next three days?

(iii) What is the mean distance travelled per day, by David, over the eight days?

8. (a) A dice was thrown 30 times. The results are recorded below.

Score	1	2	3	4	5	6
Frequency	3	4	6	8	7	2

Find the mean score.

(b) Here are the scores of three students in a computer game:

         Tim: 47, 51, 36, 78, 43, 20, 39, 27

         Frank: 35, 38, 42, 55, 28, 43, 61, 54

         Derek: 45, 51, 57, 44, 50, 48, 43, 49

(i) Which student was least consistent?
Give a reason for your answer.

(ii) One of the students scored 75 in his next game.
His range is now 32. Who was it?

9. (a) The weekly wages of the employees of a fast-food takeaway are listed below:

         €300, €250, €240, €220, €200, €1050.

Find   (i) the mean wage
        (ii) the median wage.

Why can't you find the mode?
Which of the averages – mean or median – best represents the 'typical' wage?

(b) The range for eight numbers is 40 and seven of these numbers are shown.
Find two possible values for the missing number.

27   5   33   42

11   13   19

Geometry 1: Triangles and Quadrilaterals

Key words

line line segment ray intersect collinear perpendicular parallel
straight angle acute obtuse reflex vertically opposite corresponding
alternate interior exterior isosceles equilateral quadrilateral
parallelogram rhombus diagonal Theorem of Pythagoras hypotenuse

Section 10.1 Revision of lines and angles

The diagrams below will help you recall some of the facts and terms you will have met in your study of geometry so far.

1. Lines

The **line** AB passes through the points A and B.

The **line segment** [AB] starts at A and ends at B.

The line that starts at A and continues on through B is called the **ray** [AB.

Points that lie on the same line are said to be **collinear**.

The lines l and m **intersect** at the point P.

Lines that never meet are said to be **parallel lines**.

2. Angles

The angle above is written ∠AOB (or ∠BOA).

The angle above is called a **right angle**.
A right angle = 90°.

A half a revolution makes a **straight angle**.
A straight angle = 180°.

An angle that is less than 90° is called an **acute angle**.

An angle between 90° and 180° is called an **obtuse angle**.

An angle between 180° and 360° is called a **reflex angle**.

The shaded angle, which is less than 180°, is generally referred to as an **ordinary angle**.

Vertically opposite angles are equal in measure.

Angles at a point add up to **360°**.

3. Parallel lines and angles

Angles formed when a straight line crosses a pair of parallel lines have the following properties:

Corresponding angles are equal. So, $a = b$. You can find them by looking for an 'F shape'.

Alternate angles are equal. So, $a = b$. Look for a 'Z shape'.

The **interior angles** x and y sum to 180°. So, $x + y = 180°$.

Exercise 10.1

1. Describe in words each of the following diagrams:

(i) A •————————• B

(ii) A •←———————→• B

(iii) A ←——————•——————→ B

2. Find the measure of the angle marked with a letter in each of the following diagrams:

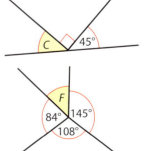

3. Work out the angles marked with a letter in each of the following diagrams:

  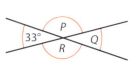

4. In each of the following diagrams, write down the number of the angle that **corresponds** to the shaded angle. (Arrows indicate parallel lines.)

(i)   (ii)   (iii)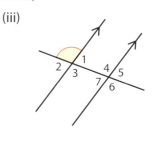

5. In each of the following figures, write down the number of the angle which is alternate to the shaded angle:

(i)   (ii)   (iii)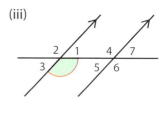

6. Write down the sizes of the angles marked with letters in each of the following diagrams, where arrows indicate parallel lines.

  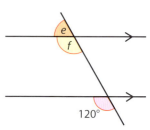

7. In each of the following, work out the size of the angle marked with a letter. Arrows indicate parallel lines.

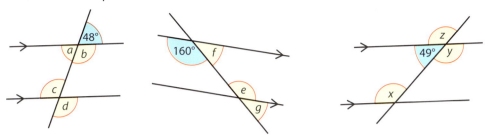

8. Find the value of the lettered angles, each time, giving reasons:

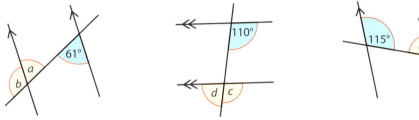

9. Find the sizes of the angles marked *a*, *b*, *c*, *d*, *e*, *f* and *g* in the given figure, where arrows indicate parallel lines.

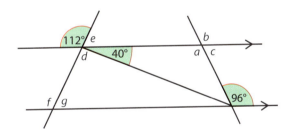

10. Find the measures of the angles marked with letters in the given diagram, where the arrows indicate parallel lines.

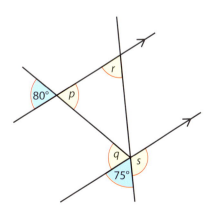

Section 10.2 **Angles of a triangle**

The diagrams below will help you recall some important facts about the angles of a triangle.

The angles of a triangle sum to 180°.
$$|\angle A| + |\angle B| + |\angle C| = 180°$$

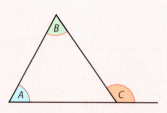

The **exterior angle** of a triangle is equal to the sum of the interior opposite angles.
$$|\angle C| = |\angle A| + |\angle B|$$

An **equilateral triangle** has
   3 equal sides
   3 equal angles.
   Each angle is 60°.

An **isosceles triangle** has
   2 equal sides
   base angles equal.

A **right-angled triangle** has
an angle of 90°.
$$a^2 = b^2 + c^2$$

It is stated in the box above that in an isosceles triangle, the angles opposite the equal sides are also equal.

Conversely, it can be shown that if a triangle contains two equal angles, then that triangle is isosceles.

> ### Example 1
>
> Find the measure of the angle marked x in
> the given triangle.
>
>
>
> The angle marked y is $180° - 110° = 70°$.
> But angle x = angle y ... isosceles triangle
> $\therefore \quad |\angle x| = 70°$
>
>

Exercise 10.2

1. For each triangle below, name:
   (i) the exterior angle
   (ii) the two interior opposite angles to the exterior angle.

(a)

(b)

(c)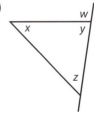

2. Find the measure of the angle marked with a letter in each of these triangles:

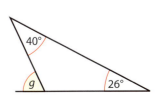

3. In the following triangles, equal sides are marked.
Find the measure of the angle marked with a letter in each triangle:

4. Work out the sizes of the missing angles in each of these isosceles triangles:

5. Find the size of the angle marked with a letter in the following figures:

  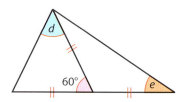

6. Calculate the size of each angle marked with a letter:

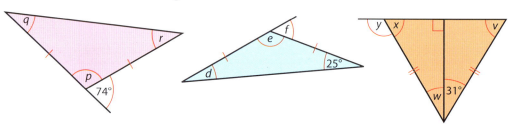

7. Find the measure of the angles marked *a* and *b* in the given triangle where equal sides are marked.

8. In each of the following triangles, the arrows indicate that the lines are parallel. Find the measure of each angle marked with a letter.

  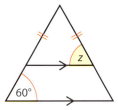

9. Find the value of x and the value of y in each of the following where the arrows indicate parallel lines.

(i)

(ii)

(iii)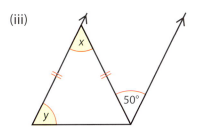

Section 10.3 **Quadrilaterals**

A figure which has four sides is called
a **quadrilateral**.
In the quadrilateral shown, the sides have different
lengths and the angles have different sizes.

However, there are quadrilaterals with special properties which you should recognise. Some of these special quadrilaterals are shown below.

A square

In a square,
> all four sides are the same length
> opposite sides are parallel
> all four angles are right angles.

A rectangle

In a rectangle,

> › each pair of opposite sides are parallel and equal in length
> › all four angles are right angles.

A parallelogram

In a parallelogram,

> › the opposite sides are parallel
> › the opposite sides are equal in length
> › the opposite angles are equal.

A rhombus

In a rhombus,

> › there are 4 equal sides
> › opposite sides are parallel
> › opposite angles are equal.

In the given parallelogram, A and B are called **interior angles** as they add up to 180°.

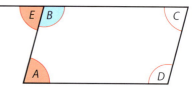

Proof: $\angle E = \angle A$ … alternate angles
          $\angle E + \angle B = 180°$ … straight angle
    $\therefore$ $\angle A + \angle B = 180°$
Similarly, $\angle B + \angle C = 180°, \angle A + \angle D = 180°$ and $\angle C + \angle D = 180°$.

The angles of a quadrilateral

The quadrilateral shown is divided into two triangles.
The angles in each triangle add up to 180°.

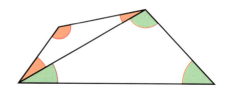

Thus the angles in a quadrilateral add up to 360°.

> The interior angles in a quadrilateral add up to 360°.

Diagonals

In the special quadrilaterals shown below, the diagonals bisect each other.

Square	Rectangle	Parallelogram	Rhombus
Diagonals are equal and bisect each other at right angles.	Diagonals are equal and bisect each other.	Diagonals bisect each other.	Diagonals bisect each other at right angles.

Theorem   The diagonals of a parallelogram bisect each other.

Example 1

In the given parallelogram ABCD,
$|\angle BAD| = 115°$ and $|\angle BDC| = 28°$.
Find   (i) $|\angle BCD|$ (ii) $|\angle ABD|$
        (iii) $|\angle ADC|$ (iv) $|\angle DBC|$
Give a reason for each answer.

  (i) $|\angle BCD| = 115°$ ... opposite angles are equal
 (ii) $|\angle ABD| = 28°$ ... alternate angles
(iii) $|\angle ADC| = 180° - 115°$ ... interior angles sum to 180°
         $= 65°$
(iv) $|\angle DBC| = 180° - 115° - 28°$ ... $|\angle BCD| = 115°$ from (i) above
         $= 37°$

Exercise 10.3

1. A, B, C and D are the four angles in the given parallelogram.
  (i) Name two pairs of equal angles.
  (ii) How many degrees are there in the angles
    $A + B$?

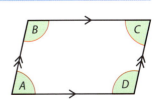

2. Find the angle marked with a letter in each of the following parallelograms:

  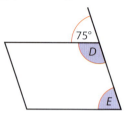

3. Find the size of the angle marked with a letter in each of these parallelograms:

  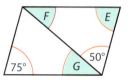

4. Find the values of *x* and *y* in the given parallelogram.

5. Find the measure of the angle marked with a letter in these parallelograms:

6. Find the value of the angle marked *x* in each of the following parallelograms:

(i) (ii) (iii)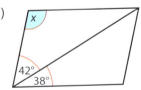

7. Find the size of the angle marked with a letter in each of these parallelograms:

  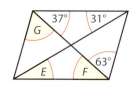

8. ABCD is a parallelogram with the diagonals intersecting at the point O.
Write down the length of
  (i) [OB]   (ii) [AB]
(iii) [AC]   (iv) [BC]

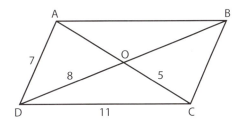

9. ABCD is a parallelogram with the diagonals intersecting at the point O.

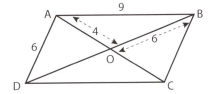

Write down the length of
  (i) [DO]   (ii) [OC]   (iii) [DC]   (iv) [BC].
Now name an angle equal in measure to
(v) ∠AOD   (vi) ∠DAB   (vii) ∠BDC   (viii) ∠CAB

10. In the given parallelogram all the sides are equal, as marked.
Calculate the values of *x*, *y*, *z* and *r*.

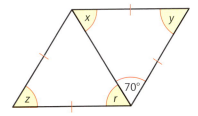

11. Copy the given diagram and mark in these angles:
    |∠BDC| = 23°, |∠DAX| = 75°, |∠DCB| = 118°.
Now find |∠AXD|.

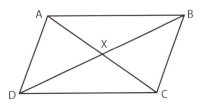

12. Find the size of the angle marked with a letter in each of these figures.

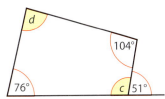

13. In the given parallelogram ABCD, parallel
lines are drawn, as shown.
Find the values of the angles
marked x, y and z.

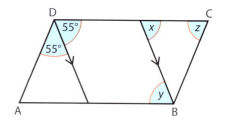

14. A square, rectangle, parallelogram and rhombus are shown below.
They are numbered 1, 2, 3, and 4.

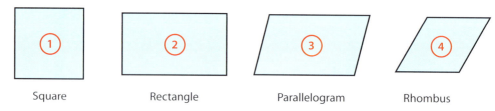

| Square | Rectangle | Parallelogram | Rhombus |

Which of these four shapes will **always** have these properties?
(The third one is done for you.)
  (i)   All angles are the same size.
 (ii)   Opposite angles are equal.
(iii)   All sides are equal in length.   1, 4
 (iv)   Opposite sides are equal.
  (v)   Opposite sides are parallel.
 (vi)   Both diagonals are equal in length.
(vii)   The diagonals bisect each other.
(viii) The diagonals intersect at right angles.

15. Find the value of x in each of the diagrams below:

(i)   (ii)   (iii)

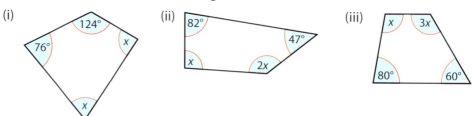

Section 10.4 The Theorem of Pythagoras

The diagram on the right shows a right-angled triangle of sides 3, 4 and 5 cm.

Squares are drawn on each of the three sides.

By counting the number of cm^2 in each of these squares, you will notice that the area of the square on the **hypotenuse** is 25 cm^2, while the other two squares have areas 16 cm^2 and 9 cm^2.

This diagram illustrates that the square on the hypotenuse is equal to the sum of the squares on the other two sides.

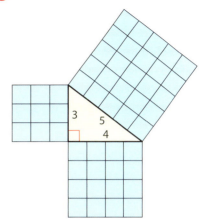

This important theorem is called the *Theorem of Pythagoras*.
Pythagoras was a Greek philosopher and mathematician who died about 500 BC.
The first formal proof of the theorem is attributed to him, although there is evidence that the theorem was well known to the Chinese and Egyptians hundreds of years before.
The Egyptian surveyors knew that a rope containing 12 equally-spaced knots could be used to form a right-angled triangle. They used this for marking fields and squaring buildings.

In a right-angled triangle, the square on the hypotenuse is equal to the sum of the squares on the other two sides.

The Theorem of Pythagoras.

The Theorem of Pythagoras can be expressed very neatly through algebra, as shown.

The converse of the Theorem of Pythagoras is also true.
It states that:

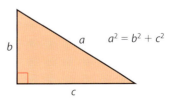

$$a^2 = b^2 + c^2$$

If the square of one side of a triangle is equal to the sum of the squares of the other two sides, then the angle opposite the first side is a right angle.

Converse of the Theorem of Pythagoras.

The triangle shown is right angled since

$$10^2 = 8^2 + 6^2,$$

i.e. $100 = 100$

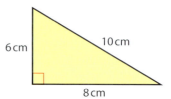

Example 1

Find the lengths of the sides marked x in the following right-angled triangles.

(i)

(ii)

By Theorem of Pythagoras:

(i) $\quad x^2 = 3^2 + 2^2$

$\qquad = 9 + 4$

$\therefore \ x^2 = 13$

$\therefore \quad x = \sqrt{13}$

$\therefore \quad x = 3.6$

(ii) $\qquad 15^2 = 12^2 + x^2$

$\therefore \quad 225 = 144 + x^2$

$225 - 144 = 144 + x^2 - 144$

$\qquad\qquad x^2 = 81$

$\therefore \quad x = \sqrt{81}$

$\therefore \quad x = 9$

Exercise 10.4

1. Write down the length of the hypotenuse in each of these triangles:

(i)

(ii)

(iii)

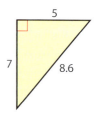

2. Use the *Theorem of Pythagoras* to find the area of the square marked with a letter in each of these figures:

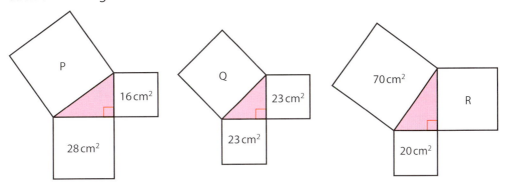

3. Find the length of the side marked with a letter in each of these triangles:

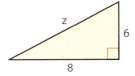

4. Find the length of the side marked with a letter in each of these triangles.
(You may leave your answer in $\sqrt{}$ form.)

5. Find the length of the diagonal in each of these squares.
(You may leave your answer in $\sqrt{}$ form.)

6. Calculate the length of the diagonal of the given rectangle.

12 cm

16 cm

7. A windowsill in an office building is 12 m above the ground. The top of a 13 m long ladder is resting against the windowsill. How far out from the wall of the office building, is the foot of the ladder?

13 m

12 m

8. A new section of road cuts off one of the dangerous right-angled bends on a country lane.
To the nearest 10 metres, how much shorter is the new section of road?

200 m

100 m

new road

9. The size of a rectangular television screen is determined by the length of the diagonal.
The screen size of this television is 54 centimetres.
If the height of the screen is 26 cm, what is the width?
Give your answer correct to 1 decimal place.

54 cm

10.

Hannah put a wooden edging around this triangular garden.
She used a 10 m length of wood for the longest side and a 6 m length for the shortest side.
What total length of wood did Hannah use?

11. A helicopter flew 24 km to the west, then 15 km to the north.
How far is the helicopter then from its starting point?
Give your answer to the nearest kilometre.

12. Semicircles are drawn on the sides of the given right-angled triangle. Investigate if the area of the semicircle on the hypotenuse is equal to the sum of the areas of the semicircles on the other two sides.

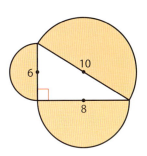

> Area of semicircle = $\dfrac{\pi r^2}{2}$.

13. Use the Theorem of Pythagoras to find the value of a and the value of b in the given right-angled triangle.

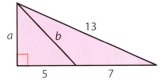

14. Alan wanted to find the width of Lake Como. He placed a stake at Z so that $|\angle YXZ| = 90°$. He found $|XZ|$ to be 450 m long and $|YZ|$ to be 780 m long.
What is the distance between X and Y?
Give your answer correct to the nearest metre.

Pythagorean triads

A triad is a group of three related objects.
A Pythagorean triad is a group of three numbers that obey Pythagoras' theorem.

(3, 4, 5) is a Pythagorean triad because $5^2 = 3^2 + 4^2$.
(5, 12, 13) and (2.5, 6, 6.5) are also Pythagorean triads. (Check them.)
Pythagoras developed a formula for finding Pythagorean triads.
If one number in the triad is x, the formulas for the other two are
$\frac{1}{2}(x^2 - 1)$ and $\frac{1}{2}(x^2 + 1)$.

15. By checking whether the square of the largest number is equal to the sum of the squares of the other two numbers, state if each of the following is a Pythagorean triad:

    (i) 6, 8, 10   (ii) 7, 11, 12   (iii) 5, 12, 13   (iv) 4, 6, 8

16. Using the formula developed by Pythagoras, find Pythagorean triads when

    (i) $x = 6$ (ii) $x = \sqrt{5}$ (iii) $x = 7$ (iv) $x = 4$

Test yourself 10

1. (a) Find the size of each angle marked with a letter in the figures below, where the arrows indicate parallel lines:

  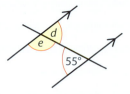

   (b) Find the size of the angle marked with a letter in each of these triangles:

2. (a) Find the values of a, b and c in the following figures:

   (b) Find the measures of the angles marked *a* and *b* in the triangles below, where equal sides are marked.

 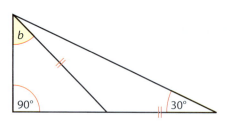

3. (a) Find the measure of each angle marked with a letter in the following parallelograms:

(b) In the given figure, equal sides are indicated. Find the sizes of the angles marked *a* and *b*.

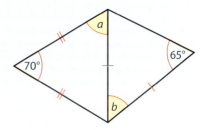

4. (a) Find the third side in each of these right-angled triangles:

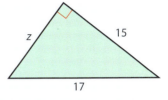

(b) Find the measure of each angle marked with a letter in each of the following figures, where the arrows indicate parallel lines.

5. (a) Find the measures of the angles marked *x*, *y* and *z* in the given parallelogram.

(b) Find the value of *x* in the given triangle. What can be deduced about the triangle?

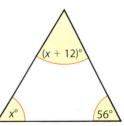

6. (a) Find the value of *a* and the value of *b* in each of these triangles:

(i)

(ii)

(iii)

(b) In the diagram on the right the arrows indicate that the lines are parallel. Calculate the measures of the angles A and B.

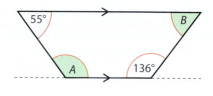

(c) In the given triangle, $|PQ| = |PR| = |RS|$. If $|\angle QPR| = 40°$, find the value of x.

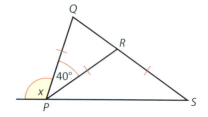

Puzzle

Find the unknown angle in each of the following triangles.
Copy the box below and match the letter of the angle to the correct given angle to answer this riddle.
How do you make varnish vanish?

| 58° | 60° | 38° | 30° | | 35° | 158° | 58° | | 58° | 42° | 30° | | 45° |

Time and Speed

Section 11.1 Time and timetables

The clock on the right shows the time to be 9.20.

This could be either 9.20 a.m. or 9.20 p.m..

When we give a time containing a.m. or p.m., we are expressing it in
12-hour clock time.

The letters **a.m.** are used to indicate times between midnight and midday.

Times between noon and midnight are indicated by **p.m.**.

> a.m.   stands for *ante meridiem* – before midday
> p.m.   stands for *post meridiem* – after midday

The **24-hour clock** is another way of telling the time.

This method uses 4 digits, e.g. 10.24.

The first two digits give the hour after midnight and the second two digits give the number of minutes after the hour.

The table below shows times expressed in 12-hour and 24-hour clock times.

12-hour clock	10 a.m.	4.30 p.m.	4.20 a.m.	9.16 p.m.	12.10 a.m.
24-hour clock	10.00	16.30	04.20	21.16	00.10

In most bus, airport and train timetables, for example, the decimal point in the 24-hour time is omitted and 21.16 is written as 2116.

Example 1

A film begins at 20.45 and ends at 22.14. How long does it last?

To calculate, we subtract 20.45 from 22.14 as follows:

$$\begin{array}{r} 22.14 \\ -\,20.45 \\ \hline \end{array}$$

When subtracting a larger number of minutes from a smaller number, change the top line by adding 60 to the minutes and then taking away one hour as follows:

$$\begin{array}{r} 22.14 \\ -\,20.45 \\ \hline \end{array} = \begin{array}{r} 21.74 \\ -\,20.45 \\ \hline 1.29 \end{array}$$ … 14 minutes after 10 p.m. = 74 minutes after 9 p.m. (22.00 = 10 p.m.)

The film lasts 1 hour 29 minutes.

Exercise 11.1

1. How many minutes are there in each of these?

(i) $\frac{1}{2}$ hour   (ii) $\frac{1}{4}$ hour   (iii) $\frac{2}{5}$ hour   (iv) $1\frac{3}{4}$ hours   (v) $\frac{7}{10}$ hour.

2. Add each of the following:

(i)	hr	min
	4	12
	3	46

(ii)	hr	min
	4	38
	3	46

(iii)	hr	min
	1	29
	3	53

3. How many minutes from 7.20 a.m. to 8.00 a.m.?

How many hours and minutes from 8.00 a.m. to 3.40 p.m.?

Now find how many hours and minutes there are between 7.20 a.m. and 3.40 p.m.

4. How many hours and minutes from

(i) 8.30 a.m. to 11.45 a.m.   (ii) 12.30 p.m. to 7 p.m.

(iii) 7.40 a.m. to 3.30 p.m.   (iv) 10.10 a.m. to 6.40 p.m.

(v) 8.45 a.m. to 3.50 p.m.   (vi) 11.50 a.m. to 7.45 p.m.?

5. Subtract the following:

(i)	hr	min
	4	53
	2	17

(ii)	hr	min
	3	12
	1	46

(iii)	hr	min
	5	35
	3	54

6. Write the following in 24-hour clock time:

(i) 6 a.m.   (ii) 10.45 a.m.   (iii) 4 p.m.   (iv) 5.20 p.m.

(v) 7.30 p.m.   (vi) 8.45 a.m.   (vii) 12 midday   (viii) 11.40 p.m.

(ix) 3.15 a.m.   (x) 3.15 p.m.

7. Write the following using a.m. or p.m.:

(i) 11.40   (ii) 15.35   (iii) 12.20   (iv) 00.30   (v) 22.15

(vi) 04.20   (vii) 10.35   (viii) 14.30   (ix) 18.45   (x) 23.12

8. Express each of these in 24-hour clock time:

(i)   (ii)   (iii)   (iv)

    a.m.   p.m.   a.m.   p.m.

9. How many hours and minutes from

(i) 10.35 to 14.45   (ii) 12.48 to 16.20   (iii) 10.36 to 18.45

(iv) 8.15 to 10.52   (v) 02.10 to 17.40   (vi) 14.42 to 18.10 ?

10. The times shown on the clocks below give hours, minutes and seconds.
Match the times on the clocks to the digital times in the blue boxes:

A   B   C   D

(i)   (ii)   (iii)   (iv)

11. A woman works from 08.45 to 12.30 and from 13.45 to 17.15 for five days each week.
Calculate how many hours she works in the week.

12. A play started at 8.20 p.m. and lasted 2hr 35 min. At what time did it finish?

13. A train leaves Tralee at 10.52 and arrives in Dublin at 14.40.
How long does the journey take?

14. A turkey needs to be cooked and ready for dinner at 18.30.

The cooking time is 28 minutes per kg, plus an extra 20 minutes.

If the turkey weighs 8 kg, what is the latest time it should be put in the oven?

15. The following is an extract from the Dublin to Westport train timetable:

		Train 1	**Train 2**
Dublin Heuston	dep.	08.30	17.10
Athlone	arr.	10.08	18.43
Athlone	dep.	10.10	18.45
Claremorris	arr.	11.25	20.08
Claremorris	dep.	11.44	20.11
Westport	arr.	12.05	20.38

   (i)   How long does it take *Train 1* to go from Dublin to Westport?

  (ii)   For how long does *Train 1* stop in Claremorris?

 (iii)   After the short stop, how long does it take *Train 2* to go from Athlone to Westport?

 (iv)   Which is the faster train from Dublin to Athlone?

  (v)   How long does it take *Train 1* to go from Dublin to Claremorris?

 (vi)   For how long does *Train 2* stop in Athlone?

(vii)   If I arrive at Heuston Station in Dublin at 07.52, how long do I have to wait for *Train 1* to depart for Westport?

(viii)   Which is the faster train from Dublin to Westport?

16. Fill in the shaded spaces marked A, B, C, D, E and F below:

Train	Time of departure	Time of arrival	Time taken
1	08.43	10.54	A
2	B	12.17	2 h 40 min
3	15.30	C	1 h 54 min
4	23.17	05.18	D
5	06.23	E	4 h 12 min
6	F	12.15	2 h 54 min

17. A car journey began at 10.40 and finished at 13.25.

   (i)   How long did the journey take?

  (ii)   If the car uses 6 litres of petrol per hour and each litre costs €1.65, calculate the cost of the petrol for the journey, correct to the nearest euro.

Section 11.2 Speed – Distance – Time

If a car travels 100 km in 2 hours, then we say that the **average speed** of the car for the journey is 50 kilometres per hour (written as 50 **km/hr**).

Again, if a train does 300 km in 3 hours, its average speed is 100 km/hr.

In each of these examples, the average speed $= \dfrac{\text{distance travelled}}{\text{time taken}}$.

The examples above could also be used to show that

(i) Time $= \dfrac{\text{Distance}}{\text{Speed}}$ ⟍ (ii) Distance = Speed × Time

The triangle on the right below could help you to remember the formulae given.

Speed $= \dfrac{\text{Distance}}{\text{Time}}$

Time $= \dfrac{\text{Distance}}{\text{Speed}}$

Distance = Speed × Time

Use your thumb to cover the value you wish to find; for example to find speed, cover S.

speed $= \dfrac{\text{distance}}{\text{time}}$

Example 1

A train travels a journey of 210 km in $2\frac{1}{2}$ hours. Find its average speed.

Average speed $= \dfrac{\text{Distance}}{\text{Time}} = \dfrac{210}{2\frac{1}{2}} = \dfrac{210 \times 2}{2\frac{1}{2} \times 2} = \dfrac{420}{5} = 84$

∴ the average speed = 84 km/hr.

Example 2

A motorist travelled 500 kilometres in six hours.
Her average speed for the first two hours was 100 km/hr.
Find her average speed, in kilometres per hour, for the last four hours.

Distance travelled in the first 2 hours is 100 km × 2 = 200 km.   ... Distance = Speed × Time

Therefore she travelled 300 km in the last 4 hours.

Average speed $= \dfrac{\text{Distance}}{\text{Time}}$

$= \dfrac{300}{4}$ ... 500 km − 200 km = 300 km and 6 hr − 2 hr = 4 hr.

$= 75$

∴ average speed for the last 4 hours = 75 km/hr.

Exercise 11.2

1. How far will a vehicle travel
   - (i) in 3 hours at an average speed of 80 km/hr
   - (ii) in 4 hours at an average speed of 65 km/hr
   - (iii) in $2\frac{1}{4}$ hours at an average speed of 88 km/hr
   - (iv) in $\frac{3}{4}$ hour at an average speed of 96 km/hr ?

2. Find the time taken to travel
   - (i) 210 km at an average speed of 70 km/hr
   - (ii) 200 km at an average speed of 80 km/hr
   - (iii) 20 km at an average speed of 60 km/hr
   - (iv) 48 km at an average speed of 64 km/hr.

3. Find the average speed, in km/hr, of a car if it does
   - (i) 250 km in 5 hours
   - (ii) 120 km in 2 hours
   - (iii) 90 km in $1\frac{1}{2}$ hours
   - (iv) 175 km in $2\frac{1}{2}$ hours
   - (v) 25 km in $\frac{1}{2}$ hour
   - (vi) 90 km in 40 mins.

4. A racing car completes a 15 km lap of a track in 5 minutes. Express the average speed in km/hr.

5. How long would it take a cyclist to travel 45 km at an average speed of 18 km/hr?

6. A car is driven on a motorway for $2\frac{1}{4}$ hours at an average speed of 84 km/hr. How far does the car travel in that time?

7. The distance from Tralee to Dublin is 312 km. If a motorist completes the journey in 4 hr 20 min, find her average speed in km/hr.

8. A train leaves Dublin at 0925 and reaches Cork at 1210. If the journey is 286 km long, find the average speed of the train.

9. A speedboat travels at 60 km/hr for two hours and then at 90 km/hr for one hour. Find its average speed over the three hours.

10. A journey takes 3 hours at an average speed of 120 km/hr. How long, in hours, would the journey take if the average speed was reduced to 80 km/hr?

11. A trip of 276 km began at 1040 hrs and ended on the same day at 1430 hrs. Find the average speed in km/hr.

12. It takes 4 hours and 20 minutes to travel a journey at an average speed of 120 km/hr. How many hours and minutes will it take to travel the same journey if the average speed is reduced to 100 km/hr?

13. A motorist travelled 320 km in five hours.
Her average speed for the first 160 km was 80 km/hr.
What was her average speed for the second 160 km?

14. A distance of 18 km is travelled in 25 minutes.
Find the average speed in metres per second.

15. A professional cyclist started a journey of 56 km at 1015 hours and finished the journey at 1135 hours.
Calculate the average speed of the cyclist in km/hr.

16. A distance of 600 metres is travelled in 30 seconds.
Find the average speed in km/hr.

17. Express 72 km/hr in metres per second.

18. Express 400 metres per minute in km/hr.

19. Express 15 metres per second in kilometres per hour.

20. A car journey of 559 kilometres took 6 hours and 30 minutes.
   (i) Calculate the average speed, in km/hr, for the journey.
  (ii) If the average petrol consumption for the journey was 8.3 km per litre, calculate the number of litres used, correct to the nearest litre.
 (iii) Find the cost of the petrol used if each litre cost €1.70.

21. The table on the right shows the times taken by some very fast animals to travel the distances given.
Arrange the animals in order, starting with the fastest.

Animal	Time taken	Distance in metres
Cheetah	18 seconds	500 m
Racehorse	16 seconds	300 m
Antelope	$4\frac{1}{2}$ min	6 000 m
Deer	42 min	32 000 m

22. A jogger sets out at midday to run to the next village, a distance of 12 km.
She wants to arrive at this village at 1330 hours.
At what average speed should she jog?

Test yourself 11

1. (a) Express each of the times shown in the 24-hour clock time.

(i)

a.m.

(ii)

p.m.

(b) Find the time taken for a journey of 100 km at an average speed of 80 km/hr.

(c) A school's lessons begin at 9.00 a.m. and end at 3.40 p.m. with an hour's break at lunchtime and 20 minutes break mid-morning.
If there are 8 lessons of equal length, how long is a lesson?

2. (a) How many hours and minutes from

(i) 9.15 a.m. to 12.30 p.m.

(ii) 09.35 to 18.10?

(b) A coach left Dublin at 09.45 and reached Limerick at 12.15.

(i) How long did the journey take?

(ii) If the length of the journey is 220 km, find the average speed of the coach in km/hr.

(c) A girl jogs for 24 minutes at an average speed of 15 km/hr.
How far does she travel?

3. (a) A television film started at 10.15 p.m. and lasted for 2 hours and 35 minutes.
At what time did the film finish?

(b) A bus travels for two hours at an average speed of 90 km/hr and then for a further hour at a speed of 60 km/hr.
Find

(i) the total distance travelled

(ii) the total time taken

(iii) the average speed of the bus for the whole journey in km/hr.

(c) Find the distance covered by an aircraft travelling at 600 km/hr for 3 hours and 36 minutes.

4. (a) Write the following times in 24-hour clock time:

(i) 6.15 a.m.   (ii) 1.45 p.m.   (iii) 9.52 p.m.   (iv) 12.15 a.m.

(b) A motorist travels at an average speed of 60 km/hr for $2\frac{1}{4}$ hours.
If his car has an average fuel consumption of 1 litre of petrol per 15 km,
find how many litres of fuel are used.

(c) A *Luas* left Tallaght at 09.45 and reached Abbey Street at 10.25.

  (i) How long did the journey take?

  (ii) If the length of the journey is 13 km, find the average speed of the
  Luas in km/hr.

5. John travelled by car from Tralee to Galway.
He left Tralee at 09.45 and arrived in Galway at 12.57.

  (i) How long did it take John to travel from Tralee to Galway?
  Give your answer in hours and minutes.

  (ii) The distance from Tralee to Galway is 200 km.
  Calculate John's average speed in km/hr.

  (iii) John had estimated it cost 22 cents per km to drive his car.
  How much did it cost him to drive his car from Tralee to Galway?

6. (a) At the Olympic Games, a swimmer completed the 1500 m freestyle race in
  15 minutes. Express this speed in km/hr.

(b) The Grand Old Duke of York, he had ten thousand men, he marched them up
to the top of the hill . . .
By 2 p.m., they were one third of the way up.
By 4 p.m., they were three quarters of the way up.
When did they set out?

(c) A *TGV* travels 567 km from Bordeaux to Paris at an average speed of 252 km/hr.
Find the arrival time in Paris, if it leaves Bordeaux at 14.10.

(d) In a Grand Prix, the winning car passed the chequered
flag 0.3 seconds ahead of the next car.
Both cars were travelling at 84 m/s.
What was the distance between the two cars?

12 Simultaneous Equations

Key words

satisfy the equation   simultaneous equations   elimination method
solving simultaneous equations graphically

Section 12.1 Simultaneous equations

Consider the equation
$$3x + y = 9.$$
The values $x = 2$ and $y = 3$ satisfy this equation.
The values $x = 1$ and $y = 6$ also satisfy the equation.
In fact, there are many pairs of values for x and y which satisfy the equation.

Now we take a second equation
$$2x - y = 1.$$
The values $x = 2$ and $y = 3$ satisfy this equation also.
Thus, the values $x = 2$ and $y = 3$ satisfy both equations
$$3x + y = 9 \text{ and } 2x - y = 1.$$
Only **one** set of values for x and y will satisfy a pair of simultaneous equations.

> When two equations are both satisfied by the same values for x and y, they are said to be simultaneous equations.

Solving a pair of simultaneous equations involves finding the values of x and y that make both equations true.

Example 1

Investigate whether $x = 6$ and $y = 2$ are the correct solutions for these simultaneous equations:

$$x + y = 8 \quad \dots ①$$
$$x + 2y = 10 \quad \dots ②$$

We substitute 6 for x and 2 for y in each equation:
Equation ①: $6 + 2 = 8$ i.e. $8 = 8$; ... correct
Equation ②: $6 + 2(2) = 10$ i.e. $10 = 10$; ... correct
Since $x = 6$ and $y = 2$ satisfy both equations, they are the correct solutions.

Exercise 12.1

For each of the following pairs of simultaneous equations, solutions are given.
Check if each solution is correct.

1. $x + y = 8$
$x - y = 4$
Solution: $x = 6, y = 2$

2. $2x + y = 11$
$x - 2y = 3$
Solution: $x = 5, y = 1$

3. $3x + 2y = 11$
$2x - 3y = 3$
Solution: $x = 3, y = 1$

4. $4x - y = 5$
$2x + 3y = 8$
Solution: $x = 2, y = 3$

5. $3x - y = 4$
$2x + y = 8$
Solution: $x = 2, y = 4$

6. $3x + y = 14$
$2x - y = 6$
Solution: $x = 4, y = 2$

7. $x + 2y = 4$
$x - y = 5$
Solution: $x = 2, y = 1$

8. $2x + 3y = 3$
$x - 4y = 7$
Solution: $x = 3, y = -1$

9. $2x - y = -8$
$x + 2y = 10$
Solution: $x = -2, y = 4$

Section 12.2 Solving simultaneous equations

There are many ways of solving simultaneous equations.
One method is called the **elimination method**.
In this method, we 'eliminate' one of the variables.
This method is discussed in the box below.

> **Discussion**
>
> $5x + 3y = 23$
> $2x - 3y = 5$ are simultaneous equations.
>
> We can illustrate them using scales.
>
> If we add the left-hand sides and then add the right-hand sides, would the scales still balance? **Discuss.**
>
> What is the left-hand side total?
> What is the right-hand side total?
> How can you use this to find x? **Discuss.**
> What is the value of x?
> How can you use this to find y? **Discuss.**

From the 'discussion' above, it can be seen that it is easy to solve simultaneous equations when one of the variables can be eliminated by adding or subtracting the two equations.

If a variable cannot be eliminated by simply adding or subtracting, then we have to multiply one or more of the equations by a number to make the elimination possible.

Example 1

Solve the simultaneous equations $\begin{aligned} x + 2y &= 10 \\ 2x - y &= 5 \end{aligned}$

(To solve these equations, we must make the number of x's or the number of y's equal. We then add or subtract as necessary.

For convenience, we will call the first equation ① and the second equation ②.)

Equation ①: $\qquad x + 2y = 10$

Equation ② $\times$ 2: $\quad 4x - 2y = 10$

Adding: $\qquad\qquad 5x \quad\ \ = 20$

$\qquad\qquad\qquad \therefore \quad x = 4$

Substituting $x = 4$ in ① we get: $\quad 4 + 2y = 10$

$\qquad\qquad\qquad\qquad\qquad\qquad 2y = 6$

$\qquad\qquad\qquad\qquad\quad \therefore \quad y = 3$

The solution is $x = 4$ and $y = 3$.

(Note: It is important to check that $x = 4$ and $y = 3$ satisfy both equations.)

Example 2

Solve these simultaneous equations $\qquad \begin{aligned} 2x - 5y &= 9 \\ 3x + 2y &= 4 \end{aligned}$

We number the equations $\quad 2x - 5y = 9 \qquad$ ①

① and ② for convenience. $\quad 3x + 2y = 4 \qquad$ ②

We now multiply equation ① by 3 and equation ② by 2 to equate the number of x's.

① $\times$ 3: $\quad 6x - 15y = 27$

② $\times$ 2: $\quad\ \ 6x + 4y = 8$

Subtract: $\qquad -19y = 19$

$\qquad\qquad\ \ 19y = -19$ ... multiply both sides by -1

$\qquad\qquad\quad\ \ y = -1$

We now substitute -1 for y in equation ①

$\qquad\qquad\qquad 2x - 5y = 9$

$\quad y = -1 \ \Rightarrow \ 2x + 5 = 9$

$\qquad\qquad \Rightarrow \ 2x = 4 \ \Rightarrow \ x = 2$

$\therefore \quad x = 2$ and $y = -1$ are the solutions.

Exercise 12.2

Solve the following simultaneous equations:

1. $x + y = 9$
$x - y = 3$

2. $2x + y = 8$
$3x - y = 2$

3. $2x - y = 4$
$x + y = 5$

4. $3x + y = 7$
$x + y = 5$

5. $4x + y = 17$
$2x + y = 11$

6. $x + 2y = 4$
$x - y = 1$

7. $x + 2y = 7$
$2x + y = 8$

8. $2x - 3y = 1$
$2x + 5y = 9$

9. $2x + 3y = 3$
$x - 4y = 7$

10. $2x - y = -8$
$x + 2y = 6$

11. $4x - y = 10$
$x - y = 1$

12. $4x - y = -9$
$2x - 3y = -7$

13. $3x - y = 3$
$x + 3y = 11$

14. $2x + y = -2$
$x + 3y = 9$

15. $2x - 3y = 14$
$2x - y = 10$

16. $3x + 4y = 5$
$2x - 3y = 9$

17. $3x + y = 5$
$5x - 4y = -3$

18. $2x - y = 12$
$3x + 2y = 11$

19. $3x + 4y = 10$
$4x + y = 9$

20. $3x - 2y = 13$
$4x + 3y = 6$

21. $3x + 5y = 6$
$2x + 3y = 5$

22. $4x + 3y = 19$
$3x - 2y = -7$

23. $2x - 5y = 1$
$5x + 3y = 18$

24. $3x = 5y + 13$
$2x + 5y = -8$

25. $x + 2y = 13$
$3x = 5y + 6$

26. $7x + 2 = 2y$
$3x = 14 - y$

27. $2x - 5y = 3$
$x = 3y + 1$

28. $3x = 22 + 2y$
$5y = 2x$

29. $2x - 3y = 8$
$3x + 4y = -22$

30. $2x - 5y = 22$
$3x + 7y = 4$

Section 12.3 Problems leading to simultaneous equations

In a later chapter, you will discover that equations such as $y = 2x + 4$ and $x + y = 5$ represent straight lines.

Discussion

The diagram on the right shows two lines intersecting at the point P.

Write down the coordinates of the point P.

Solve the simultaneous equations
$x + y = 1$
$2x - y = -4$ using the adding or subtracting equations method.

Compare the values of x and y you found with the coordinates of the point P.

What do you notice? **Discuss.**

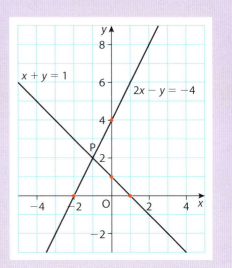

From the 'discussion' above, you should have discovered that two simultaneous equations may be solved by drawing graphs of the two equations (lines) and then reading the x-value and y-value of their point of intersection.

Using simultaneous equations to solve problems

Simultaneous equations are particularly useful for solving problems which have two unknowns. Generally, two different pieces of information enable us to write down two equations.

The following examples illustrate this procedure.

Example 1

The sum of two numbers is 19.
When twice the second number is taken from three times the first number, the result is 22.
Find the two numbers.

Let x and y be the numbers.

Equation ①: $x + y = 19$
Equation ②: $3x - 2y = 22$

Equation ① × 2: $2x + 2y = 38$
Equation ②: $3x - 2y = 22$
Adding $5x \quad\;\; = 60$
                    $x \quad\;\; = 12$

Substituting 12 for x in equation ①, we get: $12 + y = 19$
                                                  $y = 19 - 12$
                                                  $y = 7$

The two numbers are 12 and 7.

Example 2

Tickets to a movie cost either €8 or €10.
If 300 tickets were sold and the total amount of money collected was €2640, how many of each type of ticket were sold?

Let x = number of €8 tickets sold, and
      y = number of €10 tickets sold.

①   Number: $x + y = 300$
②   Money: $8x + 10y = 2640$

① × 8: $8x + 8y = 2400$
②: $8x + 10y = 2640$
Subtracting $-2y = -240$
              $\Rightarrow \quad 2y = 240$
              $\Rightarrow \quad y = 120$

Substituting 120 for y in equation ①, we get:

                    $x + y = 300$
      $y = 120$: $x + 120 = 300$
                        $x = 180$
      $\therefore \;\; x = 180$ and $y = 120$

$\therefore$ 180 €8 tickets and 120 €10 tickets were sold.

Exercise 12.3

1. The sum of two numbers is 41 and their difference is 5. Find the numbers.

2. The sum of two numbers is 12. Twice one of the numbers added to three times the other is 31. Find the two numbers.

3. The sum of two numbers x and y is 50. When twice y is taken from four times x, the result is 8. Find the value of x and the value of y.

4. Find two numbers such that the first added to three times the second is 31, while three times the first less twice the second is 16.

5. The sum of two numbers is 9. If twice the first number is added to three times the second, the answer is 15. Find the two numbers.

6. The difference of two numbers is 7. When three times the smaller number is taken from twice the larger, the result is 11. Find the two numbers.

7. The sum of two numbers is 8. When four times the second number is taken from three times the first number, the result is 3. Find the two numbers.

8. Examine the rectangle shown and write down two equations in x and y.

   Now solve these equations to find the value of x and the value of y.

9. Three nuts and six bolts have a combined weight of 72 g. Four nuts and five bolts have a combined weight of 66 g. Find the combined weight of one nut and one bolt.

10. All weights in these balance pictures are in grams.
    (i) Find the weight of a cherry.
    (ii) What is the weight of a pear?

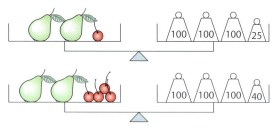

11. Three chocolate bars and four chocolate eggs weigh 465 grams. Three chocolate bars and two chocolate eggs weigh 315 grams.

    (i) Which of these pairs of equations is correct for the chocolate bars and eggs?

   A $3b + 2e = 465$ $3b + 4e = 315$
   B $b + 4e = 465$ $b + 2e = 315$
   C $3b + 4e = 465$ $3b + 2e = 315$

    (ii) Solve the pair of simultaneous equations that is correct to find the values of b and e.

12. A farmer has horses and turkeys. In total, there are 32 heads and 98 legs.

    (i) If there are x horses and y turkeys, explain why:

        (a) $x + y = 32$ (b) $4x + 2y = 98$

    (ii) How many horses and how many turkeys does the farmer have?

13. The given diagram shows the graphs of the lines $x - y = 1$ and $x + 2y = 4$.

    (i) Write down the coordinates of the point of intersection of the two lines.

    (ii) Solve the simultaneous equations $x - y = 1$ and $x + 2y = 4$.

    (iii) Explain the connection between your answers in (ii) to the answer you found in (i) above.

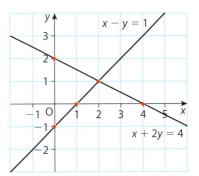

14. A sketch of the lines $2x + y = 6$ and $x + y = 5$ is shown.
Use the sketch to write down the point of intersection of the two lines.
Now use simultaneous equations to verify your answer.

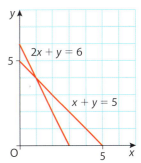

15. The length of a blue rod is x cm.

The length of a yellow rod is y cm.

    (i) The total length of 2 blue rods and 3 yellow rods is 33 cm.

        Write an equation for this diagram.

    (ii) The total length of 4 blue rods and 2 yellow rods is 46 cm.

        Write an equation for this diagram.

    (iii) Solve your equations simultaneously to find the values of x and y.

    (iv) What is the total length of 1 blue rod and 6 yellow rods?

Test yourself 12

1. (a) Solve these simultaneous equations: $3x + y = 13$
$2x - y = 2$

(b) Aisling and Zoe buy some flowers.
Aisling buys a rose and a lily.
These cost her €10.70.
Zoe buys a rose and 3 lilies.
These cost her €14.50.
What is the cost of a lily?

2. (a) Solve the equations: $3x + 2y = 17$
$x - y = 4$

(b) The diagram shows a rectangle, not drawn to scale.
All sides are measured in centimetres.
   (i) Write down a pair of simultaneous equations
   in a and b.
   (ii) Solve your pair of simultaneous equations
   to find a and b.

3. (a) Solve these simultaneous equations: $2x - y = 5$
$x - 2y = 4$

(b) The weight of a blue brick is b grams.
The weight of a red brick is r grams.

4 blue bricks and 3 red bricks weigh 58 grams.
5 blue bricks and 6 red bricks weigh 86 grams.

   (i) Write two equations to represent these diagrams.
   (ii) Solve the equations to find the weight of a blue
   brick and the weight of a red brick.
   (iii) Find the total weight of 3 blue bricks and 6 red
   bricks.

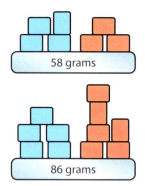

4. (a) Solve the simultaneous equations:
$5x = 4y + 10$
$2x - 3y = -3$

(b) The shape ABCD is a parallelogram.
Write two equations in x and y and
solve them to find their values.

Quadratic Equations

chapter **13**

Key words

solutions	roots	satisfy the equation	parabola
difference of two squares		mathematical sentence	forming equations

Section 13.1 Solving quadratic equations using factors

Equations such as $x^2 - 4x + 3 = 0$ or $2x^2 - x - 3 = 0$ contain a term in x^2. These are called **quadratic equations**.

Take the equation $x^2 - 5x + 6 = 0$.

When $x = 2$, then $x^2 - 5x + 6$ becomes
$$(2)^2 - 5(2) + 6, \text{ i.e. } 4 - 10 + 6 = 0$$
When $x = 3$, then $x^2 - 5x + 6$ becomes
$$(3)^2 - 5(3) + 6, \text{ i.e. } 9 - 15 + 6 = 0$$

When $x = 2$ or $x = 3$, both sides of the equation are zero. When this happens, we say that $x = 2$ and $x = 3$ are **solutions** or **roots** of the equation.

> The **roots** of an equation are the values of x which satisfy the equation.

Multiplication by zero

Any number multiplied by zero is zero.
For example, $4 \times 0 = 0$ or $0 \times 6 = 0$.
This illustrates a very important property of real numbers which is given on the right.

> If the product of two numbers is zero, then at least one of them must be zero.
> e.g. if $ab = 0$, then $a = 0$ or $b = 0$.

Thus, if $(x - 3)(x + 5) = 0$, then
$$x - 3 = 0 \text{ or } x + 5 = 0$$
$$\text{i.e. } x = 3 \text{ or } \qquad x = -5.$$

Steps for solving quadratic equations

> If necessary, rearrange the equation with one side being **zero**.
> Factorise fully the other side.
> Let each factor equal zero.
> Solve the resulting simple equations.

Example 1

Solve the equation $x^2 - 2x - 8 = 0$.

$x^2 - 2x - 8 = 0$
$(x + 2)(x - 4) = 0$ … factorise the left-hand side
$x + 2 = 0$ or $x - 4 = 0$
$\therefore$ $x = -2$ or $x = 4$

Example 2

Solve the equation $x^2 - 5x = 0$.

In this equation, there is no number term.
$x^2 - 5x = 0$
$x(x - 5) = 0$ … factorise
$x = 0$ or $x - 5 = 0$
$\therefore$ $x = 0$ or $x = 5$

Example 3

Solve the equation $x^2 - 25 = 0$.

(Here we use the *difference of two squares* to factorise $x^2 - 25$.)
$x^2 - 25 = 0$
$x^2 - (5)^2 = 0$
$(x + 5)(x - 5) = 0$
$x + 5 = 0$ or $x - 5 = 0$
$\therefore$ $x = -5$ or $x = 5$

Exercise 13.1

Solve the following quadratic equations:

1. $(x - 2)(x - 3) = 0$　　**2.** $(x - 2)(x - 5) = 0$　　**3.** $(x - 2)(x + 3) = 0$

4. $(x - 4)(x + 5) = 0$　　**5.** $(x + 2)(x + 6) = 0$　　**6.** $x(x - 4) = 0$

7. $x(x + 5) = 0$　　**8.** $(x - 3)(x + 3) = 0$　　**9.** $(x + 7)(x - 7) = 0$

10. $x^2 + 3x + 2 = 0$　　**11.** $x^2 + 5x + 6 = 0$　　**12.** $x^2 + 6x + 8 = 0$

13. $x^2 + 7x + 10 = 0$

14. $x^2 + 7x + 12 = 0$

15. $x^2 + 12x + 27 = 0$

16. $x^2 + 11x + 28 = 0$

17. $x^2 + 12x + 35 = 0$

18. $x^2 + 14x + 48 = 0$

19. $x^2 - 5x + 6 = 0$

20. $x^2 - 8x + 15 = 0$

21. $x^2 - 10x + 16 = 0$

22. $x^2 - 9x + 14 = 0$

23. $x^2 - 10x + 21 = 0$

24. $x^2 - 10x + 24 = 0$

25. $x^2 - 12x + 27 = 0$

26. $x^2 - 12x + 32 = 0$

27. $x^2 - 16x + 48 = 0$

28. $x^2 - x - 12 = 0$

29. $x^2 - 3x - 10 = 0$

30. $x^2 + 3x - 28 = 0$

31. $x^2 - 5x - 24 = 0$

32. $x^2 + 5x - 36 = 0$

33. $x^2 - x - 72 = 0$

34. $x^2 - 3x - 54 = 0$

35. $x^2 + 15x + 44 = 0$

36. $x^2 - 7x - 60 = 0$

37. $x^2 - 16 = 0$

38. $x^2 - 25 = 0$

39. $x^2 - 64 = 0$

40. $x^2 - 1 = 0$

41. $x^2 - 121 = 0$

42. $x^2 - 81 = 0$

43. $x^2 - 3x = 0$

44. $x^2 + 4x = 0$

45. $x^2 - 8x = 0$

46. $x^2 + 9x = 0$

47. $x^2 - 14x = 0$

48. $x^2 + 7x = 0$

49. $x^2 + 7x - 30 = 0$

50. $x^2 - 10x - 24 = 0$

51. $x^2 + 4x - 12 = 0$

52. $x^2 - 6x - 16 = 0$

53. $x^2 - 11x + 28 = 0$

54. $x^2 = 100$

55. $x^2 - 11x = 0$

56. $x^2 - 10x + 9 = 0$

57. $x^2 - 9x - 52 = 0$

Section 13.2 Problems leading to quadratic equations

When a problem expressed in words is changed into a mathematical sentence, it often results in a quadratic equation.

To find the equation to represent a problem,

> where relevant, draw a diagram and put all the information you are given on it
> use x to represent the unknown you are asked to find
> look for the information in the question to form an equation in x
> solve the equation to find the value or values for x; you may sometimes have to reject a negative answer.

Example 1

The sum of a number and its square is 30.
Find two numbers which satisfy this condition.

Let x be the number.

Equation:
$x + x^2 = 30$ … the square of x is x^2
$x^2 + x = 30$ … rearrange
$x^2 + x - 30 = 0$ … subtract 30 from both sides
$(x + 6)(x - 5) = 0$
$x + 6 = 0$ or $x - 5 = 0$
$\therefore \ x = -6$ or $x = 5$

The two numbers are -6 and 5.

Example 2

The length of a rectangle exceeds its breadth by 6 cm.
If the area of the rectanlge is 160 cm², find its length and breadth.

Let the breadth of the rectangle be x cm.

$\therefore$ The length is $(x + 6)$ cm.

Area $= 160$ cm²

$(x + 6)$ cm

x cm

$\therefore \ x(x + 6) = 160$ … $A = \ell \times b$
$x^2 + 6x = 160$
$x^2 + 6x - 160 = 0$
$(x - 10)(x + 16) = 0$
$x - 10 = 0$ or $x + 16 = 0$
$x = 10$ or $x = -16$

Naturally in this case, we reject the negative number -16, as a rectangle cannot have a negative breadth,
$\therefore \ x = 10$
$\therefore$ the length, $(x + 6)$ cm $= 16$ cm and the breadth, x cm $= 10$ cm

Discussion

The curve on the right is called a parabola.

It is the graph of $y = x^2 + x - 2$.

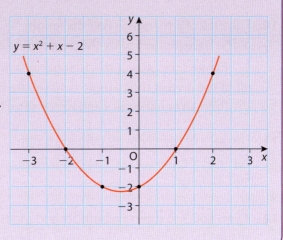

› Factorise $x^2 + x - 2$ and then solve the equation $x^2 + x - 2 = 0$.

› Can you use the graph to solve the equation $x^2 + x - 2 = 0$?

› What is the link between the two sets of answers?

› Now explain the meaning of the roots of a quadratic equation.

Exercise 13.2

1. The sum of a positive number x and its square is 42. Find the number.

2. I think of a positive number x. When I subtract four times the number from its square, the result is 21. Find the number.

3. One positive number is 4 bigger than another number.
If the product of the two numbers is 45, find these numbers.

4. Think of a positive number x. When twice the number is added to its square, the result is 48. Find the number.

5. One positive number is 3 bigger than another number.
When the larger number is added to the square of the smaller one, the result is 33.
Find the two numbers.

6. When four times a positive number is taken from its square, the result is 60.
What is this number?

7. When a number, x, is added to its square, the answer is 72.
Write an equation in x and solve it to find two numbers.
Verify that both numbers satisfy the equation.

8. The area of the given rectangle is 77 cm^2.
Form an equation in x and solve it to find the value for x.
Hence find the length and breadth of the rectangle.

$(x + 4)$ cm

x cm

9. A rectangle has length 3 cm greater than its width.
If it has an area of 28 cm², find the dimensions of the rectangle.

10. The area of a triangle is half the length
of the base multiplied by the perpendicular height.

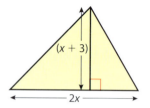

(i) Express the area of this triangle in terms of x.
(ii) If the area of the triangle is 40 square units,
form an equation in x and hence solve it to find its value.

11. The area of the given rectangle is 63 cm².
Form an equation in x and solve it to
find its value.

12. If you add 3 to a certain number and multiply the result by 4, you will get the same
answer by adding 7 to the square of the number.
Find two numbers that satisfy these conditions.

13. A square room of side x metres is
partly covered by a rectangular carpet,
as shown. If the area of the room not
covered by the carpet is 16 m², write
an equation in x and solve it to find
the value of x.

14. Alan is x years old. His mother's age is the square of his age.
If Alan's father is five years older than his mother, and the sum of all three ages is
60 years, how old is Alan?

15. Write down the roots of the equation
$x^2 + 2x - 3 = 0$ by referring to
the graph shown.

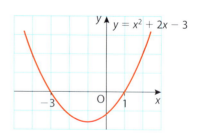

16. Which of the two graphs on the
right gives the solutions to the
equation $x^2 + 5x - 6 = 0$?
Explain your answer.

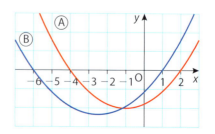

Test yourself 13

1. (a) Solve these equations:
   (i) $(x + 3)(x - 4) = 0$ (ii) $x^2 - 12x + 35 = 0$

   (b) The area of this rectangle is 7 cm².

      (i) Form an equation, in terms of x, and show that it can be written as $x^2 + 2x - 15 = 0$

     (ii) Solve this equation to find the dimensions of the rectangle.

2. (a) Solve these equations:
   (i) $x^2 + 5x = 0$ (ii) $x^2 - 9x + 8 = 0$

   (b) When twice a certain number is added to the square of the number, the result is 120. Write an equation in x and solve it to find two such numbers. Verify your answer in each case.

3. (a) Solve each of these equations:
   (i) $x^2 + 3x - 40 = 0$ (ii) $x^2 - 144 = 0$

   (b) Each of the following equations has either $x = 2$ or $x = 3$ as a solution. Which of them has both $x = 2$ and $x = 3$ as solutions?

   Ⓐ $3x + 5 = 4x + 2$ Ⓑ $2(2x - 4) = 3(2x - 4)$ Ⓒ $x^2 - 5x + 6 = 0$

   Ⓓ $(x + 1)^2 = (5 - x)^2$ Ⓔ $\dfrac{1}{x} + \dfrac{1}{2x} = \dfrac{1}{2}$

4. (a) Solve these equations:
   (i) $(x + 8) = (x - 3) = 0$ (ii) $x^2 - 5x - 14 = 0$

   (b) When five times a certain positive number is taken from its square, the result is 36. Write an equation in x and solve it to find the number.

   (c) Which one of the graphs below shows the solution of the equation $(x - 4)(x - 7) = 0$?

          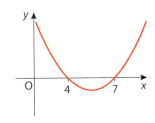

Coordinate Geometry – The Line

Key words

grid   origin   coordinates   *x*-axis   *y*-axis   quadrants   horizontal
vertical   parallel   perpendicular   slope   positive   negative
linear equation   slope-intercept   intersection   simultaneous equations

Section 14.1 The coordinated plane

In the seventeenth century, the French mathematician René Descartes developed a grid of numbers to describe the location of any point in the plane.

In the diagram on the right we have a horizontal line and a vertical line meeting at the point O. It is called the **coordinated plane** or the **Cartesian Plane** in honour of Descartes.

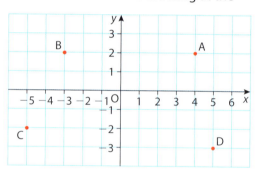

The horizontal line is called the ***x*-axis**.
The vertical line is called the ***y*-axis**.
The point where the two lines meet is called the **origin**.
The **coordinates** of A are (4, 2).
The coordinates of B are $(-3, 2)$.
The coordinates of C are $(-5, -2)$.
The coordinates of D are $(5, -3)$.

The diagram on the right shows that the *x*-axis and *y*-axis divide the plane into four quarters.

Each of these is called a **quadrant**.

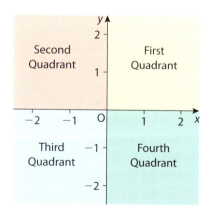

The diagram on the right shows some points plotted on the x-axis and on the y-axis.

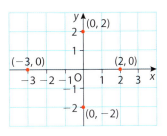

Exercise 14.1

1. Write down the coordinates of each of the points marked in the coordinated plane on the right:

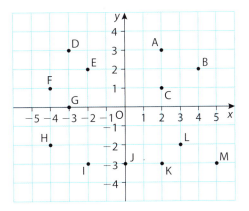

2. Draw a grid similar to that shown above and mark in the following points:

   (i) A(3, 4)   (ii) B(−1, 3)   (iii) C(4, −3)   (iv) D(−4, −3)   (v) E(1, −3)

3. The four quadrants are shown on the right. In which quadrant does each of the following points lie?

   (i) (3, 5)

   (ii) (−2, −3)

   (iii) (1, −4)

   (iv) (−3, 1)

   (v) (3, −3)

   (vi) (−1, −3).

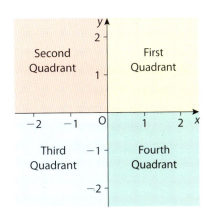

4. On which axis does each of these points lie?

   (i) A(4, 0)   (ii) B(0, 2)   (iii) C(0, −3)   (iv) D(−4, 0)   (v) E(−1, 0)

5. Write down the coordinates of the points A, B and D on the given grid.

If ABCD is a rectangle, write down the coordinates of the point C.

6. Draw an x-axis and y-axis from 0 to 5.
   (i) Plot the points (2, 1), (5, 1) and (5, 4). These are three corners of a square.
   (ii) What are the coordinates of the fourth corner of the square?

7. Draw an x-axis and y-axis from −2 to 4.
   (i) Plot the points $A(3, 2)$, $B(3, -1)$ and $C(-1, -1)$.
   (ii) Points A, B and C are three corners of a rectangle.
       Point D is the fourth corner of the rectangle. Plot point D on your diagram.
   (iii) What are the coordinates of point D?

8. (i) Plot these points on a number plane:
       $(1, -1)$, $(1, 3)$, $(3, 3)$, $(3, -1)$.
   (ii) By joining the points in order and then back to the first point again, what type of figure is formed?
   (iii) What are the lengths of the sides of this figure?
   (iv) What is its perimeter?
   (v) What is its area?

9. This triangle has been formed by joining the points shown.
   (i) What is the height h of this triangle?
   (ii) What is the length of the base b?
   (iii) Work out the area of this triangle?

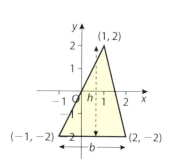

Section 14.2 **Midpoint of a line segment**

The given diagram shows the points A(2, 1) and B(6, 5).
If we join A to B we get the line segment [AB].
M is the midpoint of [AB].

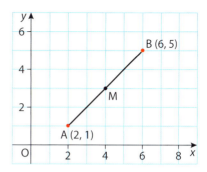

From the grid we can see that the coordinates of
M are (4, 3).

Notice that the *x*-coordinate, 4, is halfway between
the *x*-coordinates of A and B, i.e. 2 and 6.
Similarly, the *y*-coordinate of M, 3, is halfway between
1 and 5.

Thus $M = \left(\dfrac{2+6}{2}, \dfrac{1+5}{2}\right) = (4, 3)$.

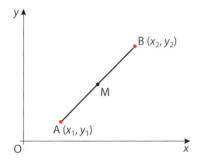

> The midpoint, M, of the line segment
> joining $A(x_1, y_1)$ and $B(x_2, y_2)$ is
>
> $$M = \left(\frac{x_1 + x_2}{2}, \frac{y_1 + y_2}{2}\right).$$

Example 1

Find the midpoint of the line segment joining A(−3, 4) and B(1, 2).

$$\text{Midpoint} = \left(\frac{x_1 + x_2}{2}, \frac{y_1 + y_2}{2}\right)$$

$$= \left(\frac{-3 + 1}{2}, \frac{4 + 2}{2}\right)$$

$$= \left(\frac{-2}{2}, \frac{6}{2}\right) = (-1, 3)$$

In words
To find the midpoint of a line
segment, we add the two
x-values and divide by 2, and add
the two *y*-values and divide by 2.

Exercise 14.2

1. A(2, 6), B(4, 2) and C(8, 4) are three points, as shown.
Find the midpoints of each of these line segments:
  (i)   [AC]
  (ii) [CB]
  (iii) [AB].

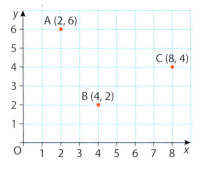

Find the coordinates of the midpoints of the line segments joining the following pairs of points:

2. (2, 1) and (4, 3)

3. (1, 1) and (5, 5)

4. (1, 3) and (3, 5)

5. (4, 3) and (6, 1)

6. (0, 4) and (6, 2)

7. (5, −2) and (1, 4)

8. (6, 2) and (−2, 0)

9. (−3, 4) and (1, −2)

10. (0, 7) and (4, 3)

11. (1, −3) and (3, 5)

12. (−3, 0) and (1, 6)

13. (4, −3) and (2, −3)

14. A(1, 1), B(5, 1), C(5, 4) and D(1, 4) are four points in the plane.
  (i) Find the coordinates of M, the midpoint of [AC].
  (ii) Show that M is also the midpoint of [BD].

15. Find the midpoint of the line segment joining A(−3, 6) and B(5, −6).
On which axis does the midpoint lie?

16. In the given diagram, M(4, 3) is the midpoint of the line segment joining A(1, 1) and B.
By trial and error, find the coordinates of the point B.

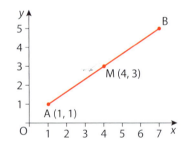

17. Show that the midpoint of the line segment joining A(4, −3) and B(−4, 7) lies on the y-axis.

18. Find the coordinates of the centre, O, of the given circle.

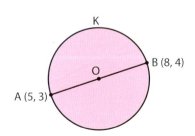

19. The given figure shows a parallelogram ABCD.
  (i) Find the coordinates of the midpoint of [AC].
  (ii) Verify that the midpoint of [AC] is also the midpoint of [BD].

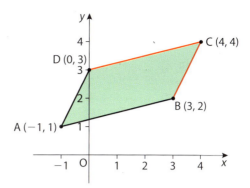

Section 14.3 Distance between two points

The given diagram shows the points $A(x_1, y_1)$ and $B(x_2, y_2)$.

$|BC| = y_2 - y_1$ and $|AC| = x_2 - x_1$

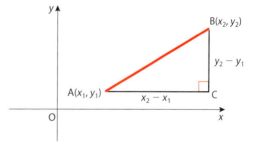

Using the Theorem of Pythagoras:

$$|AB|^2 = |AC|^2 + |BC|^2$$
$$= (x_2 - x_1)^2 + (y_2 - y_1)^2$$
$$\therefore \quad |AB| = \sqrt{(x_2 - x_1)^2 + (y_2 - y_1)^2}$$

> The distance between $A(x_1, y_1)$ and $B(x_2, y_2)$ is
> $$|AB| = \sqrt{(x_2 - x_1)^2 + (y_2 - y_1)^2}$$

Example 1

Find the distance between the points A(3, 2) and B(7, 5).

$$|AB| = \sqrt{(x_2 - x_1)^2 + (y_2 - y_1)^2}$$
$$= \sqrt{(7 - 3)^2 + (5 - 2)^2}$$
$$= \sqrt{(4)^2 + (3)^2}$$
$$= \sqrt{16 + 9}$$
$$= \sqrt{25}$$
$$= 5$$

Let   (3, 2)   and   (7, 5)
        ↓   ↓
      (x_1, y_1) (x_2, y_2)

> The distance between the points A and B is written as $|AB|$.

Exercise 14.3

Find the distances between the following pairs of points:

1. (2, 1) and (5, 4)   **2.** (1, 2) and (6, 4)   **3.** (3, 1) and (4, 5)

4. (3, 5) and (4, 7)   **5.** (2, −1) and (3, 5)   **6.** (4, 3) and (−2, 5)

7. (3, 0) and (7, 2)   **8.** (−1, 4) and (2, 1)   **9.** (3, −2) and (−2, 4)

10. (−6, 1) and (1, −4)   **11.** (0, −3) and (4, −5)   **12.** (−1, 5) and (2, 3)

13. A(1, 1), B(5, 1) and C(3, 6) are the vertices of a triangle.
Show that |AC| = |BC|.

14. Show that (2, 1) is the same distance from (5, 3) as it is from (−1, −1).

15. Use the given diagram to write down
the coordinates of A, B, C and D.
   (i) Write down the length of [DA].
   (ii) Show that |CD| = |BA|.
   (iii) Investigate if the midpoint of [AC]
       is the same as the midpoint of [DB].

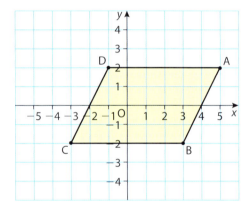

16. The points A(1, 2), B(2, 3) and C(3, 1) are the vertices of a triangle.
Find |AB|, |BC| and |AC|.
Which two sides have the same length?
Describe the triangle ABC.

17. The given figure shows the line
segment joining C(3, 1) and D(10, 4).
The Theorem of Pythagoras states
that $d^2 = \ell^2 + h^2$.
Use this theorem to find |CD|,
leaving your answer in $\sqrt{\ }$ form.
Now use the formula $\sqrt{(x_2 - x_1)^2 + (y_2 - y_1)^2}$
to find |CD|.
You should find both answers to be the same.

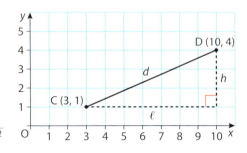

18. A sheet of wood 3.7 m by 3.7 m is needed in *Room R*.

The door of the room is 3 m high and 2 m wide.

John says that the sheet could fit in the door if it is held diagonally. Use the grid and given diagram to investigate if the sheet can be brought through the door.

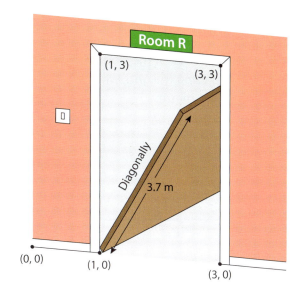

Section 14.4 **The slope of a line**

Ramp Ⓐ has a height of 3 m.
Ramp Ⓑ has a height of 4 m.

They both have a horizontal length of 9 m.

We measure slope using the value of the ratio

$$\frac{\text{height}}{\text{horizontal length}} = \frac{\text{rise}}{\text{run}}$$

We use the letter m to denote slope.

Slope of ramp Ⓐ $= \frac{3}{9} = \frac{1}{3}$

Slope of ramp Ⓑ $= \frac{4}{9}$

This shows that Ⓑ has a greater (i.e. steeper) slope than Ⓐ.

In general, the slope m of the line joining the points (x_1, y_1) and (x_2, y_2) is given by

$$m = \frac{y_2 - y_1}{x_2 - x_1}$$

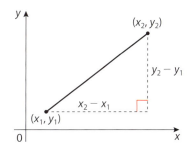

Example 1

Find the size of the slope of the given ramp using the grid, where each unit is 1 metre.

For this ramp: $h = 3$ ... Rise of 3

$\ell = 8$ ... Run of 8

Slope $= \dfrac{h}{\ell} = \dfrac{3}{8}$

1 unit = 1 m

Example 2

Find the slope of the line through the points A(1, 2) and B(3, 4).

Slope of AB $= \dfrac{y_2 - y_1}{x_2 - x_1} = \dfrac{4 - 2}{3 - 1}$

$ = \dfrac{2}{2} = 1$

$\therefore$ Slope of AB $= 1$

$(1, 2)$ $(3, 4)$

$\downarrow$ $\downarrow$

(x_1, y_1) (x_2, y_2)

Negative slopes

As we observe a line from **left to right**, it either rises or falls.

Rising   Falling

Rising lines have **positive** slopes.

Falling lines have **negative** slopes.

+

−

Positive slope   Negative slope

> ### Example 3
>
> Find the slopes of the line segments [AB] and [BC].
>
> Slope of AB $= \dfrac{y_2 - y_1}{x_2 - x_1}$ (2, 2)   (4, 5)
>
> $= \dfrac{5 - 2}{4 - 2} = \dfrac{3}{2}$ (x_1, y_1) (x_2, y_2)
>
> Slope of BC $= \dfrac{y_2 - y_1}{x_2 - x_1} = \dfrac{2 - 5}{8 - 4}$ (4, 5)   (8, 2)
>
> $= \dfrac{-3}{4} = -\dfrac{3}{4}$ (x_1, y_1) (x_2, y_2)
>
>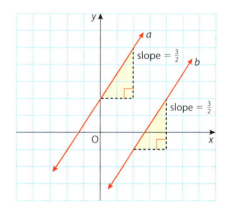
>
> (Notice that the slope of BC is negative as the line falls from left to right.)

Parallel lines

The lines a and b in the given diagram both have the slope $\frac{3}{2}$.

These lines are **parallel**.

> Parallel lines have equal slopes.

The slope of a **horizontal line** is zero. It neither rises or falls.

Exercise 14.4

1. State whether the slope of each of these lines is positive or negative:

(a)   (b)   (c)   (d)   (e)   (f)

2. The diagram shows four lines *a*, *b*, *c* and *d*.

   (i) Which lines have positive slopes?

  (ii) Which lines have negative slopes?

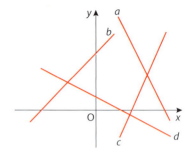

3. Use the grid and the value of $\dfrac{\text{rise}}{\text{run}}$ to find the slope of the red line in each of these diagrams:

(i)   (ii)   (iii)

4. Work out the slope of each of the lines below:

(i)   (ii)   (iii)

5. Why is the slope of the given line negative?
Use the grid to work out the slope of the line.

6. Find the slopes of the following lines:

(i)

(ii)

(iii)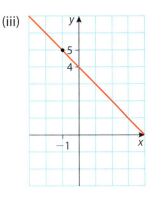

7. Using the coordinates given, calculate the slope of each of the following line segments:

(i)

(ii)

(iii)

8. Find the slope of the line through each pair of points:

   (i) (1, 2) and (4, 5)   (ii) (2, 3) and (3, 7)   (iii) (1, −3) and (4, 2)

   (iv) (−2, 4) and (2, 6)   (v) (1, 5) and (3, −1)   (vi) (−3, 2) and (1, −4)

   (vii) (−2, −6) and (1, 2)   (viii) (1, −4) and (−2, 3)   (ix) (2, −4) and (3, −1)

9. A(2, 4), B(6, 7), C(10, 5) and D(6, 2) are four points.
Show that the slope of AB is the same as the slope of CD.

10. Show that the line through A(1, 1) and B(5, −1)
is parallel to the line through C(4, 4) and D(8, 2).

> Lines with the same
> slope are parallel.

11. Find   (i) the slope of the line through A(2, 4) and B(1, 1)

        (ii) the slope of the line through C(4, 1) and D(3, −2).

    What can you say about the two lines?

12. The given diagram shows three lines a, b, and c.

    Match the lines with these slopes:

       2, $\frac{1}{2}$,   1.

13. A cyclist rides up an incline that rises
3 metres for every 60 metres it runs.

   (i) What is the slope of the incline?
  (ii) How much will the incline rise for
      a run of 120 metres?

14. A horizontal mine shaft is bored into the
side of a mountain whose slope is 0.4.
If an air vent is to be installed 150 metres
along the shaft directly up to the surface,
how long will the air vent be?

Section 14.5 The equation of a line

The diagram on the right shows that the
points $(0, 5)$, $(1, 4)$, $(2, 3)$, $(3, 2)$, $(4, 1)$ and $(5, 0)$
are all in the same straight line.

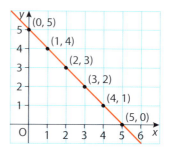

Notice that the coordinates of each
point add up to 5, that is, the
x-value and the y-value add up to 5.

Thus, for all points (x, y) on the line,
$x + y = 5$.

$x + y = 5$ is called the **equation** of the line.
The line may also be written in the form $y = -x + 5$.

The equation of a line in the form $y = mx + c$

The equation of the given line, a, is

    $y = 2x + 1$.

This line has a slope of 2.
Notice that 2 is also the coefficient of x in the equation.
The line crosses the y-axis at $(0, 1)$.
We say that the line makes an **intercept**
of 1 on the y-axis.

When a line is in the form
$y = mx + c$, it is said to
be expressed in the
slope-intercept form.

For any line expressed in the form $y = mx + c$,
  (i) the slope of the line is m
 (ii) the point where it crosses the y-axis is $(0, c)$.

For the line $y = 2x - 2$,
 (i) the slope of the line is 2
(ii) the point where it crosses
    the y-axis is $(0, -2)$, i.e. the
    y-intercept is -2.

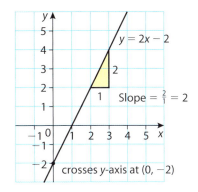

Example 1

Find the slope and y-intercept of these lines:
(i) $y = 3x + 4$
(ii) $y = -2x - 1$

(i) $y = 3x + 4$:   slope $= 3$; y-intercept is 4
(ii) $y = -2x - 1$:   slope $= -2$; y-intercept is -1

Exercise 14.5

1. Write down the slope of each of these lines:
   (i) $y = 2x + 3$ (ii) $y = 3x + 6$ (iii) $y = 2x - 1$
   (iv) $y = 5x + 2$ (v) $y = -x + 4$ (vi) $y = -3x - 2$

2. Write down the coordinates of the point where each of the lines in Question **1** above intersects the y-axis.

3. For each of the following lines, write down
   (i) the slope of the line
   (ii) the point at which it crosses the y-axis.
   (a) $y = 3x + 1$ (b) $y = 2x - 4$ (c) $y = -3x + 5$

4. The slope of each of these lines is given.
Write the equation of each line in the form $y = mx + c$.

(i)

(ii)

(iii)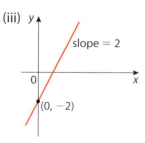

5. For the given line, write down
  (i) the slope of the line
  (ii) the coordinates of the point at which
      the line crosses the y- axis
  (iii) the equation of the line in the form
      $y = mx + c$.

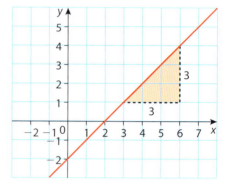

6. By reading off the slope and the y-intercept, write down the equations of the
following lines in the form $y = mx + c$.

(a)

(b)

(c)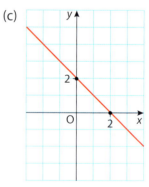

7. By finding the slope and y-intercept,
write down the equation of the
given line.

8. The equations of six lines are given below:

a: $y = 2x - 3$ c: $y = x + 3$ e: $y = -\frac{1}{2}x + 4$

b: $y = \frac{1}{2}x + 5$ d: $y = -2x - 4$ f: $y = 2x - 2$

(i) Which two lines are parallel?
(ii) Which line has a slope of $\frac{1}{2}$?
(iii) Which line crosses the y-axis at $(0, -4)$?
(iv) At what point does the line marked a cross the y-axis?
(v) What is the slope of the line c?

Section 14.6 The equation of a line containing (x_1, y_1) with slope m

If we know a point (x_1, y_1) on a line and its slope m, the equation of the line is:

$$y - y_1 = m(x - x_1)$$

Example 1

Find the equation of the line which has a slope of 2 and which contains the point $(3, 1)$.

The equation is
$$y - y_1 = m(x - x_1)$$
$$y - 1 = 2(x - 3)$$
$$y - 1 = 2x - 6$$
$$y = 2x - 6 + 1$$
$$y = 2x - 5$$

$m = 2$
$(x_1, y_1) = (3, 1)$

[Note: The equation may also be written in the form $2x - y - 5 = 0$.]

Given two points on a line

If we are given two points on a line but no slope, we first find the slope of the line through the two given points. We then use this slope and any **one** of the two points to find the equation of the line.

Example 2

Find the equation of the line which passes through the points $(-2, 1)$ and $(1, 5)$.

$$m = \frac{y_2 - y_1}{x_2 - x_1} = \frac{5 - 1}{1 + 2} = \frac{4}{3}$$

$$\begin{array}{cc} (x_1, y_1) & (x_2, y_2) \\ \downarrow & \downarrow \\ (-2, 1) & (1, 5) \end{array}$$

We will now use this slope and the point $(-2, 1)$.

Equation: $y - y_1 = m(x - x_1)$ $\qquad m = \frac{4}{3} \quad (-2, 1)$

$$\begin{array}{c} \downarrow \\ (x_1, y_1) \end{array}$$

$$y - 1 = \tfrac{4}{3}(x + 2)$$

$$y - 1 = \frac{4x}{3} + \frac{8}{3}$$

$$y = \frac{4x}{3} + \frac{8}{3} + 1$$

$$y = \frac{4x}{3} + \frac{8}{3} + \frac{3}{3}$$

$$y = \frac{4x}{3} + \frac{11}{3} \quad \text{is the required equation}$$

Exercise 14.6

Use the formula $y - y_1 = m(x - x_1)$ to find the equation of each of the lines below.
Give each equation in the form $y = mx + c$.

1. Slope = 2; point = $(1, 3)$

2. Slope = 3; point = $(5, 2)$

3. Slope = 4; point = $(1, 4)$

4. Slope = -2; point = $(4, 3)$

5. Slope = 3; point = $(-3, 2)$

6. Slope = 4; point = $(-3, 4)$

7. Slope = -2; point = $(-1, 3)$

8. Slope = 3; point = $(-1, -3)$

9. Slope = -4; point = $(0, -2)$

10. Slope = 2; point = $(-2, 0)$

11. Slope = $\frac{2}{3}$; point = $(1, 2)$

12. Slope = $\frac{1}{3}$; point = $(-3, 2)$

13. Slope = $\frac{5}{2}$; point = $(1, -2)$

14. Slope = $-\frac{3}{4}$; point = $(0, 3)$

15. Find the slope of the line containing A$(1, 2)$ and B$(2, 5)$.
Now use this slope and the point A$(1, 2)$ to find the equation of the line.
Now use the slope and the point B$(2, 5)$ to find the equation of the line.
(Both your answers should be the same.)

16. A$(2, -1)$ and B$(4, 5)$ are two points. Find
   (i) the slope of AB
   (ii) the equation of AB.

17. Find the slope and hence the equation of the line through the given pairs of
points:

    (i) $(-1, 3)$ and $(1, 7)$ (ii) $(1, -2)$ and $(2, 3)$

    (iii) $(-2, 1)$ and $(-3, 5)$ (iv) $(2, -3)$ and $(5, 2)$

18. A$(-1, 3)$ and B$(2, 1)$ are two points. Find

    (i) the slope of AB   (ii) the equation of AB

19. Find the equation of the line which passes through the points $(-4, 1)$ and $(0, 5)$.

20. Find the equation of the line through the origin $(0, 0)$ with slope $= -2$.

21. Find the midpoint of the line segment R$(-1, 3)$ and S$(5, 5)$.
    Now find the equation of the line through the midpoint of [RS] with slope $= 4$.

Section 14.7 Graphing lines

1. Lines parallel to the x-axis or y-axis

The lines $x = 2$ and $x = 4$ are shown.

Notice that the x-value of each point on the line
$x = 4$ is 4.

Similarly, the x-value of each point on the line $x = 2$ is 2.

All lines with equations of the form $x = a$ will be parallel
to the y-axis.

The diagram on the right shows the line $y = 2$.

Again, notice that the y-value of each of the
points on this line is 2.

All lines with equations of the form $y = a$
will be parallel to the x-axis.

2. Graphing lines

To draw a line such as $2x + 3y = 6$, we need to know at least two points on the
line.

The easiest points to find are those at which the line crosses the x-axis and y-axis.

On the x-axis, $y = 0$; on the y-axis, $x = 0$.

Take the line $2x + 3y = 6$.

When $x = 0$, then $2(0) + 3y = 6$

$$3y = 6$$

$$\Rightarrow \quad y = 2$$

∴ $(0, 2)$ is one point on the line

When $y = 0$, then $2x + 3(0) = 6$

$$2x = 6$$

$$x = 3$$

∴ $(3, 0)$ is a second point on the line

A sketch of the line is shown on the right.

Sketch of line $2x + 3y = 6$

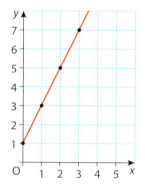

Another way to draw a line such as $y = 2x + 1$ is to set out a table of values, as shown below.

$y = 2x + 1$

$x =$	0	1	2	3
$y =$	1	3	5	7

Four points on the line are:

$(0, 1), (1, 3), (2, 5)$ and $(3, 7)$.

A sketch of the line is shown.

Exercise 14.7

1. Write down the equations of the lines marked a to d on the given diagram.

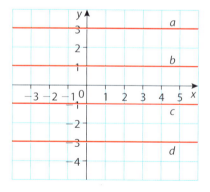

2. Write down the equations of the lines marked e, f, g and h in the given diagram.

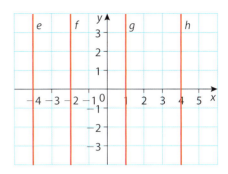

3. Draw a coordinate grid with the x-axis and y-axis each labelled from -5 to 5. On the grid draw and label these lines:

    (i) $x = 5$ (ii) $x = -2$ (iii) $y = 2$ (iv) $y = -3$

4. Write down the equations of the lines marked Ⓐ to Ⓕ on the given diagram.

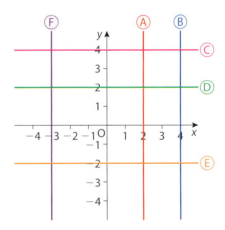

5. (i) What is the equation of the x-axis?
    (ii) What is the equation of the y-axis?

6. $y = 2x - 4$ is the equation of a line.
    (i) If $x = 0$, find the value for y.
        Now write down the coordinates of the point at which the line crosses the y-axis.
    (ii) If $y = 0$, find the value for x.
        Now write down the coordinates of the point at which the line crosses the x-axis.

7. Find the coordinates of the point where each of these lines cuts the x-axis:

    (i) $y = x + 2$ (ii) $y = 3x - 6$ (iii) $y = \frac{1}{2}x + 3$

8. Find the coordinates of the point where each of these lines cuts the y-axis:

   (i) $y = 2x - 3$ (ii) $y = x + 5$ (iii) $y = 3x - 4$

9. Find the points at which the line $y = 2x - 5$ intersects the x-axis and y-axis. Now draw a sketch of the line.

10. Find the points at which the following lines intersect the x-axis and y-axis. Hence draw a sketch of each line.

   (i) $y = x + 3$ (ii) $y = 4x + 2$ (iii) $y = 6x - 6$

11. Find the points at which the line $y = \frac{3}{2}x - 3$ intersects the x-axis and y-axis. Now draw a sketch of the line and mark in the coordinates of the points where the line crosses the x-axis and y-axis.

12. ℓ is the line $y = \frac{1}{2}x - 2$ and it cuts the x-axis at the point K.

  (i) Find the coordinates of K.
  (ii) ℓ intersects the y-axis at P. Find the coordinates of P.
 (iii) Find the slope of the line PK.
 (iv) Find the length of [PK].

13. Which of the three lines below intersects

   (i) the x-axis at $(2, 0)$ (ii) the y-axis at $(0, -1)$?

       A: $y = \frac{1}{2}x + 2$ B: $y = 2x - 1$ C: $y = 2x - 4$

14. By finding where the line crosses the x-axis and y-axis, match each of these equations with the correct graph:

   (i) $x + y = 3$ (ii) $x - y = 3$ (iii) $y = 2x - 3$

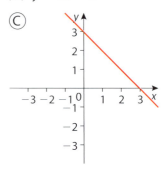

Section 14.8 **Intersection of lines**

A sketch of the lines $x + y = 4$ and $x + 3y = 6$ is shown on the right. The point of intersection of the two lines can be read from the diagram. This point is (3, 1).

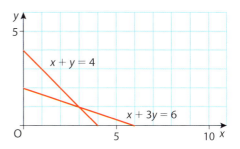

The point of intersection of any two lines can be found by sketching the lines on a grid and then reading their point of intersection from this grid.

To verify that a point is on a given line

To investigate if the point $(3, -2)$ is on the line $x + 2y + 1 = 0$, we substitute 3 for x and -2 for y in the equation.

$x + 2y + 1 = 0$

$x = 3$ and $y = -2$

> If a point is on a line, then the coordinates of the point will satisfy the equation of the line.

Test: $3 + 2(-2) + 1$

$\quad\quad 3 - 4 + 1 = 0$

Since both sides of the equation are zero, we say that $(3, -2)$ **satisfies** the equation $x + 2y + 1 = 0$.

However, $(-3, 4)$ is not on the line $x - 3y + 7 = 0$ since $-3 - 12 + 7 \neq 0$, i.e. it does not satisfy the equation.

Example 1

Is (i) (2, 3) (ii) $(-4, 1)$ on the line $2x + y = 7$?

(ii) (2, 3): Here we substitute 2 for x and 3 for y in the equation
$\quad\quad\quad 2x + y = 7$
$\quad\quad\therefore\ 2(2) + (3) = 7$, i.e. $7 = 7$
$\quad\quad\therefore\ (2, 3)$ is on the line because (2, 3) satisfies the equation.

(ii) $(-4, 1)$: $2x + y = 7$
$\quad\quad\quad 2(-4) + 1 : 7$
$\quad\quad\quad -8 + 1 : 7$
$\quad\quad\therefore\ -7 \neq 7$
$\quad\quad\therefore\ (-4, 1)$ is not on the line because $(-4, 1)$ does not satisfy the equation.

Exercise 14.8

1. Use the diagram on the right to write down the point of intersection of the lines

   $x + y = 4$ and $2x - y = -1$.

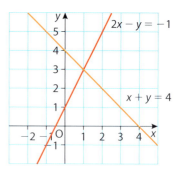

2. The diagram shows three lines **A**, **B** and **C**. The equations of the lines are:

   A: $x + y = 3$ **B**: $y = 2x$ **C**: $x - 2y = 3$.

   Use the diagram to write down the point of intersection of these lines
   (i) $x + y = 3$ and $y = 2x$
   (ii) $x - 2y = 3$ and $x + y = 3$
   (iii) $y = 2x$ and $x - 2y = 3$

3. Using the one diagram, sketch the lines
   $$x + y = 5 \quad \text{and} \quad x + 4y = 8.$$
   Use your sketch to write down the point of intersection of the two lines.

4. On the same pair of axes, sketch the lines
   $$x + y = 3 \quad \text{and} \quad 2x - y = 3$$
   From your graph, write down the point of intersection of the two lines.

5. By graphing the two lines $x + y = 5$ and $2x - y = 4$, find the coordinates of their point of intersection.

6. Show that the point $(2, 1)$ is on the line $3x - y = 5$.

7. Verify that the point $(2, -3)$ is on the line $y = x - 5$.

8. Show that $(-3, 1)$ is not on the line $x - 3y + 1 = 0$.

9. Investigate if $(2, 0)$ is on the line $2x - y + 3 = 0$.

10. Show that $(-3, 1)$ is on the line $2x + 4y + 2 = 0$.

11. If $(1, 4)$ is on the line $2x + y + k = 0$, find the value of k.

12. If $(2, -3)$ is on the line $x + ky + 7 = 0$, find the value of k.

13. (i) Find the value of k if the line $2x + ky - 8 = 0$ contains the point $(3, 1)$.
    (ii) If $(1, t)$ lies on the line $y = 2x + 3$, find the value of t.

Test yourself 14

1. (a) A($-2, 4$) and B($1, 5$) are the two points.
   (i) Find the slope of AB.   (ii) Find the equation of the line AB.

   (b) The equation of the line ℓ is $y = 2x - 4$.
   The line ℓ intersects the x-axis at P and the y-axis at Q.
   (i) Find the coordinates of P and Q.
   (ii) Find the length of the line segment [PQ].

2. (a) (i) Find the coordinates of M, the midpoint of the line segment joining
   A($-1, 6$) and B($5, -6$).
   On which axis does M lie?
   (ii) P($6, 2$), Q($-1, 3$) and R($1, -3$) are three points.
   Show that $|PQ| = |PR|$.

   (b) (i) Write down the slope of the
   given line k.
   (ii) Write the equation of k in
   the form $y = mx + c$.

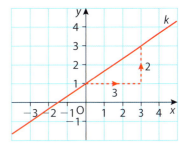

3. (a) Four lines ℓ, m, n, k are shown in
   the given figure.
   Name the line that is represented
   by each of these equations:
   (i) $x = 4$
   (ii) $x = -3$
   (iii) $y = 3$
   (iv) $y = -2$

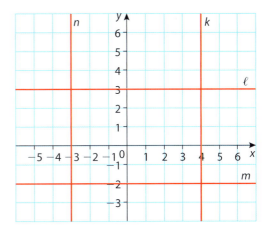

   (b) Find the slope of the line k whose equation is $y = 3x - 2$.
   Now find the equation of the line through ($2, -1$) and which has the same
   slope as k.

4. A(5, 4) is shown in the diagram.

    (i) Plot the point B(1, 2) on a copy of this diagram and then find the slope of AB.

    (ii) Find the equation of AB.

    (iii) The line AB intersects the x-axis at the point C. Find the coordinates of C.

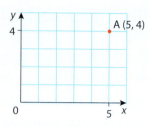

5. (a) The diagram shows two lines ℓ_1 and ℓ_2.

    (i) Which line has a positive slope?

    (ii) Find the slope of ℓ_2.

    (iii) Find the equation of ℓ_1.

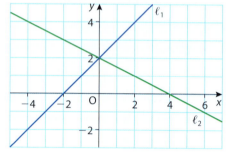

  (b) Write all these equations in the form $y = mx + c$.

    A: $y + 4 = 3x$ **B:** $y - 2x = 5$ **C:** $2y = 4x + 6$

    (i) Which line has a slope of 3?

    (ii) Which two lines are parallel?

    (iii) Which line intersects the y-axis at (0, 5)?

    (iv) Which line intersects the x-axis at $\left(-2\tfrac{1}{2}, 0\right)$?

6. (a) Find the equation of the line shown. Give your answer in the form $y = mx + c$.

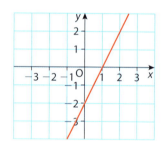

  (b) The equations of the lines ℓ, m, n and p are given on the right. Say if each of the following is true or false. Explain each answer.

    (i) p intersects the x-axis at $(-3, 0)$.

    (ii) n is parallel to the y-axis.

    (iii) ℓ intersects the y-axis at $(0, -5)$.

    (iv) the slope of the line m is -3.

$\ell:\ y = 3x - 5$
$m:\ y = 2x - 3$
$n:\ x = 4$
$p:\ y = \tfrac{2}{3}x - 2$

Statistics 3 – Presenting Data

Chapter 15

Key words

line plot   outlier   clustered   bar chart   pie chart

sector   stem and leaf plot   histogram   misleading graphs

Section 15.1 Line plots and bar charts revisited

1. Line plots

The following data shows the daily maximum temperatures (in °C) in Barcelona during the month of June.

27	28	26	25	26	27	22	30	28	29
28	26	24	22	28	24	27	29	28	27
19	25	26	29	29	26	28	28	31	25

These temperatures are shown in the **line plot** below:

Each temperature is represented by a dot

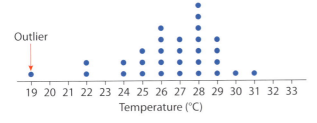

The **range** is 19°C to 31°C, i.e., 12°C.

The **mode** is 28°C as it occurs most frequently.

19°C is referred to as an **outlier** as it is significantly different from the rest of the scores.

The temperatures are bunched or **clustered** between 25°C and 29°C.

2. Bar charts

Bar charts are a simple but effective way of displaying data.

A bar chart consists of a series of bars of the same width, drawn either vertically or horizontally from an axis.

The heights (or lengths) of the bars always represent the frequencies.

The bars are generally separated by narrow gaps of equal width.

The bar chart below shows the numbers of text messages received by a group of students on a particular Saturday.

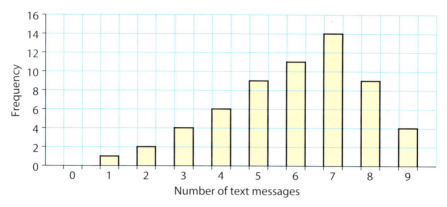

Number of text messages

The total number of text messages received was

$$1 + 2 + 4 + 6 + 9 + 11 + 14 + 9 + 4 = 60.$$

The modal number is 7 and the range is 1 to 9, i.e. 8.

Exercise 15.1

1. The line plot below illustrates the number of goals scored per match by a hockey team.

Goals scored

- (i) How many matches has the team played?
- (ii) Which number of goals scored is the mode?
- (iii) What is the range of the number of goals scored?
- (iv) What percentage of their matches were scoreless?

2. The daily maximum temperatures (in °C) at the Eiffel Tower during April are shown in this line plot:
- (i) What is the mode?
- (ii) What is the outlier?
- (iii) On how many days was the maximum temperature 25°C?

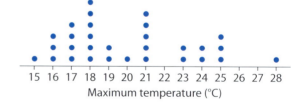

Maximum temperature (°C)

- (iv) On what percentage of days did the maximum temperature drop below 20°C?
- (v) If a day is selected at random, what is the probability that the maximum temperature is less than 18°C?

3. This line plot shows the scores (out of 50) of a group of students in a maths exam:

(i)   Which score was the most common?
(ii) How many students scored 34?
(iii) How many students scored 45 or more?
(iv) What percentage of students scored 35 or less?
(v)   If a student was selected at random, what is the probability that he scored 40?

4. This bar chart shows the number of pictures remembered by each student in a memory experiment.

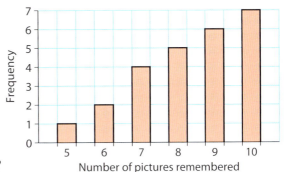

(i)   How many students took part in the experiment?
(ii) What is the modal number of pictures remembered?
(iii) How many students remembered less than 7 pictures?
(iv) What is the range of the number of pictures remembered?
(v)   What is the median number of pictures remembered?

5. The bar chart shows the numbers of hours spent on homework each week by a group of second-year students.

The numbers of hours a group of second-year students spent doing homework

(i)   How many students spent 6 hours doing homework?
(ii) What was the greatest number of hours a student spent doing homework?

(iii)   How many students spent less than 7 hours doing homework?
(iv)   How many students spent more than 10 hours doing homework?
 (v)   How many students were surveyed?
(vi)   What percentage of students spent 8 hours doing homework?
(vii)   If a student is selected at random, what is the probability that the student
         spent 10 hours doing homework?

6. Six coins were tossed 30 times and the number of heads showing each time was
        recorded.
        The results are shown in the given bar chart.

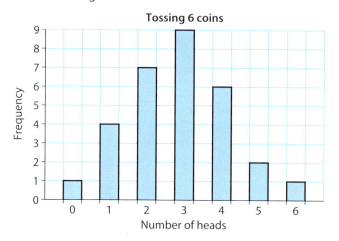

Tossing 6 coins

 (i)   How many times were 4 heads showing?
 (ii)   What was the modal number of heads showing?
(iii)   If, for a particular toss, there were 2 heads, how many tails showed?
(iv)   Write down the experimental probability of getting 4 heads.

7.

Computer game scores

This graph shows scores in a computer game.
 (i)   Scores of 250 or more won a prize. How many people won a prize?
 (ii)   How many people played altogether?
(iii)   What is the greatest number of people who could have scored more than 220?
(iv)   What is the smallest number of people who could have scored less than 160?

8. The numbers of goals scored in a series of football matches is represented in the bar chart shown on the right.

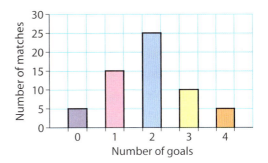

   (i) How many matches were played?

  (ii) Calculate the total number of goals scored.

 (iii) Calculate the mean number of goals scored per match, correct to one decimal place.

9. A survey was conducted to determine the numbers of hours students spend on the Internet per week. The results were as follows:

17	14	9	28	8	27	23	16	10	18
15	23	5	38	27	19	6	25	24	36
16	5	7	17	8	9	3	4	27	28
16	7	8	18	9	4	9	8	6	35

   (i) Arrange this information in a frequency distribution table, using class intervals (1–10), (11–20), (21–30) and (31–40).

  (ii) Draw a bar chart to represent this information.

 (iii) How many students used the Internet for more than 30 hours per week?

 (iv) What percentage of students used the Internet for 25 hours or more per week?

  (v) What percentage of students used the Internet for fewer than 21 hours per week?

10. A group of 20 male and 20 female teenagers were asked their opinion on whether physical education should be compulsory. The results are displayed in this double-column bar chart.

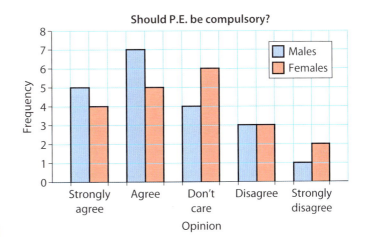

   (i) How many females strongly agree with compulsory physical education?

237

(ii) How many males strongly agree with compulsory physical education?

(iii) What is the total number of teenagers who strongly disagree with compulsory physical education?

(iv) If a teenager was selected at random, what is the probability that the student strongly agreed that physical education should be compulsory?
Give your answer as a decimal.

Section 15.2 Pie charts

Another way of showing information in diagram form is by using a **pie chart**.

A pie chart is generally used when we want to show how a given quantity is shared out or divided into different categories. The 'pie', or circle represents the total quantity and each 'slice' or **sector** represents the size of the share. The size of each 'slice' or sector is in proportion to the size of the angle at the centre of the sector.

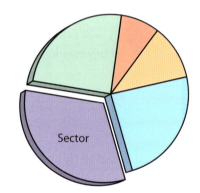

Sector

The angle at the centre of a circle or pie is 360°.

A half share will have an angle $\frac{1}{2} \times 360° = 180°$.

The diagram on the right shows how different shares are represented by sectors in a pie chart.

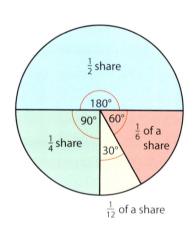

$\frac{1}{2}$ share

180°

90°   60°

$\frac{1}{4}$ share $\frac{1}{6}$ of a share

30°

$\frac{1}{12}$ of a share

If the fraction of a share is $\frac{1}{6}$, the angle at the centre is found by getting $\frac{1}{6}$ of 360°.

$\frac{1}{6}$ of 360° = 360° ÷ 6 = 60°.

Similarly, if the fraction is $\frac{1}{10}$, the angle at the centre is $\frac{1}{10}$ of 360° = 36°.

The pie chart on the right shows how Derek spent 24 hours over a weekend.

From the pie chart we can see that

(i)   he spent about $\frac{1}{3}$ of the time sleeping

(ii) he spent about $\frac{1}{4}$ of the time playing with friends.

Example 1

120 first-year girls were asked to name their favourite sport. The results are shown in the given pie chart.
How many girls named
  (i)   tennis
  (ii) athletics
  (iii) hockey
  (iv) netball
as their favourite sport?

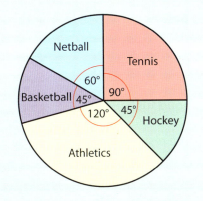

Here we express each of the angles in the sectors required as a fraction of 360°.

(i) **Tennis:** 90° ; $\dfrac{90°}{360°} = \dfrac{1}{4}$ and $\dfrac{1}{4}$ of 120 = 30

   ∴   30 girls named tennis

(ii) **Athletics:** 120° ; $\dfrac{120°}{360°} = \dfrac{1}{3}$ and $\dfrac{1}{3}$ of 120 = 40

   ∴   40 girls named athletics

(iii) **Hockey:** 45° ; $\dfrac{45°}{360°} = \dfrac{9}{72} = \dfrac{1}{8}$ and $\dfrac{1}{8}$ of 120 = 15

   ∴   15 girls named hockey

(iv) **Netball:** 60° ; $\dfrac{60°}{360°} = \dfrac{1}{6}$ and $\dfrac{1}{6}$ of 120 = 20

   ∴   20 girls named netball

Example 2

In a survey, 72 people were asked what type of heating they had in their homes. The results are given in the table below:

Type of heating	Oil	Gas	Electricity	Solid fuel
Number of households	30	24	12	6

Draw a pie chart to illustrate this information.

The angle in each sector is found as follows:

Oil: $\quad \frac{30}{72} = \frac{5}{12}$ and $\frac{5}{12}$ of $360° = \frac{5}{\overset{1}{12}} \times \frac{\overset{30}{360}}{1} = 150°$

Gas: $\quad \frac{24}{72} = \frac{1}{3}$ and $\frac{1}{3}$ of $360° = 120°$

Electricity: $\frac{12}{72} = \frac{1}{6}$ and $\frac{1}{6}$ of $360° = 60°$

Solid fuel: $\frac{6}{72} = \frac{1}{12}$ and $\frac{1}{12}$ of $360° = 30°$

The results are represented by the pie chart on the right.

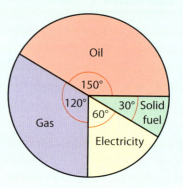

Exercise 15.2

1. A pie chart is shown on the right.
   (i) What percentage is yellow?
   (ii) What fraction is yellow?
   (iii) What percentage is red?
   (iv) What fraction is red?

The pie chart represents 12 coloured counters.
   (v) How many of the counters are yellow?
   (vi) How many of the counters are red?

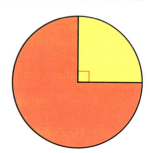

2. The contents of a box of mixed sweets are shown in this pie chart.

Contents of a box of mixed sweets

  (i) What percentage are fruit chews?
  (ii) What fraction are toffees?
The box contains 60 sweets.
  (iii) How many toffees are there?
  (iv) How many chocolates are there?

3. The pie chart on the right shows the different types of accommodation in a holiday village.
If the total number of 'units' in the village was 600, find

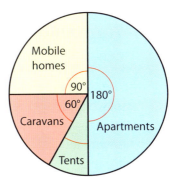

  (i) the number of apartments in the village
  (ii) the number of mobile homes in the village
  (iii) the number of caravans in the village
  (iv) the angle in the sector representing tents.

4. Find the value of x in each pie chart shown.

(i)

(ii)

(iii)

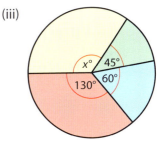

5. On returning to Dublin, 240 holiday makers were asked to name the countries they had visited.
The results are shown in the pie chart on the right.

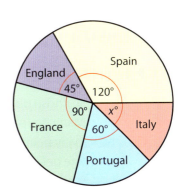

  (i) What is the size of the angle marked $x°$?
  (ii) How many people visited Portugal?
  (iii) Which country was visited by the most people?
  (iv) Which country was visited by $\frac{1}{4}$ of the people questioned?
  (v) Which two countries combined accounted for one half of the holiday makers questioned?

6. One hundred and eighty women were asked how
many children they had in their families. The results
are shown in the pie chart on the right.

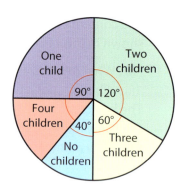

   (i) How many families had two children?

  (ii) How many families had no children?

 (iii) How many families had three children?

 (iv) What is the angle in the sector representing
      four children?

  (v) How many families had four children?

7. A packet of breakfast cereal weighing 600 g contains 4 ingredients as follows:

Oats	Barley	Wheat	Rye
150 g	100 g	75 g	275 g

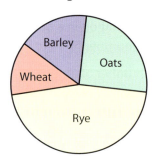

In the pie chart on the right, find the
angle in the sector representing

  (i) oats

 (ii) wheat

(iii) rye.

8. Sixty people were asked how they generally travel to work and the results are given
in the following table:

Transport	Bus	Car	Train	Walk	Bicycle
Number of people	20	15	12	8	5

  (i) Calculate the angle in each of the sectors.

 (ii) Draw a pie chart to illustrate the data.

9. Some senior citizens were asked about their
favourite pets.
The results are shown in the pie chart.

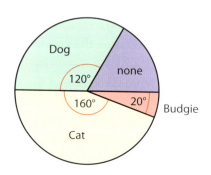

  (i) What fraction of the citizens liked a
      dog best?

If 30 people chose dog,

 (ii) how many people were asked altogether?

(iii) how many people chose a cat as their
      favourite pet?

 (iv) how many chose a budgie as their
      favourite pet?

10. This pie chart represents the colours of eyes in a group of children. The angles for blue, green and hazel are shown in the chart.

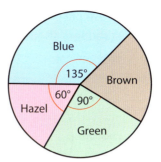

   (i) What is the angle in the sector representing brown?

  (ii) If there are 30 children with green eyes, how many in total are in the group?

 (iii) How many children have blue eyes?

11. This pie chart shows the proportions of guests at a wedding who selected the various desserts listed on the menu.

   (i) What proportion of the guests chose peach melba?

  (ii) What percentage of the guests chose trifle?

 (iii) If there were 288 guests at the wedding, how many of them had ice-cream?

12. A shop that sells mobile phones noted the colours of the phones sold in one month. The owner of the shop wanted to draw a pie chart to show the results. Find the values of the angles marked A, B, C and D in the table below.

Mobile phone colour	Number of mobile phones	Pie chart angle
black	75	A
yellow	5	B
grey	25	C
blue	15	D
Total	**120**	**360°**

Draw a circle of radius 4 cm.
Represent the information in the table above on your pie chart.

13. Which of these sets of data are very suitable to display on a pie chart?

   (i) The countries chosen by people in which to go on a skiing holiday.

  (ii) The midday temperatures taken in a seaside resort over a 30-day period.

 (iii) The favourite colour named by each student in a class of 30.

 (iv) The marks (out of 100) scored by the students in first-year.

  (v) The proportion of people who had chosen hotel, camping or self-catering for their most recent holiday.

14. These pie charts show the types of cards on sale in two
stationery shops.

Cardworld had 200 cards and *Card Den* had 600 cards.
  (i) Approximately how many birthday cards were at
       Card Den?
  (ii) Jenny thought that the pie charts above showed
       there were more *Congratulations* cards at *Cardworld*
       than at *Card Den*.
Explain why the pie charts show that this is not so.

Section 15.3 Stem and leaf plots

A **stem and leaf plot** is a very useful way of presenting data. It is useful because it shows all
the original data and also gives you the overall picture or shape of the distribution.

It is similar to a horizontal bar chart, with the numbers themselves forming the bars.

Stem and leaf diagrams are suitable only for small amounts of data.

If data consists of 2 digits, the first digit is used as the stem and the second digit as the leaf.

The number 42 is written as 4|2.

A typical stem and leaf diagram is shown below.

```
0 | 6  9
1 | 2  5  (7) ◄──────────── This represents 17.
2 | 3  3  6  8
3 | 0  2  7
4 | 1  2  6
5 | 3                    Key: 3|2 = 32
```

> You must always add a
> key to show how the stem
> and leaf combine.

The data represented above is:

   6, 9, 12, 15, 17, 23, 23, 26, 28, 30, 32, 37, 41, 42, 46, 53

Notice that all the numbers are in order of size, starting with the smallest and finishing with the largest.

This is called an **ordered** stem and leaf plot.

Example 1

Use a stem and leaf plot to show the following ages of the 21 musicians in an orchestra:

| 25 | 35 | 28 | 47 | 52 | 33 | 50 | 28 | 33 | 35 | 48 |
| 55 | 29 | 50 | 39 | 41 | 32 | 29 | 56 | 26 | 35 |

(i) What is the mode of the data?
(ii) What is the median age?

The ages range from 25 to 56.
We write 2, 3, 4 and 5 down the first column to make the stem.
The leaves are the single digits written next to the stem:
25 is shown by writing a 5 next to the 2 stem.

Stem	Leaf
2	5 8 8 9 9 6
3	5 3 3 5 9 2 5
4	7 8 1
5	2 0 5 0 6

This is an **unordered** stem and leaf plot.

In a stem and leaf plot, the numbers must align beneath one another.

It is more useful to rearrange the scores so they are in order, from smallest to largest. This results in an **ordered** stem and leaf plot.

Stem	Leaf
2	5 6 8 8 9 9
3	2 3 3 5 5 5 9
4	1 7 8
5	0 0 2 5 6

Key: $3|2 = 32$

(i) The mode is 35 as it occurs most frequently.
(ii) The median is the value that is halfway through the distribution.
There are 21 values altogether.
The median value is the 11th value.
This value is 35, i.e. the median is 35.

Exercise 15.3

1. The stem and leaf diagram below shows the ages, in years, of 25 people who wished to enter a 10 km walking competition.

```
1 | 4  4  6  9
2 | 1  3  7  7  7  8
3 | 3  6  6  7  9
4 | 0  2  3  3  8  8
5 | 1  3  4  7          Key: 1|6  means 16 years old
```

   (i)   How many people were less than 20 years old?
   (ii) Write down the modal age.
   (iii) How many people were between 35 and 45 years old?
   (iv) What was the median age?
   (v)   What percentage of people were under 20 years of age?

2. The stem and leaf plot below shows the times, in seconds, taken by a group of first-year pupils to complete a 200-metre race.

```
2 | 6  8  9
3 | 1  5  6  8  9
4 | 0  2  5  5  8  9
5 | 1  3  6  7
6 | 2  5  7  8
7 | 0  1                Key: 4|0 = 40 seconds
```

   (i)   What was the fastest time recorded?
   (ii)   How many pupils ran the race in less than 40 seconds?
   (iii) How many pupils took part in the race?
   (iv)   What was the time of the 8th fastest pupil?
   (v)   What was the time of the 3rd slowest pupil?
   (vi)   What was the difference between the times of the fastest and slowest pupils?
   (vii) If a time of 45 seconds or less qualifies a pupil for a further race, how many pupils qualified?

3. Here are the marks of 20 students in a maths test displayed in a stem and leaf diagram.
   (i) What is the lowst mark?
   (ii) What is the difference between the lowest and highest marks?
   (iii) If marks between 40 and 60 inclusive achieve grade C, how many got this grade?
   (iv) What percentage of the students got a mark between 50 and 60?

stem	leaf
2	6 8
3	3 7 9
4	0 5 7 8
5	3 5 7 9
6	1 2 4 8
7	1 3 5

Key: 5|3 = 53

4. The stem and leaf diagram on the right shows the marks obtained by a group of students in a Spanish test.
   (i) How many students took this test?
   (ii) How many students got between 70 and 79 marks?
   (iii) What is the range of the marks obtained?
   (iv) Find the median mark.
   (v) What percentage of students got a mark between 70 and 80 inclusive?

stem	leaf
5	1 4 6
6	2 3 3 6
7	2 3 5 7 8
8	0 0 2 4 6 6
9	3 4

Key: 7|3 means 73 marks

5. This stem-and-leaf plot shows the height, in centimetres, of 22 women at a gym.
   (i) What is the range of the heights of the women?
   (ii) How many women are more than 170 cm in height?
   (iii) How many women are between 150 cm and 160 cm, inclusive, in height?
   (iv) What is the median height of the women?
   (v) What is the ratio of women under 150 cm to women over 180 cm?

stem	leaf
14	7 8 8
15	0 1 2 3 6 6 8
16	1 5 8 9 9 9
17	2 3 3 5
18	1 1

Key: 14|7 = 147 cm

6. The number of points scored per match by the *Dragons* basketball team are shown below:

85	67	56	69	99	97	59	65	84	97
49	72	89	78	66	81	92	88	53	73

Copy and complete the stem and leaf plot on the right.
- (i)   Write down the range of the scores.
- (ii) Find the median score.
- (iii) In how many matches did the *Dragons* score 80 points or more?
- (iv) In what percentage of their matches did the *Dragons* score less than 70 points?

stem	leaf
4	9
5	3 6
6	
7	
8	
9	

7. Twenty four pupils were asked how many CDs they had in their collection. The results are shown below:

23	2	18	14	7	4	25	21	32	26	31	6
17	6	18	19	31	21	12	1	0	8	14	15

- (i)   Draw a stem and leaf diagram to represent this information.
- (ii) How many pupils had more than 20 CDs?
- (iii) What percentage of the pupils had between 10 and 20 CDs in their collections?
- (iv) What is the median number of CDs in the collections?
- (v)   What is the mean number of CDs in the collections? Give your answer to the nearest whole number.

8. The stem and leaf diagram on the right shows the marks achieved by 20 students in a test.
- (i)   Write down the range of the marks.
- (ii) If students who got 65 marks or more achieved a grade C, how many students got this grade?
- (iii) What percentage of students got 70 marks or more?
- (iv) Find the median mark.
- (v)   Calculate the mean mark.

stem	leaf
2	2
3	4 6
4	2 7 9
5	3 4 5 8 9
6	0 2 6 7
7	2 6 7
8	1 4

Key: $4|2 = 42$ marks

Section 15.4 Histograms

One of the most common ways of representing a frequency distribution is by means of a **histogram**.

Histograms are very similar to bar charts but there are some important differences:
> there are no gaps between the bars in a histogram
> histograms are used to show **continuous data**
> the data is always **grouped**; the groups are called **classes**
> the **area** of each bar or rectangle represents the frequency.

Histograms may have equal or unequal class intervals.

For our course, we will confine our study to histograms with **equal class intervals**.

When the class intervals are equal, drawing a histogram is very similar to drawing a bar chart.

Example 1

Fifty children were asked to solve a puzzle.
The table below records the time, in minutes, taken by the children.

Time (in mins)	0–5	5–10	10–15	15–20	20–25
Number of children	6	10	16	12	6

All the groups have the same interval of 5 minutes.
To draw the histogram, you start by drawing the two axes.

The horizontal axis shows the time. Each group or class is 5 minutes.
The vertical axis is labelled 'Number of children'.
We now draw the rectangles or bars for each class.
Notice that the heights of the bars represent the frequencies.
The **modal class** is (10–15) minutes because there are more children in this class than any other class.

Exercise 15.4

1. A supermarket opens at 08:00. The histogram opposite shows the times that employees arrive for work.

(i) How many employees arrive before 07:30?

(ii) How many employees arrive after 08:00?

(iii) How many employees arrive between 07:30 and 08:00?

(iv) What is the modal class?

(v) Find the total number of employees turning up for work.

2. The histogram shows information about the weights of 100 people.

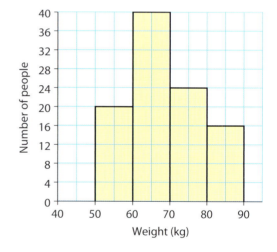

(i) How many people weigh between 60 kg and 70 kg?

(ii) How many people weigh 70 kg or more?

(iii) What is the modal class?

3. The histogram on the right shows the distances, in kilometres, travelled to work by people in an office block.

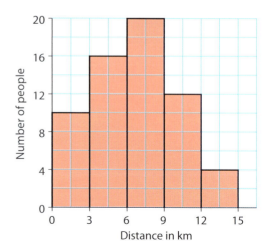

(i) How many people travelled between 6 km and 9 km to work?

(ii) How many people had to travel more than 9 km?

(iii) What is the modal class?

(iv) What is the total number of people included in the survey?

4. A Garda officer recorded the speeds of cars passing a school.

The table below shows the speeds that he recorded.

Speed (in km/hr)	20–30	30–40	40–50	50–60
Number of cars	8	20	16	12

(i) Draw a histogram to illustrate this data.

(ii) How many cars were travelling at less than 40 km/hour?

(iii) If the speed limit was 55 km/hr, what is the maximum number of cars that could have exceeded this limit?

5. The histogram shows the number of people who used a snack bar before lunch one weekday.

(i) At what time do you think the snack bar opened?

(ii) How many people used the snack bar during the first hour?

(iii) Why do you think that the people used the snack bar at this time?

The snack bar had another busy hour.

(iv) When was it busy again?

(v) Why do you think that the snack bar was busy for a second time?

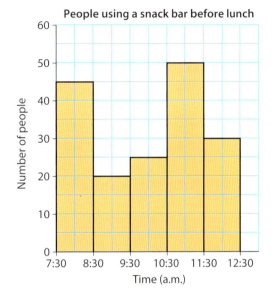

6. *AB United* played 28 matches away from home last season.

The table below gives the distances travelled to these matches.

Distance (in km)	0–20	20–40	40–60	60–80
Number of matches	6	10	8	4

[0–20 means ⩾ 0 to <20]

(i) Draw a histogram to illustrate this data.

(ii) For how many of the matches did they travel less than 40 km?

(iii) What was the modal distance–class travelled?

(iv) At the end of the season, the club realised that they had drawn half of the matches and had lost one third of the matches that involved journeys of 40 km or more.

How many of these matches did they win?

7. The histogram below shows the times taken by a group of pupils to complete a puzzle.

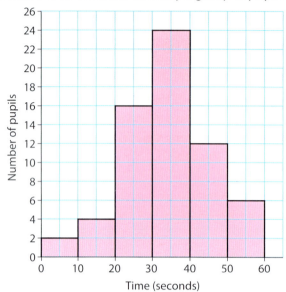

(i)   How many pupils took between 20 and 30 seconds to complete the puzzle?
(ii)   How many pupils completed the puzzle?
(iii)   What is the modal class?
(iv)   What is the greatest number of pupils that could have completed the puzzle in less than 25 seconds?

8. The histogram below shows the ages of people living in a village.

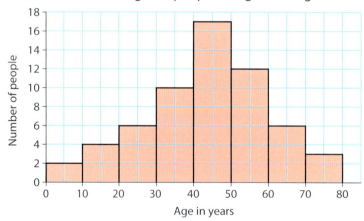

(i)   How many people are aged under 30 years?
(ii)   How many people live in the village?
(iii)   Which interval contains 20% of the people?
(iv)   If a person is selected at random, what is the probability that he/she is aged between 60 and 70 years?
(v)   What is the greatest number of people who could be older than 55 years?

Section 15.5 **Misleading graphs**

Because graphs and tables are based on information gathered and presented, people tend to believe the impressions they give. However, graphs can be used by unscrupulous people to give a false or misleading impression.

The following three graphs were used by *Munchies* dog food to compare its sales figures to those of *Doggo's* dog food.

We will use these graphs to highlight some of the more common ways of drawing graphs that may be used to give a false impression.

1. This graph does not have a scale on the vertical axis. You cannot tell how big the difference is between *Munchies* sales and *Doggo's* sales.

> The vertical axis must be labelled.

2. This graph shows only **part** of a scale. The scale does not start at 0. This makes the difference between *Munchies* sales and *Doggo's* sales look much bigger than it actually is.

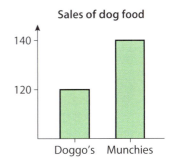

> If an axis does not start from zero, or the zero is put in the wrong place, it can mislead people.

3. This graph uses pictures instead of columns. The *Munchies* dog is twice as tall as the *Doggo's* dog, but it is also twice as wide, making it seem much bigger (four times bigger).

> Using area or volume will mislead when only height is needed.

4. This graph shows the information correctly.
The scale is regular and begins at 0.
Notice that the difference in sales figures is
not as large as it seemed in the misleading
graphs on the previous page.

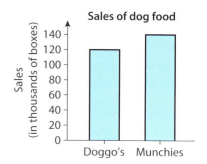

Sales of dog food

Exercise 15.5

1.

Boxit's Production of boxes 2001–2003

(i)   How many times greater is the height of box 2 than the height of box 1?
(ii) How many times greater is the area of box 2 than the area of box 1?
(iii) How many times greater is the volume
      of box 2 than the volume of box 1?
(iv) How many times greater is the height
      of box 3 than the height of box 1?
(v)   How many times greater is the area of
      box 3 than the area of box 1?
(vi) How many times greater is the volume
      of box 3 than the volume of box 1?
(vii) Draw a vertical bar chart to represent
      the information shown here.

- Box 2 is meant to
  represent twice what box 1
  represents, but it appears
  to be 8 times as big.
- Box 3 is meant to represent
  3 times what box 1
  represents, but it appears
  to be 27 times as big.

2. Give one reason why the graph
on the right is misleading.

3. Describe the misleading or poor features of each of the following graphs:

(i)

Fish sold at markets

(ii)

Milk production

(iii)

Intercity bus fares

(iv)

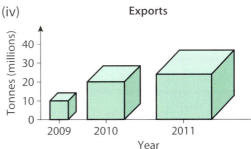

Exports

4. The bar chart on the right gives the correct representation of the sales of three soft drinks.

The company produced the following graph to represent the sales.

Name two ways in which this graph is misleading.

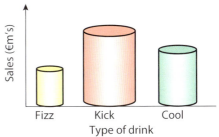

5. The Government released the following graph showing the increase in employment in the tourism industry over recent years.

   (i) Explain why the graph is misleading.

  (ii) Redraw the graph in a way that more accurately indicates the increase in employment.

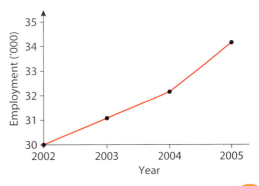

Test yourself 15

1. (a) The bar chart below shows the day of birth for a group of children.

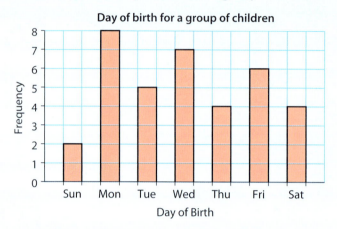

(i) How many children are there in the group?

(ii) On which day were one sixth of the children born?

(iii) In which two consecutive days was there the highest number of births?

(iv) Give one reason why you think the births were low on the Sunday.

(b) The data below shows the ages of 20 employees in a business.

| 19 | 17 | 26 | 33 | 31 | 41 | 41 | 27 | 25 | 28 |
| 40 | 31 | 29 | 29 | 39 | 26 | 36 | 26 | 35 | 38 |

(i) Construct a stem and leaf diagram to show these ages.

(ii) What is the modal age?

(iii) What is the range of the ages of the employees?

(iv) What percentage of the employees were 25 years of age or younger?

2. (a) This dot plot shows the scores of a group of students in a maths exam:

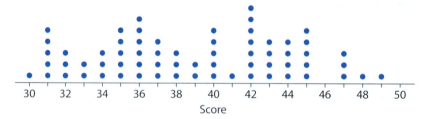

(i) Which score was the most common?

(ii) How many students scored 34?

(iii) How many students scored 45 or more?

(iv) Convert this information to a grouped frequency table.
Use class intervals of (30–34), (35–39), (40–44) and (45–49).

(b) Neil records the number of emails he receives every day for 35 days.
The data he collects is shown in the stem and leaf diagram.

```
0 | 6 7 9 9
1 | 4 7 7 8 8 9 9
2 | 2 3 5 5 6 7 8 9 9 9
3 | 1 5 6 6 6 6 7
4 | 3 6 8 9
5 | 2 3 3
```
Key: 3|1 = 31

(i) Write down the mode of the data.
(ii) Find the median.
(iii) On how many days did he receive more than 30 emails?
(iv) Write down the range of the data.

3. (a) The pie chart shows how 120 pupils in first-year travel to school.
   (i) How many pupils walk to school?
   (ii) What is the value of the angle marked $x°$?
   (iii) How many pupils cycle to school?
   (iv) What percentage of the pupils travel by bus?

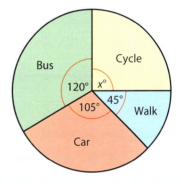

(b) The histogram below shows information about the training times taken by some 100 m runners before the Olympic Games.
   (i) Write down the reason why there are no gaps between bars.
   (ii) Write down the number of runners that took between 10 and 12 seconds.
   (iii) Work out the number of runners that took 12 seconds or more.
   (iv) Work out how many runners there were altogether.

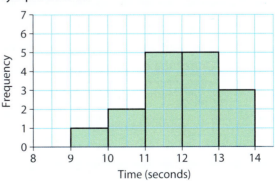

4. (a) A total of 25 adults sat a Driver Theory Test.
Their results are shown in the line plot below.

Score

  (i) Find the highest and the lowest scores from this line plot.

  (ii) Find the number of adults who got 35 marks or below.

  (iii) If 35 marks is the pass score, find the percentage that passed.

(b) The favourite colours of a group of 72 school children are shown in the following table:

Favourite colour	Red	Blue	Green	Purple	Others
Number of students	24	18	15	9	6

  (i) If the information is represented by a pie chart, work out the angle in each sector.

  (ii) Draw a pie chart to illustrate the data.

  (iii) Name another diagram that could be used to illustrate this information.

5. (a) This pie chart shows how the cost of a holiday
was shared between various items.
The flights cost €300.

  (i) Calculate the total cost of the holiday.

  (ii) (a) Calculate the size of the angle
which represents the cost of
the hotel.

    (b) Calculate the cost of the hotel.

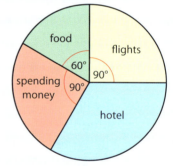

(b) The president of a college sent a questionnaire to each head of department.
One of the questions was as follows:

> How many hours do you think you are working each week?

The results are shown in the table.

  (i) Draw a histogram to represent this data.

  (ii) What is the greatest number who could
have worked more than 43 hours?

  (iii) Is the given data discrete or continuous?

  (iv) In which interval do you think the
median lies?
Give a reason for your answer.

Hours worked each week, t	Number of heads of department
$30 \leqslant t < 35$	2
$35 \leqslant t < 40$	3
$40 \leqslant t < 45$	8
$45 \leqslant t < 50$	6
$50 \leqslant t < 55$	1

Indices – Scientific Notation – Reciprocals

chapter 16

Key words

index   indices   order of operations   simplest form   standard form

scientific notation   significant figures   approximation   reciprocals

squares   square root   cube root

Section 16.1 The laws of indices

$2^3 = 2 \times 2 \times 2 = 8$

2^3 is called '2 cubed' or '2 to the power of 3'.

3 is the **power** or **index** which tells us how many times the number 2 is multiplied by itself.

> **Power** is another word for **index**.

1. Multiplication

$4^2 \times 4^3 = (4 \times 4) \times (4 \times 4 \times 4)$

$\qquad = 4^5$

Similarly, $x^2 \times x^3 = (x \times x) \times (x \times x \times x) = x^5$

So, $x^2 \times x^3 = x^{2+3} = x^5$

> To **multiply** powers of the same number, **add** the indices.

2. Division

$\dfrac{3^5}{3^2} = \dfrac{3 \times 3 \times 3 \times 3 \times 3}{3 \times 3} = 3^3$

Similarly, $\dfrac{x^5}{x^2} = \dfrac{x \times x \times x \times x \times x}{x \times x} = x^3$

Thus, $\dfrac{x^5}{x^2} = x^{5-2} = x^3$

> To **divide** powers of the same number, **subtract** the indices.

3. A power to a power

Consider $(2^3)^2$.

$(2^3)^2 = 2^3 \times 2^3$

$\qquad = 2^{3+3} = 2^6$

Similarly, $(x^2)^4 = x^2 \times x^2 \times x^2 \times x^2$

$\qquad = x^{2+2+2+2}$

$\qquad = x^8$

Thus, $(x^2)^4 = x^{2 \times 4} = x^8$

> To **raise** a power to a further power, **multiply** the indices.

259

4. The power of zero

$$\frac{2^3}{2^3} = \frac{8}{8} = 1 \quad \text{and} \quad \frac{2^3}{2^3} = 2^{3-3} = 2^0$$

This shows that $2^0 = 1$.

> Any number to the power of zero is 1, i.e. $a^0 = 1$.

5. The meaning of $a^{\frac{1}{2}}$

We use the laws of indices to show that $2^{\frac{1}{2}} = \sqrt{2}$.

$2^{\frac{1}{2}} \times 2^{\frac{1}{2}} = 2^{\frac{1}{2} + \frac{1}{2}} = 2^1 = 2$.

Also, $\sqrt{2} \times \sqrt{2} = 2$.

This shows that $2^{\frac{1}{2}} = \sqrt{2}$.

Similarly, $2^{\frac{1}{3}} = \sqrt[3]{2}$.

Thus (i) $25^{\frac{1}{2}} = \sqrt{25} = 5$ (ii) $81^{\frac{1}{2}} = \sqrt{81} = 9$.

> $2^{\frac{1}{2}} = \sqrt{2}$
> $2^{\frac{1}{3}} = \sqrt[3]{2}$

Example 1

Express each of the following as a single number:

(i) $2^2 \times 2^3$ (ii) $\dfrac{3^7}{3^3}$ (iii) $(3^2)^3$ (iv) $(3 \times 5)^2$

(i) $2^2 \times 2^3 = 2^{2+3} = 2^5 = 2 \times 2 \times 2 \times 2 \times 2 = 32$

(ii) $\dfrac{3^7}{3^3} = 3^{7-3} = 3^4 = 3 \times 3 \times 3 \times 3 = 81$

(iii) $(3^2)^3 = 3^{2 \times 3} = 3^6 = 3 \times 3 \times 3 \times 3 \times 3 \times 3$
$= 9 \times 9 \times 9 = 81 \times 9 = 729$

(iv) $(3 \times 5)^2 = 15^2 = 15 \times 15 = 225$

Order of operations

When performing operations containing powers, brackets, multiplication and division, the correct order of operations is given on the right.

> **Order of operations**
> 1. Brackets
> 2. Powers or square roots
> 3. Multiplication and division
> 4. Addition and subtraction

Example 2

Find the value of $12(5 - 3) + 3 \times 2^2 - 4\sqrt{25}$.

$12(5 - 3) + 3 \times 2^2 - 4\sqrt{25} = 12(2) + 3 \times 4 - 4 \times 5$ ... brackets, powers and
square roots first

$= 24 + 12 - 20$ ... multiplication

$= 36 - 20$ ... addition and subtraction

$= 16$

Exercise 16.1

1. Write each of these in index form:
   - (i) $2 \times 2 \times 2$
   - (ii) $5 \times 5 \times 5 \times 5$
   - (iii) $6 \times 6 \times 6 \times 6 \times 6$
   - (iv) $a \times a \times a$
   - (v) $k \times k \times k \times k$
   - (vi) $(-2) \times (-2) \times (-2)$

2. Write each of these as a single number without a power:
   - (i) 3^2
   - (ii) 2^3
   - (iii) 4^3
   - (iv) 10^3
   - (v) $(-2)^4$

3. Write each of the following as a single number to a power:
   - (i) 3×3
   - (ii) $6 \times 6 \times 6$
   - (iii) $3^2 \times 3^3$
   - (iv) $5^4 \times 5^2$
   - (v) 5×5^2
   - (vi) $3^4 \times 3^3$
   - (vii) $5 \times 5^2 \times 5^3$
   - (viii) $2^4 \times 2 \times 2^3$

4. Find the missing power in each of these:
   - (i) $2^\square = 8$
   - (ii) $3^\square = 27$
   - (iii) $2^\square = 16$
   - (iv) $10^\square = 100$
   - (v) $6^\square = 36$
   - (vi) $5^\square = 125$
   - (vii) $10^\square = 1000$
   - (viii) $2^\square = 32$

5. Work out the value of each of these:
   - (i) 3×2^2
   - (ii) 2×3^2
   - (iii) 4×2^3
   - (iv) 2×5^2
   - (v) $2^2 \times 3^2$
   - (vi) 2×6^2
   - (vii) $4^2 \div 2$
   - (viii) $4^3 \div 2^2$

6. Evaluate each of these:
   - (i) $(-2)^2$
   - (ii) $(-3)^3$
   - (iii) $-2 \times (-3)^2$
   - (iv) $4 \times (-2)^3$

7. Write each of these in the form $a^n \times b^n$:
   - (i) $2 \times 2 \times 3 \times 3$
   - (ii) $3 \times 3 \times 4 \times 4 \times 4$
   - (iii) $5 \times 5 \times 5 \times 3 \times 3$
   - (iv) $4 \times a \times a \times 4$
   - (v) $3 \times a \times a \times a \times 3^2$
   - (vi) $5^2 \times 5a^2 \times a$

8. Express as a single number to a power:
   - (i) 9
   - (ii) 25
   - (iii) 27
   - (iv) 1000
   - (v) 81
   - (vi) 64

9. Express as a single number in index form:

(i) $\dfrac{5^4}{5^2}$ (ii) $\dfrac{3^5}{3}$ (iii) $\dfrac{7^5}{7^3}$ (iv) $\dfrac{3^8}{3^4}$ (v) $\dfrac{5^8}{5}$ (vi) $\dfrac{7^6}{7^4}$

10. Find the value of each of these:

(i) 8×10^2 (ii) 1.5×10^2 (iii) 7.6×10^3 (iv) 0.3×10^3 (v) 0.07×10^2

11. Simplify each of these and express your answer as a whole number:

(i) $\dfrac{2^4 \times 2^2}{2^3}$ (ii) $\dfrac{4^3 \times 4}{4^2}$ (iii) $\dfrac{3^7 \times 3}{3^6}$ (iv) $\dfrac{7^6 \times 7^2}{7^5}$

12. Write each of these as a whole number:

(i) $(2^2)^2$ (ii) $(2^2)^3$ (iii) $(3^2)^2$ (iv) $(2^3)^2$ (v) $(10^2)^2$

13. State whether each of the following statements is true or false:

(i) $5^2 = 5 \times 2$ (ii) $3^2 > 2^3$ (iii) $2^6 < 5^2$ (iv) $3^4 < 6^2$

14. Express as a single number:

(i) $(2 \times 3)^2$ (ii) $(4 \times 2)^2$ (iii) $(2 \times 5)^2$ (iv) $(\frac{1}{3} \times 9)^2$ (v) $\left(\dfrac{20}{5}\right)^3$

15. Express each of these as a single number:

(i) $\sqrt{9}$ (ii) $3\sqrt{4}$ (iii) $\sqrt{81}$ (iv) $2\sqrt{64}$

(v) $\sqrt{9} \times \sqrt{36}$ (vi) $6\sqrt{4}$ (vii) $\dfrac{\sqrt{36}}{\sqrt{4}}$ (viii) $\dfrac{2\sqrt{144}}{\sqrt{36}}$

(ix) $\dfrac{\sqrt{81} \times \sqrt{4}}{\sqrt{9}}$ (x) $\dfrac{6\sqrt{49}}{14}$

16. Find the value of each of these:

(i) $2^2 + \sqrt{25}$ (ii) $3^3 \times 4 + \sqrt{36}$ (iii) $3 \times 2^3 + 2\sqrt{25}$ (iv) $2^3(\sqrt{81} - 7)$

17. Find the value of each of these:

(i) $4^{\frac{1}{2}}$ (ii) $9^{\frac{1}{2}}$ (iii) $100^{\frac{1}{2}}$ (iv) $\dfrac{64^{\frac{1}{2}}}{4^{\frac{1}{2}}}$ (v) $\dfrac{144^{\frac{1}{2}}}{16^{\frac{1}{2}}}$

18. Evaluate each of the following:

(i) $3(2^2 + \sqrt{16})$ (ii) $3 \times 2^2 - 3 \times \sqrt{9}$

(iii) $4 \times \sqrt{25} + 2^2(\sqrt{4} + 2)$ (iv) $\sqrt{25} \times 2^2 + 2(\sqrt{16} - 2)$

(v) $2^4 + 3 \times 4^2 - \sqrt{144}$ (vi) $2^2 \times 3 + \dfrac{3 \times \sqrt{36}}{9}$

19. Find the value of the index n in each of these:

(i) $4^n = 16$ (ii) $2^n = 8$ (iii) $3^n = 27$ (iv) $2^2 \times 2^4 = 2^n$

(v) $3^4 \times 3^n = 3^7$ (vi) $3^5 \times 3^n = 3^8$ (vii) $\dfrac{5^4 \times 5^2}{5^n} = 5^3$ (viii) $64 = (4 \times 2)^n$

20. Copy and complete these:

(i) $3^2 \times 5^3 \times 5^4 \times 3^6 = 3^\square \times 5^\square$ (ii) $2 \times 9^2 \times 2^5 \times 9^3 = 2^\square \times 9^\square$

(iii) $4^7 \times 3^\square \times 4 \times 3^2 = 3^{10} \times 4^\square$ (iv) $3^4 \times 11^\square \times 3^\square \times 11^5 = 3^5 \times 11^8$

21. Which of these statements is false?

A $2^5 \times 3^4 \times 2^2 = 2^7 \times 3^4$ **B** $5^2 \times 6^3 \times 5^4 \times 6 = 5^6 \times 6^4$ **C** $2^2 \times 3^5 = 6^7$

22. If $a = 4$ and $b = 3$, find the value of the following:

(i) $a^2 + 2b$ (ii) $\sqrt{a} + b^2$ (iii) $2a + b^2$ (iv) $\sqrt{a^2 + b^2}$

(v) $2a^2 + b$ (vi) $2b^2 + 3\sqrt{a}$ (vii) $a^2b - 2b$ (viii) $\dfrac{2a + 3\sqrt{a}}{b^2 - 2}$.

Section 16.2 Numbers in standard form

If you use your calculator to perform the operation $60\,000 \times 4\,600\,000$, the screen will display the number 2.76×10^{11}.

This represents the number 2.76 multiplied by 10 eleven times.

The number 2.76×10^{11} is written in **scientific notation** or **standard form**.

Standard form is a convenient kind of shorthand for writing very large and very small numbers.

Definition

> A number in the form $\boldsymbol{a \times 10^n}$, where $1 \leqslant a < 10$, and n is an integer, is said to be expressed in scientific notation or standard form.

Example

$$6.8 \times 10^4$$

This part is written as a number between 1 and 10.

This part is written as a power of 10.

Here are some numbers written in standard form:

(i) $450 = 4.5 \times 100 = 4.5 \times 10^2$

(ii) $5000 = 5 \times 1000 = 5 \times 10^3$

(iii) $64\,000 = 64 \times 1000 = 6.4 \times 10\,000 = 6.4 \times 10^4$

(iv) $380\,000 = 3.8 \times 10^5$

Notice that if you move the decimal point

(i) 1 place to the **left**, multiply by 10^1

(ii) 2 places to the **left**, multiply by 10^2

(iii) 3 places to the **left**, multiply by 10^3 …

 On your calculator, there is an $\boxed{\text{EXP}}$ or $\boxed{\times 10^x}$ key which stands for 'exponential' or 10 to any power.

To change the number 2.54×10^3 to decimal form, key in $2.54 \boxed{\text{EXP}} 3 \boxed{=}$.

The calculator will display 2540.

Adding and subtracting numbers in standard form

To add or subtract numbers expressed in standard form, convert each number to a decimal number and then perform the addition or subtraction.
You may also use a calculator, as shown in the following example.

Example 1

Express in standard form: $1.84 \times 10^2 + 8.7 \times 10^3$.

$1.84 \times 10^2 = 184$ and $8.7 \times 10^3 = 8700$

$\therefore$ $1.84 \times 10^2 + 8.7 \times 10^3 = 184 + 8700$

$= 8884$

$= 8.884 \times 10^3$

 Key in $1.84 \boxed{10^x} 2 + 8.7 \boxed{10^x} 3 \boxed{=}$

The result displayed is 8884 which is 8.884×10^3.

Multiplying and dividing numbers in standard form

To multiply (or divide) numbers expressed in standard form, first multiply (or divide) the 'a parts' and then multiply (or divide) the numbers expressed as powers of 10.
The calculator is particularly useful in these operations.

Thus, $(2.6 \times 10^2) \times (5.5 \times 10^3) = (2.6 \times 5.5) \times (10^2 \times 10^3)$

$$= 14.3 \times 10^{2+3}$$
$$= 14.3 \times 10^5$$
$$= 1.43 \times 10^6$$

This number ('a part') must be less than 10.

Example 2

Express $(3.6 \times 10^5) \div (1.2 \times 10^3)$ in standard form.

$$(3.6 \times 10^5) \div (1.2 \times 10^3) = \frac{3.6 \times 10^5}{1.2 \times 10^3}$$
$$= \frac{3.6}{1.2} \times \frac{10^5}{10^3}$$
$$= 3 \times 10^{5-3} = 3 \times 10^2$$

Exercise 16.2

1. Which of the following numbers are written in scientific notation?
  (i) 2.4×10^2 (ii) 0.8×10^4 (iii) 27.4×10^3 (iv) 8.9×10^4

2. Write each of the following as a decimal number:
  (i) 2×10^2 (ii) 3.4×10^2 (iii) 5.7×10^3 (iv) 2.84×10^4
  (v) 5.81×10^2 (vi) 2.94×10^3 (vii) 1.837×10^4 (viii) 9.843×10^3

3. Explain why 30×10^3 is not written in standard form.

4. Write each of these numbers in standard form:
  (i) 28   (ii) 64   (iii) 80   (iv) 150   (v) 467

5. Express these numbers in standard form:
  (i) 400   (ii) 650   (iii) 2000   (iv) 2700   (v) 6920

6. Express these numbers in the form $a \times 10^n$, where $1 \leqslant a < 10, n \in N$;
  (i) 7800   (ii) 946   (iii) 15 400   (iv) 38 900

7. Express each of these in scientific notation:
  (i) 2400   (ii) 12 800   (iii) 80×10^2 (iv) 12.9×10^3

8. (i) Add 643 and 78 and express your answer in scientific notation.

    (ii) Multiply 320 by 0.8 and express your answer in scientific notation.

9. Write each of the following as a single whole number:

    (i) $3 \times 10^2 + 2.8 \times 10^2$ (ii) $1.4 \times 10^2 + 3.7 \times 10^2$

    (iii) $5.4 \times 10^3 + 9.6 \times 10^3$ (iv) $4.7 \times 10^3 + 8.3 \times 10^3$

10. Express $6.8 \times 10^3 - 5.2 \times 10^2$ in the form $a \times 10^n$, where $1 \leqslant a < 10, n \in N$.

Add or subtract each of the following and express your answer in standard form:

11. $5 \times 10^2 + 8.9 \times 10^2$ **12.** $6.87 \times 10^2 + 1.92 \times 10^2$

13. $3.4 \times 10^3 + 5.8 \times 10^2$ **14.** $8.94 \times 10^3 + 6.24 \times 10^2$

15. $9.4 \times 10^3 - 6.4 \times 10^2$ **16.** $1.8 \times 10^3 - 9.4 \times 10^2$

17. $9.46 \times 10^4 + 1.8 \times 10^3$ **18.** $6.85 \times 10^3 + 9.84 \times 10^2$

Write each of the following as a single whole number:

19. $(4 \times 10) \times (3 \times 10^2)$ **20.** $(1.4 \times 10^2) \times (5 \times 10)$

21. $(3.8 \times 10^2) \times (4 \times 10^2)$ **22.** $(5.3 \times 10^2) \times (2 \times 10^2)$

Express each of the following as a single number expressed in scientific notation:

23. $(6 \times 10^2) \times (4 \times 10^2)$ **24.** $(5 \times 10^2) \times (3 \times 10^3)$

25. $(7 \times 10^2) \times (8 \times 10^4)$ **26.** $(1.5 \times 10^2) \times (5 \times 10^3)$

27. $(4.7 \times 10^3) \times (7 \times 10^2)$ **28.** $(8.5 \times 10^3) \times (9 \times 10^4)$

29. $(6 \times 10^2) \times (3.8 \times 10^4)$ **30.** $(4.8 \times 10^4) \times (8 \times 10^2)$

Simplify each of the following and express your answer in scientific notation:

31. $\dfrac{5 \times 10^3}{2 \times 10^2}$ **32.** $\dfrac{8 \times 10^6}{4 \times 10^3}$ **33.** $\dfrac{7.2 \times 10^4}{6 \times 10^2}$ **34.** $\dfrac{9.5 \times 10^4}{5 \times 10}$

35. The Earth's diameter is 1.27×10^4 km and the diameter of Mars is 6.8×10^3 km.

    (i) Which planet has the larger diameter?

    (ii) What is the difference between their diameters?

    (iii) What is the total if the two diameters are added? Give your answer in standard form.

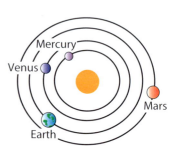

36. This table shows the lengths of five well-known rivers.

River	km (thousands)
Nile	6.65
Yangtze-Kiang	6.3
Congo	4.7
Danube	2.84
Seine	0.78

   (i)   In kilometres, the length of the Nile is 6650 km. Write the lengths of the other rivers in kilometres.

   (ii)   Express the length of the Congo in scientific notation.

   (iii) Express the length of the Seine in scientific notation.

   (iv) What is the missing number in this statement?
   'The length of the Congo is about ☐ times the length of the Seine.'

Section 16.3 Reciprocals and use of calculator

1. Reciprocals

The **reciprocal** of a number is $\dfrac{1}{\text{number}}$.

The reciprocal of 5 is $\frac{1}{5}$; the reciprocal of 1.8 is $\frac{1}{1.8}$.

When a number and its reciprocal are multiplied, the result is 1, e.g., $\dfrac{\overset{1}{3}}{\underset{1}{4}} \times \dfrac{\overset{1}{4}}{\underset{1}{3}} = 1$.

The reciprocal of 12.8 is $\frac{1}{12.8}$.

This can be found using your calculator by keying in 1 ÷ 12.8 = .

The result is 0.078.

2. Powers and roots

The examples below show the procedures for finding powers and roots of numbers on your calculator.

Operation	Example
(i) To find the **square root** of a number, use the $\sqrt{\ }$ key.	To find $\sqrt{28}$, key in $\sqrt{\ }$ 28 = The result is 5.29.
(ii) To find the **cube root** of a number, use the $\sqrt[3]{\ }$ key.	To find $\sqrt[3]{27}$, key in SHIFT $\sqrt[3]{\ }$ 27 = The result is 3.
(iii) To find the **square** of a number, use the x^2 key.	To find 24^2, key in 24 x^2 = The result is 576.
(iv) To find 8^5 (or any power), use the $x^{\blacksquare}$ key.	To find 8^5, key in 8 $x^{\blacksquare}$ 5 = The result is 32768.

3. Operations on the calculator

When using your calculator to find the value of $\dfrac{14 \times 15}{50 - 29}$, always enclose the denominator in brackets.

Now try $\dfrac{14 \times 15}{(50 - 29)}$. You should get 10.

If you omit the brackets, you will get -28.4, an incorrect answer.

Example 1

Use your calculator to evaluate $\dfrac{12.42 \times 23.47}{13.48 + 5.73}$, correct to two decimal places.

Insert brackets around the denominator and key in

$12.42 \boxed{\times} 23.47 \boxed{\div} \boxed{(} 13.48 \boxed{+} 5.73 \boxed{)} \boxed{=}$

The result is 15.17.

Example 2

Use your calculator to find the value of $\dfrac{3}{17.4} + 2\sqrt{74}$, correct to 2 decimal places.

In this example, the calculator will perform the operations in the correct order.

Key in $3 \boxed{\div} 17.4 \boxed{+} 2 \boxed{\times} \boxed{\sqrt{}} 74 \boxed{=}$

The result is 17.3770 …

$\qquad\qquad = 17.38$

Exercise 16.3

1. Write down the reciprocal of each of these numbers:

    (i)   4   (ii)   12   (iii) $\dfrac{1}{3}$ (iv) $\dfrac{2}{5}$ (v) $\dfrac{5}{4}$

2. Use your calculator to find the value of each of these, correct to two decimal places.

    (i) $\dfrac{1}{9}$ (ii) $\dfrac{1}{12}$ (iii) $\dfrac{1}{23}$ (iv) $\dfrac{1}{12.6}$ (v) $\dfrac{3}{8.9}$

Use your calculator to find the value of each of the following:

3. $(15)^2$ **4.** $(34)^2$ **5.** $(6.3)^2$ **6.** $(12.4)^2$ **7.** $(32)^2$

8. $(26.1)^2$ **9.** $(1.8)^2$ **10.** $(0.9)^2$ **11.** $(9.2)^2$ **12.** $(0.54)^2$

Evaluate each of the following, correct to 1 decimal place:

13. $\sqrt{12}$ **14.** $\sqrt{54}$ **15.** $\sqrt{158}$ **16.** $\sqrt{923}$ **17.** $\sqrt{58.5}$

18. $\sqrt{98.62}$ **19.** $\sqrt{1596}$ **20.** $\sqrt{2348}$ **21.** $\sqrt{0.84}$ **22.** $\sqrt{0.68}$

Evaluate these correct to 2 decimal places, where necessary:

23. $3\sqrt{48}$ **24.** $5\sqrt{105}$ **25.** $3 \times (18)^2$ **26.** $23 \times (4.8)^2$

27. $6\sqrt{96.4}$ **28.** $0.7 \times (5.6)^2$ **29.** $68 \div \sqrt{14}$ **30.** $2.5 \times (4.3)^2$

31. Use your calculator to verify that $\dfrac{48 \times 64}{16 + 24} = 76.8$.

32. Use your calculator to evaluate each of these, correct to one decimal place:

     (i) $\dfrac{12.4 \times 5.9}{(3.7 \times 2.5)}$ (ii) $\dfrac{42.3 + 18.4}{16.7 \times 0.4}$ (iii) $\dfrac{81.73 - 21.4}{3.87 \times 1.25}$

33. Evaluate each of these correct to 2 decimal places:

     (i) $\dfrac{32}{14^2}$ (ii) $\dfrac{\sqrt{26}}{4}$ (iii) $\dfrac{2 \times \sqrt{40}}{3}$ (iv) $\dfrac{(12.8)^2}{3.7}$ (v) $\dfrac{15.4}{\sqrt{38}}$

Section 16.4 Significant figures – Approximation

There are many occasions when it is either desirable or necessary to **round off** large or small numbers to a reasonable degree of accuracy. If there were 12 946 people at a football match, it would be reasonable to state that the attendance was about 13 000. We say that 13 000 is given 'correct to the nearest thousand'. Similarly, 1.823 could be rounded off to 1.8.

With the widespread use of calculators, it is important that we have some idea or estimate of the answer we expect to get. Then we will know whether the answer shown on the calculator is reasonable or not. To make a rough estimate of a calculation, we generally give decimals correct to 1 or 2 decimal places and we round whole numbers to the nearest 10, 100 or 1000, as appropriate.

1. Decimal places

When writing a decimal correct to a given number of decimal places, count each digit, including zero, after the decimal point. If the last digit is 5 or more, increase the previous digit by 1. If the last digit is 4 or less, leave the previous digit as it is.

Thus, 6.8537 = 6.854, correct to 3 decimal places
               = 6.85, correct to 2 decimal places
               = 6.9, correct to 1 decimal place.

2. Significant figures

If the attendance at a football match was 34 176, it would be reasonable to write down 34 200 or 34 000 or even 30 000.

> 34 200 is written correct to 3 significant figures.
> 34 000 is written correct to 2 significant figures
> 30 000 is written correct to 1 significant figure.

When expressing a whole number correct to a given number of significant figures, zeros at the end of the number are not counted but must be included in the final result. All other zeros are significant.

Thus, 52 764 = 52 760, correct to 4 significant figures
               = 52 800, correct to 3 significant figures
               = 53 000, correct to 2 significant figures
               = 50 000, correct to 1 significant figure.

The number 70 425 = 70 400, correct to 3 significant figures.
Notice here that the zero between the 7 and 4 is significant, but the two final zeros are not.

If a number is less than 1, then the zeros immediately after the decimal point are not significant.

Thus, (i) 0.07406 = 0.0741, correct to 3 significant figures.
      (ii) 0.00892 = 0.0089, correct to 2 significant figures.

Here are some numbers written correct to 1 significant figure:

| 376.2 | 72.81 | 4.053 | 0.632 | 0.0873 |
| 400 | 70 | 4 | 0.6 | 0.09 |

3. Making an Estimate

If a calculation involves a mixture of numbers greater than and less than 1, then to make an estimate of the answer,
 (i) round numbers greater than 1 correct to one significant figure
(ii) round numbers less than 1 correct to one decimal place.

Example 1

Make a rough estimate of $\dfrac{10.25 + 29.83}{0.24 \times 46}$.

$$\frac{10.25 + 29.83}{0.24 \times 46} \approx \frac{10 + 30}{0.2 \times 50} = \frac{40}{10} = 4$$

A rough estimate is 4.
(The result, using a calculator is 3.63…)

Exercise 16.4

1. Write each of the numbers correct to the nearest 10:

(i) 84   (ii) 97   (iii) 31   (iv) 128   (v) 434

2. Write these numbers to the nearest 100:

(i) 283   (ii) 134   (iii) 675   (iv) 1852   (v) 7355

3. Write these numbers to the nearest 1000:

(i) 796   (ii) 2359   (iii) 9215   (iv) 17 592   (v) 28 199

4. Write each of these numbers correct to one decimal place:

(i) 1.37   (ii) 12.32   (iii) 0.48   (iv) 12.06   (v) 0.678

5. How many significant figures are there in each of these numbers?

(i) 60   (ii) 240   (iii) 700   (iv) 2500   (v) 31 800

6. Round these numbers to one significant figure:

(i) 68   (ii) 41   (iii) 326   (iv) 587   (v) 2851

7. Round these numbers to two significant figures:

(i) 584   (ii) 989   (iii) 2926   (iv) 5884   (v) 24 676

8. Write a headline for each of these stories, with each number rounded to one significant figure.

(i) 5182 people join a protest march.

(ii) 38 426 people attend an open-air concert.

9. Round these numbers to two significant figures:

(i) 0.473   (ii) 0.06312   (iii) 2.384   (iv) 0.669   (v) 54.839

10. To what number is the arrow pointing?
Now write this number

(i) correct to 2 significant figures

(ii) correct to 1 significant figure.

11. Round each number correct to one significant figure and hence make an estimate of each of these:

(i) $\dfrac{56 \times 18}{28}$ (ii) $\dfrac{19.48 + 43.2}{10.4 \times 2.8}$ (iii) $\dfrac{183 \times 46.4}{77.4}$

12. Round all the numbers to the nearest whole number and hence estimate the answer to each of these:

(i) $\dfrac{2.75 \times 8.34}{5.24 + 2.74}$ (ii) $\dfrac{0.73 \times 12.42}{1.75 + 2.38}$ (iii) $\dfrac{6.28 + \sqrt{4.3}}{0.65 \times \sqrt{8.57}}$

13. Sally estimates the value of $\dfrac{42.8 \times 63.7}{285}$ to be 8.

Write down three numbers Sally could use to get her estimate: $\dfrac{\cdots \cdots \times \cdots \cdots}{\cdots \cdots}$

14. By rounding numbers less than 1 correct to one decimal place and other numbers to one significant figure, make a rough estimate of these calculations:

(i) $\dfrac{807}{391.3 \times 0.37}$ (ii) $\dfrac{31.69 \times 6.25}{0.473}$ (iii) $\dfrac{324 \times 2.76}{196 \times 0.54}$

Test yourself 16

1. (a) The attendance at a football match was 46 374.
   Write this number correct to
   (i) the nearest 100   (ii) the nearest 1000   (iii) the nearest ten thousand.

   (b) Find the value of each of these:
   (i) 3×4^2 (ii) $3^2 \times 4 - \sqrt{16}$ (iii) $2^3 \times 3^2$.

   (c) (i) Write 7400 in scientific notation.
   (ii) Express $1.8 \times 10^2 + 6.7 \times 10^3$ as a single whole number.

2. (a) Put 2^5, 3^4, 4^2 and $\sqrt{144}$ in order of size, starting with the smallest.

   (b) Find x in the following:
   (i) $100 = 10^x$ (ii) $36 = 6^x$ (iii) $x^3 = 27$ (iv) $x^4 = 16$

   (c) Write (i) 4×10^2 (ii) 7.3×10^3 as single numbers.
   Now write $(4 \times 10^2) + (7.3 \times 10^3)$ as a single number in scientific notation.

3. (a) Find the value of each of these:

(i) $4 \times 5^2 - 3 \times 4$ (ii) $5\sqrt{16} + 2 \times (6)^2$

(b) (i) Write 2.83×10^3 as a single number.

(ii) Write 7930 in scientific notation.

(c) Which two of the following have the same value?

(i) 2^4 (ii) $64^{\frac{1}{2}}$ (iii) $4\sqrt{16}$ (iv) $2 \times \sqrt{9}$ (v) $\dfrac{8^2}{\sqrt{4}}$

4. (a) Express as a single number $\dfrac{2 \times 3^2 + 2^4}{2^2 \times 5 - 3}$

(b) By rounding each number to the nearest 100, find an estimate of the value of

$$\frac{236 \times 453}{202 \times 149}$$

(c) Express 6.8×10^2 and 9×10^3 as whole numbers.
Hence express $6.8 \times 10^2 + 9 \times 10^3$ in the form $a \times 10^n$,
where $1 \leqslant a < 10, n \in N$.

5. (a) Find the value of each of these:

(i) $3\sqrt{25} - 2^2 \times 3$ (ii) $\dfrac{3^4}{3^2}$

(b) Simplify each of these:

(i) $\dfrac{x^2 \times x^4}{x^3}$ (ii) $2a^2 \times 4a^3$ (iii) $\dfrac{4a^3 \times 3a^4}{2a^2}$

(c) Use your calculator to evaluate the following correct to 2 decimal places:

$$\frac{4}{17} + (18.3)^2 - 3\sqrt{47}.$$

6. (a) Find the value of $2^3 + 4\sqrt{9} - 16^{\frac{1}{2}} + 3^2 \times 2\sqrt{25}$.

(b) (i) Write 3.74×10^3 as a whole number.

(ii) Express 5820 in standard form.

(c) Use your calculator to evaluate, correct to two decimal places:

$$\frac{14.8}{27.3} + 3 \times (2.9)^2 - \sqrt{38}.$$

(d) Sort these into four matching pairs.

 A $4 \times 10\,000$
B $4.7 \times 10\,000\,000$
C 4.7×10^6
D $47 \times 100\,000$

E 400×1000
F 40×10^3
G 0.47×10^8
H 4×10^5

17 Circles and Cylinders

Key words

circumference   centre   area   radius   diameter   sector
arc   segment   quadrant   semicircle   cylinder   volume
curved surface area

Section 17.1 The circumference of a circle

The **circle** on the right was drawn by placing the point of a compass at O.

The point O is called the **centre** of the circle.

The line that traces the circle is called the **circumference**.

The terms that we will use when dealing with circles are given in the diagrams below:

Length of circumference

> Mark a point on the circumference of a 20 cent coin.
> Place the coin on the ruler with the mark pointing to the scale, as shown.
> Roll the coin along the ruler until the mark returns again to the scale.
> Read the length of the circumference from the ruler and you will find that it is a little more than three times the length of the diameter.

The circumference is slightly more than 3 diameters.

The number by which we multiply the diameter to get the circumference is represented by the greek letter π (pronounced 'pie').

π has no exact decimal or fraction value.

However, when using decimals, we generally use **3.142** as an approximate value.

When using fractions, we use $\frac{22}{7}$ as an approximate value.

> **Approximate values for π**
>
> $\pi = 3.142$ or $\pi = \frac{22}{7}$

Circumference of a circle

> The length of the circumference of a circle is
> $$2\pi r \quad \text{or} \quad \pi d$$
> where r = radius and d = diameter

 The π key on your calculator gives a more exact value than 3.142 or $\frac{22}{7}$. When using your calculator, you should use this key unless told otherwise.

Perimeter of a sector

A **sector** is part of a circle that is bounded by two radii and an arc.

To find the arc length, ℓ, of a sector, we divide the angle in the sector by 360° to get a fraction.

Then we find this fraction of the circumference.

> Length of arc:
> $$\ell = \frac{\theta}{360°} \times 2\pi r$$

Example 1

Find the length of the circumference of this circle using 3.14 as an approximation for π.

$$\begin{aligned}
\text{Circumference} &= 2\pi r \\
&= 2 \times 3.14 \times 12 \quad \text{... } r = 12 \\
&= 75.36 \text{ cm} \\
&= 75.4 \text{ cm, correct to 1 decimal place}
\end{aligned}$$

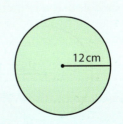

12 cm

Example 2

The diagram on the right shows a sector of a circle of radius 21 cm.
Find the length of the perimeter of this figure.
Use $\frac{22}{7}$ as an approximation for π.

The perimeter consists of the arc AB and two radii.
$60° = \frac{1}{6}$ of 360°, so the arc AB is $\frac{1}{6}$ of the circumference.

Length of arc AB $= \frac{1}{6} \times 2\pi r$

$= \frac{1}{6} \times \frac{2}{1} \times \frac{22}{7} \times \frac{21}{1}$

$= 22$ cm

Total perimeter $= 22 + 21 + 21 = 64$ cm

Exercise 17.1

1. Name the feature shown, in red, on each circle.

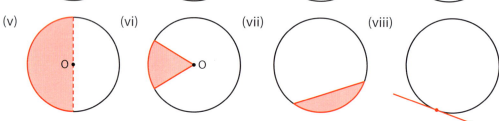

(i) (ii) (iii) (iv)

(v) (vi) (vii) (viii)

2. Calculate the circumference of each of these circles, using $\pi = 3.14$.

(i) 10 cm (ii) 4 cm (iii) 12 cm (iv) 9 cm

3. Using the approximation $\pi = \frac{22}{7}$, find the circumference of each circle:

(i)

14 cm

(ii)

21 cm

(iii)

35 cm

(iv)
14 cm

4. Using the π key on your calculator, find the circumference of each of these circles. Give each answer correct to 1 decimal place.

(i)

8 cm

(ii)

21 cm

(iii)

11 cm

(iv)

18 cm

5. Using 3.14 as an approximate value for π, calculate the lengths of the circumferences of these circles.

  (i) radius = 13 cm   (ii) diameter = 30 cm   (iii) radius = 40 cm

6. Find the length of the arc AB in each of these sectors, taking $\pi = \frac{22}{7}$.

(i)

A
B
21 cm

(ii)

A
45°
14 cm
B

(iii)

A
120°
28 cm
B

7. Find the perimeters of these shapes, taking $\pi = \frac{22}{7}$.

(i)

28 cm

(ii)

60°
14 cm

(iii)

7 cm

8. Find the perimeter of each of these shapes.
Give each answer correct to the nearest whole number.

(i)

(ii)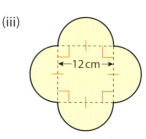

(iii)

9. Taking $\pi = 3.142$, work out the perimeter of the given shaded figure, correct to the nearest cm.

10. Which is the shorter path from A to B

(i) along the 4 semicircles, or
(ii) along the larger semicircle ?

11. Tape has been placed along all lines of this indoor hockey pitch.
How much tape was used?
Give your answer correct to the nearest metre.

12. Kevin's dad has a measuring wheel with a 5-digit counter.
The radius of the wheel is 12 cm.

(i) Find the circumference of the measuring wheel in metres, correct to two decimal places.
(ii) Kevin and his dad use this to measure the length of the school football pitch.
The counter shows a reading of 106 revolutions.
How long is the pitch?
Give your answer to the nearest metre.

Section 17.2 **The area of a circle**

If the 12 sectors of the circle below are cut neatly, they can be formed into a 'rectangle', as shown.

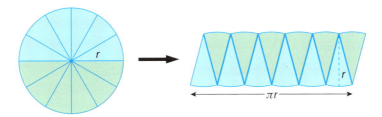

Explain why the length of the rectangle is πr and its height is r.

What is the area of the rectangle?

Explain why the area of the circle is πr^2.

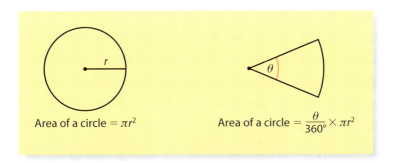

Area of a circle $= \pi r^2$

Area of a circle $= \dfrac{\theta}{360°} \times \pi r^2$

Example 1

(i) Find the area of a circle of radius 14 cm. (Take $\pi = \frac{22}{7}$)

(ii) Find the radius of a circle of area 1386 cm².
Use the π key on your calculator and give your answer correct to the nearest whole number.

(i) Area $= \pi r^2$

$\qquad = \dfrac{22}{7} \times 14^2$

$\qquad = \dfrac{22}{1\,7} \times \dfrac{14^{\,2}}{1} \times \dfrac{14}{1}$

$\qquad = 616 \text{ cm}^2$

(ii) $\pi r^2 = 1386$

$\qquad r^2 = \dfrac{1386}{\pi}$

$\qquad r^2 = 441.178$

$\qquad r = \sqrt{441.178} = 21.004$

$\qquad r = 21 \text{ cm}$

Exercise 17.2

1. Find the area of each of these circles, using $\pi = 3.14$.

(i)
10 cm

(ii)
4 cm

(iii)

12 mm

(iv)

9 cm

2. Using the approximation $\pi = \frac{22}{7}$, find the area of each circle:

(i)
14 cm

(ii)

21 cm

(iii)

35 m

(iv)
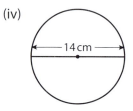
14 cm

3. Use the π key on your calculator to find the area of each of these circles, correct to 1 decimal place:

(i)
8 cm

(ii)
21 cm

(iii)

11 cm

(iv)

18 mm

4. What fraction of the area of a complete circle is each of these sectors?

(i)

(ii)
120°

(iii)

60°

(iv)
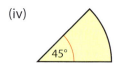
45°

5. Using $\pi = \frac{22}{7}$, find the area of each of these sectors:

(i)

42 cm

(ii)

45°
14 cm

(iii)

120°
28 cm

6. Using $\pi = 3.14$, find the area of each of these shapes.

(i)

(ii)

(iii)

Give each answer correct to one place of decimals.

7. The area of each circle below is given in terms of π.
Find the length of the radius of each circle.

(i)

(ii)

(iii)

8. The area of a circle is 154 cm². Taking $\pi = \frac{22}{7}$, find
  (i) the length of the radius
  (ii) the length of the circumference.

9. Write down the formula for the length of the circumference of a circle.
The circumference of a circle is 88 cm. Taking $\pi = \frac{22}{7}$, find
  (i) the length of the radius
  (ii) the area of the circle.

10. (i) Write down the length of the side of
     the given square.
  (ii) Taking $\pi = \frac{22}{7}$, find the area of the
     shaded part of the figure.

11. The circumference of a circle is 220 cm.
Taking $\pi = \frac{22}{7}$, find
  (i) the radius
  (ii) the area of the circle.

12. Work out the area of each of these figures.
Take $\pi = 3.14$ and give each answer correct to the nearest cm².

(i)

← 8 cm →

(ii)

7 cm

10 cm

(iii)

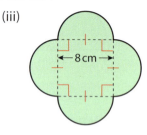

8 cm

13. Work out the area of the shaded region
between the given pair of circles.
Take $\pi = 3.142$ and give your answer correct
to two decimal places.

5 cm   2 cm

14. A circle was cut out of the square, as shown in the diagram.
Using $\pi = = 3.14$, the area of the circle was found to be
28.26 cm².

(i) What was the side length of the square?

(ii) What area of cardboard was left after the circle had
been removed?

Section 17.3 Cylinders

The cylinder on the right has a circular top and base,
and vertical sides.
The volume of this cylinder is the area of the base
multiplied by its height.

$\therefore$ volume $= \pi r^2 h$

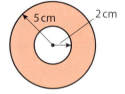

r

h

Surface area of closed cylinder

The surface area of a cylinder consists of the top and bottom circles added to the curved
surface area.

To calculate the area of the curved surface, imagine that the cylinder is hollow.
If we cut the curved surface along the dotted line and flattened it out, it would
form a rectangle.

The area of this rectangle would obviously be the same as the area of the curved surface.

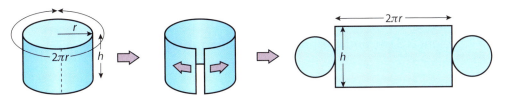

From the series of diagrams above, we see that the curved surface area is equivalent to a rectangle that has a length equal to the circumference of the cylinder and a width equal to the height of the cylinder. Using the formula for the area of a rectangle, we obtain:

Curved surface area $= 2\pi r \times h = 2\pi rh$

The total surface area $=$ curved surface area $+$ area of 2 circles
$$= 2\pi rh + 2\pi r^2$$

Cylinder

Volume $= \pi r^2 h$

Curved surface area $= 2\pi rh$

Total surface area $= 2\pi rh + 2\pi r^2$

Example 1

Find (i) the volume
    (ii) the total surface area
        of the cylinder shown, taking $\pi = \frac{22}{7}$.

14 cm
24 cm

Volume $= \pi r^2 h$

$= \pi \times 7^2 \times 24$ ... $r = \frac{14\,cm}{2}$, i.e. 7 cm

$= \frac{22}{7_1} \times \frac{7^1}{1} \times \frac{7}{1} \times \frac{24}{1}$

Volume $= 3696\,cm^3$

Total surface area $= 2\pi rh + 2\pi r^2$

$= 2 \times \left(\frac{22}{7} \times 7 \times 24\right) + \left(2 \times \frac{22}{7} \times 7^2\right)$

$= 1056 + 308$

Total surface area $= 1364\,cm^2$

Example 2

The volume of a cylinder is 1232 cm³.
If its height is 8 cm, find the length of its radius taking $\pi = 3.14$.
Give your answer correct to the nearest centimetre.

Volume $= 1232$ cm³ $\Rightarrow \pi r^2 h = 1232$

$$3.14 \times r^2 \times 8 = 1232$$

$$r^2 = \frac{1232}{3.14 \times 8}$$

$$r^2 = 49.04$$

$$r = \sqrt{49.04} = 7.0029$$

$$r = 7 \text{ cm}$$

The radius $= 7$ cm

Exercise 17.3

1. Taking $\pi = \frac{22}{7}$, find the volume of each of the cylinders shown below:

(i)

12 cm

7 cm

(ii)

14 cm

16 cm

(iii)

30 mm

28 mm

2. Find the total surface areas of the solid cylinders in Question **1.** above, taking $\pi = \frac{22}{7}$.
Give your answer correct to the nearest whole number where necessary.

3. Taking $\pi = 3.14$, find the volume of each of these cylinders.
Give your answers correct to the nearest whole numbers.

(i)

30 cm

24 cm

(ii)

8 m

4 m

(iii)

6 cm

50 cm

4. Taking $\pi = \frac{22}{7}$, find the volume of the
cylinder shown on the right.

If 1 litre = 1000 cm³, find the capacity of the
cylinder, correct to the nearest litre.

40 cm

28 cm

5. The figure on the right shows a solid
cylinder cut along its diameter.
Taking $\pi = 3.14$, find the volume of the figure in cm³.

5 cm

18 cm

6. The volume of the given cylinder is 350π cm³.
   (i) Write down the formula for the volume of
       a cylinder.
   (ii) Write in all the known values in the formula,
        given that the height is 14 cm.
   (iii) Now find the length of the radius of the cylinder.

14 cm

Volume =
350π cm³

7. The two given cylinders have the same
volume.
Find the height, h cm, of the cylinder on
the right.
All dimensions are in centimetres

9

8

h cm

6

8. The volume of a cylinder is 288π cm³.
If the height of the cylinder is 8 cm, find its radius.

9. The volume of a cylinder is 360π cm³.
If the radius of the cylinder is 6 cm, find its height.

10. Write down the formula for the curved surface area of a cylinder.
The curved surface area of a certain cylinder is 110 cm².
If the height of the cylinder is 5 cm, find the length of the radius correct to
1 decimal place.

11. The volume of a cylinder is 1848 cm³.
If the height of the cylinder is 12 cm, find its radius, taking $\pi = \frac{22}{7}$.

12. A hole of radius 4 cm is bored through this
    rectangular solid, as shown.
    Using the π key on your calculator, find the
    volume of the remaining solid, correct to
    the nearest cm^3.

13. A cylindrical metal pipe has an external diameter
    of 6 cm and an internal diameter of 4 cm, as shown.
    The pipe is 1 m long.
    Taking $\pi = 3.14$, find

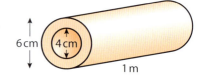

    (i) the volume of the pipe in cm^3
    (ii) the mass of the pipe, in kg, if 1 cm^3 of the metal has a mass of 9 g.

14. A cylindrical pencil holder has a diameter
    4 cm and height 14 cm. Taking $\pi = \frac{22}{7}$,
    find the volume of the holder in cm^3.

    Eight pencil holders are packed tightly
    into a rectangular box as shown.
    Find the volume of this box in cm^3.

15. Rain falls into a flat rectangular
    container 88 cm by 42 cm by 6 cm.
    When the container is full, it is
    poured into an empty cylinder of
    radius 21 cm. The depth of water
    in the cylinder is h cm.
    Find the value of h.
    Take $\pi = \frac{22}{7}$.

Test yourself 17

1. (a) Find   (i) the circumference
                   (ii) the area
of the given circle. Take $\pi = \frac{22}{7}$.

(b) Using $\pi = 3.14$, find

   (i) the volume

   (ii) the curved surface area of the given cylinder,
   correct to the nearest whole number.

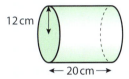

2. (a) The figure shown on the right has a
semicircular end.

Using $\pi = \frac{22}{7}$, find the area of the
figure in cm².

(b) The diagram shows a quadrant, AOB, of a
circle of radius 14 cm.

Taking $\pi = \frac{22}{7}$, find the area of the shaded
portion of the figure.

3. (a) The given figure consists of a square and a semicircle.
Taking $\pi = 3.14$, find correct to 1 decimal place,

   (i) the area of the figure
   (ii) the perimeter of the figure.

(b) A Christmas cracker has length 25 cm
and diameter 5 cm. A box contains
10 identical crackers arranged in
two layers, as shown.
What is the volume of the box?

4. (a) Find the area of the shaded part of the given
diagram if the radius of the larger circle is
10 cm and the radius of the smaller circle
is 5 cm.
Take $\pi = 3.14$.

(b) A cylindrical water tank has internal
diameter 40 cm and height 50 cm.
A cylindrical mug has internal diameter
8 cm and height 10 cm.

   (i) Find the volume of the tank
in terms of π.
   (ii) Find the volume of the mug in terms of π.
   (iii) How many mugs can be filled from a full tank?

5. (a) What fraction of a full circle is shown?
Taking $\pi = 3.14$, find the area of this sector.

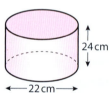

(b) Taking $\pi = 3.14$, find the volume of the given
cylinder, correct to the nearest cm^3.
If 1 litre $= 1000\ cm^3$, find the capacity of this
cylinder correct to the nearest litre.

6. (a) Circular tops for yoghurt cartons are cut from a strip of metal foil as shown below.
The radius of each top is 4 cm.
The gap between each top is 1 cm.
The gap between each top and the
edge of the strip is also 1 cm.

   (i) How many tops can be cut from a
strip of foil 7.02 metres long?
   (ii) Find the area of the remainder of the
strip is cm^2, correct to the nearest whole number.

(b) A cylindrical tank has radius 10 cm,
as shown. If the volume of the cylinder
is $4400\ cm^3$, find the height, h, of the tank.
Take $\pi = \frac{22}{7}$.

Geometry 2: Triangles and Circles

Key words

congruence	corresponding sides and angles	similar triangles
equiangular	theorem	converse of theorem	proportional
circumference	diameter	semicircle	segment	sector

Section 18.1 Congruent triangles

Two shapes are said to be **congruent** if they have the **exact same size and shape**.
One shape may be thought of as being an exact copy or duplicate of the other.
The following diagrams illustrate some pairs of congruent shapes, even though some of
these shapes are turned over or upside down.

The two triangles below are congruent because all the angles and sides of one triangle
are exactly the same as the angles and sides of the other triangle.

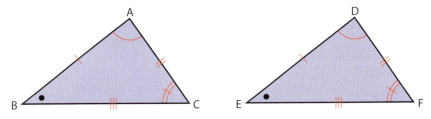

The angles marked with the dot ● are called **corresponding** angles.
Similarly, the sides [AC] and [DF] are corresponding because they are opposite
corresponding angles.

Sometimes it is not very obvious that two triangles are congruent.

Take, for example, these two triangles.

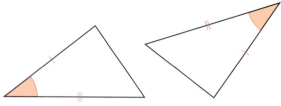

These two triangles are in fact congruent but it is not immediately obvious.

Tests for congruent triangles

To help us identify congruent triangles, at least **one** of the following conditions must be found to exist:

1. Two triangles are congruent if three sides in one triangle are equal in measure to three sides in the other triangle (SSS).

   Case 1
   SSS.

   In the diagram below, each pair of triangles is congruent.

2. Two triangles are congruent if two sides and the included angle in one are equal to two sides and the included angle in the other (SAS).

   Case 2
   SAS.

   Remember that the equal angles must be between the equal sides. In the diagram below, each pair of triangles is congruent.

3. Two triangles are congruent if two angles and the side between them are equal in measure in each (ASA).

   Case 3
   ASA.

   In the diagram below, each pair of triangles is congruent.

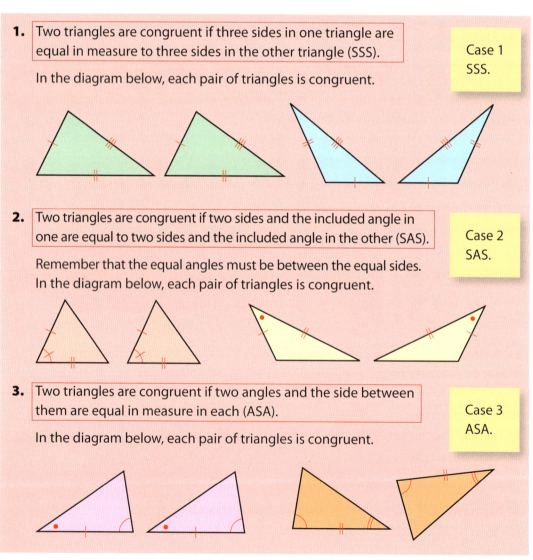

4. Two triangles are congruent if both contain a right angle, and the hypotenuse and one other side in both triangles are equal.

Case 4
RHS.

This is known as the right-angle-hypotenuse-side condition (RHS). In the diagram below, each pair of triangles is congruent.

Corresponding sides and angles

The two triangles below are congruent (ASA).

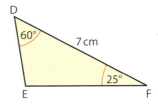

The side [DE] corresponds to the side [AB] as they are both opposite the 25° angle.

Similarly, [EF] corresponds to [BC] as they are both opposite the 60° angle.

The angle ABC corresponds to the angle DEF as they are both opposite the side of length 7 cm.

Note: If the triangles ABC and DEF are congruent, it can be written as △**ABC** ≡ △**DEF**.

Example 1

Explain why the two triangles shown are congruent.

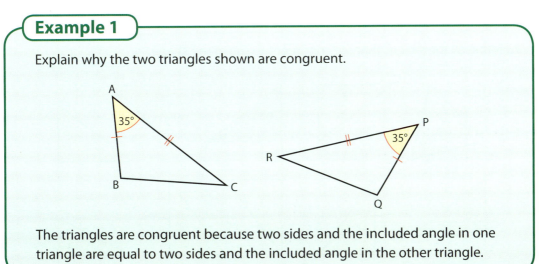

The triangles are congruent because two sides and the included angle in one triangle are equal to two sides and the included angle in the other triangle.

Many geometry theorems and other geometric problems are solved by showing that two triangles are congruent.

The worked example below shows how congruent triangles can be used to prove a very important property of equilateral triangles.

Example 2

Given the triangle ABC in which
$|AC| = |AB|$ and [AD] bisects $\angle CAB$.
Prove that $|\angle ACD| = |\angle ABD|$.

In the triangles ACD and ABD,

$|AC| = |AB|$ ... given
$|AD| = |AD|$ ... common side
$|\angle CAD| = |\angle BAD|$ ... given [AD] is bisector of $\angle CAB$
∴ △ACD ≡ △ABD ... SAS
∴ $|\angle ACD| = |\angle ABD|$ ... corresponding angles, both opposite [AD].

Exercise 18.1

1. Write down the letters of the pairs of shapes that are congruent.

A   B   C   D

2. Name all the shapes that are congruent to the green shape.

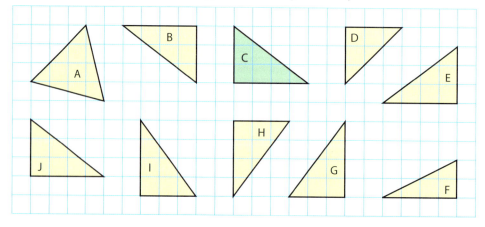

3. The given triangles ABC and DEF
are congruent.
Which side corresponds to
  (i) [AB]   (ii) [EF]
(iii) [AC]   (iv) [DE]?

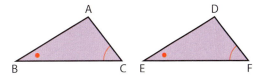

4. The two given triangles are congruent.
   (i) Which side corresponds to [XZ]?
  (ii) Which side corresponds to [LN]?
 (iii) Which angle corresponds to ∠XYZ?
 (iv) Which angle corresponds to ∠LMN?

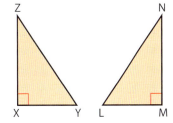

5. These two triangles are congruent.
The equal angles are marked.
   (i) Which side corresponds to [MN]?
  (ii) Which side corresponds to [AG]?
 (iii) Which side corresponds to [LM]?

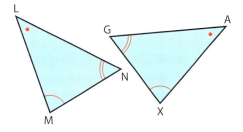

6. Explain why the two triangles
shown are congruent.

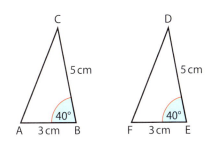

7. State why each of the following pairs of triangles are congruent, using SSS, SAS,
ASA or RHS as reasons for your answers:

(i)

(ii)

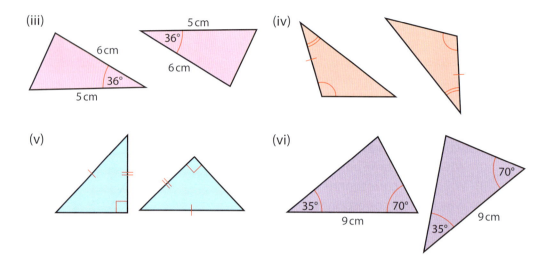

(iii)

5 cm
36°
6 cm
6 cm
36°
5 cm

(iv)

(v)

(vi)

35°   70°
9 cm
70°
9 cm
35°

8. Which two of these triangles are congruent to each other?
   Give a reason for your answer.

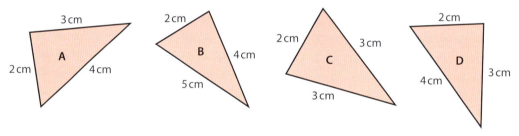

3 cm
A
2 cm   4 cm

2 cm
B
4 cm
5 cm

2 cm   3 cm
C
3 cm

2 cm
D
4 cm   3 cm

9. Are the triangles on the right congruent?
   Give a reason for your answer.

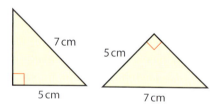

7 cm
5 cm

5 cm
7 cm

10. Explain why the two triangles ABD and ADC
    on the right are congruent.

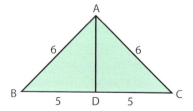

A
6   6
B   5 D 5   C

11. Are the triangles ABD and BCD on the right congruent?
Give a reason for your answer.

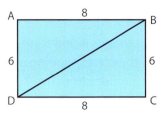

12. Explain why the triangles AOB and COD are congruent.

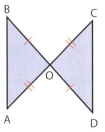

13. Explain why the two triangles shown below are congruent.

 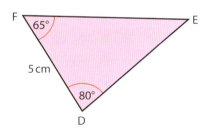

(i) Which side corresponds to [BC]?
(ii) Which side corresponds to [DE]?
(iii) Find $|\angle DEF|$.

14. These triangles are congruent.
Write down the values of x and y.

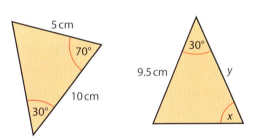

15. ABCD is a parallelogram.

Show that the triangles ABC and ACD are congruent.

Hence explain why the angles ABC and ADC are equal in size.

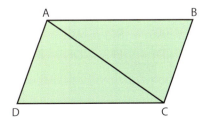

Section 18.2 Similar triangles

The shapes A and B are similar.
All the corresponding angles are the same and
all the sides in shape B are twice as long as the
corresponding sides in shape A.

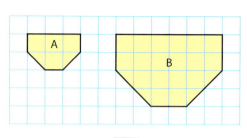

When two figures are **similar**,
> their **shapes** are the **same**
> their **angles** are **equal**
> corresponding **lengths** are in the **same ratio**.

All the sides in figure B are $1\frac{1}{2}$ times longer than
the corresponding sides in figure A.

Similar triangles

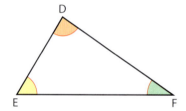

> Similar triangles have
> the same shapes but
> different sizes.

The triangles ABC and DEF above have equal angles.
Notice that they have the same shape but are different
in size.
These triangles are said to be **similar** or **equiangular
triangles**.

> Equiangular means
> all the corresponding
> angles are equal.

The sides [BC] and [EF] are said to be **corresponding sides**
since they are opposite equal angles.
The sides [AB] and [DE] are also corresponding.

Since each side in the triangle DEF is twice the length of the corresponding side in the
triangle ABC, we say that the sides are in the **same ratio** or are **proportional**.

In the triangles above, |AB| is half |DE|.
Similarly, $|BC| = \frac{1}{2}|EF|$ and $|AC| = \frac{1}{2}|DF|$.

Thus, $\dfrac{|AB|}{|DE|} = \dfrac{|BC|}{|EF|} = \dfrac{|AC|}{|DF|} = \dfrac{1}{2}$

This important result for similar triangles is stated in the theorem on the right.

> **Theorem**
> If two triangles ABC and DEF are similar, then their sides are proportional, in order,
> $$\frac{|AB|}{|DE|} = \frac{|BC|}{|EF|} = \frac{|AC|}{|DF|}$$

The **converse** of this theorem is also true.

> If the sides of two triangles are proportional, in order, then the triangles are similar.

Note: Two triangles are similar if two angles in one triangle are equal to two angles in the other triangle. The triangles are equiangular or similar because the third angles must be equal.

Example 1

The given triangles ABC and DEF are similar.
Find the lengths of the sides
  (i) [DE]
  (ii) [DF].

 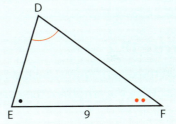

  (i) [DE] corresponds to [AB].
  Each side of the triangle DEF is $1\frac{1}{2}$ times the length of the corresponding side in the triangle ABC since 9 is $1\frac{1}{2}$ times 6.
  $$\therefore \quad |DE| = 1\tfrac{1}{2}|AB|$$
  $$|DE| = 1\tfrac{1}{2}(4) = 6$$
  (ii) $|DF| = 1\frac{1}{2}|AC|$
  $$|DF| = 1\tfrac{1}{2}(5) = 7\tfrac{1}{2}$$

Example 2

(i) Show that triangle ABC is similar to triangle EFG.
(ii) Find the length of side [FG].

(i) Find the missing angles:

$$|\angle ACB| = 180° - 80° - 43° = 57°$$
$$|\angle FEG| = 180° - 80° - 57° = 43°$$

Since each triangle has angles measuring 80°, 57° and 43°, the triangles are similar.

(ii) [FG] corresponds to the side [BC] ... opposite equal angles

Since $|EG| = 2\tfrac{1}{2}|AC| \Rightarrow |FG| = 2\tfrac{1}{2}|BC|$ ... $15\,cm = 6\,cm \times \left(\tfrac{5}{2}\right)$
$$= 2\tfrac{1}{2}(5\,cm)$$
$$|FG| = 12.5\,cm$$

Exercise 18.2

1. In the given figures, each side in PQRS is twice the length of the corresponding side in KLMN.

(i) What side corresponds to [NM]?
(ii) What side corresponds to [QR]?
(iii) If $|KL| = 4$, find $|PQ|$.
(iv) If $|NM| = 8.2$, find $|SR|$.
(v) If $|QR| = 15$, find $|LM|$.

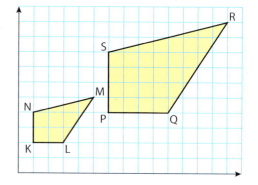

2. The triangles ABC and DEF are similar.

(i) Complete this ratio:
$$|BC| : |EF| = 6 : 12 = \ldots : \ldots$$
(ii) If $|AC| = 7.2$, find $|DF|$.
(iii) If $|DE| = 8$, find $|AB|$.

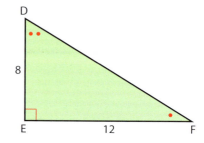

3. The given triangles are similar.
Find the lengths of the sides
marked x and y.

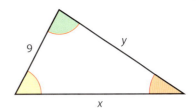

4. The diagrams opposite show three
squares A, B and C drawn on squared
paper.
Complete each of these ratios:
  (i) Side of square A : side of square
       B = 2 : …
  (ii) Side of square A : side of square
       C = 2 : …
If the side of square A is 6 cm, find
  (iii) the length of the side of square B
  (iv) the length of the side of square C
If the length of the diagonal of B is 17 cm, find
  (v) the length of the diagonal of A.

5. The shapes in (i) and (ii) below are similar.
Find the lengths of the sides marked with letters.
  (i)
  (ii)

6. The two given triangles are similar.
  (i) Copy and complete this statement:
       'Each side of the bigger triangle is … times
       the length of the corresponding side of
       the smaller triangle'.
  (ii) Find the values of x and y.

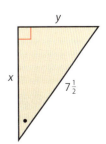

7. Explain why the triangles ABC and DEF are similar.
Find the values of *x* and *y*.

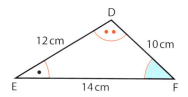

8. The triangles ABC and PQR are similar.
In the triangle PQR, which side
corresponds to
  (i) [AB]
  (ii) [AC]
  (iii) [BC]?

If |AC| = 8, |PR| = 12 and |BC| = 6,
find |PQ|.

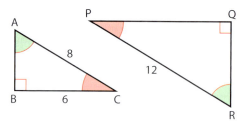

9. The triangles DEF and KLM are
similar.
  (i) Which side corresponds
      to [DF]?
  (ii) Which side corresponds
      to [ML]?
  (iii) Find |KM|.

10.

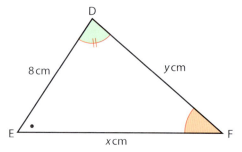

  (i) Explain why the triangles ABC and DEF are similar.
  (ii) Which side of the triangle DEF corresponds to the side [AC]?
  (iii) Find the values of *x* and *y*.

11. Which of these *shape families* are always similar?

   (i) all squares   (ii) all rectangles

 (iii) all parallelograms   (iv) all circles

  (v) all equilateral triangles   (vi) all isosceles triangles

12. When James planted a tree 5 m from a window, the tree just blocked from view a building 50 m away.
If the building was 20 m tall, how tall was the tree?

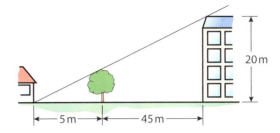

Section 18.3 Angles and circles

The diagrams below will help remind you of the meanings of the terms frequently used when dealing with circles.

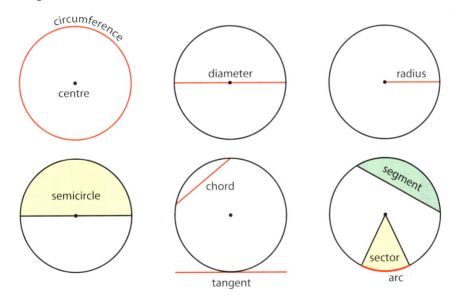

1. The angle in a semicircle

The shaded angle shown is called the **angle in a semicircle** because [AB] is a diameter. We will show below that the angle in a semicircle is a right angle.

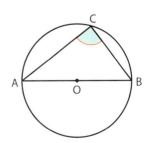

Explanation

In the given circle,

$$|OB| = |OA| = |OC| = \text{radius.}$$

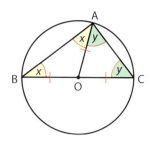

The angles marked x are equal because the triangle AOB is isosceles.

Similarly, the angles marked y are equal.

$2x + 2y$ make up the three angles of the $\triangle$ABC.

$$\therefore \qquad 2x + 2y = 180°$$
$$\therefore \qquad 2(x + y) = 180°$$
$$\therefore \quad |\angle x| + |\angle y| = 90°$$
$$\text{Thus,} \qquad |\angle BAC| = 90°.$$

> The angle in a semicircle is a right angle.

Converse

The angle ACB is said to be standing on the chord [AB].
If $|\angle ACB| = 90°$, then [AB] is a diameter of the circle.

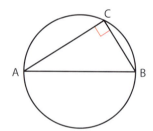

Example 1

Find the value of x in the given diagram where O is the centre of the circle.

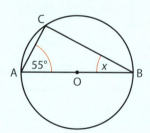

$$|\angle ACB| = 90° \quad \text{... the angle in a semicircle}$$
$$\angle x + 55° = 90° \quad \text{... } 180° \text{ in a triangle}$$
$$\angle x = 90° - 55°$$
$$\angle x = 35°$$

Example 2

A, B and C are three points on a circle with centre O.
If $|\angle OCB| = 65°$, find

(i) $|\angle OBC|$ (ii) $|\angle AOB|$ (iii) $|\angle OBA|$.

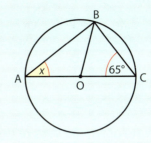

(i) The triangle OCB is isosceles since $|OC| = |OB| =$ radius.

∴ $|\angle OBC| = |\angle OCB| = 65°$

(ii) $|\angle BOC| = 180° - 65° - 65°$

∴ $|\angle BOC| = 50°$

∴ $|\angle AOB| = 180° - 50° = 130°$

(iii) Since $|OA| = |OB| =$ radius, $|\angle OAB| = |\angle OBA| = x$

∴ $x + x + 130° = 180°$ … $|\angle AOB| = 130°$ … from (i) above

$2x = 50°$

$x = 25°$

$|\angle OBA| = 25°$

Exercise 18.3

1. In the given circle, O is the centre.
If the diameter of the circle is 10 cm, find

(i) $|AB|$ (ii) $|DC|$

(iii) $|OA|$ (iv) $|OC|$

What type of triangle is AOD?

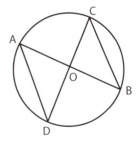

2. [AB] is a diameter of the given circle.

(i) Explain why $\angle ACB$ is a right angle.

(ii) Find $|\angle CAB|$.

(iii) Describe the triangle ABC in two ways.

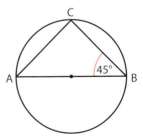

3. Find the value of *x* in each of these circles where O is the centre:

(i)

(ii)

(iii)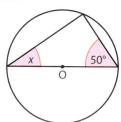

4. Write down the sizes of the angles marked with a letter in each of the following circles with O as centre:

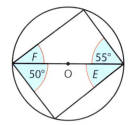

5. Find the values of *x* and *y* in each of the following circles with O as the centre:

(i)

(ii)

(iii)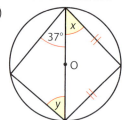

6. In the given circle, O is the centre.
- (i) Why is |OA| = |OB|?
- (ii) What is |∠ABC|?
- (iii) What is |∠ABO|?
- (iv) Now find |∠OBC|.
- (v) Explain why the triangle OBC is isosceles.

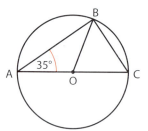

7. In the given circle, O is the centre and |∠AOC| = 120°.
Explain why |OB| = |OC|.
Now find
- (i) |∠COB|
- (ii) |∠OCB|

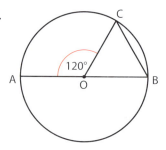

8. Find the values of *x* and *y* in each of the following diagrams, where O is the centre of the circle.

(i)   (ii)   (iii)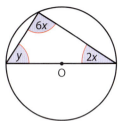

9. Find the value of the angle marked *x* in each of these circles with O as centre:

(i)   (ii)   (iii)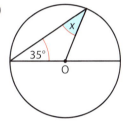

10. What sort of triangle is ABC if O is the centre of the circle?

If $|AC| = 8$ and $|BC| = 6$, find $|AB|$.

Now write down the length of the radius of the circle.

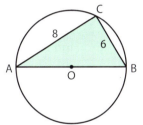

11. [AB] is the diameter of a circle of centre O.

$|OC| = 10\,cm$ and $|\angle CAB| = 30°$

Write down

  (i) $|AB|$ (ii) $|\angle OCA|$

 (iii) $|\angle ACB|$ (iv) $|\angle OCB|$

12. OAB is a quarter circle with O as centre. OXYZ is a rectangle.

If $|XZ| = 8\,cm$, write down (by examining the diagram) the length of the radius of the circle.

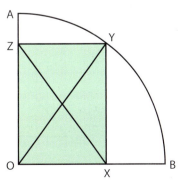

Test yourself 18

1. (a)   Find the values of *x*, *y* and *z* in these circles where O is the centre:

(b)   Which two of the following triangles are congruent? Give a reason for your answer.

(i)   (ii)   (iii)   (iv)

2. (a)   Find the values of *x* and *y* in the given circle with O as centre.

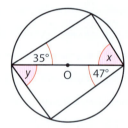

(b)   Two of these triangles are congruent. Which two? Give the reason.

3. (a)   Explain why the two triangles shown are congruent.

(b) In the given figure, O is the centre of the circle.
Find the values of *a* and *b*.
Explain your answers.

4. (a) In the given circle, O is the centre, $|\angle ACD| = 65°$ and $|AB| = |BC|$.

(i) Name two right angles in the figure.

(ii) Find $|\angle BAC|$.

(iii) Find $|\angle BAD|$.

(b) In the given triangles, the marked angles are equal.

(i) Explain why the two triangles are similar.

(ii) Find the values of *x* and *y*.

5. (a) Find the values of *x* and *y* in each of the following circles with O as centre:

(i)

(ii)

(iii)

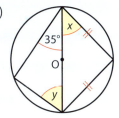

(b) Explain why the triangles ABE
and BCD are congruent.

(i) Which side matches [BE]?

(ii) Which side matches [CD]?

(iii) Which angle matches $\angle AEB$?

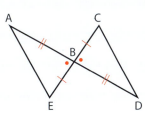

Chapter 19

Patterns and Sequences

Key words

sequence   term   position   term-to-term rule   repeating pattern
linear sequence   position-to-term rule   the *n*th term   quadratic sequence
first difference   second difference   exponential sequence

Section 19.1 Sequences

Whole numbers can produce some very interesting patterns when some basic operations are applied to them. Patterns exist all around us in the real world if we know where to look.

Number patterns can be simple like these:

1   3   5   7   9 …   … Each number is formed by adding 2 to the previous
+2   +2   +2   +2   number.

2   6   18   54 …   … Each number is formed by multiplying the previous
×3   ×3   ×3   number by 3.

1   2   4   7   11 …   … Each number is formed by adding 1 to the difference
+1   +2   +3   +4   between the previous two numbers, and then adding
                                        that.

Here is another simple pattern:

0, 4, 8, 12, 16, 20, 24, 28, 32, 36, 40, 44, …

However, if we take the last digit in each of the numbers above, we get another pattern which is as follows:

0, 4, 8, 2, 6, 0, 4, 8, 2, 6, 0, 4, …

The first pattern continues on with each number 4 bigger than the number before it.
The second pattern is a little more complex.
The numbers repeat in **blocks** of 5 with a particular pattern in each block.

308

In about the year 1200 AD, Leonardo Fibonacci of Pisa discovered a sequence of numbers that is very common in nature.

The sequence is: 1, 1, 2, 3, 5, 8, 13, 21, …

Each number after the first is obtained by adding the two previous numbers.

The number patterns above are called **sequences**.
A sequence is a set of numbers in a particular order.

> 1, 3, 5, 7, 9, … is a sequence

1st term   4th term   the dots indicate that the sequence continues on.

Each number is called a **term**.
Each number's place in the sequence is called its **position**.

The pattern below is made of squares.

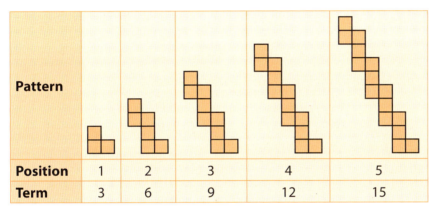

Pattern					
Position	1	2	3	4	5
Term	3	6	9	12	15

The terms form the sequence.

The fifth term is 15. It is made of 15 squares.
The pattern increases by 3 each time.
The sixth pattern in the sequence is made of 18 squares.
Thus, the sixth term in the sequence is 18.

The **term-to-term rule** describes how to get from one term to the next.

The term-to-term rule for 4, 8, 12, 16, 20, … is 'add 4'.
The term-to-term rule for 2, 6, 18, 54, … is 'multiply by 3'.
The term-to-term rule for 30, 25, 20, 15, … is 'subtract 5'.

A sequence can be **described in words** by giving the first term and then the term-to-term rule.

Example 1

  (i) A sequence starts at 7 and increases in steps of 4.
      Write down the first six terms of the sequence.

 (ii) Describe in words this sequence:
          27, 24, 21, 18, …

  (i) The first six terms of the sequence are: 7, 11, 15, 19, 23, 27.

 (ii) The sequence begins at 27 and goes down in steps of 3.

Exercise 19.1

1. Write down the next four terms of each of these sequences:

    (i) 3, 5, 7, 9, 11, …   (ii) 2, 5, 8, 11, 14, …   (iii) 4, 8, 12, 16, 20, …
  (iv) 20, 18, 16, 14, …   (v) 50, 45, 40, 35, …   (vi) 12, 8, 4, …

2. Write down the next three terms in each of these sequences:

    (i) 1, 2, 4, 8, …   (ii) 2, 6, 18, …   (iii) 3, 9, 27, …
  (iv) 1, 4, 9, 16, …   (v) $\frac{1}{3}$, 1, 3, …   (vi) $\frac{1}{2}, \frac{2}{3}, \frac{3}{4},$ …

3. Look at this sequence:

         4, 7, 10, 13, …

The rule to find the next term of this sequence is *add 3 to the previous term*.
Write down the next three terms in this sequence.

4. Write down the first four terms of these sequences:

    (i) Start with 2 and count forwards in steps of 4.
   (ii) Start with 5 and count forwards in steps of 3.
  (iii) Start with 3 and count forwards in steps of 5.
  (iv) Start with 30 and count back in steps of 4.
   (v) Start with -10 and count forwards in steps of 3.

5. Describe in words the rule for each of these sequences:

    (i) 3, 6, 9, 12, …   (ii) $-8, -4, 0, 4,$ …   (iii) 10, 15, 20, 25, …
  (iv) 16, 14, 12, 10, …   (v) $-6, -3, 0, 3,$ …   (vi) $2, 3\frac{1}{2}, 5, 6\frac{1}{2},$ …

6. For each of these sequences, the first four terms and the rules are given.
Write down the next three terms of each sequence.

    (i) 2, 4, 6, 8, …   Add 2 to the last term.
    (ii) 2, 4, 6, 10, …   Add the previous two terms together.
    (iii) 2, 4, 8, 16, …   Double the last term.
    (iv) 2, 4, 10, 28, …   Multiply the last term by 3 and then take off 2.

7. A sequence begins 3, 4, 6, 10, …
The rule for continuing the sequence is

> Double the last number and subtract 2.

What is the next number in this sequence?

8. The first term of a sequence is 5.
The term-to-term rule is 'add 6'.

    (i) What is the second term of the sequence?
    (ii) What is the fifth term?

9. Copy and complete this table:

1st term	Term-to-term rule	2nd, 3rd, 4th and 5th terms
8	+5	
	+4	9, 13, 17, 21
		12, 15, 18, 21
0	−3	
−12		−7, −2, 3, 8

10. The sixth term of a sequence is 11.
The term-to-term rule is 'subtract 3'.

    (i) What is the fifth term of the sequence?
    (ii) What is the first term?

11. Here are three sequences:
    (a) 7, 14, 21, 28, …   (b) 6, 11, 16, 21, 26, …   (c) 3, 7, 11, 15, 19, …
What goes in the box in each of the following?

    (i) In sequence (a), the terms of the sequence are multiples of ☐.
    (ii) In sequence (b), the terms are all ☐ more than a multiple of ☐.
    (iii) In sequence (c), the terms are all ☐ less than a multiple of ☐.

12. In the sequence shown below, you add the previous two numbers to get the next number.

...   5   8   13   21   ...   ...

   (i) Write down the next two numbers of the sequence.

  (ii) Write down the number that came before 5.

13. Here is the rule for finding a term in a sequence.

> Multiply the previous term by 3 and add 2.

The first three terms in the sequence are 2, 8 and 26.
Work out the next two terms.

14. Each term in the sequence of patterns below is the number of squares in the pattern.
Copy and complete the shaded boxes below.

Pattern					
Position	1	2	3		
Term	5	8			

15. Write down the first six terms of this sequence.

> I am thinking of a sequence.
> The third term is 4.
> The rule is 'multiply by 2'.

16. The rule for a sequence is 'multiply the previous term by 2 and add 1'.
The first term of the sequence is 3.

   (i) Write down the second term.

  (ii) Work out the sixth term.

17. In each of the sequences below, the difference between the terms is constant.
Copy each sequence and fill in the missing numbers.

   (i) 4, 6, ___, ___, ___, 14, ...

  (iii) 1, ___, 11, ___, 21, ___, ...

  (ii) 25, ___, 19, ___, 13, 10, ...

  (iv) ___, 10, ___, ___, 19, ___, ...

18. Examine these number patterns.
Write down the next line in each pattern without using a calculator.
Now use a calculator to check that you are correct.

(i) $1 \times 9 + 2 = 11$ (ii) $3 \times 11 = 33$ (iii) $9 \times 1 = 9$

         $11 \times 9 + 2 = 101$ $33 \times 11 = 363$ $9 \times 12 = 108$

         $111 \times 9 + 2 = 1001$ $333 \times 11 = 3663$ $9 \times 123 = 1107$

         $1111 \times 9 + 2 = 10\,001$ $3333 \times 11 = 36\,663$ $9 \times 1234 = 11\,106$

- - - - - - - - - - - - - - - - - -   - - - - - - - - - - - - - - - - - -   - - - - - - - - - - - - - - - - - -

Section 19.2 Repeating patterns ——————————————

The pattern of the coloured circles above is green, pink, blue, yellow, green, pink, …
The pattern repeats in blocks of 4.
The pattern of green circles is 1, 5, 9, …
The pattern of yellow circles is 4, 8, 12, …

What colour is the 35th circle?
Since the pattern repeats every 4 circles, we find how many blocks of 4 there are in 35
and then see how many circles are left over.

     $35 \div 4 = 8$ and remainder 3

When the remainder is 3, we look for the colour of the 3rd circle in the block of 4.

This colour is blue. Therefore, the 35th circle is blue.

> **Example 1**
>
> A repeating pattern is made up of letters as follows:
>
>
>
> (i)   What is the 25th letter?
> (ii)   What is the 43rd letter?
> (iii)   What is the 61st letter?
>
> (i)   The pattern repeats in blocks of 5.
>   To find the 25th letter, divide 25 by 5.
> $25 \div 5 = 5$, i.e. five complete blocks.
>   The 25th letter is therefore the last letter in the block.
>   Thus, the 25th letter is E.

(ii) The 43rd letter is 43 ÷ 5. This is 8 and remainder 3.
Remainder 3 means it is the 3rd letter in the block.
This letter is C.
The 43rd letter is C.

(iii) The 61st letter is 61 ÷ 5. This is 12 and remainder 1.
Remainder 1 means the first letter in the block.
The 61st letter is A.

Exercise 19.2

1. Here is a repeating pattern of geometric shapes:

(i) What are the next two shapes?
(ii) List the positions of the first three circles. Is there a pattern?
(iii) Which shape forms the pattern 3, 7, …?
(iv) What is the 21st shape?
(v) What is the 37th shape?
(vi) If the 61st shape is a square, what is the 62nd shape?

2. Here is a repeating pattern of coloured tiles:

(i) What is the next colour in the pattern?
(ii) What colour is the 30th tile?
(iii) What colour is the 48th tile?
(iv) If the 63rd tile is red, what colour is the 65th tile?
(v) Write down the pattern formed by the blue tiles.
(vi) In what position is the 6th blue tile?

3. The pattern below is the multiples of 6.

6, 12, 18, 24, 30, 36, 42, 48, 54, 60, 66, 72, …

The last digit in each number forms this pattern:

6, 2, 8, 4, 0, 6, 2, 8, 4, 0, 6, 2, …

Notice that this is a repeating pattern.

    (i)   What are the next two numbers of this pattern?

    (ii) What is the 24th number of this pattern?

    (iii) What is the 51st number of this pattern?

    (iv) What is the position of the fifth 8 of this pattern?

4. Here is a repeating pattern of geometric shapes.

    (i)   What is the next shape in the pattern?

    (ii) List the positions of the first three triangles.
         Now write down the position of the fourth triangle.

    (iii) What is the 26th shape?

    (iv) What is the 38th shape?

    (v) Which shape forms the sequence 3, 8, 13, … ?

5. Write down the first ten multiples of 8.

    (i)   Show that the last digits of these multiples form a repeating pattern.

    (ii) After how many digits does the pattern start repeating?

    (iii) What number appears in the 100th position in the pattern?

Section 19.3 **Linear sequences**

Look at this sequence:

    12, 9, 6, 3, …   The term-to-term rule is '−3' or 'subtract 3'.

When the term-to-term rule involves adding or subtracting a constant (a fixed number), it is known as a **linear sequence**.

> A linear sequence is also known as an **arithmetic sequence**.

Here are some examples of linear sequences:

 (i)   5, 8, 11, 14, … the constant difference is $+3$.

(ii) 24, 20, 16, 12, … the constant difference is -4.

The following sequences are not linear because the term-to-term rule does not involve adding or subtracting a constant.

 (i)   2, 4, 8, 16, 32, …   The term-to-term rule is $\times 2$.

(ii) 27, 9, 3, 1, $\frac{1}{3}$, …   The term-to-term rule is $\div 3$.

How to find any term of a sequence

We can calculate the value of a term from its position in the sequence by using a **position-to-term rule**. This helps us avoid having to add or subtract the constant a lot of times.

Examine the sequence below:

Position → ×3 → +4 → Term

Position	1	2	3	4	5	...	n
Term	7	10	13	16	19	...	$n \times 3 + 4$

> The position-to-term rule may also be called the **nth-term rule**.

The example above shows that any term may be found by using the rule ×3 → +4

From this, the 6th term (T_6) is 6 ×3 $+$ 4 , i.e. $T_6 = 22$.

The position-to-term rule for a sequence can be obtained by writing an expression for T_n, the nth term.

In the example above, $T_n = n$ ×3 $+$ 4

$$\therefore T_n = 3n + 4$$

When we know T_n we can write down any term of the sequence.

Example 1

The nth term of a sequence is given by $T_n = 3n - 4$.
(i) Write down the first three terms of the sequence and also T_{20}.
(ii) Explain why the sequence is linear.

(i) $T_n = 3n - 4$
$T_1 = 3(1) - 4 = 3 - 4 = -1$ ... substitute 1 for n.
$T_2 = 3(2) - 4 = 6 - 4 = 2$
$T_3 = 3(3) - 4 = 9 - 4 = 5$
$T_{20} = 3(20) - 4 = 60 - 4 = 56$

The first three terms are $-1, 2, 5$ and $T_{20} = 56$.

(ii) Since the difference between the terms is a constant, i.e. 3, the sequence is linear.

Exercise 19.3

1. The *n*th terms of some sequences are given.
Write out the first four terms of each sequence.

(i) $T_n = 2n$ 　　　　(ii) $T_n = 3n + 1$ 　　　　(iii) $T_n = 4n - 3$
(iv) $T_n = 2n + 5$ 　　(v) $T_n = 5n - 4$ 　　　　(vi) $T_n = 7 - 2n$

2. Explain why each of these sequences is linear:

(i) 6, 10, 14, 18, … 　　(ii) 1, 6, 11, 16, … 　　(iii) 20, 17, 14, 11, …

3. The *n*th term of a sequence is $T_n = 2n + 3$.

(i) Write down the first five terms of the sequence.
(ii) Find T_{20} and T_{100}.
(iii) Explain why the sequence is linear.

4. If $T_n = 2n - 6$, show that $T_1 + T_5 = 0$.

5. Write out the first four terms of the sequence given by $T_n = n^2 + 1$.
Is the sequence linear? Explain your answer.

6. The *n*th term of a sequence is $3n + 2$.

(i) Write down the first six terms of the sequence.
(ii) Calculate the 100th term.

7. Linear sequences can be found on this grid.
Two are highlighted on the diagram.

(i) Write down each of these two sequences,
starting with the smallest number in each
case.

(ii) Find seven more linear sequences that
have four terms or more.

44	34	24	14	4	3	6	9	12
40	30	5	20	10	11	5	8	1
44	37	30	23	16	9	2	7	3
4	11	23	21	22	12	1	6	9
1	7	26	20	28	9	8	5	0
3	31	10	15	34	30	12	4	8
36	6	11	13	40	0	1	3	2

8. Examine the number of sides used for each group of triangles.

 , , , …

Copy and complete the given
table of values which shows
how the number of sides used
is related to the number of triangles.
Explain why the sequence formed by the number of sides is linear.

Number of triangles	1	2	3	4	5
Number of sides	3	5			

317

Section 19.4 Finding the *n*th term of a sequence

To find the *n*th term of a linear sequence, we look at the differences between terms.

The sequence is linked to 3-times tables because the terms go up in 3s.
So 3*n* will be part of the *n*th term.
T_n will be $3n \pm$ some number.

To work out what to add to or subtract from 3*n*, we compare the first term of
$T_n = 3n$ and the given sequence 7, 10, 13, …

For $T_n = 3n$, $T_1 = 3(1) = 3$.
We need to add 4 to this 3 in order to get 7, the first term of the given sequence.

$$\therefore\ T_n = 3n + 4 \qquad\qquad n \longrightarrow \boxed{\times 3} \xrightarrow{3n} \boxed{+4} \longrightarrow 3n+4$$

Example 1

Find the *n*th term of the sequence 3, 7, 11, 15, …

In the sequence 3, 7, 11, 15, …, the difference between the terms is +4.
So $T_n = 4n \pm$ some number.
If $T_n = 4n$, then $T_1 = 4(1) = 4$.

What do I need to add to or subtract from 4 in order to get the first term, i.e. 3,
of the given sequence?
I need to subtract 1, since $4 - 1 = 3$.
So $T_n = 4n - 1$.

Note: Having found an expression for T_n, always check that it works for T_2 or T_3,
for example.

If we know the *n*th term of a sequence, we can use this information to find which
particular term of the sequence any given number is.

Example 2

The nth term of a sequence is given by $T_n = 5n - 4$.
Which term of the sequence is 21?

Let $T_n = 21$
$\therefore 5n - 4 = 21$
$\qquad 5n = 25$
$\qquad\; n = 5$

Thus, 21 is the 5th term of the sequence.

Exercise 19.4

1. A given sequence is 5, 9, 13, 17, …

    (i) Write down the constant difference between the terms.

    (ii) If $T_n = \boxed{}n \pm$ a number, what number goes in the box?

    (iii) Now find an expression for T_n, the nth term.

    (iv) Write down the value of T_{20}.

2. Each of the following sequences is linear.
By finding the constant difference between the terms in each sequence, write down the number in the red box for T_n in each case:

    (i) 2, 5, 8, 11, … ; $T_n = \boxed{}n \pm ?$ (ii) 3, 7, 11, 15, … ; $T_n = \boxed{}n \pm ?$

    (iii) 6, 12, 18, 24, … ; $T_n = \boxed{}n \pm ?$ (iv) 5, 10, 15, 20, … ; $T_n = \boxed{}n \pm ?$

3. Complete T_n, the nth term, for each of the following:

(i)

Position	1	2	3	4	5
Term	3	6	9	12	15

$T_n = \boxed{}n$

(ii)

Position	1	2	3	4	5
Term	4	7	10	13	16

$T_n = \boxed{}n + 1$

(iii)

Position	1	2	3	4	5
Term	5	10	15	20	25

$T_n = \boxed{}n$

(iv)

Position	1	2	3	4	5
Term	3	8	13	18	23

$T_n = \boxed{}n - \boxed{}$

(v)

Position	1	2	3	4
Term	7	9	11	13

$T_n = \boxed{}n + \boxed{}$

(vi)

Position	1	2	3	4	5
Term	5	9	13	17	21

$T_n = \boxed{}n + \boxed{}$

4. Find an expression for the nth term of each of these sequences:

    (i) 5, 7, 9, 11, ...   (ii) 5, 8, 11, 14, ...   (iii) 6, 10, 14, 18, ...

5. Find an expression for the nth term of this sequence:

        7, 11, 15, 19, ...

Use the expression for the nth term to find T_{10} and T_{20}.

6. Find an expression for the nth term of the sequence:

        8, 12, 16, 20, ...

Now find the value of   (i) T_{10} (ii) T_{30}.

Use the expression for T_n to find which term of the sequence is 80.

7. Consider the sequence 12, 10, 8, 6, ...

    (i) What is the term-to-term rule for this sequence?

    (ii) If $T_n = \boxed{} n \pm$ a number, what number goes in the box?

    (iii) Use this to find an expression for T_n.

    (iv) Find T_{10} of the sequence.

    (v) Which term of the sequence is -14?

8. Find an expression for the nth terms of these sequences:

    (i) -3, 0, 3, 6, 9, ...   (ii) 20, 15, 10, 5, ...

Section 19.5 Sequences formed from shapes

So far in this chapter we have dealt mainly with number patterns.

In this section we will examine some geometric figures and the patterns they form.

Example 1

The figure on the right shows some photo frames made with rods.

1 photo   2 photos   3 photos

    (i) Draw the frame that holds 4 photos.

    (ii) How many rods are there in the frame that holds 5 photos?

    (iii) Find an expression for the number of rods in the nth frame.

    (iv) Which frame uses 41 rods?

(i) This is the frame that holds 4 photos:

(ii) The sequence is 3, 5, 7, 9, 11, …
Therefore, the 5th frame has 11 rods.

(iii) The difference between the terms is $+2$.
Thus, the nth term will be $2n \pm$ a number.
If $T_n = 2n$, $T_1 = 2$ and so 1 must be added to get the first term 3.
∴ $T_n = 2n + 1$

(iv) Let $T_n = 41 \Rightarrow 2n + 1 = 41$
$$2n = 40$$
$$n = 20$$
The 20th frame uses 41 rods.

Exercise 19.5

1. Here is a pattern made from sticks.

6 sticks   11 sticks   16 sticks

(i) Draw the 4th pattern in this sequence.
(ii) Write down the sequence of numbers generated by the sticks in the first six patterns.
(iii) Show that the number of sticks in the nth pattern is given by $T_n = 5n + 1$.
(iv) How many sticks are required for the 20th pattern?
(v) For which pattern are 51 sticks required?

2. Here are three diagrams made with triangles.

Diagram 1   Diagram 2   Diagram 3

3 triangles   5 triangles   7 triangles

(i) Draw diagram 4.
(ii) How many triangles will be in diagram 7?
(iii) Find an expression for the number of triangles in the nth diagram.
(iv) Which diagram will contain 33 triangles?

321

3. Complete the table of values for this sequence of matchstick patterns.

Number of squares	1	2	3	4	5
Number of matchsticks	4	7			

   (i) How many matchsticks are required for the 6th pattern?
  (ii) Find an expression in n for the number of matchsticks in the nth pattern.
(iii) Use the expression found to ascertain the number of matchsticks required for the 50th pattern.

4. Here is a pattern made with matchsticks.

         Pattern 1   Pattern 2   Pattern 3

   (i) How many matchsticks will be in Pattern 5?
  (ii) Find an expression for the number of matchsticks in the nth pattern.
(iii) In which pattern are there 51 matchsticks?

5. Here is another pattern made with matchsticks.

         Pattern 1   Pattern 2   Pattern 3

   (i) How many matchsticks will there be in pattern 4?
  (ii) What is the term-to-term rule for the pattern?
(iii) How many matchsticks will there be in the nth pattern?
(iv) Which pattern will contain exactly 66 matchsticks?
 (v) Will any pattern use exactly 88 matchsticks?

Section 19.6 Quadratic sequences

1, 4, 9, 16, 25, … is the sequence of square numbers.
Since $T_1 = 1^2, T_2 = 2^2, T_3 = 3^2, …, T_n = n^2$.

Sequences that have an nth term containing **n^2** as the highest power are called **quadratic sequences**.

Let us examine the first seven terms of the sequence $T_n = n^2$.

Notice that the **second difference** is a constant, i.e. 2.

Quadratic sequences always have a **constant** second difference.

Now we will examine the sequence 1, 6, 15, 28, 45, … by finding the first and second differences:

Here again the second differences are all the same, i.e. 4.

Quadratic sequences

> In a quadratic sequence, the second difference between the terms is always constant.

Example 1

By finding the second difference between the terms, investigate if the sequence 2, 5, 10, 17, 26, … is quadratic.

Since the second difference is constant (i.e. 2), the sequence is quadratic.

Example 2

Find the next two terms of the quadratic sequence 5, 7, 10, 14, … by finding the first and second differences.

In the given sequence, the difference between the terms is increasing by 1 each step.

The next two terms are $(14 + 5)$ and $(19 + 6)$.

∴   the next two terms are 19 and 25.

Exponential sequences

Here is a special type of sequence formed by the powers of 2:

$2^1, 2^2, 2^3, 2^4, 2^5 \ldots$ or $2, 4, 8, 16, 32, \ldots$

Notice that the values of the terms increase very quickly.
This is an example of an **exponential sequence**.

If $T_n = 3^n$, then the sequence is

$3^1, 3^2, 3^3, 3^4, 3^5, \ldots$ or $3, 9, 27, 81, 243, \ldots$

Exponent is another word for power.

In everyday language, **exponential growth** is used to indicate 'very fast growth'.

When the sequence $2, 4, 8, 16, \ldots$ is plotted on a graph, it can be seen that the curve rises very steeply.

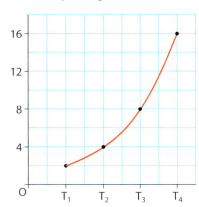

Exercise 19.6

1. The nth term of a sequence is given by $T_n = n^2 + 3$.
   Write out the first five terms of this sequence.
   By finding the second difference between these terms, explain why the sequence is quadratic.

2. Work out the first four terms of each of these quadratic sequences:
   (i) $T_n = n^2 + 1$ (ii) $T_n = n^2 - 2$ (iii) $T_n = 2n^2 - 1$

3. Find the first and second differences between the terms of these sequences. Hence state if each sequence is quadratic.

(i) 3, 4, 6, 9, 13, …   (ii) 3, 6, 11, 18, 27, …   (iii) 2, 7, 14, 23, 34, …

4. By examining the pattern in the first differences, write down the next two terms of each of these sequences:

(i) 6, 8, 12, 18, 26, …   (ii) 4, 7, 12, 19, 28, …

5. Here are the first 3 diagrams of a matchstick pattern.

(i) How many matchsticks will there be in Diagram 4?

(ii) Using the sequence formed, write down the number of matchsticks in Diagram 5.

Diagram 1   Diagram 2   Diagram 3

(iii) Explain why the sequence is quadratic.

6. Here are the first three terms of an exponential sequence: 3, 9, 37, …

(i) Write out the next three terms.

(ii) Investigate if the second difference between the terms is a constant.

7. Write down the first six terms of the sequence, given that $T_n = 2^n$. Describe the sequence you have found.

8. Work out the first four terms of the sequence defined by $T_n = 3(2^n)$. By finding the second differences between the terms, show that the sequence is not quadratic.

Section 19.7 Graphing linear sequences

Here is a linear pattern: 1, 4, 7, 10, 13, …

It can be seen that $T_1 = 1, T_2 = 4, T_3 = 7, …$

These may be written as ordered pairs as follows:

$(T_1, 1), (T_2, 4), (T_3, 7), (T_4, 10), …$

On the right, we have plotted the terms on the horizontal axis and the values of the terms on the vertical axis.
When the term and its value are plotted, and the points joined, the result is a **straight line**.

This illustrates why the sequence is called **linear**.

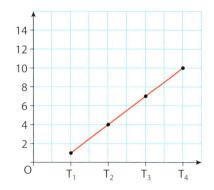

Exercise 19.7

1. The diagram below shows the fare structures of two taxi companies, A and B.

Use the graph to find

   (i)   how much Company A charges for a journey of 10 km
  (ii)   how far you could travel with Company B for €16
 (iii)   the distance for which both companies charge the same amount
 (iv)   the difference in the charges when the distance is 4 km.

2. The table on the right shows the first four terms of a sequence and the values of these terms.

Term	1	2	3	4
Value	4	7	10	13

Putting the terms on the horizontal axis and the values on the vertical axis, draw a graph of the sequence.
Explain why the sequence is linear.

3. If $T_n = 2n + 1$, write out the first five terms of the sequence.
Illustrate this sequence on a graph, putting the term numbers on the horizontal axis.
Describe the graph you have drawn.

4. A fast-growing plant is 4 cm in height when purchased.
It grows 2 cm per day each day afterwards.
Copy and complete the table on the right showing
the height of the plant during its first seven days.

Day	Height (cm)
1	4
2	6
3	8
......	......

 (i) Draw a graph to show the height of the plant
      for Day 1 ..... Day 7.
 (ii) How many days will it take for the plant to
      reach a height of 30 cm?
 (iii) The plant will stop growing when it reaches a height of 60 cm.
      How many days will this take?

5. The graph on the right shows a
plumber's charges when called out
to do a repair job on a boiler.

 (i) What is the initial or 'call out' charge?
 (ii) How much does he charge for a
      job that lasts for $3\frac{1}{2}$ hours?
      (Include 'call out' charge.)
 (iii) If he charges €135 in total,
      how many hours, roughly,
      has he worked?
 (iv) Use the sequence of charges
      for 1 hour, 2 hours, 3 hours, …
      to find approximately what the
      charge would be for 8 hours work.

6. The table on the right shows the total
amounts of money Cara has saved after
weeks 1, 2, 3, ...
Draw a graph to illustrate these savings,
putting the week number on the x-axis.

Week number	Amount saved
1	€10
2	€20
3	€30
4	€40
5	€50
......	......

 (i) Use the pattern to find the amount
      she will have saved at the end of the
      10th week.
 (ii) Use the graph to find at the end of which
      week she will have saved €80.

7. One candle is 50 cm long and burns at the rate of 5 cm/hour.
A second candle is 40 cm long and burns at the rate of 2 cm/hour.

Make an enlarged copy of this grid and mark
on it the height of each candle after 2 hours,
4 hours, 6 hours, 8 hours and 10 hours.

Draw two lines to show the rates at which
the candles burn.

Use the graph to estimate after how many
hours of burning both candles are the same
length.

8. This pattern is made from cubes.
The outside faces of the cubes in each block are painted.

The table below shows the number of faces painted in each block.

Block number (*n*)	1	2	3	4
Number of painted faces	6	10	14	18

(i) Explain why the sequence formed by the numbers of faces painted forms a
linear sequence.
(ii) Now find an expression for the *n*th term of the sequence.
(iii) Draw a graph of the sequence, putting the block numbers on the
horizontal axis.
(iv) Copy and complete this sentence:
"The graph of a linear sequence is always a … ."

Test yourself 19

1. (a) Find the missing number in each of these sequences:

   (i) 3, 7, 11, ☐, 19, …   (ii) 10, 6, 2, ☐, −6, …   (iii) 4, 12, 36, ☐, …

   (b) A sequence begins 1, 2, 6, 16, …
   Here is the rule to continue the sequence:

   > Add the previous two numbers together, then multiply the answer by two.

   Work out the next two terms of the sequence.

   (c) The first two terms of a sequence are 3, 9, … .
   (i) If the sequence is linear, write down the next three terms.
   (ii) If the sequence is quadratic, write down what the next three terms could be.
   (iii) If the sequence is exponential, write down the next three terms.

2. (a) Here is a repeating pattern of coloured tiles:

   (i) What are the colours of the next two tiles?
   (ii) Write down the sequence formed by the positions of the yellow tiles in the pattern.
   (iii) In what position is the 10th yellow tile?
   (iv) What is the colour of the 72nd tile?

   (b) By finding the second difference between the terms, investigate if the sequence 1, 6, 12, 19, 27, … is quadratic.
   Explain your result.

3. Kevin has €20 saved. He gets €7 a week for doing jobs at home.
   He spends €2 on sweets every week and saves the rest in a piggybank.
   (i) How much money, in total, has he saved at the end of week 1?
   (ii) Complete the table below to show how his savings grow in the first five weeks.

	Week 1	Week 2	Week 3	Week 4	Week 5
€20		€30			

   (iii) Write down a formula (in words) to represent the amount he has saved at the end of each week.
   (iv) Kevin would like to buy a mobile phone costing €100. Use your formula to find out for how many weeks he needs to save in order to have enough money to buy the phone.

     (v) Imagine Kevin stopped buying the sweets after five weeks.
          How much could he then save each week after that?

    (vi) Kevin thinks he can now buy his phone three weeks sooner with the extra savings.
          Do you agree with Kevin? Explain your answer.

4. (a) What number goes in the box in each of these sequences?

      (i) 10, 7, 4, 1, ☐, ...   (ii) -2, 1, ☐, 7, ...

     (iii) 81, 27, ☐, 3, ...   (iv) 3, 5, 9, ☐, 23, ...

   (b) Look at these matchstick shapes.

             5 matchsticks   9 matchsticks

     (i) Copy and complete the table below:

Shape number	1	2	3	4	5
Number of matchsticks	5	9	...	...	...

     (ii) How many matchsticks are there in Shape 7?

    (iii) Find an expression for the number of matchsticks in Shape n?

    (iv) Use this expression for the nth term to find which shape contains exactly 101 matchsticks.

5. (a) Which **one** of the following sequences is linear?

      (i) 6, 4, 0, ...   (ii) -3, -1, 3, 6, ...   (iii) -5, -3, -1, 1, ...

   (b) A sequence of numbers begins 36, 20, 12, 8, ...
      The rule for the sequence is 'add 4 to the previous term and then halve the result'.

      (i) Work out the next three terms.

     (ii) Is the sequence linear? Explain your answer.

    (iii) Is the sequence quadratic? Explain your answer.

   (c) Look at the sequence of these triangle patterns:

      (i) Draw the next triangle in the sequence.

     (ii) How many dots will there be in the 5th pattern?

    (iii) Find an expression for the nth term for this sequence.

    (iv) Use the expression for the nth term to find which pattern has 63 dots.

Algebra 2: Inequalities – Algebraic Fractions

20

Key words

natural numbers   integers   real numbers   number line   equation
inequality   algebraic fractions   lowest common multiple (LCM)
mathematical sentence

Section 20.1 Plotting numbers on the number line

In your study of numbers so far, you will have dealt with **natural numbers** and
integers. These numbers are described again below and illustrated on the number
line.

1. **Natural numbers** are the counting numbers starting at 1.
   They are denoted by the capital letter **N**.

   $N = 1, 2, 3, 4, 5, \ldots$

   The arrow indicates that the dots continue indefinitely.

2. **Integers** are whole numbers which may be positive or negative.
   They are denoted by the capital letter **Z**.
   The integers are illustrated here on the
   number line.

   $Z = \ldots, -3, -2, -1, 0, 1, 2, 3, \ldots$

3. **Real numbers** describe all the numbers on the number line.
   These numbers include natural numbers, integers, fractions, decimals and numbers
   such as $\sqrt{5}, \sqrt{7}, \pi, \ldots$

   Since every number on the number line is a real number, we say that real numbers
   'fill' the number line. For this reason, real numbers are represented on the number
   line by a heavy or 'bold' line as shown below.
   The capital letter **R** is used to denote the set of real numbers.

Inequalities

The speed limit for cars driving in a city is
generally 50 km/hr.
This could be written as speed $\leqslant 50$ or $S \leqslant 50$.
This means that S could be 48, 46, 42, 40, …
The statement $S \leqslant 50$ is an example of an **inequality**.

$x + 3 = 7$ is an example of an **equation** since one side is *equal* to the other.
However, $x + 3 > 7$ is an example of an **inequality** since one side is **not equal** to the
other side.

Here are the four inequality signs we will use.

>	<	⩾	⩽
is greater than	is less than	is greater than or equal to	is less than or equal to

We will now use these inequality signs to show how different numbers can be shown on
the number line.

1. Natural numbers

The inequality $x \geqslant 4, x \in N$ means that x may be any whole number greater than or
equal to 4, i.e. 4, 5, 6, 7, …
These are represented on the number line below:

2. Integers

The inequality $x > -2, x \in Z$ represents all the integers greater than -2,
i.e. $-1, 0, 1, 2, 3, …$
These are represented on the number line below:

3. Real numbers

The inequality $x \geqslant 3, x \in R$ is the set of all real numbers greater than or equal to 3.
The inequality $x \geqslant 3$ is represented on the number line as follows:

The 'bold' line indicates that all the points on the line are included and the closed
circle at 3 shows that the number 3 is **included**.

The inequality $x > -2, x \in R$ is shown below.
The 'empty' circle at -2 is used to show that -2 is **not included**.

Changing the order in an inequality

It is clear that $7 > 4$ but $4 < 7$.
This illustrates that when the two parts of an inequality are interchanged, the inequality
sign must also be changed.

Thus, (i) if $8 > 3$, then $3 < 8$ (ii) if $x \geqslant 5$, then $5 \leqslant x$.

Exercise 20.1

1. State whether each of the following is true or false:
    (i) $3 \in N$ (ii) $4 \in Z$ (iii) $-5 \in N$ (iv) $2.5 \in R$
    (v) $-3\frac{1}{2} \in N$ (vi) $0.5 \in N$ (vii) $2\frac{3}{8} \in R$ (viii) $\sqrt{17} \in R$

2. Insert $>$ or $<$ in each of the boxes below:
    (i) $6 \;\square\; 4$ (ii) $-5 \;\square\; 2$ (iii) $6 \;\square\; -2$ (iv) $-4 \;\square\; 3$

3. Write a mathematical sentence for each of these:
    (i) x is less than 4   (ii) 2 is greater than -3
    (iii) the speed limit (S) is 40 km/hr   (iv) b is less than or equal to -5
    (v) the minimum age (A) is 18   (vi) the maximum age (A) is 60

4. If $x \in N$, state the values x may have in each of the following inequalities:
    (i) $x < 4$ (ii) $x \leqslant 5$ (iii) $x < 6\frac{1}{2}$
    (iv) $x > 2$ and $x < 7$ (v) $x \geqslant 1$ and $x \leqslant 4$ (vi) $x \geqslant 2$ and $x < 8$

5. If $x \in Z$, state the values x may have in each of the following inequalities:
    (i) $x \geqslant -2$ and $x \leqslant 1$ (ii) $x \geqslant 0$ and $x \leqslant 4$ (iii) $x \geqslant -3$ and $x \leqslant 0$
    (iv) $x \geqslant -4$ and $x < 1$ (v) $x > -5$ and $x < 2$ (vi) $x > -2\frac{1}{2}$ and $x < 3\frac{1}{4}$

6. Graph each of the following inequalities on the number line:
    (i) $x \geqslant 3, x \in N$ (ii) $x \leqslant 4, x \in N$ (iii) $x > 3, x \in N$
    (iv) $x \leqslant 2, x \in Z$ (v) $x \geqslant -3, x \in Z$ (vi) $x > -2, x \in Z$

7. Choose one of $x = 3, x \leqslant 3, x < 3, x > 3$ or $x \geqslant 3$ to describe each graph below,
where $x \in R$.

(i)   −1   0   1   2   3   4   5 x
                                                     (ii)   −1   0   1   2   3   4   5 x

(iii)   −1   0   1   2   3   4   5 x
                                                     (iv)   −1   0   1   2   3   4   5 x

8. Write the inequality represented by each of these number lines:

(i) $-3 \ -2 \ -1 \ 0 \ 1 \ 2 \ 3 \ \ x$

(ii) $-3 \ -2 \ -1 \ 0 \ 1 \ 2 \ 3 \ \ x$

(iii) $-1 \ 0 \ 1 \ 2 \ 3 \ 4 \ 5 \ \ x$

(iv) $-9 \ -6 \ -3 \ 0 \ 3 \ 6 \ 9 \ \ x$

(v) $0 \ 2 \ 4 \ 6 \ 8 \ 10 \ 12 \ \ x$

(vi) $-3 \ -2 \ -1 \ 0 \ 1 \ 2 \ 3 \ \ x$

9. Graph each of the following on the number line:

(i) $x \geqslant 1, x \in R$ (ii) $x \geqslant -3, x \in R$ (iii) $x \leqslant 4, x \in R$

(iv) $x > 3, x \in R$ (v) $x < -1, x \in R$ (vi) $x < 4, x \in R$

10. Write each of the following statements as a mathematical sentence.
Let n stand for the number in each case.

(i)   I have at least 6 shirts in my wardrobe.

(ii)   The temperature in a fridge must be 5°C or less.

(iii)   Hand baggage must not exceed 10 kg.

(iv)   Gillian has more than 5 DVDs.

Section 20.2 **Solving inequalities**

Here are scales that show $10 > 8$.

$10 > 8$

Would the scales stay as they are if

> the same amount is added to both sides
> the same amount is subtracted from both sides
> the mass on each side is doubled
> the mass on each side is halved ?

The answer to each question is 'yes'.

The answers to the four questions above illustrate two very important results for inequalities:

Rules for inequalities

1. An inequality remains true when the same number is added to or subtracted from both sides.

2. An inequality remains true when both sides are multiplied or divided by the same **positive** number.

Here are some numerical examples:

We know that the inequality	**$6 > 4$**
Add 4 to both sides:	$10 > 8$ … true
Subtract 3 from both sides:	$3 > 1$ … true
Multiply both sides by 3:	$18 > 12$ … true
Divide both sides by 2:	$3 > 2$ … true

Multiplication by a negative number

Consider again the inequality $6 > 4$.
Multiply both sides by -2: $\quad -12 > -8 \ldots$ false $\ldots$ as $-12 < -8$.

This illustrates that the inequality sign must be changed (i.e. reversed) when both sides of an inequality are multiplied or divided by the same **negative** number.

(i) $2 < 5$,
but $2 \times (-2) > 5 \times (-2)$,
i.e. $-4 > -10$

(ii) $8 > 6$, but $\dfrac{8}{-2} < \dfrac{6}{-2}$,
i.e. $-4 < -3$.

> If an inequality is multiplied or divided by the same negative number, the inequality sign must be reversed.

Example 1

Solve the inequality $5x - 3 \geqslant 12, x \in N$ and graph the solution on the number line.

$$5x - 3 \geqslant 12$$
$$5x \geqslant 12 + 3 \quad \ldots \text{add 3 to both sides}$$
$$5x \geqslant 15$$
$$x \geqslant 3 \quad \ldots \text{divide both sides by 5}$$

The solution is graphed on the number line below.

Example 2

Solve the inequality $2x - 3 < 5, x \in R$ and graph the solution on the number line.

$$2x - 3 < 5$$
$$2x - 3 + 3 < 5 + 3 \quad \ldots \text{add 3 to each side}$$
$$2x < 8$$
$$x < 4 \quad \ldots \text{divide each side by 2}$$

Exercise 20.2

1. Which of the following inequalities are equivalent to $a \geqslant 10$?

Ⓐ $a - 5 \geqslant 5$ **Ⓑ** $2a \geqslant 20$ **Ⓒ** $a + 5 \geqslant 5$ **Ⓓ** $\frac{1}{2}a \geqslant 5$ **Ⓔ** $a + \frac{1}{2} \geqslant 10\frac{1}{2}$

2. Which of the following inequalities are equivalent to $m < 3$?

Ⓐ $m + 2 < 5$ **Ⓑ** $2m < 4$ **Ⓒ** $3 > m$ **Ⓓ** $8 > m + 5$ **Ⓔ** $6 > 2m$

Solve the following inequalities and graph the solution on the number line in each case:

3. $x - 1 \leqslant 4, x \in N$

4. $3x - 2 \leqslant 10, x \in N$

5. $4x - 5 \leqslant 11, x \in N$

6. $3x + 5 \leqslant 14, x \in N$

7. $2x + 5 \leqslant 1, x \in Z$

8. $3x - 5 \leqslant 7, x \in Z$

9. $3x - 1 < -10, x \in Z$

10. $5x - 2 \leqslant 8, x \in Z$

11. $3x - 8 \leqslant 7, x \in R$

12. $2x + 2 \leqslant 8, x \in R$

13. $5x + 7 < 17, x \in R$

14. $3 - x \leqslant 4, x \in R$

15. $5 - 2x \geqslant -7, x \in R$

16. $1 - 5x > -14, x \in R$

17. $3x + 1 \geqslant 2x + 2, x \in R$

18. $4x + 2 \leqslant 2x + 8, x \in R$

19. $4x - 5 \leqslant x + 7, x \in R$

20. $2x - 1 < x + 2, x \in R$

21. $3x - 7 \geqslant x - 1, x \in R$

22. $5x + 7 < 3x + 3, x \in Z$

23. $1 - 2x \leqslant 5, x \in R$

24. $4 - 3x \geqslant 13, x \in R$

25. (i) For the set of values $x \leqslant 1$, which of the numbers in the bubble are values of x?
(ii) Which are values of n for the set $n > 3$?

26. If we know that $x > 3$, decide if each of the following is

- **always** true   or   - **sometimes** true   or   - **never** true

(i) $x > 4$ (ii) $x > 2$ (iii) $x > -1$ (iv) $x < 1$
(v) $x + 5 > 8$ (vi) $x - 1 < 4$ (vii) $2x > 3$ (viii) $3x + 1 > 10$

Section 20.3 Adding algebraic fractions

To add $\frac{3}{4} + \frac{4}{5}$, we first find the LCM of 4 and 5, i.e. 20.

We now express each fraction with 20 as denominator.

$$\therefore \quad \frac{3}{4} + \frac{4}{5} = \frac{5(3)}{20} + \frac{4(4)}{20} = \frac{15}{20} + \frac{16}{20} = \frac{15 + 16}{20} = \frac{31}{20} = 1\frac{11}{20}$$

Similarly, $\frac{6}{7} - \frac{2}{3} = \frac{3(6) - 7(2)}{21} = \frac{18 - 14}{21} = \frac{4}{21}$

Algebraic fractions can be added or subtracted in the same way as numerical fractions.

Example 1

Express each of these as a single fraction:

(i) $\frac{x}{4} + \frac{x}{6}$ (ii) $\frac{x+3}{5} + \frac{x-1}{3}$

(i) $\frac{x}{4} + \frac{x}{6}$

The smallest number into which 4 and 6 divide is 12.

$$\frac{x}{4} + \frac{x}{6} = \frac{3(x)}{12} + \frac{2(x)}{12} = \frac{3x + 2x}{12} = \frac{5x}{12}$$

(ii) $\frac{x+3}{5} + \frac{x-1}{3}$

The smallest number into which 5 and 3 divide is 15.

$$\therefore \quad \frac{x+3}{5} + \frac{x-1}{3} = \frac{3(x+3)}{15} + \frac{5(x-1)}{15}$$

$$= \frac{3x+9}{15} + \frac{5x-5}{15}$$

$$= \frac{3x+9+5x-5}{15} = \frac{8x+4}{15}$$

Example 2

Express as a single fraction: $\frac{5x-3}{2} - \frac{2x+1}{3}$

The LCM of 2 and 3 is 6.

$$\frac{5x-3}{2} - \frac{2x+1}{3} = \frac{3(5x-3) - 2(2x+1)}{6}$$

$$= \frac{15x - 9 - 4x - 2}{6} = \frac{11x - 11}{6}$$

> LCM is the lowest common multiple.

Exercise 20.3

Express each of the following as a single fraction:

1. $\frac{1}{2} + \frac{2}{3}$

2. $\frac{3}{4} + \frac{3}{5}$

3. $\frac{5}{12} + \frac{2}{12} + \frac{1}{12}$

4. $\frac{7}{8} - \frac{3}{4}$

5. $\frac{x}{2} + \frac{x}{3}$

6. $\frac{x}{5} + \frac{x}{3}$

7. $\frac{3x}{4} + \frac{5x}{2}$

8. $\frac{3x}{5} + \frac{2x}{3}$

9. $\frac{x}{4} - \frac{x}{6}$

10. $\frac{x}{2} - \frac{x}{5}$

11. $\frac{7x}{5} - \frac{x}{2}$

12. $\frac{3x}{4} - \frac{2x}{5}$

13. $\frac{x+1}{2} + \frac{x}{2}$

14. $\frac{x+1}{2} + \frac{x+4}{2}$

15. $\frac{x+4}{3} + \frac{2x+1}{3}$

16. $\frac{3x-4}{5} + \frac{5x-2}{5}$

17. $\frac{3x-2}{4} + \frac{5x+6}{4}$

18. $\frac{2x+1}{3} + \frac{2x-3}{3}$

19. $\frac{2x+1}{3} + \frac{x+4}{2}$

20. $\frac{2x-1}{3} + \frac{x+2}{4}$

21. $\frac{2x-1}{6} + \frac{x-3}{4}$

22. $\frac{5x-1}{5} - \frac{x}{2}$

23. $\frac{3x-2}{3} - \frac{x+4}{2}$

24. $\frac{5x-3}{4} - \frac{2x+1}{3}$

25. $\frac{2x+1}{3} - \frac{2x-1}{4}$

26. $\frac{7x-2}{7} - \frac{x-5}{14}$

27. $\frac{2x-1}{12} - \frac{3x-4}{6}$

28. $\frac{3x-1}{2} + \frac{2x-6}{5}$

29. $\frac{3x+1}{4} - \frac{2x-3}{6}$

30. $\frac{2x-3y}{3} - \frac{x-2y}{5}$

31. $\frac{2x-3}{2} + \frac{x-1}{4} - \frac{5}{6}$

32. $\frac{x-6}{3} + \frac{3}{4} - \frac{3x-4}{2}$

Section 20.4 Solving equations involving fractions

Consider the equation $\frac{x-1}{5} = 4$.

To get rid of the fraction, we multiply both sides by 5.

$$\therefore \frac{{}^1\cancel{5}(x-1)}{\cancel{5}_1} = 4 \times 5$$

$$x - 1 = 20$$
$$x - 1 + 1 = 20 + 1$$
$$x = 21$$

> If an equation contains more than one fraction, we multiply each part by the lowest common multiple (LCM) of the denominators.

Example 1

Solve each of these equations:

(i) $\dfrac{3x}{4} - \dfrac{x}{2} = 3$

(ii) $\dfrac{2x-5}{3} = \dfrac{x-2}{2}$

(i) The LCM of 4 and 2 is 4.
Multiply each term by 4.

$$\frac{\mathbf{4}(3x)}{4} - \frac{\mathbf{4}(x)}{2} = 3 \times \mathbf{4}$$

$$3x - 2x = 12$$

$$x = 12$$

(ii) The LCM of 3 and 2 is 6.
Multiply each term by 6.

$$\frac{\mathbf{6}(2x-5)}{3} = \frac{\mathbf{6}(x-2)}{2}$$

$$2(2x-5) = 3(x-2)$$

$$4x - 10 = 3x - 6$$

$$4x - 3x - 10 = 3x - 3x - 6$$

$$x - 10 = -6$$

$$x - 10 + 10 = -6 + 10$$

$$x = 4$$

Example 2

Solve the equation: $\dfrac{3x-1}{6} - \dfrac{x-3}{4} = \dfrac{4}{3}$

The LCM of 6, 4 and 3 is 12.
We now multiply each term by 12.

$$\frac{\mathbf{12}(3x-1)}{6} - \frac{\mathbf{12}(x-3)}{4} = \frac{\mathbf{12}(4)}{3}$$

$$2(3x-1) - 3(x-3) = 4(4)$$

$$6x - 2 - 3x + 9 = 16$$

$$3x + 7 = 16$$

$$3x + 7 - 7 = 16 - 7$$

$$3x = 9$$

$$x = 3$$

Exercise 20.4

Solve the following equations:

1. $\dfrac{x}{2} = 3$

2. $\dfrac{x}{4} = 5$

3. $\dfrac{2x}{3} = 6$

4. $\dfrac{3x}{5} = 3$

5. $\dfrac{2x}{3} = \dfrac{14}{3}$

6. $\dfrac{2x}{5} = \dfrac{6}{5}$

7. $\dfrac{x}{2} = \dfrac{6}{4}$

8. $\dfrac{2x}{9} = \dfrac{2}{3}$

9. $\dfrac{3x}{4} = \dfrac{9}{2}$

10. $\dfrac{5x}{3} = 10$

11. $\dfrac{3x}{8} = \dfrac{3}{2}$

12. $\dfrac{x-3}{2} = 4$

13. $\dfrac{3x-1}{4} = 4$

14. $\dfrac{2x+1}{5} = 1$

15. $\dfrac{4x-3}{7} = 3$

16. $\dfrac{3x-1}{4} = 8$

17. $\dfrac{4x+2}{7} = 2$

18. $\dfrac{3x-2}{3} = \dfrac{16}{3}$

19. $\dfrac{x-3}{3} = \dfrac{x-2}{4}$

20. $\dfrac{4x-7}{6} = \dfrac{x+2}{4}$

21. $\dfrac{x-1}{2} = \dfrac{2x+1}{5}$

22. $\dfrac{x}{2} + \dfrac{x}{3} = 5$

23. $\dfrac{x}{3} + \dfrac{x}{6} = 2$

24. $\dfrac{x}{2} + \dfrac{2x}{5} = \dfrac{9}{2}$

25. $\dfrac{x}{3} - \dfrac{x}{5} = \dfrac{4}{3}$

26. $\dfrac{x}{3} - \dfrac{x}{12} = \dfrac{1}{4}$

27. $\dfrac{2x}{3} - \dfrac{x}{4} = \dfrac{5}{6}$

28. $\dfrac{3x}{4} - \dfrac{x}{2} = 3$

29. $\dfrac{x}{3} + \dfrac{2x}{5} = \dfrac{11}{15}$

30. $\dfrac{3x}{4} - \dfrac{5x}{8} = \dfrac{1}{2}$

31. $\dfrac{3x}{4} - \dfrac{2x}{3} = \dfrac{1}{4}$

32. $\dfrac{3x}{2} + \dfrac{2x}{3} = 13$

33. $\dfrac{2x}{3} - \dfrac{x}{4} = \dfrac{5}{2}$

34. $\dfrac{5x}{6} - \dfrac{x}{2} = 3$

35. $\dfrac{3x}{4} - \dfrac{2x}{3} = \dfrac{5}{12}$

36. $\dfrac{4x}{5} - \dfrac{x}{2} = \dfrac{3}{4}$

37. $\dfrac{2x-1}{5} = \dfrac{x}{3} + \dfrac{1}{3}$

38. $\dfrac{2x+3}{5} + \dfrac{x}{2} = 6$

39. $\dfrac{x+1}{4} - \dfrac{x}{3} = \dfrac{1}{12}$

40. $\dfrac{2x-1}{3} + \dfrac{x}{4} = \dfrac{6}{4}$

41. $\dfrac{x+4}{3} - \dfrac{x}{4} = 2$

42. $\dfrac{x}{5} - \dfrac{3}{2} = \dfrac{x-3}{6}$

43. The diagram shows an isosceles triangle ABC.

If $|AB| = |AC|$,

   (i) write down an equation in terms of x

   (ii) work out the length of [AB].

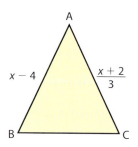

Section 20.5 Solving problems involving fractions ———

The ability to change a problem expressed in words into a mathematical sentence is very important in mathematics.

You will already have changed statements like that shown on the right into mathematical sentences.

> I think of a number.
> I take off 5.
> I multiply the result by 3.
> My answer is 21.
> What is my number?

Discuss which one of these equations you should use to solve this puzzle.

$$3x - 5 = 21 \qquad 3(x - 5) = 21 \qquad x - 5 \times 3 = 21$$

In this section we will deal with some simple problems that involve the use of fractions.

Example 1

If the sum of a quarter of a number and a fifth of the same number is 18, find the number.

Let x be the number.

$\frac{1}{4}$ of the number $= \frac{x}{4}$ $\frac{1}{5}$ of the number $= \frac{x}{5}$

The equation is: $\frac{x}{4} + \frac{x}{5} = 18$

Multiply each term by 20, the LCM of 4 and 5.

$$\frac{20(x)}{4} + \frac{20(x)}{5} = \frac{20(18)}{1}$$

$$5x + 4x = 360$$

$$9x = 360$$

$$x = 40$$

The required number is 40.

Exercise 20.5

1. The sum of a number and half the number is 12. Find the number.

2. If the sum of half a number and a third of the same number is 15, find the number.

3. The sum of half and three quarters of a certain number is 20. What is this number.

4. When half a certain number is taken from three quarters of the number, the result is 5. Find the number.

5. One number is 5 bigger than another number. When one third of the smaller number is added to half the bigger number, the answer is 10. Find the smaller number.

6. When 5 is added to a number and the result is divided by 4, the answer is 3. Work out what this number is.

7. When 3 is taken from four times a certain number and the result is divided by 7, the answer is 3. Find the number.

8. When two thirds of a certain number is taken from three quarters of the number, the answer is 2. Find the number.

9. I think of a number x. I add 8 to the number and then divide the total by 3. The result is the same as half the number I thought of. Find the value of x.

10. One number is 3 greater than another number. When one sixth of the bigger number is taken from one third of the smaller one, the result is 2. Find the two numbers.

Section 20.6 Simplifying algebraic fractions

The fraction $\frac{8}{12}$ can be simplified by dividing the numerator and denominator by 4, as shown.

$$\frac{^2\cancel{8}}{_3\cancel{12}} = \frac{2}{3}$$

Similarly, the algebraic fraction $\frac{4ab}{2b}$ can be simplified by dividing the numerator and denominator by any common factors.

Thus, $\dfrac{4ab}{2b} = \dfrac{^2\cancel{4} \times a \times \cancel{b}^1}{_1\cancel{2} \times \cancel{b}_1} = \dfrac{2 \times a}{1} = 2 \times a = 2a$

Example 1

Simplify each of the following:

(i) $\dfrac{9x^2y}{3x}$

(ii) $\dfrac{12a^3b}{ab^2}$

(i) $\dfrac{9x^2y}{3x} = \dfrac{{}^{3}9 \times \overset{1}{\cancel{x}} \times x \times y}{{}_{1}3 \times \cancel{x}_{1}}$

$= 3xy$

(ii) $\dfrac{12a^3b}{ab^2} = \dfrac{12 \times a \times a \times \overset{1}{\cancel{a}} \times \overset{1}{\cancel{b}}}{{}_{1}\cancel{a} \times b \times \cancel{b}_{1}}$

$= \dfrac{12a^2}{b}$

Using factors to simplify algebraic fractions

The expression $\dfrac{x^2 - 4}{x + 2}$ can be simplified by first factorising the numerator and then dividing above and below by a common factor.

$$\dfrac{x^2 - 4}{x + 2} = \dfrac{\overset{1}{\cancel{(x + 2)}}(x - 2)}{\underset{1}{\cancel{(x + 2)}}} = x - 2$$

Example 2

Simplify (i) $\dfrac{5a - 10b}{2a - 4b}$

(ii) $\dfrac{a^2 + 2a}{a^2 + 3a + 2}$.

(i) $\dfrac{5a - 10b}{2a - 4b} = \dfrac{5\overset{1}{\cancel{(a - 2b)}}}{2\underset{1}{\cancel{(a - 2b)}}}$

$= \dfrac{5}{2}$

(ii) $\dfrac{a^2 + 2a}{a^2 + 3a + 2} = \dfrac{a\overset{1}{\cancel{(a + 2)}}}{\underset{1}{\cancel{(a + 2)}}(a + 1)}$

$= \dfrac{a}{a + 1}$

Exercise 20.6

1. Simplify each of the following algebraic fractions:

(i) $\dfrac{10ab}{2b}$

(ii) $\dfrac{8xy}{4x}$

(iii) $\dfrac{15cd}{5d}$

(iv) $\dfrac{18ab}{6a}$

(v) $\dfrac{8x^2y}{4xy}$

(vi) $\dfrac{16b^2c}{2c}$

(vii) $\dfrac{14x^3y}{2x^2y}$

(viii) $\dfrac{28ab^2}{7ab}$

2. Simplify these expressions:

(i) $\dfrac{3}{x} \times \dfrac{4x}{9}$ (ii) $\dfrac{km}{4n} \times \dfrac{2n}{m}$ (iii) $\dfrac{ab}{3} \times \dfrac{6b}{a}$ (iv) $\dfrac{2ab \times 6a}{3a}$

(v) $\dfrac{x}{3} \div \dfrac{x}{6}$ (vi) $\dfrac{3}{2x} \div \dfrac{1}{3x}$ (vii) $\dfrac{3ab^2}{2} \div \dfrac{ab}{6}$ (viii) $\dfrac{8a \times 3ak}{2a \times 6k}$

3.

A	E	G	L	M	N	O	P	R
$2b$	$4bc$	bc^2	$4d$	cd	$2b^2$	$3bd$	$3c$	$2b^2d$

Simplify each expression below as far as you can.
Use the code above to find a letter for each expression.

Rearrange each set of letters to spell a fruit.

(i) $\dfrac{8cd}{2c}$ $\dfrac{12bc}{3}$ $\dfrac{15cd}{5d}$ $\dfrac{4bc}{2c}$ $\dfrac{9c^2b}{3cb}$

(ii) $\dfrac{18b^2d}{6b}$ $\dfrac{10ab^2}{5a}$ $\dfrac{20b^2c^2}{5bc}$ $\dfrac{12cd^5}{3cd^4}$ $\dfrac{5c^2d}{5c}$

Simplify each of the following, using factors where necessary:

4. $\dfrac{6(a + b)}{3}$ **5.** $\dfrac{4x + 4y}{4}$ **6.** $\dfrac{12(a + b)}{3(a + b)}$

7. $\dfrac{3(x + y)}{6x + 6y}$ **8.** $\dfrac{4a - 8b}{3(a - 2b)}$ **9.** $\dfrac{3x + 12}{x(x + 4)}$

10. $\dfrac{2a - 3b}{6a - 9b}$ **11.** $\dfrac{3(x + y)(x + y)}{3x + 3y}$ **12.** $\dfrac{x(x - 2y)}{3x - 6y}$

13. $\dfrac{2x + 4y}{x^2 + 2xy}$ **14.** $\dfrac{x + 2y}{(x + y)(x + 2y)}$ **15.** $\dfrac{x^2 - y^2}{2(x + y)}$

16. $\dfrac{x + 3}{x^2 + 6x + 9}$ **17.** $\dfrac{x^2 + 5x + 4}{x + 1}$ **18.** $\dfrac{x^2 - 2x - 3}{2(x - 3)}$

19. $\dfrac{x + 4}{x^2 + 2x - 8}$ **20.** $\dfrac{x^2 + 2x - 24}{x - 4}$ **21.** $\dfrac{x^2 - x}{x - 1}$

22. $\dfrac{x^2 - 9}{x^2 - x - 6}$ **23.** $\dfrac{x^2 + 3x - 10}{x^2 - 4}$ **24.** $\dfrac{x^2 + 4x - 5}{x - 1}$

25. $\dfrac{3(x^2 - 4y^2)}{9(x + 2y)}$ **26.** $\dfrac{x^2 - 2x - 15}{4x + 12}$ **27.** $\dfrac{x^2 + 2x - 35}{x^2 - 25}$

Test yourself 20

1. (a) (i) For what values of x is $2x - 3 \leqslant 7, x \in N$?

(ii) Express as a single fraction $\dfrac{x + 3}{4} + \dfrac{2x}{3}$.

(b) (i) Simplify $\dfrac{5ab}{c} \times \dfrac{ac}{10b}$.

(ii) Solve the equation $\dfrac{2x}{5} = 4$.

(c) If $x \in N$, state the values x may have in each of the following:

(i) $x \leqslant 6$ (ii) $x \geqslant 2$ and $x < 9$ (iii) $2x + 1 < 13$.

2. (a) (i) Solve the following inequality and graph the solution on the number line:

$$3x - 2 \geqslant 4, x \in N$$

(ii) List all the integers, x, for which $x^2 < 17$.

(b) Express as a single fraction $\dfrac{2x + 3}{3} + \dfrac{x - 1}{2}$.

(c) Use factors to simplify $\dfrac{x^2 - x - 6}{x + 2}$.

3. (a) Simplify each of these:

(i) $\dfrac{6x^2y}{3xy}$ (ii) $\dfrac{10x}{7} \times \dfrac{14y^2}{5xy}$

(b) Solve the following inequality and graph the solution on the number line:

$$3x - 7 \geqslant x - 3, x \in R.$$

(c) Solve the equation $\dfrac{3x}{4} - \dfrac{5x}{8} = \dfrac{3}{8}$.

4. (a) Write down the inequality represented by each of the following number lines, where $x \in Z$ in each case:

(i)

(ii)

(b) Solve each of these equations:

(i) $\dfrac{2x + 1}{3} = 7$ (ii) $\dfrac{4x + 4}{3} = \dfrac{3x - 1}{2}$

(c) Simplify each of these:

(i) $\dfrac{11a^2b}{33ab^2}$ (ii) $\dfrac{x^2 + 3x - 18}{x + 6}$

5. (a) Solve this inequality and graph your solution on the number line:

$$4x + 2 \leqslant -10,\, x \in Z.$$

(b) Express as a single fraction $\dfrac{2x + 4}{3} - \dfrac{x - 6}{4}$.

(c) One number is 5 bigger than another number. When twice the smaller number is added to two thirds of the bigger number, the result is 14.
Find the two numbers.

6. (a) (i) If $x \in Z$, state the values x may have for this inequality:

$$x \geqslant -3 \text{ and } x < 3.$$

(ii) Write down all the values of x for which $4x - 5 < x + 10,\, x \in N$.

(b) Use factors to simplify $\dfrac{x^2 + 3x - 10}{x - 2}$.

(c) The equal sides in this triangle are marked.
Write an equation in x and solve it to find its value.
Hence find the length of the equal sides.

Functions

Key words

function rule   input   output   function machine   mapping diagram

domain   range   codomain   couples   ordered pairs

Section 21.1 Functions

Each term in the number sequence below is found by adding 4 to the previous term:

3   7   11   15   19

+4   +4   +4   +4   ... 'Add 4' is the **rule** for finding the next term.

Now consider this sequence:

2   6   18   54

×3   ×3   ×3   ... Here the rule is 'multiply by 3'

The next number in the sequence is 54×3, i.e. 162.
When the operation '$\times 3$' is applied to 54, we get 162.
We use the words **input** for 54 and **output** for 162.

The chain of diagrams below shows how we can find the output if we are given the input by means of a **function machine** or **flowchart**.

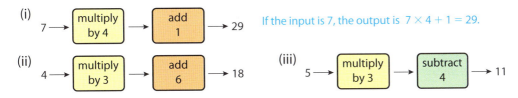

(i) $7 \to$ multiply by 4 $\to$ add 1 $\to 29$ If the input is 7, the output is $7 \times 4 + 1 = 29$.

(ii) $4 \to$ multiply by 3 $\to$ add 6 $\to 18$

(iii) $5 \to$ multiply by 3 $\to$ subtract 4 $\to 11$

If we call the input number *x* and the output number *y*, we can then write the 'rule' in terms of *x* and *y*.

$x \to$ multiply by 3 $\to$ add 2 $\to y$

The rule for this function machine is 'multiply by 3, then add 2'.

We can write this as $x \times 3 + 2 = y$ or $y = 3x + 2$.

Here are the rules for these function machines:

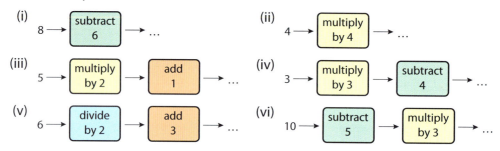

$x \longrightarrow$ multiply by 2 $\longrightarrow$ add 4 $\longrightarrow y$ Rule: $y = 2x + 4$

$x \longrightarrow$ multiply by 8 $\longrightarrow$ subtract 7 $\longrightarrow y$ Rule: $y = 8x - 7$

The rule $y = 2x + 4$ may also be written as $x \longrightarrow 2x + 4$.

Exercise 21.1

1. Find the output for each of these:

(i) $8 \longrightarrow$ subtract 6 $\longrightarrow$ ...

(ii) $4 \longrightarrow$ multiply by 4 $\longrightarrow$ ...

(iii) $5 \longrightarrow$ multiply by 2 $\longrightarrow$ add 1 $\longrightarrow$ ...

(iv) $3 \longrightarrow$ multiply by 3 $\longrightarrow$ subtract 4 $\longrightarrow$ ...

(v) $6 \longrightarrow$ divide by 2 $\longrightarrow$ add 3 $\longrightarrow$ ...

(vi) $10 \longrightarrow$ subtract 5 $\longrightarrow$ multiply by 3 $\longrightarrow$ ...

2. Describe in **words** the rule for each function machine in Question **1.** above.

3. Find the outputs for these:

(i) $3 \longrightarrow$ $7 \longrightarrow$ $8 \longrightarrow$ multiply by 2 $\longrightarrow$ subtract 4 $\longrightarrow$ ...

(ii) $2 \longrightarrow$ $1 \longrightarrow$ $0 \longrightarrow$ add 4 $\longrightarrow$ multiply by 2 $\longrightarrow$ ...

4.

$x \longrightarrow$ add 2 $\longrightarrow$ multiply by 3 $\longrightarrow y$ is a function machine.

Use a copy of this table and fill in the values for y.

x	1	2	3	4	5
y					

Write in words what this function machine does.

5. Write the rules for these function machines as $y = \ldots$

(i) $x \longrightarrow$ multiply by 2 $\longrightarrow$ add 6 $\longrightarrow y$

(ii) $x \longrightarrow$ multiply by 8 $\longrightarrow$ subtract 9 $\longrightarrow y$

(iii) $x \longrightarrow$ divide by 4 $\longrightarrow$ subtract 3 $\longrightarrow y$

(iv) $x \longrightarrow$ add 3 $\longrightarrow$ multiply by 4 $\longrightarrow y$

6. Write the rules for these function machines in the form $x \to \ldots$

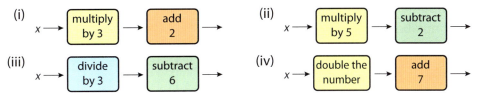

7. Find the missing operation in each of these:

8. Find the missing operations in these function machines:

9. What numbers went into each of these function machines?

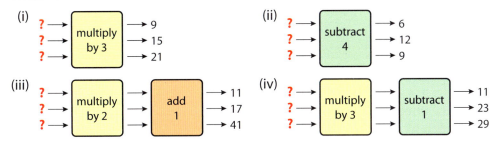

Section 21.2 Mapping diagrams

Consider this function machine: $\ldots \to$ [multiply by 3] $\to$ [subtract 4] $\to \ldots$

We will input all the numbers from the set $\{1, 3, 5, 7, 9\}$ into the function machine.

The output numbers are: $\{-1, 5, 11, 17, 23\}$.

The set of input numbers is called the **domain**.

The set of output numbers is called the **range**.

The input numbers and output numbers can be represented by a special type of diagram called a **mapping diagram**.
Each input number is mapped onto its corresponding output number.

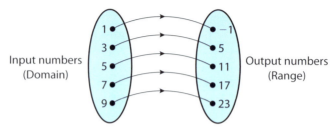

In the mapping diagram above, notice that there is one and **only one output number for each input number**.

In mathematics, we use the word **function** for any rule that produces one output value only for each input value.

Notation for a function

Consider this rule for a function: "Double the number and add 4".
If we input x, the output will be $2x + 4$.
The rule for this function may be written in any one of these three ways:

(i) $f(x) = 2x + 4$
(ii) $f: x \rightarrow 2x + 4$
(iii) $y = 2x + 4$.

These three notations tell us that if the input is 3, the output $(2x + 4)$ is $[(2 \times 3) + 4]$, i.e. 10.
This can be written as $f(3) = 10$.

The codomain

Take the two sets $A = \{1, 2, 3\}$ and $B = \{1, 3, 5, 7, 9, 11\}$.
If we are asked to list the couples of the function $f: x \rightarrow 2x - 1$, where the input numbers come from set A and the output numbers come from set B, we could set up a mapping diagram as follows:

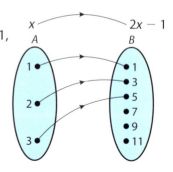

The couples are (1, 1), (2, 3) and (3, 5).

The set A is the **domain**, i.e. $\{1, 2, 3\}$.

The **range** is $\{1, 3, 5\}$.

The set B is called the **codomain**, that is, the set of allowable outputs.

∴ the codomain = {1, 3, 5, 7, 9, 11}.

The set of inputs is called the **domain**.

The set of outputs is called the **range**.

The set of possible outputs is called the **codomain**.

Example 1

A function f is defined as $f: x \rightarrow 3x - 2$.
The domain of f is {0, 1, 2, 3, 4}.
Represent f on a mapping diagram and write out the couples generated.
What is the range of f?

x	$3x - 2$	$f(x)$
0	$0 - 2$	-2
1	$3 - 2$	1
2	$6 - 2$	4
3	$9 - 2$	7
4	$12 - 2$	10

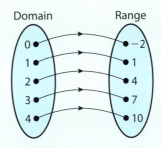

The couples are: {(0, −2), (1, 1), (2, 4), (3, 7), (4, 10)}.

The range is {−2, 1, 4, 7, 10}.

Identifying functions

When a function is represented by a mapping diagram, each element of the domain maps onto **one and only one** element of the range.

Consider these two mapping diagrams:

(i)   (ii)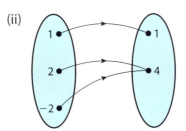

Diagram (i) is not a function because the element b is paired with 2 elements (e and f) in the range.

Diagram (ii) is a function because each element in the domain is mapped onto one and only one element in the range.

Couples

We have already seen that a function can be written as a set of **couples** or **ordered pairs**, i.e. (input, output).

When a function is written as a set of couples, no two distinct couples will have the same input.

> {(1, 4), (2, 5), (3, 6), (4, 7)} is a function as no two couples have the same input.

> {(2, 7), (3, 8), (3, 9), (4, 12)} is **not** a function as the input 3 has two different outputs.

Exercise 21.2

1. Use the given mapping diagram to write down

    (i) the domain

    (ii) the range

    (iii) the set of couples formed

    (iv) the rule that gives the outputs.

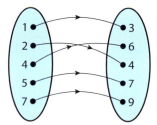

2. Copy and complete the mapping diagrams below.
Write down the domain and range of each function.

(i)

Rule: Add 5

(ii)

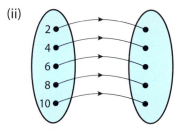

Rule: $x \rightarrow 2x + 1$

3. State whether each of the following mapping diagrams represents a function.
Give a reason for your answer in each case:

(i)

(ii)

(iii) 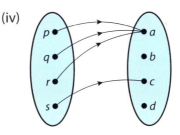 (iv)

4. Say why the following set of couples is a function:

{(1, 7), (2, 8), (3, 9), (4, 10)}.

5. Say why the following set of couples is not a function:

{(2, 5), (3, 6), (5, 8), (2, 10)}.

6. Investigate if each of these sets of couples represents a function.
If it is not a function, state the reason why.

   (i) {(0, 0), (1, 1), (2, 4), (3, 9), (4, 16)}

  (ii) {(−2, 1), (−1, 3), (−2, 5), (1, 6), (2, 9)}

 (iii) {(−3, 4), (0, 7), (2, 9), (4, 11)}

7. The flowchart $x \longrightarrow$ [add 3] $\longrightarrow$ [multiply by 2] $\longrightarrow y$ shows how to find the output (y)

for any input (x).

Express this in the form $y = \ldots\ldots$.

Use this function to find the values
of the outputs in the given table.

Input (x)	Output (y)
1	
2	
3	
4	
5	

8. For each of the mapping diagrams below, write down

   (i) the domain   (ii) the range   (iii) the codomain.

(a) 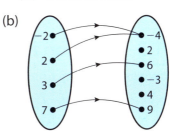 (b)

9. The rule for a function is: 'Multiply by 2 and add 3'.
   If the domain of the function is {0, 1, 3, 5}, write down

   (i) the range
   (ii) the couples generated.

10. A function f is defined as $f: x \rightarrow 3x - 1$.
    The domain of the function is {1, 2, 4, 6}.
    Write down the range of the function.

11. A function f is defined as $f(x) = 4x - 5$.
    The domain of the function is {−2, 0, 2, 4}.

    (i) What is the range of f?
    (ii) Write f as a set of couples.

12. Make a copy of this table.
    Fill it in for the function machine shown below.

x	1	2	3	4	5
y					

    $x \longrightarrow$ | multiply by 2 | $\longrightarrow$ | add 7 | $\longrightarrow y$

    Write the function in the form $y = \ldots\ldots$.

13. This is a function machine:
    Write the function in the form
    $f(x) = \ldots\ldots$.

    $x \longrightarrow$ | multiply by 4 | $\longrightarrow$ | add 10 | $\longrightarrow y$

    If the input is 5, what is the output?
    Use the function rule to find the input when the output is 22.

14. $x \longrightarrow$ | multiply by 2 | $\longrightarrow$ | add 4 | $\longrightarrow y$ describes a function.

    Copy the table on the right and fill in
    the missing input and output numbers.

Input (x)	Output (y)
3	
−2	
	14
	−8

Section 21.3 Notation for functions

We have already seen that a function can be written in any of these ways:

(i) $f(x) = 3x - 2$ (ii) $f: x \rightarrow 3x - 2$ (iii) $y = 3x - 2$

In each case, the output is $(3x - 2)$ when the input is x.

The notation **f(3)** is used to represent the output number when 3 is the input number.
If $f(x) = 3x - 2$, then $f(3) = 3(3) - 2 = 9 - 2 = 7$.
Thus, $f(3) = 7$.

While $f(x)$ is generally used to describe a function, other letters such as $g(x)$ and $h(x)$ are used when we are dealing with more than one function.

Example 1

The functions f and g are defined as follows
$$f: x \rightarrow x + 5 \quad \text{and} \quad g: x \rightarrow x^2 - 1.$$
Find (i) $f(3)$ (ii) $f(-4)$ (iii) $3f(-2)$ (iv) $g(4)$ (v) $g(-3)$

(i) $f(x) = x + 5$
$f(3) = 3 + 5 = 8$

(ii) $f(x) = x + 5$
$f(-4) = -4 + 5 = 1$

(iii) $f(x) = x + 5$
$3f(-2) = 3(-2 + 5)$
$= 3(3) = 9$

(iv) $g(x) = x^2 - 1$
$g(4) = 4^2 - 1 = 16 - 1 = 15$

(v) $g(x) = x^2 - 1$
$g(-3) = (-3)^2 - 1 = 9 - 1 = 8$

Example 2

$f(x) = 3x - 4$ defines a function.

(i) If $f(x) = 5$, find the value of x.
(ii) If $f(a) = 11$, find the value of a.
(iii) If $f(x) = 2f(-1)$, find the value of x.

(i) $f(x) = 3x - 4$
$\therefore 3x - 4 = 5$
$3x = 9$
$x = 3$

(ii) $f(a) = 3a - 4$
$\therefore 3a - 4 = 11$
$3a = 15$
$a = 5$

(iii) $f(x) = 2f(-1)$
$\therefore 3x - 4 = 2[3(-1) - 4]$
$3x - 4 = 2[-7]$
$3x - 4 = -14$
$3x = -10$
$x = -\frac{10}{3} = -3\frac{1}{3}$

Exercise 21.3

1. If $f(x) = 3x$, find
   (i) $f(1)$ (ii) $f(3)$ (iii) $f(4)$ (iv) $f(6)$ (v) $f(-2)$

2. If $f(x) = 2x + 3$, find
   (i) $f(2)$ (ii) $f(3)$ (iii) $f(5)$ (iv) $f(0)$ (v) $f(-3)$

3. If $f(x) = 3x - 1$, find
   (i) $f(1)$ (ii) $f(2)$ (iii) $f(4)$ (iv) $f(5)$ (v) $f(-1)$

4. If $f(x) = x^2 - 3$, find
   (i) $f(0)$ (ii) $f(1)$ (iii) $f(2)$ (iv) $f(-2)$ (v) $f(-4)$

5. If $f(x) = 5 - 2x$, find
   (i) $f(0)$ (ii) $f(2)$ (iii) $f(-3)$ (iv) $f(-\frac{1}{2})$ (v) $f(k)$

6. If $f(x) = 5x - 2$, solve the following equations:
   (i) $f(x) = 8$ (ii) $f(x) = 3$ (iii) $f(k) = -12$

7. If $f(x) = 2x - 5$, find
   (i) $f(3)$ (ii) $f(0)$ (iii) $f(1) + f(4)$ (iv) $2f(-3)$ (v) $f(3) + f(-3)$

8. If $f(x) = 3x - 2$ and $g(x) = 2 - 4x$, solve the following equations:
   (i) $f(x) = 4$ (ii) $g(x) = -10$ (iii) $g(x) = f(4)$

9. If $f(x) = 5x - 2$ and $x \in \{1, 2, 3, 4\}$, write down the four couples of the function.

10. A function is defined by $f : x \to x^2 + 3x - 2$. Find
    (i) $f(1)$ (ii) $f(2)$ (iii) $f(3)$ (iv) $f(0)$ (v) $f(-2)$

11. A function is defined by $f(x) = 5x - 4$.
    If the domain of f is {0, 1, 2, 3, 4}, find the range of f.

12. $f : x \to 3x + 4$ is a function.
    (i) Find $f(4)$.   (ii) If $f(x) = 10$, find x.   (iii) If $f(k) = -2$, find k.

13. If $f(x) = 3x - 5$ which *one* of the following is not a couple of the function?
    (i) $(2, 1)$ (ii) $(4, 7)$ (iii) $(2, -1)$ (iv) $(0, -5)$

14. The domain of the function $f : x \to x^2 - 3x + 4$ is {-2, -1, 0, 1, 2).
    (i) List the five couples of the function.
    (ii) Write down the range of the function.

Test yourself 21

1. (a) If $f(x) = 3x - 2$, find
    (i) $f(2)$ (ii) $f(0)$ (iii) $f(-2)$ (iv) $2f(2) + 3f(-1)$.

(b) For the set of couples $\{(2, 3), (3, 6), (4, 8), (5, 18)\}$, write down
    (i) the domain   (ii) the range

(c) $f(x) = 4x - 3$ defines a function.
    (i) Find $f(-2)$.
    (ii) If $f(x) = 9$, find the value of x.
    (iii) If $f(k) = -7$, find the value of k.

2. (a) Use a copy of this table.
Fill it in for the function machine,

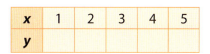

x	1	2	3	4	5
y					

(b) State whether each of these mapping diagrams represents a function, giving a reason for your answers:

  (i)

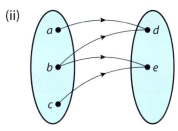

  (ii)

(c) A function is defined by $f : x \rightarrow 4x - 5$.
    (i) Find $f(3)$ and $f(10)$.
    (ii) Find the value of k when $f(10) = kf(3)$.

3. (a) A function f is defined by $f : x \rightarrow 5x - 1$.
If the domain of $f = \{0, 1, 2, 3\}$, find the range of f.

(b) State why the set of couples $\{(1, 3), (2, 7), (3, 10), (1, 12)\}$ is not a function.

(c) $f(x) = ax - 6$ is a function.
If $f(2) = -2$, find the value of a.

4. (a) What operation does the question mark stand for in the given function machine?

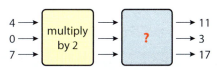

(b) $f(x) = 3x - 4$ defines a function.
If the domain of f is $\{-3, -2, -1, 0\}$,
what is the range of f?

(c) The cost €C of hiring a taxi is given by $C = 5k + 3$, where k is the number of kilometres travelled.

(i) Find the cost of hiring a taxi for a journey of 8 kilometres.

(ii) If the cost of a journey was €23, how long was the journey?

5. (a) Find the output number for each input number in the function machines below:

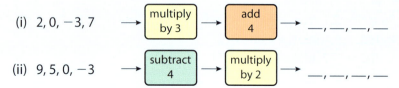

(i) $2, 0, -3, 7$ → | multiply by 3 | → | add 4 | → __, __, __, __

(ii) $9, 5, 0, -3$ → | subtract 4 | → | multiply by 2 | → __, __, __, __

(b) A function is defined as $f: x \rightarrow 4x - 2$.
Copy the mapping diagram and fill in the missing numbers a, b and c.

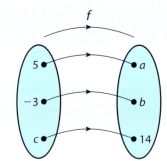

(c) If $f(x) = 2x - 3$ and $g(x) = 3 - 5x$, solve these equations:

(i) $f(x) = 7$

(ii) $g(x) = -7$

(iii) $f(x) = g(-3)$.

6. (a) A function f is defined by $f: x \rightarrow 5x - 3$.
Copy and complete these three couples of f:
$(1, *), \ (3, *), \ (0, *)$.

(b) A function machine and three output numbers are given below.
Find the three input numbers.

__, __, __ → | subtract 4 | → | multiply by 3 | → 3, 12, 24

(c) The function f is defined by $f(x) = 7 - 3x$.
If $f(24) = kf(-2)$, find the value of k.

Graphing Functions

Key words

linear function   domain   intercept method   parabola   axis of symmetry
quadratic function   intersecting graphs

Section 22.1 Graphing linear functions

Consider the function $f(x) = x + 3$.
This function can be written as a set of couples by taking different values for x.

$f(1) = 1 + 3 = 4 \Rightarrow (1, 4)$ is one couple.
$f(2) = 2 + 3 = 5 \Rightarrow (2, 5)$ is another couple.

Other couples are $(0, 3), (-3, 0), \ldots$
When these couples are plotted and joined,
they will form a line as shown.

Since the graph of $f(x) = x + 3$ is a line,
we say that $f(x)$ is a **linear function**.

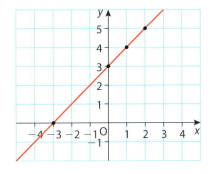

A line is the most straightforward function to
graph as we need only two points to plot it.

Usually we are given the **domain** in which to draw any function.
The domain $x = -2$ to $x = 3$, both included, is written as $-2 \leqslant x \leqslant 3$.

When plotting a line, two points are sufficient to enable us to plot it, but we generally
take three points in case any errors are made.

Example 1

Graph the function $f(x) = 2x - 4$ in the domain $-1 \leqslant x \leqslant 4$.
Use your graph to find
(i) $f(3)$ (ii) the value of x for which $f(x) = -2$.

To find three points, we generally select the smallest and largest x-values in the given domain and one value for x in between those two.

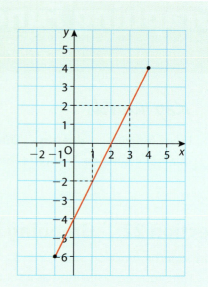

x	$2x - 4$	y
-1	$-2 - 4$	-6
0	$0 - 4$	-4
4	$8 - 4$	4

The three points are $(-1, -6)$, $(0, -4)$ and $(4, 4)$.
Join these points to give a line.

(i) $f(3)$ represents the y-value when $x = 3$.
   From the graph, this is 2, i.e. $f(3) = 2$.

(ii) $f(x) = -2 \Rightarrow y = -2$
   The value of x in the graph when $y = -2$ is $x = 1$.

The intercept method for drawing a line

If the equation of a line is in a form such as $3x - 4y = 12$, it is more convenient to find the two points where the line intersects the x-axis and y-axis.

$$3x - 4y = 12$$

$$x = 0 \Rightarrow 0 - 4y = 12 \Rightarrow y = -3$$

∴ $(0, -3)$ is one point on the line.

$$y = 0 \Rightarrow 3x = 12 \Rightarrow x = 4$$

∴ $(4, 0)$ is a second point on the line.

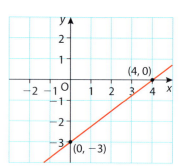

These points are joined to give the required line.

This method is generally called the **intercept method**.

Exercise 22.1

1. Copy and complete the table on the right and use the table to draw the graph of the line $y = 2x - 3$ in the domain $-1 \leqslant x \leqslant 4$.

x	2x − 3	y
−1		
0		
1		
2		
3		
4		

2. Copy and complete the table on the right and hence draw the graph of the function $f(x) = 3x - 4$ in the domain $-1 \leqslant x \leqslant 3$.

x	3x − 4	y
−1		
0		
3		

3. The equation of a line is $f(x) = 2x - 1$.
Find $f(1), f(2)$ and $f(3)$ and write down three points on the line.
Hence draw the graph of the line.

4. $f(x) = 3x - 2$ is the equation of a line.
Find $f(0), f(1)$ and $f(2)$ and hence draw the graph of the line.

5. $f(x) = 3x - 4$ is the equation of a line.
Find $f(1), f(2)$ and $f(3)$.
Plot the three points and hence draw the graph of the line.

6. Draw the graph of the function $f(x) = 6 - x$ in the domain $0 \leqslant x \leqslant 6$ by finding only three points on the line.

7. Draw the graph of the function $f(x) = 2x - 2$ in the domain $-2 \leqslant x \leqslant 3$.

8. Copy and complete the table on the right and hence draw the graph of the function $f(x) = 4 - 2x$ in the domain $0 \leqslant x \leqslant 3$.

x	4 − 2x	y
0		
1	4 − 2	2
2		
3		

9. Draw the graph of $f(x) = 6 - 2x$ in the domain $0 \leqslant x \leqslant 5$.

10. Draw the graph of the line $f(x) = 3x - 5$ in the domain $0 \leqslant x \leqslant 3$.

By finding the couples (*, 0) and (0, *), sketch each of the following lines:

11. $y = 4 - x$ **12.** $y = x - 6$ **13.** $y = 2x + 4$ **14.** $2y = x + 2$

15. Drawn on the right is the graph of a function $y = f(x)$.

Use this graph to write down

(i) $f(3)$ (ii) $f(0)$ (iii) $f(-4)$
(iv) the value of x when $f(x) = -2$
(v) the value of x when $f(x) = 6$.

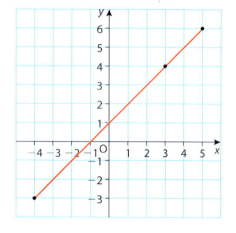

16. On the same diagram, draw the lines $y = 5 - x$ and $y = 2x - 4$, in the domain $0 \leqslant x \leqslant 4$.

Use your graph to write down the point of intersection of the two lines.

Section 22.2 **Graphs of quadratic functions**

The curve on the right is called a **parabola**.
The name parabola comes from the Greek word for throw, because when a ball, for example, is thrown high in the air, its path makes a parabolic shape.

Ball
Ground

Suspension bridges, such as the **Golden Gate Bridge** in San Francisco, form parabolic curves.

The simplest quadratic function is $y = x^2$.
Its graph can be drawn from a table of values from $x = -3$ to $x = 3$.

x	-3	-2	-1	0	1	2	3
y	9	4	1	0	1	4	9

The points shown on this curve are:

$(-3, 9), (-2, 4), (-1, 1), (0, 0), (1, 1), (2, 4), (3, 9)$.

When these points are joined, a smooth curve called a parabola is formed.

Notice that the curve is symmetrical about the y-axis. Hence the y-axis is called **the axis of symmetry**.

The function shown above may be written in one of these three ways:

(i) $y = x^2$ (ii) $f(x) = x^2$ (iii) $f : x \rightarrow x^2$

A function in the form $f(x) = ax^2 + bx + c$, where a, b and c are constants and $a \neq 0$, is called a **quadratic function**.

It is called a quadratic function because it contains a term in x^2.

To draw the **graph of a quadratic function**, we take a given number of x-values and find the corresponding $f(x)$-values (or y-values) and then plot the resulting points.

When asked to draw the graph of a function, we are usually given the x-values we are to use. The values of x from -2 to 3 inclusive are written as $-2 \leqslant x \leqslant 3$.

The steps used in drawing a quadratic graph are given in the following example.

Example 1

Draw the graph of the quadratic function $f(x) = x^2 - 2x - 3$ in the domain $-2 \leqslant x \leqslant 4$.

We set out a table of ordered pairs as follows:

x	$x^2 - 2x - 3$	y
-2	$4 + 4 - 3$	5
-1	$1 + 2 - 3$	0
0	$0 + 0 - 3$	-3
1	$1 - 2 - 3$	-4
2	$4 - 4 - 3$	-3
3	$9 - 6 - 3$	0
4	$16 - 8 - 3$	5

Plotting these ordered pairs, we get the following curve:

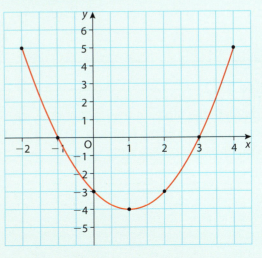

The ordered pairs found are:

$(-2, 5), (-1, 0), (0, -3), (1, -4),$
$(2, -3), (3, 0), (4, 5)$.

Graphing functions when the coefficient of x^2 is negative

If the coefficient of x^2 is negative in a quadratic function, e.g. $f(x) = -3x^2 + 4$, then the graph of the function will take the shape shown on the right.

x^2 negative

Example 2

Draw the graph of the function $f(x) = -x^2 + 3x + 4$ in the domain $-2 \leqslant x \leqslant 5$.

The table of values is set out below:

x	$-x^2 + 3x + 4$	y
-2	$-4 - 6 + 4$	-6
-1	$-1 - 3 + 4$	0
0	$0 + 0 + 4$	4
1	$-1 + 3 + 4$	6
2	$-4 + 6 + 4$	6
3	$-9 + 9 + 4$	4
4	$-16 + 12 + 4$	0
5	$-25 + 15 + 4$	-6

The required points are:
$(-2, -6), (-1, 0), (0, 4), (1, 6), (2, 6),$
$(3, 4), (4, 0), (5, -6).$
The graph of the function is shown below:

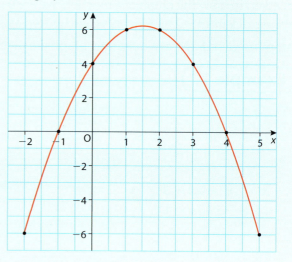

Exercise 22.2

1. Complete the table on the right and hence draw the graph of the function $f(x) = x^2 - 4$ in the domain $-3 \leqslant x \leqslant 3$.

x	$x^2 - 4$	y
-3		
-2		
-1		
0		
1		
2		
3		

2. Draw the graph of the function $f : x \rightarrow x^2 - 4x$ in the domain $-1 \leqslant x \leqslant 4$.

3. Draw the graph of the function $f(x) = x^2 + x - 2$ in the domain $-3 \leqslant x \leqslant 3$.

4. Draw the graph of the function $f(x) = 2x^2 - x - 3$ in the domain $-2 \leqslant x \leqslant 3$.

5. Draw the graph of the function $f(x) = 2x^2 + 3x - 4$ in the domain $-3 \leqslant x \leqslant 2$.

6. Draw the graph of the function $f(x) = 2x^2 - 5x - 3$ in the domain $-2 \leqslant x \leqslant 4$.
   Use your graph to write down the coordinates of the points at which the graph crosses the x-axis.
   Now write down the coordinates of the point where the graph crosses the y-axis.

7. Draw the graph of the function $y = -x^2$ in the domain $-2 \leqslant x \leqslant 2$.

8. Draw the graph of the function $f : x \rightarrow -x^2 + 2x + 3$ in the domain $-2 \leqslant x \leqslant 4$.
   Use your graph to find the coordinates of the points where the graph crosses the x-axis.

9. Draw the graph of the function $f : x \rightarrow -2x^2 + x + 3$ in the domain $-2 \leqslant x \leqslant 3$.
   Write down the values of x at which the curve crosses the x-axis.

10. Graph the function $f(x) = -2x^2 + 7x - 3$ in the domain $-1 \leqslant x \leqslant 4$.
    (i) Use the graph to write down the coordinates of the points at which the graph intersects the x-axis.
    (ii) Write down the coordinates of the point where the graph crosses the y-axis.

Section 22.3 **Using quadratic graphs**

1. **Solving the equation** $f(x) = 0$

The graph on the right shows the curve $f(x) = x^2 - 2x - 3$ intersecting the x-axis at A and B.

The x-values of these points are the roots of the associated quadratic equation
$$x^2 - 2x - 3 = 0.$$
Why is this?

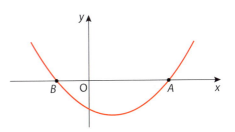

$f(x) = x^2 - 2x - 3$ may be also written as $y = x^2 - 2x - 3$.
When $y = 0$, then $x^2 - 2x - 3 = 0$.
$y = 0$ is another name for the x-axis.

Thus, the solution of the equation $x^2 - 2x - 3 = 0$ gives the x-values of the points at which the curve crosses the x-axis.

The curve on the right is the graph of
the function

$$f(x) = x^2 + 2x - 5$$

The roots of the equation $x^2 + 2x - 5 = 0$
are found by reading from the graph the
x-values of the points at which the graph
intersects the x-axis.

These values are

$$x = -3.5 \text{ and } x = 1.5$$

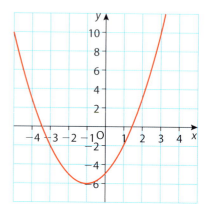

2. Solving the equation $f(x) = k$, where $k \in R$

The graph of the function $f(x) = x^2 - 3x$ is drawn below.

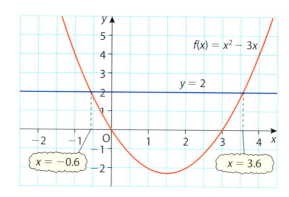

This graph can be used to solve the equation $f(x) = 2$ or $y = 2$ by drawing
the line $y = 2$ and then reading from the graph the x-values of the points
where the line $y = 2$ intersects the curve.

These values are $x = -0.6$ or $x = 3.6$.

3. Finding $f(k)$ from a graph

The graph of the function $f(x) = x^2 + 5x - 1$ is shown.

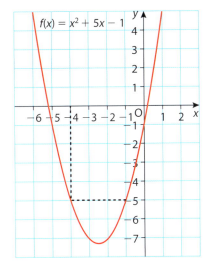

$f(-4)$ is the value of y when $x = -4$.
To find $f(-4)$, we draw the broken line $x = -4$ and then read the y-value of the point where this line intersects the curve.

This y-value is -5.

Thus, $f(-4) = -5$.

4. Intersecting graphs

Graphed below are the functions

$f(x) = x^2$ (i.e. $y = x^2$) and $g(x) = x + 2$ (i.e. $y = x + 2$)

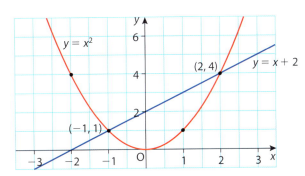

Notice that the curve $f(x)$ and the line $g(x)$ intersect at the points $(-1, 1)$ and $(2, 4)$.

We will now solve the equation $x^2 = x + 2$.

$$x^2 = x + 2 \Rightarrow x^2 - x - 2 = 0$$
$$\Rightarrow (x + 1)(x - 2) = 0$$
$$\Rightarrow x + 1 = 0 \text{ or } x - 2 = 0, \text{ i.e. } x = -1 \text{ or } x = 2.$$

Notice that these are the x-values of the points where the two graphs intersect.

Remember

When we solve the equation $f(x) = g(x)$, we are finding the x-values of the points of intersection of the graphs $y = f(x)$ and $y = g(x)$.

5. Axis of symmetry

The diagram on the right is the graph of the function $y = x^2 - 2x - 3$.

The broken red line is called the **axis of symmetry** of the curve.

The equation of this axis of symmetry is **$x = 1$**.

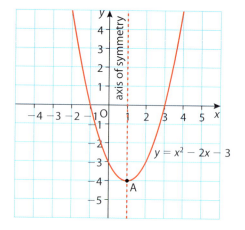

Exercise 22.3

1. The curve on the right is the graph of the function

$$y = x^2 - 4x + 3.$$

From the graph, write down

   (i)   the coordinates of the points where the curve crosses the x-axis

   (ii) the value of y when $x = 2$

  (iii) the values of x when $y = 8$

  (iv) the equation of the axis of symmetry of the curve.

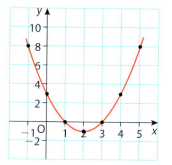

2. The curve on the right is the graph of the function

$$f(x) = x^2 - 1.$$

Use the graph to find

   (i)   the values of x when $f(x) = 0$

   (ii) the values of x when $f(x) = 3$

  (iii) the value of $f(x)$ when $x = 2$

  (iv) the value of $f(x)$ when $x = 0$.

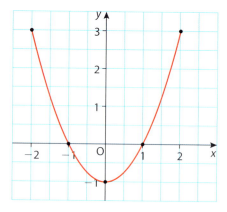

3. The graph of $f(x) = x^2 - 2x - 5$
is given on the right.
Use the graph to estimate

   (i)   the values of x for which $f(x) = 0$
   (ii)   the values of x for which $f(x) = 6$
   (iii)   the value of $f(-3)$
   (iv)   the value of $f(1)$

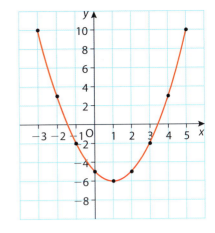

4. Drawn below is the graph of the function:

$$f : x \rightarrow 3 + 2x - x^2 \text{ for } -2 \leqslant x \leqslant 4, x \in R.$$

Use the graph to write down

   (i)   the roots of the equation $f(x) = 0$
   (ii)   the values of x for which $f(x) = 3$
   (iii)   the values of x for which $f(x) = -2$
   (iv)   the value of $f(2)$
   (v)   the value of $f(-1\frac{1}{2})$
   (vi)   the equation of the axis of
       symmetry of the curve.

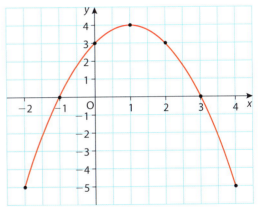

5. Draw the graph for the function $f(x) = 2x^2 - x - 3$ in the domain $-2 \leqslant x \leqslant 3$.
Use your graph to find

   (i)   the values of x for which $f(x) = 0$
   (ii)   the values of x for which $f(x) = 6$
   (iii)   the value of $f(0)$
   (iv)   the value of $f(2)$.

6. The graphs of the functions $f(x) = x^2$ and $g(x) = 2x + 3$ are shown below.

(i) Write down the coordinates of the points where the curve and line meet.

(ii) Solve the equation $x^2 = 2x + 3$.

(iii) What is the connection between the answers in (i) and (ii) above?

(iv) Explain the meaning of the equation $f(x) = g(x)$.

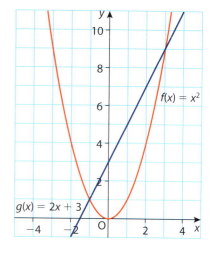

7. Drawn on the right are the graphs of $f(x) = x^2 - 2x$ and $g(x) = x - 1$ in the domain $-1 \leqslant x \leqslant 3$.

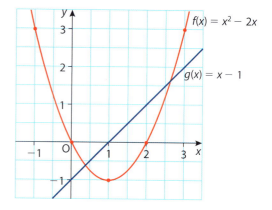

Use the graph to write down

(i) the values of x for which $f(x) = 0$

(ii) the values of x for which $f(x) = 3$

(iii) the value of x for which $g(x) = 0$

(iv) the value of x for which $g(x) = 2.5$

(v) the values of x for which $f(x) = g(x)$

(vi) the equation of the axis of symmetry of the curve.

8. Drawn below are the graphs $f(x) = x^2 + x - 6$ and $g(x) = 3x - 3$.

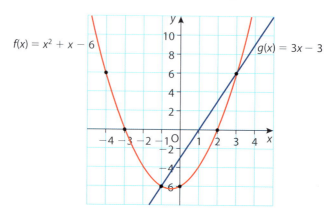

Use the graph to estimate
   (i) $f(-2)$
   (ii) $g(3)$
   (iii)   the values of x for which $f(x) = 0$
   (iv)   the values of x for which $f(x) = 4$
   (v)   the value of x for which $g(x) = 0$
   (vi)   the values of x for which $f(x) = g(x)$.

Solve algebraically the equation $f(x) = g(x)$.
Explain the connection between the values for x you have just found and the values
for x in (vi) above.

9. Using the same axes and the same scales, graph the functions

$$f: x \rightarrow x^2 + 3x - 3 \quad \text{and} \quad g: x \rightarrow x - 2 \text{ in the domain } -4 \leqslant x \leqslant 2, x \in R.$$

Use the graph to estimate
   (i)   the values of x for which $x^2 + 3x - 3 = 0$
   (ii)   the values of x for which $x^2 + 3x - 3 = -2$
   (iii)   the values of x for which $f(x) = g(x)$.

10. On the right is the graph of the function
$f(x) = -x^2 + 4x + 12$.

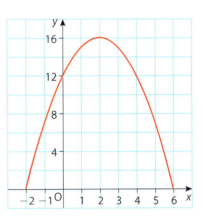

$f(x)$ represents the number of taxis at a
taxi-rank from 10 a.m. $(x = -2)$ to 6 p.m. $(x = 6)$.
Each unit on the x-axis represents one hour
and each unit on the y-axis represents one taxi.

Use the graph to estimate
   (i)   the number of taxis at the rank at 12 noon
   (ii)   the times when there were 14 taxis at the rank
   (iii)   the times when there were no taxis at the rank
   (iv)   the number of hours when there were 10 taxis or more at the rank.

Test yourself 22

1. (a) Draw the graph of the function $f(x) = 3x - 1$ in the domain $-2 \leqslant x \leqslant 3$.
Use your graph to estimate
   (i) $f(-1.5)$ (ii) the value of x when $f(x) = 3.5$.

(b) Copy and complete the table on the right for the function $f(x) = 2x^2 + 3x - 6$.

Hence draw the graph of the function in the domain $-4 \leqslant x \leqslant 3$.

Use your graph to estimate
   (i) the values of x when $f(x) = 0$
   (ii) the values of x when $f(x) = -3$
   (iii) the value of $f(1.5)$.

x	$2x^2 + 3x - 6$	y
-4		
-3	$18 - 9 - 6$	3
-2		
-1		
0		
1		
2	$8 + 6 - 6$	8
3		

2. (a) Draw the graph of $f(x) = 2x - 5$ in the domain $0 \leqslant x \leqslant 5$.

(b) The graph of $y = x^2 - 2x$ has been drawn on the given grid.

Use the graph to find estimates for the solutions of these equations:
   (i) $x^2 - 2x = 0$
   (ii) $x^2 - 2x = 3$.

Write down the equation of the axis of symmetry of the curve.

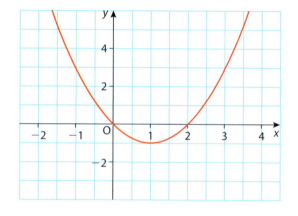

3. (a) $x - 2y = 6$ is the equation of a line.
If $x = 0$, find the value of y.
If $y = 0$, find the value of x.
Plot the two points you have found and draw the graph of the line $x - 2y = 6$.

(b) Draw the graph of the function $f : x \rightarrow x^2 + 2x - 4$ in the domain $-4 \leqslant x \leqslant 2$, $x \in R$.
Use your graph to find
   (i) $f(0.5)$
   (ii) the values of x when $f(x) = 0$
   (iii) the values of x for which $f(x) = 3$.

4. (a) The graph of the function $f(x) = 2x + 5$ is shown.

Use the graph to write down

   (i) $f(0)$ (ii) $f(1)$ (iii) $f(-1)$

  (iv) the value of x when $y = 3$

   (v) the value of y when $x = -2.5$.

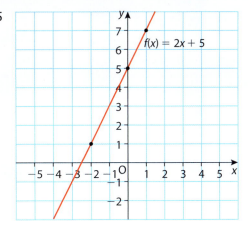

(b) Which sketch graph fits which equation?
Give reasons for your answers.

$$y = 2x$$

$$y = x^2 - 2$$

$$y = 2 - x^2$$

Ⓐ
Ⓑ
Ⓒ

5. (a) Copy and complete the table on the right and hence draw a graph of the function $f(x) = 3 - 2x$ in the domain $-1 \leqslant x \leqslant 3$.

x	$3 - 2x$	y
-1		
0		
3		

(b) Draw the graph of the function $f : x \rightarrow 6x - x^2$ in the domain $0 \leqslant x \leqslant 6$.

$f(x)$ represents the height above ground, in metres, reached by a golf ball from the time it was struck $(x = 0)$ to the time it hit the ground $(x = 6)$.

If each unit on the x-axis represents 1 second and each unit on the y-axis represents 5 metres, use your graph to estimate

  (i) the greatest height reached by the golf ball

  (ii) the height of the golf ball after $1\frac{1}{2}$ seconds

 (iii) after how many seconds the ball was 10 metres above ground (two times)

 (iv) after how many seconds the ball reached its maximum height.

Key words

| Pythagoras | hypotenuse | opposite side | adjacent side | sine |
| cosine | tangent | angle of elevation | angle of depression |

Section 23.1 **The Theorem of Pythagoras**

In your study of geometry, you may have heard of Pythagoras and his wonderful discovery about right-angled triangles. He was a famous Greek mathematician who lived around 500 BC and his discovery is now known as the *Theorem of Pythagoras*. This theorem is given below.

Theorem of Pythagoras

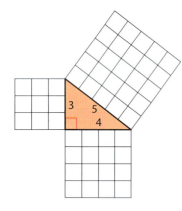

The square on the hypotenuse of a right-angled triangle is equal to the sum of the squares on the other two sides.

$$a^2 = b^2 + c^2$$

The **hypotenuse** is opposite the right angle.

Example 1

Find the area of the square marked A in the given figure.

$A = 64\,\text{cm}^2 + 36\,\text{cm}^2$

$A = 100\,\text{cm}^2$

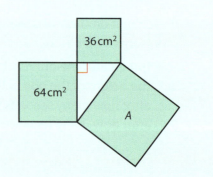

Example 2

Find the length of the side marked x in each of these right-angled triangles:

(i)

(ii)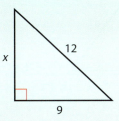

(i) $x^2 = 8^2 + 6^2$
       $= 64 + 36$
    $x^2 = 100$
    $x = \sqrt{100} = 10$

(ii) $12^2 = 9^2 + x^2$
           $144 = 81 + x^2$
      $144 - 81 = x^2$
            $63 = x^2$
           $x^2 = 63$
            $x = \sqrt{63}$

Exercise 23.1

1. Find the area of the shaded square in each of the following right-angled triangles:

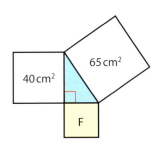

2. Find the length of the hypotenuse in each of the following right-angled triangles:

  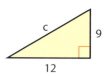

3. Find the length of the side marked with a letter in each of the following right-angled triangles:

(You may leave your answers in $\sqrt{}$ form.)

  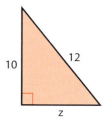

4. Find the length of the side marked with a letter in each of these triangles:

(Give each answer correct to one decimal place.)

  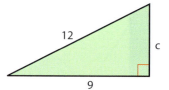

5. Find the length of the hypotenuse in each of these triangles:

(Give each answer correct to 1 decimal place.)

  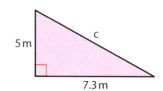

6. Use the Theorem of Pythagoras to determine whether each of these triangles is right-angled:

(i)

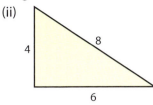

(ii)

> If a triangle is right-angled, the square on the hypotenuse must be equal to the sum of the squares on the other two sides.

(iii)

(iv)

(v)

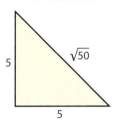

7. Name the hypotenuse in the given triangle. Now find the length of the side [BC].

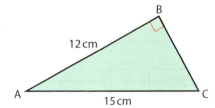

8. A vertical tree 16 metres tall casts a shadow that is 14 metres in length. What is the distance from the top of the tree to the tip of the shadow, represented by the line marked, ℓ? (Give your answer to the nearest metre.)

9. The size of a television screen is the length of its diagonal. The size of this television screen is 80 cm. If the height of the screen is 42 cm, find the width of the screen in centimetres, correct to the nearest whole number.

10. Seven lengths of wood are needed to make this gate.
Find the total length of wood needed, giving your answer in metres, correct to one decimal place.

Section 23.2 Sides of a right-angle triangle

The **hypotenuse**, the **opposite side** and the **adjacent side** have all been labelled in the two triangles below for the angle A and the angle B.

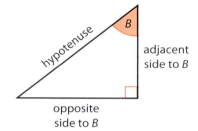

> ### Example 1
>
> For the angle *A* in the given figure, write down
>   (i) the length of the opposite side
>   (ii) the length of the adjacent side
> (iii) the fraction $\dfrac{\text{opposite side}}{\text{hypotenuse}}$.
>
>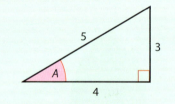
>
>   (i) Opposite side to angle *A* is 3.　　(ii) Adjacent side is 4.
> (iii) $\dfrac{\text{opposite side}}{\text{hypotenuse}} = \dfrac{3}{5}$.

Exercise 23.2

1. Write down the length of the hypotenuse in each of the following triangles:

(i)

(ii)

(iii)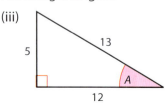

2. Write down the length of the side adjacent to the angle *A* in each of the triangles in Question 1 above.

3. Write down the length of the side opposite the angle *A* in each of the triangles in Question 1 above.

4. Write down the length of the hypotenuse in each of the triangles below:

(i)   (ii)   (iii)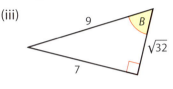

5. Write down the length of the side opposite the angle *B* in each of the triangles in Question 4 above.

6. Write down the length of the side adjacent to the angle *B* in each of the triangles in Question 4 above.

7. In relation to the angle *A* in the given triangle, express as a fraction the length of

(i) $\dfrac{\text{opposite side}}{\text{hypotenuse}}$ (ii) $\dfrac{\text{adjacent side}}{\text{hypotenuse}}$.

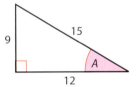

8. In relation to the angle *B* in the given triangle, express as a fraction the length of

(i) $\dfrac{\text{opposite side}}{\text{adjacent side}}$ (ii) $\dfrac{\text{opposite side}}{\text{hypotenuse}}$.

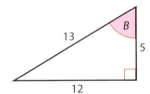

Section 23.3 **Sine, Cosine and Tangent ratios**

The sine ratio

The three triangles below are all different sizes but each contains an angle marked A which is the same size in all the triangles.

      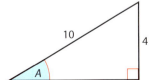

In each triangle the length of the side opposite the angle A and the length of the hypotenuse are given.

In each triangle the ratio $\dfrac{\text{opposite side}}{\text{hypotenuse}}$ is the same, that is 0.4.

The ratio $\dfrac{\text{opposite side}}{\text{hypotenuse}}$ is called the **sine** of the angle.

sin is used for **sine**.

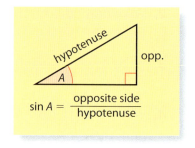

$$\sin A = \frac{\text{opposite side}}{\text{hypotenuse}}$$

The cosine ratio

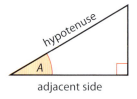

In the given right-angled triangle the ratio

$$\frac{\text{adjacent side}}{\text{hypotenuse}}$$

is called the **cosine** of the angle A.

cos is used for **cosine**.

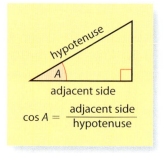

$$\cos A = \frac{\text{adjacent side}}{\text{hypotenuse}}$$

The tangent ratio

In the given right-angled triangle, the ratio

$$\frac{\text{opposite side}}{\text{adjacent side}}$$

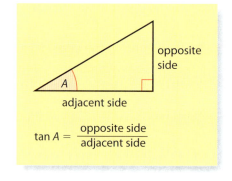

is called the **tangent** of the angle A.

tan is used for **tangent**.

$$\tan A = \frac{\text{opposite side}}{\text{adjacent side}}$$

Example 1

Find the values of sin A, cos A and tan A in the given right-angled triangle.

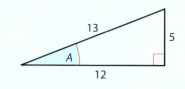

$$\sin A = \frac{\text{opposite}}{\text{hypotenuse}} = \frac{5}{13}$$

$$\cos A = \frac{\text{adjacent}}{\text{hypotenuse}} = \frac{12}{13} \qquad \tan A = \frac{\text{opposite}}{\text{adjacent}} = \frac{5}{12}$$

Exercise 23.3

1. Write down the value of sin A in each of the following triangles:

(i)   (ii)   (iii)

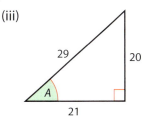

2. Write down the value of cos A in each of the triangles in Question 1.

3. Find the value of tan A in each of the triangles in Question 1.

4. Find the value of sin B in each of the triangles below:

(i)   (ii)   (iii)

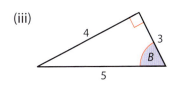

5. Write down the value of cos B in each of the triangles in Question 4.

6. Write down the value of tan B in each of the triangles in Question 4.

7. From the given triangle, write down the value of
    (i)   sin A   (ii)   cos B
    (iii)   tan A   (iv)   cos A
    (v)   tan B   (vi)   sin B.

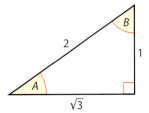

8. Use the Theorem of Pythagoras to find the length
of the side marked x in the given triangle.
Now write down the value of
    (i)   sin A
    (ii)   cos A
    (iii)   tan A.

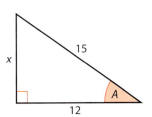

Section 23.4 **Using your calculator to find ratios**

The value of the sine, cosine and tangent of any angle can be found by using an electronic calculator. When using a calculator make sure that it is in degree mode.

Example 1

Use your calculator to find, correct to two decimal places, the value of
(i) sin 58°   (ii) cos 74°   (iii) tan 37°.

(i) Key in [sin] [5] [8] [=]   The answer is 0.8480 = 0.85.

(ii) Key in [cos] [7] [4] [=]   The answer is 0.2756 = 0.28.

(iii) Key in [tan] [3] [7] [=]   The answer is 0.7536 = 0.75.

How to find the angle when given its sin, cos or tan

When you use your calculator you will find that sin 60° = 0.8660.
If you are asked the question: 'What angle has a sine of 0.8660?',
of course the answer is 60°.

If we are given sin A = 0.8660, we use the [sin⁻¹] key on the calculator to find the value of the angle A.

The [sin⁻¹] key is found by keying in [SHIFT] [sin].

So to find the angle A when sin A = 0.8660, key in

[SHIFT] [sin] [.] [8] [6] [6] [0] [=]

Your answer is 59.99° = 60°, correct to the nearest degree.

Example 2

(i) If sin A = 0.5786, find A correct to the nearest degree.
(ii) If tan B = 1.8453, find B correct to the nearest degree.

(i) sin A = 0.5786
To find A, key in [SHIFT] [sin] [.] [5] [7] [8] [6] [=].
The result is 35.35° = 35°, correct to the nearest degree.

(ii) tan B = 1.8453
To find B, key in [SHIFT] [tan] [1] [.] [8] [4] [5] [3] [=].
The result is 61.55° = 62°, correct to the nearest degree.

Exercise 23.4

Use your calculator to find the value of each of the following, correct to 4 decimal places:

1. sin 34°   **2.** sin 74°   **3.** sin 12°   **4.** cos 28°

5. tan 56°   **6.** tan 74°   **7.** tan 18°   **8.** sin 67°

9. cos 80°   **10.** tan 19°   **11.** sin 54°   **12.** cos 58°

13. tan 68°   **14.** tan 32°   **15.** sin 18°   **16.** cos 63°

17. Find the angle A in each of the following, correct to the nearest degree:

    (i) sin A = 0.7453   (ii) sin A = 0.2154   (iii) sin A = 0.8416

    (iv) sin A = 0.5129   (v) sin A = 0.1684   (vi) sin A = 0.9154.

18. Find the angle B in each of the following, correct to the nearest degree:

    (i) cos B = 0.4587   (ii) cos B = 0.7416   (iii) cos B = 0.2153.

19. Find the angle C in each of the following, correct to the nearest degree:

    (i) tan C = 0.5286   (ii) tan C = 1.4251   (iii) tan C = 2.4127.

20. Find the angle A in each of the following, correct to the nearest degree:

    (i) tan A = 2.0416   (ii) sin A = 0.7463   (iii) cos A = 0.4197

21. Verify that   (i) sin 27° = cos 63°   (ii) sin 51° = cos 39°.

22. Use your calculator to find the value of these, correct to 2 decimal places:

    (i) 3 × sin 54°   (ii) 5 × cos 14°   (iii) 7 × tan 44°   (iv) 8 × sin 55°.

23. Look at the triangle on the right and say which ratio $\frac{3}{5}$ represents.

Express $\frac{3}{5}$ as a decimal and then find the value of the angle A, correct to the nearest degree.

Section 23.5 **Finding sides and angles of a triangle**

If we know the angles and one side of a right-angled triangle, we can then find the lengths of the other sides.

For example, we could calculate the height of a tree if we know the angle to the top of the tree as well as the distance from the base of the tree.

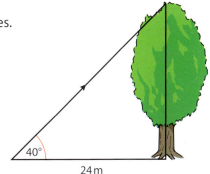

40°

24 m

Example 1

Find the value of the side marked x in the
given triangle.
Give your answer correct to 1 decimal place.

In relation to the angle 40°, we have the **opposite** side and the **hypotenuse**
which gives us the **sine** ratio.

$$\frac{x}{8} = \sin 40°$$

$$\frac{x}{8} = 0.6428 \ \ldots \text{(to find sin 40°, key in } \boxed{\text{sin}}\,\boxed{4}\,\boxed{0}\,\boxed{=} \text{.)}$$

$$x = 8 \times 0.6428 \ \ldots \text{multiply both sides by 8}$$

$$x = 5.1, \text{ correct to 1 decimal place.}$$

Example 2

Find the length of the side marked y in the
given triangle.
Give your answer correct to 1 decimal place.

$$\frac{y}{12} = \tan 32° \ \ldots \tan = \frac{\text{opposite}}{\text{adjacent}}$$

$$\frac{y}{12} = 0.6249$$

$$y = 12 \times (0.6249) \ \ldots \text{multiply both sides by 12}$$

$$y = 7.499$$

$$y = 7.5 \text{ cm}$$

Example 3

Find the measure of the angle A in the given triangle.
Give your answer correct to the nearest degree.

Relative to the angle A, we have the adjacent side and the hypotenuse.

$\cos A = \frac{8}{11}$

$\cos A = 0.7273$

$$\frac{\text{adjacent}}{\text{hypotenuse}} = \cos A$$

To find A, key in SHIFT cos • 7 2 7 3 =

This gives $A = 43.34°$.
    $A = 43°$, correct to the nearest degree

Note: If $\cos A = \frac{8}{11}$, you could also find the angle A by keying in

SHIFT cos 8 ÷ 1 1 =

The answer again is $43.34° = 43°$.

Exercise 23.5

1. Which ratio (sine, cosine or tangent) would you use to find x in each of these triangles?

(i)   (ii)   (iii)   (iv)

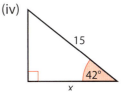

2. Use the sine ratio to find the length, correct to one decimal place, of the side marked x in each of these triangles:

(i)   (ii)   (iii)

3. Use the tangent ratio to find the length of the side marked with a letter in each of these triangles. Give each answer correct to one decimal place.

  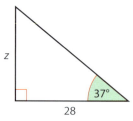

4. Use the cosine ratio to find, correct to the nearest whole number, the length of the side marked *a* in each of these triangles:

(i)   (ii)   (iii)

5. Find the length of the side marked with the letter *x* in each of these triangles: Give your answers correct to one decimal place.

(i)   (ii)   (iii)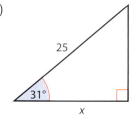

6. Find in metres, correct to the nearest whole number, the height of the office block shown.

7. A ladder 8 m in length is placed at an angle of 60° against a vertical wall. How far is the foot of the ladder from the wall?

8 m

60°

8. Jack is fishing from the straight bank of a river. He lets out 18 m of line and this is carried down stream so that the line makes an angle of 22° with the bank where Jack is standing. What is the shortest distance from the hook to the bank? Give your answer in metres, correct to one decimal place.

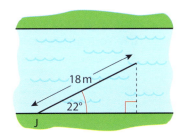

18 m

22°

J

9. Find the height of the church tower in the given diagram.

30°

100 m

Give your answer correct to the nearest metre.

10. In the given triangle ABC, $|AB| = 10$ and $|\angle BAC| = 41°$. Find, correct to 1 decimal place
  (i) $|BC|$
  (ii) $|AC|$.

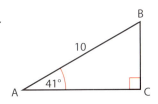

B

10

41°

A

C

11. Which trigonometric ratio links 5, 8 and B in the given right-angled triangle? Use this ratio to find the measure of the angle B, correct to the nearest degree.

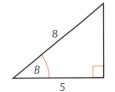

8

B

5

12. Find the angle marked with a letter in each of these triangles.
Give each angle correct to the nearest degree.

  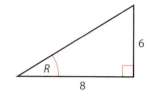

13. Find the measure of the angle between the kite-line
and the ground in the given figure.
Give your answer correct to the nearest degree.

14. A plane, which took off from Dublin Airport, had gained a height of 1.8 km after it
had travelled 8 km.

At what angle was the plane climbing?
Give your answer correct to the nearest degree.

Section 23.6 Using trigonometry to solve problems

Today, trigonometry is used by engineers, architects and surveyors who need to work
out relationships between distances and angles.

In this section we will use trigonometry to solve
some very simple problems involving right-
angled triangles.

Some of the terms we will use are explained
below.

An **angle of elevation** is an angle formed by a
horizontal line and the line of sight above
the horizontal line.

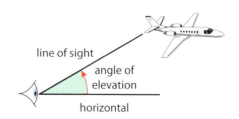

When we look down at something, the angle between the horizontal line and the direction in which we are looking is called the **angle of depression**.

A **clinometer** is often used to measure angles of elevation or depression. The clinometer shown on the left is being used to measure an angle of elevation as the observer is looking upwards.

Example 1

From a point P on level ground, the angle of elevation of the top of a tower is 42°. If P is 40 metres from the foot of the tower, find h, the height of the tower, correct to the nearest metre.

$$\frac{h}{40} = \tan 42° \quad \Rightarrow \quad \frac{h}{40} = 0.9004$$

$$h = 40 \times 0.9004$$

$$\therefore \quad h = 36 \text{ metres}$$

Exercise 23.6

1. When the angle of elevation of the sun is 22°, the length of the shadow cast by a tower is 15 m. Find the height h of the tower, in metres, correct to one decimal place.

2. From a point on the ground 200 m from the middle of the base of the Eiffel Tower, the angle of elevation of the top is 58°. Use this information to find the height of the tower, correct to the nearest metre.

58°

200 m

3. A boy is flying a kite from a string of length 30 m. If the string makes an angle of 71° with the ground, find the height h of the kite, correct to the nearest metre.

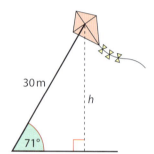

30 m

h

71°

4. When the angle of elevation of the sun is 42°, a tree casts a shadow 14 m long on level ground. Find the height of the tree, correct to the nearest integer.

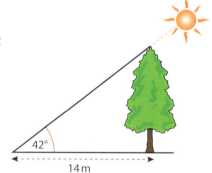

42°

14 m

5. The distance from the roof of an office block to the point C on level ground is 40 m. If $|\angle ACB| = 32°$, find correct to the nearest metre,
(i) the height of the block   (ii) the length [BC].

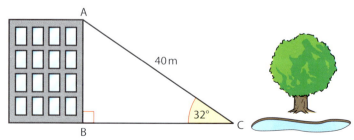

A

40 m

32°

C

B

6. Daniel lies down 25 m away from his house, which is built on flat ground. He uses a clinometer to measure the angle between the ground and the top of his house. The angle is 20°.

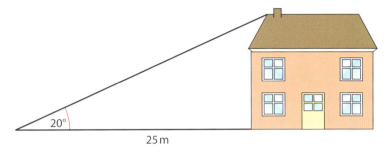

20°

25 m

Estimate the height of Daniel's house, correct to the nearest metre.

7. A ladder of length 5 metres rests against a wall so that the base of the ladder is 3 m from the wall. Find the angle between the ladder and the ground, correct to the nearest degree.

5 m

3 m

8. From the top of a rig 80 m high, the angle of depression of a boat at sea is 25°.
Explain why the shaded angle is also 25°.
Now find the distance from the middle of the base of the rig to the boat.
Give your answer correct to the nearest metre.

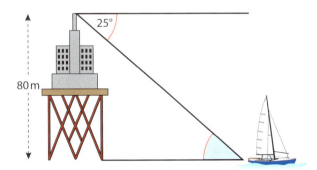

25°

80 m

Test yourself 23

1. (a) In the given triangle, write down

    (i) the length of the hypotenuse

    (ii) the length of the side adjacent to the angle A.

    (iii) the value of sin A

    (iv) the value of tan A.

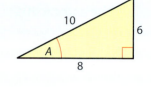

(b) Use the diagram on the right to write down

    (i) cos 60°

    (ii) sin 30°

    (iii) tan 60°.

2. (a) Use the *Theorem of Pythagoras* to find the length of the side marked x in the given right-angled triangle. Use the length found to write down the value of

    (i) sin A (ii) cos A (iii) tan B.

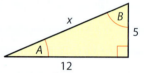

(b) Andy stands at A, directly under the end of a crane.

From A, he walks 12 m to B. At B, he measures the angle of elevation of the end of the crane as 70°.

How high is the end of the crane, h?

Give your answer correct to the nearest metre.

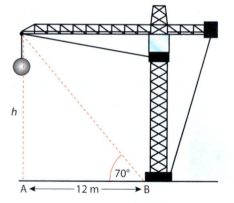

3. (a) Find, correct to one decimal place, the length of the side marked y in the given triangle.

(b) A playground slide has a 6 m sloped side. It makes an angle of 52° with the ground, as shown.

How high is the top of the slide above the ground?

Give your answer in metres, correct to one decimal place.

4. (a) (i) If cos A = 0.5592, find A correct to the nearest degree.

   (ii) A wire runs from the top of a pole 10 metres in height to the ground.
   The end of the wire is 15 m from the bottom of the pole.
   What angle does the wire make with the ground?
   Give your answer correct to the nearest degree.

10 m

15 m

(b) The angle of elevation of a tree top is 38° when measured from a point 20 m from its base.
Find the height of the tree in metres, correct to one decimal place.

38°

20 m

5. (a) A see-saw is made from a 4-metre plank of wood, pivoting about the middle on a stand.
The piece of wood makes an angle of 30° with the ground when one side of the see-saw is touching the ground.
How high is the top of the pivot stand?

(b) The diagram shows a roofing frame ADC with BD perpendicular to AC.
   (i) Find |AD|, in metres, correct to one decimal place.
   (ii) Find the size of the angle BAD correct to the nearest degree.

D

3 m

A   7 m   B   5 m   C

6. A flagpole is on the top of a building. From the point D, 4 m from the base of the building, Joanne measures the angles of elevation of the top, A, and the bottom, B, of the flagpole. Her measurements are shown on the diagram.

(i) Find the length |AC|.

(ii) Find the length |BC| and hence the height of the flagpole.
Give each answer in metres, correct to one decimal place.

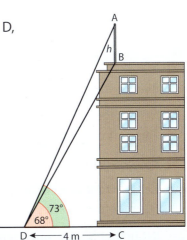

A

h B

73°
68°
D ←— 4 m —→ C

Drawing and Interpreting Real-life Graphs

Key words

distance–time graphs   average speed   steepness   directly proportional

conversion   real-life graphs   interpret   constant rate

Section 24.1 Distance–time graphs

> A **distance–time graph** (or travel graph) is a special type of line graph used to describe a journey.

> The vertical axis represents the distance from a certain point, while the horizontal axis represents time.

The distance–time graph below shows the journey of a cyclist who set out from town *A*.

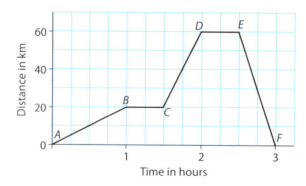

(i)   From *A* to *B* he cycled a distance of 20 km in 1 hour.

(ii) At B he stopped for half an hour which is represented by [*BC*].

(iii) At *C* he took a lift on a lorry and travelled to *D*, a distance of 40 km. This part of the journey took half an hour.

(iv) He then rested for half an hour. This is represented by [*DE*].

(v)   He then took a train back to the town he had originally left and completed the 60 km return journey in half an hour. This is represented by [*EF*].

      (Note that both *A* and *F* represent town *A*.)

Distance–time graphs

> ❯ A change in steepness represents a change in speed.
> ❯ The steeper the line, the faster the speed.
> ❯ The flatter the line, the slower the speed.
> ❯ A horizontal line indicates that the person or object is stopped.

The formulae that connect distance (D), time (T) and average speed (S) are given on the right.

$$D = S \times T \qquad S = \frac{D}{T} \qquad T = \frac{D}{S}$$

Exercise 24.1

1. The distance–time graph given shows Olivia's 3-hour journey.

   (i) How far did she travel in the first hour?

   (ii) For how long was she stopped?

   (iii) How far did she travel in the third hour?

   (iv) What was the total length of the journey?

2. The graph below shows Mr. Desmond's journey from Town A to Town B and back.

   (i) Find the distance travelled in the first two hours.

   (ii) Find his average speed for these two hours.

   (iii) For how long did he rest?

   (iv) How long did the return journey take?

   (v) What was his average speed on the return journey?

3. This travel graph gives the distance of a boy from home.

   (i) When did the boy leave home? When did he return?

   (ii) How far was he from home at 1.00 p.m.?

   (iii) At what times was he 15 km from home?

   (iv) At what times did he rest?

   (v) When was he travelling most quickly?

4. The travel graph shows the distance of a cyclist from his home between the times of 10. a.m. and 4.30 p.m.

   (i) How far does the cyclist travel in the first 2 hours?

   (ii) How far from home is he when he stops to rest?

   (iii) At what time does he commence the return journey?

   (iv) At 3.00 p.m. his speed changes.
   Does it increase or decrease?
   How can you tell without calculating the actual speeds?

   (v) How far does he travel altogether?

5. The graph shows the journey taken by Joseph to cycle from Town *P* to Town *Q*.
Use the graph to find
  (i)   the time taken to travel from Town *P* to Town *Q* including rest time
  (ii) what is the length of his rest
  (iii) the distance from Town *Q* when he stopped to rest.
  (iv) What was his average speed for the part of the journey before he took a rest?

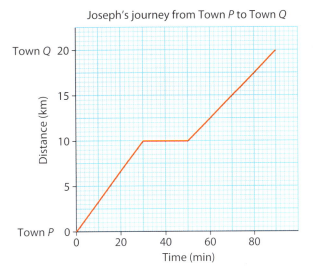
Joseph's journey from Town *P* to Town *Q*

6. Match the graph to the story.

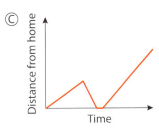

  (i)   I am walking steadily to school. After a while, I meet a friend and we walk together. We walk slower than when I was by myself.
  (ii) I am part-way to school when I remember that I have left my homework at home. I run back home to get it and then run to school.
  (iii) I start to walk to school, then I accept a ride with a friend.

7. The given distance–time graph shows the journey from his office undertaken by a sales representative to the countryside.

  (i)   At what time did he leave his office?
  (ii) How far did he travel to Town *A*?
  (iii) What was his average speed for this leg of the journey?
  (iv) How far is it from Town *A* to Town *B*?
  (v)   He had his lunch in Town *B*. How long did it last?
  (vi) What was his overall average speed, excluding the breaks?

8. The graph shows the journeys of two motorists, Conor and Adam. They are travelling on the same road and in the same direction, leaving town *A* at 9.00 a.m.

   (i)   Who travels faster in the first hour?
   (ii) How many times do they pass each other?
   (iii) At what time do they pass each other for the second time?
   (iv) How far apart are they at 3.00 p.m.?
   (v)   How far does each man travel altogether?

9. Use the graph below to answer the following question.

Jill's Sunday drive

Write a paragraph to describe Jill's journey to and from her destination, including:
   (i)   her departure and arrival times
   (ii) when and where the rest stop is taken
   (iii) the time spent driving
   (iv) her average speed for the return part of the journey.

10. The graph shows the journeys of two tourists and gives their distances from their hotel.

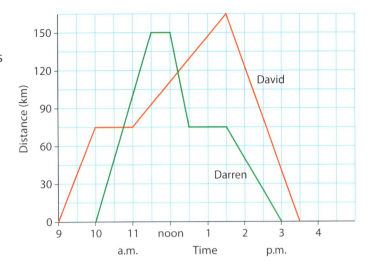

(i) How far is David from the hotel when Darren starts his journey?

(ii) At approximately what times do their paths cross?

(iii) At what time does David begin his return journey?

(iv) How far is Darren from his hotel when David begins his return journey?

(v) Who returns to the hotel first?
What time elapses before the other tourist arrives?

Section 24.2 **Directly proportional graphs**

Lucy is paid for the hours that she works at the rate of €12 per hour.
If she works 2 hours, she is paid €12 × 2 = €24.
If she works 5 hours, she is paid €12 × 5 = €60.

The hours worked and the pay received are said to be **directly proportional**.

When two quantities are in direct proportion, a graph is particularly useful for illustrating how one quantity increases (or decreases) relative to the second quantity.

Directly proportional graphs are always straight lines through the origin.

Example 1

The graph below shows the relationship between kilograms and pounds.

Use the graph to approximately convert
  (i)   20 pounds to kilograms (kg)
  (ii) 14 pounds to kilograms
  (iii) 4 kg to pounds
  (iv) 7.5 kg to pounds.

From the graph,

  (i)   20 pounds = 9.1 kg
  (ii) 14 pounds = 6.4 kg
  (iii) 4 kg = 8.8 pounds
  (iv) 7.5 kg = 16.5 pounds

Exercise 24.2

1. In which of these graphs is h directly proportional to t?

(i)

(ii)

(iii)

(iv)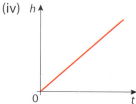

Explain your answers.

2. The graph below shows the relationship between kilometres and miles.

Use the graph to convert approximately

(i) 60 km to miles

(ii) 80 km to miles

(iii) 30 miles to km

(iv) 15 miles to km.

Is the given graph a directly proportional one?

3. The graph below shows the relationship between degrees Celsius (°C) and degrees Fahrenheit (°F).

Is this a directly proportional graph? Explain your answer.

Use the graph to convert approximately

(i) 35°C to Fahrenheit

(ii) 15°C to Fahrenheit

(iii) 50°F to Celsius

(iv) 100°F to Celsius.

If the temperature in a city on a particular day ranges between 55°F and 90°F, express this range in °C.

4. Television repair charges depend on the length of time taken for the repair, as shown on the graph.

(i)   What is the charge for a repair that took 60 minutes?
(ii) What is the charge for a repair that took 30 minutes?
(iii) If the charge was €80, how long did the repair take?
(iv) If the charge was €60, how long did the repair take?

The standing charge is the basic charge before the time charge is added.

(v)   What is this standing charge?

5. The graph below shows the typical weight for a man of medium build and given height.

Use the graph to estimate:

(i)   the weight of a man whose height is 165 cm
(ii) the weight of a man whose height is 175 cm
(iii) the height of a man whose weight is 78 kg.

If a group of men are all between 160 cm and 170 cm in height, what is the range of their weights likely to be?

6. The graph below can be used to convert between litres and pints.

(i) Use the graph to find the number of pints equivalent to 90 litres.
(ii) Use the graph to find the number of litres equivalent to 80 pints.
(iii) A petrol tank contains 95 litres of fuel.
Use the graph to express this in pints, correct to the nearest 10 pints.
(iv) The average yearly milk-yield for a dairy cow in Ireland is roughly 10 000 pints.
Use your graph to convert this figure to litres, correct to the nearest 1000 litres.

7. The given diagram shows that the length of the shadow cast by a tree at midday is directly proportional to the height of the tree.

(i) What is the length of the shadow when the tree is 8 m in height?
(ii) By using two points on the line, find the equation of the line in terms of s and h.
(iii) Use the equation you have found to write down the length of the shadow when the tree is 15 metres in height.

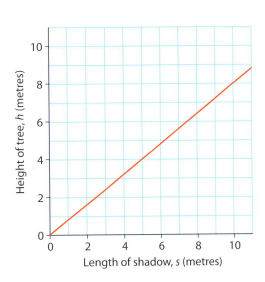

8. The graph on the right represents taxi fares for journeys of up to 9 km.

   (i) What is the fare for a journey of 5 km?

   (ii) What is the fare for a journey of 9 km?

   (iii) The taxi fare for a certain journey is €21.
   What is the length of this journey?

   (iv) Suggest a reason why the graph does not pass through the origin.

9. This graph shows how much petrol two cars consume.

   ——————— David's car

   – – – – – – – Stephen's car

   (i) David's car travelled 80 km. How much petrol did it use?

   (ii) Stephen's car used 9 litres of petrol one day. How far did it go?

   (iii) How much more petrol does Stephen's car use than David's car when each car travels 60 km?

   (iv) Is each line graph directly proportional? Explain your answer.

   (v) Find the equation of the broken red line in the form $y = mx$.
   Now use this equation to find the number of litres used when the car travels 300 km.

Section 24.3 **Real-life graphs**

When water is poured into the vessel below **at a steady rate**, the water will rise in the vessel also at a steady rate.

The graph of the water's height as time passes is shown on the right below.

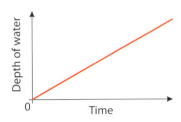

The graph is a straight line because the water rises at a **constant rate**.

The thinner the container, the steeper the graph.

You can see the differences in the graphs of the containers below.
They all have the same height.

Containers with sides that bulge out have a curved line graph. They may start steeply, get less steep and then get steep again.

The graph of the water's height for the given container is shown on the right.
The top part of the graph is a straight line because the water rises at a constant rate due to the uniform shape of the container at the top.

Example 1

Match these containers to their graphs when they are filled with liquid at a constant rate.

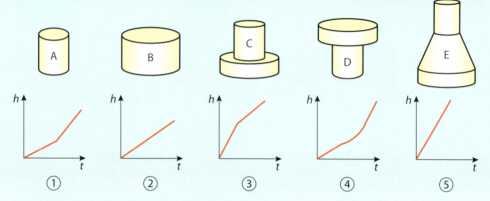

A is matched to ⑤ since A has straight parallel sides and is thin. It rises faster than container B.

B is matched to ② since B has straight parallel sides but is wider than A.

C is matched to ① since C is initially wide with straight sides and then narrow with straight sides – hence two line segments.

D is matched to ③ since D is initially narrow with straight sides and then wide with straight sides.

E is matched to ④ since E has three distinct sections which can be identified on the graph.

Exercise 24.3

1. Which of these best describes what this graph tells us?

  (i) The pulse rate is steady, then decreases, then is steady.

  (ii) The pulse rate increases, then stops, then decreases.

  (iii) The pulse rate increases, then stays steady, then decreases with time.

Going on a run

2. Water is added to the tank shown at a steady rate.
Which graph best represents the increase in the water level *h*?

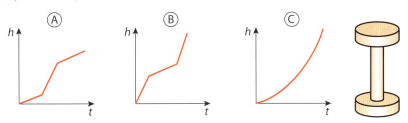

3. Here are three different-shaped bowls.

(i) Which description of filling the bowls with water goes with which bowl?
 (a) *The water level goes up fast at first and then suddenly goes up more slowly.*
 (b) *The water level goes up slowly at first, then changes to go up more quickly.*
 (c) *The water level starts by going up quickly, but gets slower and slower.*

(ii) Which graph goes with which bowl?

4. There are three routes from Appleville to Peartown.
Match the route descriptions to the appropriate *distance–time graphs*:

 Route A: A two-lane highway direct with a maximum speed limit of 110 km/hour. A thirty minute wait at bridge-works.

 Route B: A winding mountain road with steep gradients and curves requiring you to travel at a constant slower speed.

 Route C: A two-lane highway with a maximum speed limit of 110 km/hour and then a winding detour to avoid bridge-works.

(i)

(ii)

(iii)

5. This graph shows the temperatures in a greenhouse during 24 hours in summer.

The temperature in a greenhouse falls during the night and rises during the day. There are windows in this greenhouse to help keep the temperature down when it gets too hot.

(i) At roughly what time in the morning does the temperature in the greenhouse start to go up?

(ii) About when during the day is the temperature going up fastest?

(iii) About when is it going down fastest?

(iv) Because it was getting too hot, the gardener opened the windows in the greenhouse. Later she closed them again.
  (a) At about what time do you think she opened the windows?
  (b) Roughly when did she close them?

(v) What was the highest temperature in the greenhouse during the day?

(vi) What was the lowest temperature in this 24-hour period?

6. (i)

(ii)

(iii)

(iv)
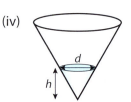

These containers are being filled with liquid.
The graphs below show how the diameter of the surface of the liquid changes as the height of the liquid increases.
Which graph belongs to which container?

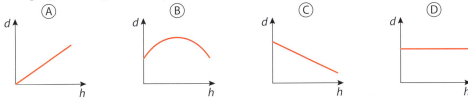

7. Match the graph to the story.

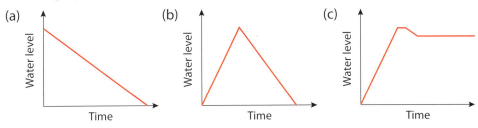

(i) I fill a bucket with water. After a few minutes, my dog drinks some of the water. I decide to leave the water in the bucket in case he wants a drink later.

(ii) I quickly fill a bucket with water but the bucket is spilt over and the water runs out.

(iii) I start with a full bucket of water and pour the water steadily over my seedlings until the bucket is empty.

8. The graph gives the shortest braking distances that should be between cars at different speeds.

   (i) Ed is driving in bad weather at 60 km per hour. What is the shortest distance he should be from the car in front?

   (ii) Fay is driving in good weather at 90 km per hour. What is the shortest distance she should be from the car in front?

   (iii) Mr Shaw is driving 70 metres behind another car. The weather is bad. What is the fastest he should be driving?

Geometry 3: Transformations – Constructions

Key words

transformation   object   image   translation   axial symmetry
central symmetry   symmetrical   axis of symmetry   centre of symmetry
construction   perpendicular bisector   ray   hypotenuse

Section 25.1 Transformation geometry

The figure marked A in the diagram below has been moved to different positions. All the figures have the same shape and size. Some are upside-down and some are back-to-front.

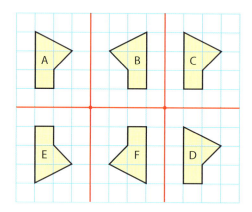

Each of the figures B, C, D, E and F is an **image** of the figure A under a **transformation**.
The original figure A is called the **object**.
The new position is called the **image**.
In this chapter we consider three transformations.
These are **translations**, **axial symmetry** and **central symmetry**.

Translations

A translation is movement in a straight line.
It may also be described as a 'sliding movement'.

The shape A on the left has been moved in the direction PQ and by a distance equal to |PQ|.
The translation PQ is written $\overrightarrow{\mathbf{PQ}}$.

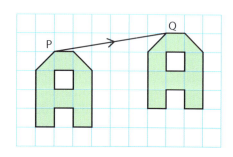

The image of the given figure is found by moving 4 units to the right and 3 units up. Notice that the size and shape of the figure is unchanged.

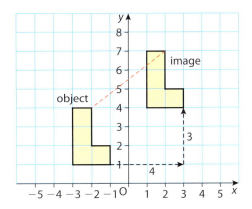

Here is the image of a line segment [AB] under the translation $\vec{t}$.

The image is labelled **A'B'**.

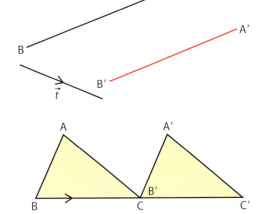

The image of the triangle ABC under the translation $\overrightarrow{BC}$ is shown on the right.

The image is A'B'C'.

Exercise 25.1

1. Describe the translation that maps the blue shape onto the red shape in each of the following. Use words such as right, left, up and down.

2.

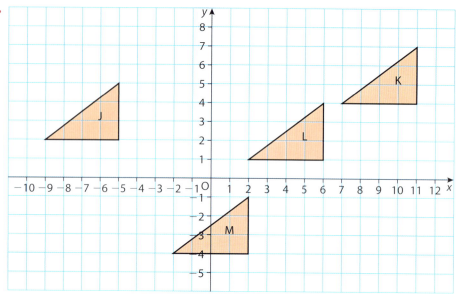

Describe fully the translation that maps
  (i)   shape L onto shape K
 (ii)   shape J onto shape L
(iii)   shape M onto shape L
(iv)   shape J onto shape M
 (v)   shape L onto shape M.

3. Construct the image of the letter T
under the given translation $\overrightarrow{AB}$.

4. Draw the triangle ABC twice and
construct its image under

  (i) $\overrightarrow{BC}$ (ii) $\overrightarrow{AC}$.

5. ABCD is a square, as shown.
Copy the diagram and draw a rough
sketch of the image of ABCD

  (i) under $\overrightarrow{AB}$ (ii) under $\overrightarrow{DB}$.

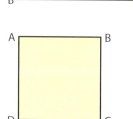

6. ABCD is a rectangle with the diagonals intersecting at the point O.
Find each of the following:

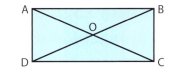

   (i) the image of A under $\overrightarrow{DC}$

  (ii) the image of [AB] under $\overrightarrow{BC}$

 (iii) the image of D under $\overrightarrow{OB}$

 (iv) the image of [DC] under $\overrightarrow{DA}$.

7. ABCD and ABEC are parallelograms.
Under the translation $\overrightarrow{CE}$, write down the image of

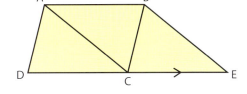

   (i) the point A   (ii) [AD]

 (iii) △ADC   (iv) [AC].

8. In the given figure, ABCD is a square and BECD is a parallelogram.

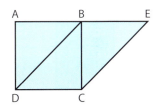

   (i) What is the image of [BD] under $\overrightarrow{DC}$?

  (ii) What is the image of C under $\overrightarrow{DB}$?

 (iii) What is the image of △ABD under $\overrightarrow{BE}$?

 (iv) Of what point is B the image under $\overrightarrow{CE}$?

  (v) Of what line segment is [BC] its image under $\overrightarrow{DC}$?

 (vi) Of what triangle is ABD the image under $\overrightarrow{CD}$?

9.

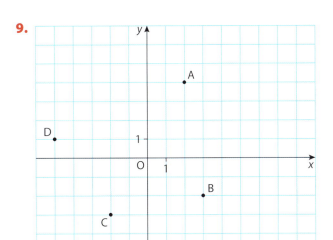

   (i) Write down the coordinates of A, B, C and D.

  (ii) Each point is translated 5 units to the right and 2 units up.
      What are the coordinates of the image points A', B', C' and D'?

Section 25.2 **Symmetries**

1. Symmetrical shapes

Each of the figures below is **symmetrical**.

The broken line(s) in each figure is called an **axis of symmetry**.

A figure will have an axis of symmetry if it can be reflected in a line so that each half of the figure is reflected exactly onto the other half of the figure.

Here are some well-known geometrical figures and their axes of symmetry.

Equilateral triangle	A square	A rectangle	Isosceles triangle
(3 axes of symmetry)	(4 axes of symmetry)	(2 axes of symmetry)	(one axis of symmetry)

A parallelogram with unequal sides and no right angle has no axis of symmetry.

2. Axial symmetry

In the given diagram, the blue figure is the image of the green figure under reflection in the broken line ℓ.

We name the image figure A′B′C′D′.

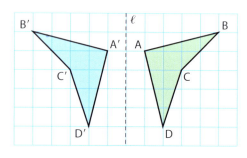

Here is another reflection in the horizontal broken red line.

The word MAM has line symmetry.
Can you think of any other words
that have line symmetry?

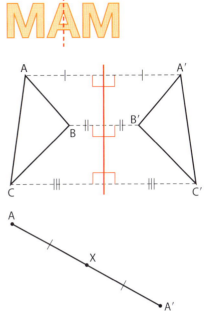

The diagram on the right illustrates how
the image of a figure is constructed under
reflection in a line.

3. Central symmetry

In the diagram on the right, the
point A is joined to the point X
and produced to A′ such that
$$|XA'| = |AX|.$$
We say that the point A′ is the image of A under
reflection in the point X or **central symmetry** in X.

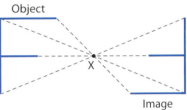

This diagram on the right shows the letter F and
its image under central symmetry in the point X.

Notice that the image appears **upside-down and
back-to-front** in relation to the given figure.

4. Centre of symmetry

All the figures below are mapped onto themselves under central symmetry in the point X.

   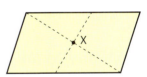

In each case, the point X is the **centre of symmetry**.

Exercise 25.2

1. Use a set square and ruler to construct the image of the point X under reflection in
the line ℓ in each of the following:

2. Use a set square and ruler to draw a rough sketch of the images of these triangles under reflection in the line *m*.

  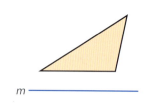

3. The rectangle DCFE is the image of the rectangle ABCD under axial symmetry in the line *k*.

Write down the image of each of the following under reflection in the line *k*.

(i) the point B   (ii) [AB]   (iii) [DB]
(iv) △DCB   (v) △ABD   (vi) [CB]

4. Which of the following transformations represent reflection in a line?

(i)   (ii)   (iii)   (iv)

5. Which of the letters in the word below have an axis of symmetry?

6. Sketch the image of the triangle ABC under central symmetry in the point C in each of the following.

   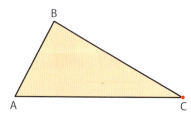

7. ABCD is a rectangle with the diagonals intersecting at the point O.

Find the image of each of the following under central symmetry in the point O.

(i) D   (ii) C   (iii) [BC]   (iv) $\triangle$AOB

(v) [AO]   (vi) $\triangle$ADB   (vii) [OC]   (viii) ABCD.

8. Which of the four faces shown below could be the image of the face shown on the right under a central symmetry?

(A)   (B)   (C)   (D)

9. Which of the four faces in question 8 could be the image of the given face under
(i) reflection in a vertical line
(ii) a translation?

10. In the diagram on the right, describe fully the single transformation which will map

(i) shape P onto shape P_1
(ii) shape P_1 onto shape P_2
(iii) shape P onto shape P_2.

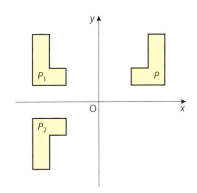

11. On the right is a circle of centre C. Name two transformations, each of which maps the circle onto itself.

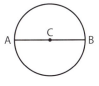

12. The diagram on the right shows a pattern and a line n.

Which one of the following diagrams is the reflection of the pattern in n?

A   B   C   D

13. The diagram on the right shows the
triangle ABC.
The image of ABC under reflection in
the y-axis is A′B′C′.

(i) Find the coordinates of A′, B′ and C′.

A″, B″ and C″ are the images of A, B and C
under reflection in the x-axis.

(ii) Find the coordinates of A″, B″ and C″.

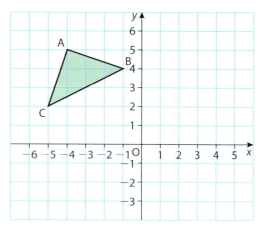

14. How many axes of symmetry has each of the following figures?

(i)   (ii)   (iii)   (iv)

15. Which of the figures in question 14 have a centre of symmetry?

16.

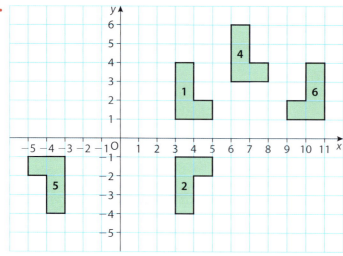

Which of the transformations – axial symmetry, central symmetry or translation
– will map

(i) L_1 onto L_2 (ii) L_1 onto L_4

(iii) L_5 onto L_2 (iv) L_1 onto L_6

(v) L_1 onto L_5?

Section 25.3 **Constructions 1**

Here are the instruments you will need to do various geometrical constructions.

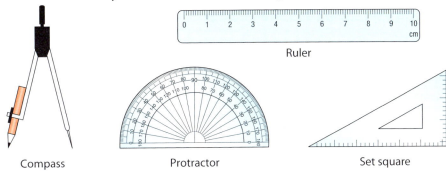

Compass   Protractor   Set square

Note: The words 'ruler' and 'straightedge' are used interchangeably.

1. Bisector of a given angle using only compass and straightedge

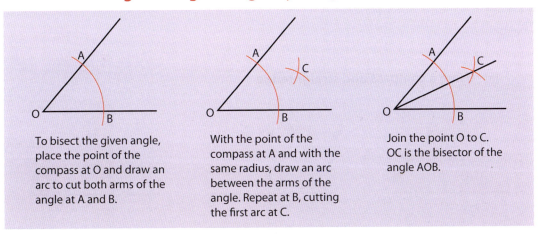

To bisect the given angle, place the point of the compass at O and draw an arc to cut both arms of the angle at A and B.

With the point of the compass at A and with the same radius, draw an arc between the arms of the angle. Repeat at B, cutting the first arc at C.

Join the point O to C. OC is the bisector of the angle AOB.

2. How to construct the perpendicular bisector of a line segment

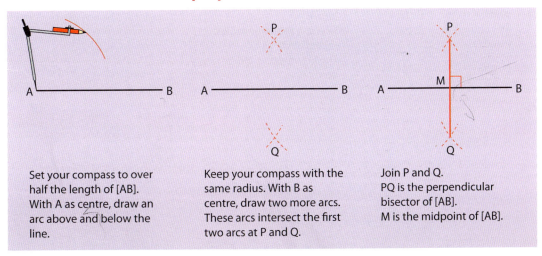

Set your compass to over half the length of [AB]. With A as centre, draw an arc above and below the line.

Keep your compass with the same radius. With B as centre, draw two more arcs. These arcs intersect the first two arcs at P and Q.

Join P and Q. PQ is the perpendicular bisector of [AB]. M is the midpoint of [AB].

3. Line perpendicular to a given line ℓ, passing through a given point on ℓ

(i) Using a set square and straightedge

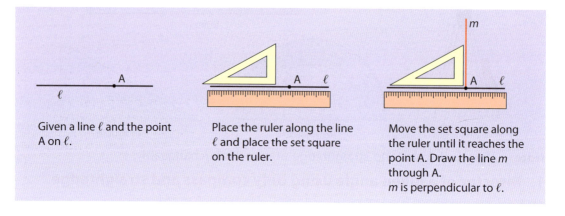

Given a line ℓ and the point A on ℓ.

Place the ruler along the line ℓ and place the set square on the ruler.

Move the set square along the ruler until it reaches the point A. Draw the line m through A. m is perpendicular to ℓ.

(ii) Using a compass and straightedge

With the point of the compass at A and with a suitable radius, draw two arcs cutting the line ℓ at P and Q.

With the point of the compass at P, draw an arc above A.
Keeping the same radius, repeat at Q.
The arcs meet at the point X.

Using a straightedge, draw a line through X and the point A. The line XA is perpendicular to ℓ and contains A.

4. How to draw a line parallel to a given line, through a given point

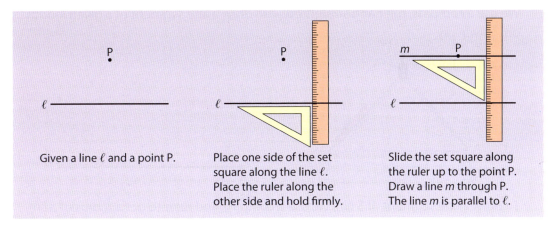

Given a line ℓ and a point P.	Place one side of the set square along the line ℓ. Place the ruler along the other side and hold firmly.	Slide the set square along the ruler up to the point P. Draw a line m through P. The line m is parallel to ℓ.

5. Division of a line segment into three equal parts

Draw a line segment [XY]. Draw a line through X making an acute angle with [XY].	Use a compass with X as centre and draw an arc crossing the line at A. With A as centre and with the same radius, draw another arc crossing the line. Mark this point B. Repeat the process at point B and mark the new point C.	Join C to Y. Using a set square and ruler, draw lines through B and A parallel to CY. These lines meet [XY] at the points V and U, respectively. U and V divide [XY] into three equal parts.

6. Line segment of a given length on a given ray

We use a compass, ruler and straightedge to draw a line segment of a given length on a given ray.

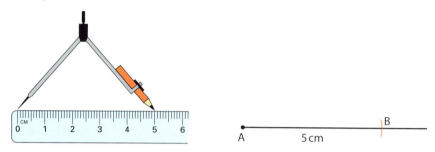

To draw a line segment of 5 cm, we use a compass and ruler to get a radius of 5 cm. We now place the compass at the point A and without changing the radius, draw an arc intersecting the line at B.

[AB] is 5 cm in length.

7. Angle of a given number of degrees with a given ray as one arm

We use a protractor to measure angles and draw angles of given sizes. The diagrams below show how to draw an angle of 74°.

Draw a line (or ray). Mark the vertex of the angle.

Position the protractor as if you were measuring an angle. Mark a dot at 74°.

Draw a line from the vertex through the dot.

Exercise 25.3

1. Using only a compass and straightedge, construct the bisector of each of the angles shown below:

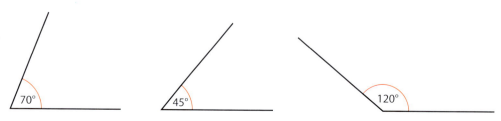

2. Use your set square to draw a right angle.
    Now use your compass and straightedge to divide the angle into two equal parts.
    Use your protractor to verify that each part is 45°.

3. Draw a line segment 6 cm in length.
    Use your compass and straightedge to construct the perpendicular bisector of this
    line segment.
    Verify that each half is 3 cm in length.

4. Draw a line segment 7 cm in length.
    Bisect the line and verify that both halves are equal in length.

5. Draw a line segment [AB], 8 cm in length.
    Use a compass and straightedge to construct the perpendicular bisector of this line
    segment.
    Pick any point on the perpendicular bisector and verify that it is the same distance
    from A and B.

6. Using a set square and straightedge, construct a line perpendicular to the given
    line through the given point for each of the lines shown below:

7. Using diagrams similar to those in question 6 above, construct a line perpendicular
    to the given line through the given point using only a compass and straightedge.

8. Using a set square and straightedge, draw a
    line through the point P parallel to the line ℓ.

    P.

    ℓ ————————————————

9. Draw any line segment and plot a point P not on the line.
    Now, using a set square and straightedge, draw a line through P parallel to the line
    segment you have drawn.

10. The diagram on the right shows a line segment [AB]
and a line AY in which |AX| = |XY|.
Use your set square and ruler to draw XM parallel to YB.
Verify that M is the midpoint of [AB].

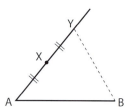

11. Draw a line segment 9 cm in length.
Now use your compass, ruler and set square to divide the line into 3 equal parts.
Use your ruler to verify that each part is 3 cm in length.

12. Use your protractor to draw an angle of 65° (∠BAC).
Now use a compass and straightedge to construct
the bisector of this angle.
If X is any point on the bisector of the angle BAC and
XB ⊥ AB and XC ⊥ AC, use congruent triangles to
show that |XB| = |XC|.

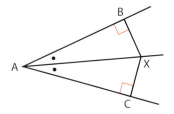

Section 25.4 **Constructing triangles and rectangles**

1. **Triangle given lengths of the three sides**

Make an accurate drawing of triangle ABC with |AB| = 6 cm,
|BC| = 5 cm and |CA| = 4 cm.

Make a rough sketch first, to get an idea of what
your finished drawing should be like.

Start with the longest side. Using a ruler, draw a line segment 6 cm long and label its ends A and B.

Set your compass to a radius of 5 cm. Put the point at B and draw an arc.

Set your compass to 4 cm. Put the point at A and draw a second arc. Point C is where the two arcs cross.

Join C to A and B to complete the triangle.

2. Triangle given side, angle and side measurements

Construct a triangle ABC with [BC] as base,
where |BC| = 4 cm, |AB| = 3 cm and |∠ABC| = 60°.
Measure the side [AC].

A rough sketch is shown on the right.

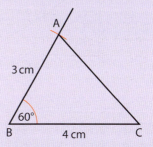

Draw a horizontal line and use your compass to mark off 4 cm. This gives the base [BC] = 4 cm.	Use your protractor to measure ∠CBA = 60° and draw the line BA. Place the point of your compass at B and draw an arc using a radius of 3 cm. The point where the arc cuts the line BA gives us the required point A.	Join A to C. ABC is the required triangle. If we measure |AC|, we get 3.6 cm.

3. Triangle given angle, side, angle measures

Construct a triangle ABC with |BC| = 5 cm, |∠ABC| = 40°
and |∠ACB| = 50°.

A rough sketch is shown.

Draw a line segment [BC], 5 cm in length.

Use a protractor to make
|∠ABC| = 40° and |∠BCA| = 50°.
The lines meet at the point A.
ABC is the required triangle.

4. Right-angled triangle, given the length of the hypotenuse and one other side

Construct the triangle ABC so that $|\angle ABC| = 90°$, $|BC| = 5$ cm and $|AC| = 6$ cm.
A rough sketch of the triangle is shown.

Draw a line segment [BC],
5 cm in length.

Use a protractor to make an angle of 90° at B.
Draw a vertical line BA.
Set your compass to a radius of 6 cm.
With C as centre, draw an arc cutting the vertical line.
Mark this point A and join AC.
ABC is the required triangle.

5. Right-angled triangle, given one side and one of the acute angles

Construct the triangle ABC so that the base $[BC] = 5$ cm, $|\angle ABC| = 90°$ and $|\angle ACB| = 40°$. A rough sketch is shown.

Draw a line segment [BC],
5 cm in length.

Use a protractor to make an angle of 90° at B.
Draw a vertical line BA.
Now use your protractor to make an angle of 40° at C.
Mark the point A where the arm of the angle meets the vertical line.
ABC is the required triangle.

6. Constructing rectangles

Construct a rectangle of sides 5 cm and 3 cm in length.

| Draw a horizontal line and mark a point A on it. Use a set square or protractor to draw a line perpendicular to the given line at A. | Use a compass to measure 5 cm on the horizontal line and 3 cm on the vertical line. Mark the points D and B, respectively. | Draw a line through B parallel to AD. Draw a line through D parallel to AB. These lines meet at the point C. ABCD is the required rectangle. |

Exercise 25.4

1. Draw an accurate construction of each of the following triangles.
All construction lines must be shown.

2. Draw a rough sketch of each of the following triangles.
Use [BC] as base in each case.
Now draw an accurate construction of each triangle.

   (i)   △ABC in which |BC| = 6 cm, |AB| = 5 cm and |AC| = 4 cm.
   (ii) △ABC in which |BC| = 8 cm, |AB| = 5.5 cm and |AC| = 6 cm.

3. Draw a triangle of sides 3 cm, 5 cm and 6 cm.
Measure the three angles and verify that
   (i)   the smallest angle is opposite the shortest side
   (ii) the largest angle is opposite the longest side.

4. Construct the following triangles based on the dimensions shown in the rough sketches below.

Measure |AC| Measure |DE| Measure |XZ|

5. Construct a triangle ABC, with [BC] as base, in each of the following cases.
(First draw a rough sketch.)
Measure the third side in each triangle.

   (i) |BC| = 4 cm, |AB| = 3 cm and |∠ABC| = 50°.
   (ii) |BC| = 6 cm, |∠BCA| = 60° and |AC| = 4.5 cm.

6. Draw accurate diagrams of the sketches shown below:

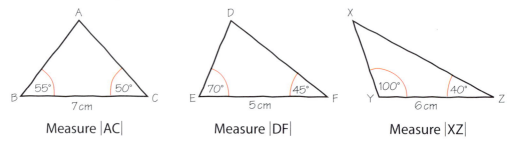

Measure |AC| Measure |DF| Measure |XZ|

7. Draw an accurate construction of each of the following right-angled triangles:

8. Construct the triangle DEF with base [EF], in which |DE| = 5 cm, |EF| = 6.5 cm and |∠DEF| = 90°.

9. Construct the triangle ABC, with [BC] as base, in which |BC| = 7 cm, |∠ABC| = 90° and |∠ACB| = 50°.
Measure |AC|.

10. Draw a rectangle of sides 6 cm and 4 cm in length.
Verify that both diagonals are equal in length.

11. Draw a rectangle of sides 70 mm and 45 mm in length.
Measure the length of the diagonal.

12. Construct the rectangle ABCD with base [AB] = 7 cm in length, where the area of
the rectangle is 28 cm².

13. (i) Draw an accurate plan of this
park, using a scale of 1 cm
to 10 m.
(ii) There are two straight paths
in the park, one from Main
Gate to Honeysuckle Gate
and the other from Archway
to Dewdrop Gap.

What is the length, in metres,
of the longer path?

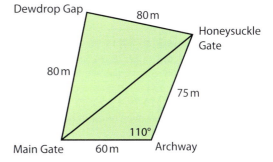

Answers

Chapter 1: Number Revisited

Exercise 1.1

1. (i) Y   (ii) N   (iii) N
   (iv) N   (v) N   (vi) Y
2. 5, 10, 15, 20, 25, 30
3. (i) 6, 12, 18, 24, 30, 36, 42, 48
   (ii) 7, 14, 21, 28, 35, 42, 49, 56
   (iii) 42
4. (i) 1, 2, 4, 7, 14, 28
   (ii) 1, 2, 3, 5, 6, 10, 15, 30
   (iii) 1, 3, 5, 9, 15, 45
   (iv) 1, 2, 3, 4, 5, 6, 10, 12, 15, 20, 30, 60
   (v) 1, 2, 3, 4, 6, 8, 9, 12, 18, 24, 36, 72
5. (i) 6   (ii) 6   (iii) 4   (iv) 4
6. 54, 60, 66
7. (i) 2, 3, 5, 7, 11, 13, 17, 19, 23, 29
   (ii) As every other even number has at least 3 factors, e.g. 6, 12
8. 13, 23, 31, 53
9. (i) $2^3 \times 3$ (ii) $2^2 \times 3^2$ (iii) $2 \times 3 \times 7$
   (iv) $2 \times 3 \times 11$ (v) $2^2 \times 5^2$
10. 13, 17, 37
11. 17, 29
12. 3 and 8 (or 6 and 8)
13. 6, 9 and 12
14. 1 minute (60 sec)
15. 6732

Exercise 1.2

1. (i) $-7°C, -4°C, 0°C, 3°C, 10°C$
   (ii) $-5°C, -4.5°C, -1°C, 6°C, 7.5°C$
2. (i) $-4°C$ (ii) $-9°C$ (iii) $-2°C$ (iv) $-10°C$
3. (i) 5   (ii) -1
   (iii) -9 (iv) -8
   (v) -2 (vi) -19
   (vii) -2 (viii) 4
4. SUBARU
5. (i) 7, -4 (ii) 7, -12
   (iii) $-4, -12$ (iv) 10, -5
6. (i) -12 (ii) -18
   (iii) 6   (iv) -40
   (v) -120 (vi) -56
   (vii) -24 (viii) -48
7. (i) 2   (ii) -5 (iii) -3
   (iv) -7 (v) 8   (vi) 5

8. (i) -7 (ii) 4   (iii) -9 (iv) 9
9. (i) SHEEP   (ii) RABBIT   (iii) HAMSTER
10. (i) 19   (ii) 7   (iii) 12   (iv) 14
    (v) 40   (vi) 6   (vii) 15   (viii) 34
    (ix) 58
11. (i) Fine as it is
    (ii) $54 \div (6 + 3) + 2 = 8$
    (iii) $(6 + 34 \div 2 + 3) \div 2 = 13$
    (iv) $42 \div (5 + 2) \times 5 = 30$
    (v) $15 + 4 \times (5 - 5) = 15$
    (vi) $(81 \div 9) \div (2 + 1) = 3$
12. (i) F   (ii) F   (iii) T   (iv) F
13. (i) $+, \div$ (ii) $-, \times$ (iii) $\times, -$
    (iv) $+, \div$ (v) $-, +$ (vi) $-, \div$
14. (i) 8   (ii) 5   (iii) 57   (iv) 1
15. (i) $-5 \times 4 \times -3$ (i.e. 60)
    (ii) $-5 \times 4 \times 3$ (i.e. -60)
16.

Exercise 1.3

1. (i) $\frac{5}{10}$ (ii) $\frac{3}{12}$ (iii) $\frac{8}{20}$ (iv) $\frac{4}{6}$
2. (i) $\frac{1}{2}$ (ii) $\frac{2}{3}$ (iii) $\frac{3}{4}$ (iv) $\frac{3}{5}$ (v) $\frac{5}{7}$
3. (i) $\frac{5}{3}$ (ii) $\frac{21}{8}$ (iii) $\frac{15}{4}$ (iv) $\frac{28}{5}$ (v) $\frac{61}{8}$
4. (i) $1\frac{3}{5}$ (ii) $5\frac{3}{4}$ (iii) $2\frac{2}{7}$ (iv) $3\frac{1}{4}$ (v) $6\frac{1}{2}$
5. $\frac{9}{2}$ $\left(\text{i.e. } 4\frac{1}{2}\right)$
6. $\frac{8}{7}, \frac{17}{10}, \frac{11}{4}, \frac{15}{5}, \frac{10}{3}$
7. (i) $\frac{6}{7}$ (ii) $\frac{2}{3}$ (iii) $\frac{2}{5}$ (iv) $\frac{1}{4}$
8. (i) 6   (ii) 12   (iii) 18   (iv) 24
9. (i) $\frac{9}{10}$ (ii) $\frac{5}{8}$ (iii) $\frac{7}{12}$ (iv) $1\frac{5}{12}$
   (v) $\frac{13}{18}$ (vi) $1\frac{1}{15}$ (vii) $1\frac{3}{28}$ (viii) $\frac{31}{36}$
10. (i) $\frac{1}{12}$ (ii) $\frac{17}{40}$ (iii) $\frac{7}{30}$ (iv) $\frac{2}{3}$
11. (i) $\frac{1}{10}, \frac{1}{4}, \frac{2}{5}, \frac{1}{2}, \frac{3}{5}$ (ii) $\frac{7}{12}, \frac{5}{8}, \frac{2}{3}, \frac{17}{24}, \frac{3}{4}, \frac{5}{6}$
12. (i) $3\frac{11}{12}$ (ii) $4\frac{3}{10}$ (iii) $6\frac{1}{5}$
    (iv) $4\frac{7}{12}$ (v) $1\frac{3}{10}$ (vi) $2\frac{1}{15}$
    (vii) $\frac{5}{8}$ (viii) $2\frac{1}{6}$
13. (i) $\frac{5}{8}$ (ii) $\frac{2}{7}$ (iii) $\frac{3}{7}$ (iv) $\frac{1}{9}$

14. (i) 4   (ii) 25   (iii) 20   (iv) 21

15. (i) $\frac{3}{2}$ (ii) $4\frac{2}{7}$ (iii) $\frac{10}{11}$ (iv) $8\frac{1}{4}$

16. (i) $1\frac{1}{4}$ (ii) $3\frac{1}{2}$ (iii) $1\frac{1}{5}$ (iv) $\frac{7}{8}$
   (v) $4\frac{2}{3}$ (vi) 6   (vii) $1\frac{1}{2}$ (viii) $\frac{18}{35}$

17. (i) $\frac{1}{2}$ (ii) 6   (iii) $\frac{5}{6}$ (iv) $2\frac{5}{8}$

18. (i) $\frac{11}{12}$ of 60 (55)   (ii) Both the same (18)

19. (i) Ⓐ and Ⓡ, Ⓑ and Ⓠ, Ⓒ and Ⓟ
   (ii) $\frac{3}{10}$, $\frac{5}{12}$, $\frac{2}{15}$

20. GLASGOW   **21.** Ⓒ

22. 14 students   **23.** 5 tins

24. (i) 48   (ii) 84

25. Thirty   **26.** 13

27. €81

28. (i) $1\frac{3}{4}$ m; $\frac{7}{20}$ m

29. $\frac{5}{24}$

30. Largest $=\frac{115}{3}\left(3\frac{5}{6}\div\frac{1}{10}\right)$, smallest $=\frac{1}{80}\left(\frac{1}{8}\times\frac{1}{10}\right)$

Exercise 1.4

1. (i) $\frac{4}{5}$ (ii) $\frac{1}{4}$ (iii) $\frac{3}{4}$
   (iv) $\frac{7}{20}$ (v) $\frac{1}{20}$

2. (i) 0.7   (ii) 0.65   (iii) 0.87
   (iv) 0.05   (v) 0.035

3. (i) 16   (ii) 134   (iii) 104   (iv) 20

4. (i) 7.4   (ii) 3.45   (iii) 0.015   (iv) 0.184

5. (i) 0.9   (ii) 6   (iii) 7.2
   (iv) 12.3   (v) 16.3

6. (i) 9.525   (ii) 0.9525   (iii) 0.9525

7. (i) 12   (ii) 27   (iii) 1.2
   (iv) 300   (v) 120   (vi) 3
   (vii) 0.21   (viii) 0.84

8. (a) $= 7.4$,   (b) $= 8.2$,   (c) $= 8.8$,
   (d) $= 0.75$,   (e) $= 1.5$,   (f) $= 2.25$

9. (i) $\frac{3}{5}$ (ii) $\frac{1}{4}$ (iii) $\frac{3}{4}$ (iv) $\frac{13}{20}$ (v) $\frac{1}{8}$

10. (i) 14   (ii) 24
   (iii) 27   (iv) 24

11. (i) 60   (ii) 30
   (iii) 24   (iv) 6

12. (i) 75   (ii) 161
   (iii) 60   (iv) 210

13. 10% of 40 & 5% of 80 ; 30% of 10 & 50% of 6;
   20% of 50 & 25% of 40 ; 30% of 50 & 75% of 20

14. (i) $\frac{3}{10}$ (ii) 30%
   (iii)

15. (i) 0.15   (ii) 0.4
   (iii) 0.09, 15%, 0.2, $\frac{2}{5}$

16. (i) 0.18, $\frac{1}{4}$, 28%, 0.3   (ii) 8%, 0.55, 0.6, $\frac{7}{10}$
   (iii) 0.09, $\frac{3}{4}$, 78%, 0.8   (iv) 0.19, 0.4, 48%, $\frac{1}{2}$

17.

Percentage	Fraction	Decimal
21%	$\frac{21}{100}$	0.21
57%	$\frac{57}{100}$	0.57
41%	$\frac{41}{100}$	0.41
9%	$\frac{9}{100}$	0.09
3%	$\frac{3}{100}$	0.03
8%	$\frac{8}{100}$	0.08

18. (i) 87.5%, 85%, 80%, 90%, 87.5%
   (ii) Business

19. (i) 75 m²   (ii) $41\frac{1}{4}$ m²   (iii) 8%

20. €239 616

Exercise 1.5

1. (i) 5:4   (ii) 3:2   (iii) 2:5
   (iv) 2:4 (1:2)   (v) $\frac{1}{8}$ (vi) $\frac{1}{4}$
   (vii) 12.5%

2. (i) 1:2   (ii) 1:3   (iii) 4:5
   (iv) 4:7   (v) 5:4   (vi) 2:5
   (vii) 5:9   (viii) 2:3

3. (i) 9   (ii) 15   (iii) 6   (iv) 2
   (v) 3   (vi) 28

4. (i) 1:4   (ii) 3:14   (iii) 1:5

5. (i) 1:4   (ii) 1:2   (iii) 3:2   (iv) 6:7

6. (i) 1:10   (ii) 1:4   (iii) 10:1   (iv) 3:4
   (v) C   (vi) B

7. (i) 2:3   (ii) 2:3   (iii) 4:9

8. Lighter

9. 320 boys, 240 girls

10. Tom – €1050, Gerry – €840

11. €40:€60:€100

12. 75 kg

13. €1400

14. (i) (a) 750 g   (b) 270 g   (c) 360 g
   (ii) 10   (iii) 12

15. €73.60

16. (i) $13\frac{1}{3}$ km   (ii) 60 km
   (iii) 200 km ; 1 hr 15 min

17. (i) 9 km   (ii) 126 km
   (iii) 10 ℓ

18. Adam – €3240, Emer – €2160; Adam – €3000,
   Emer – €2400

19. 3:1

20. (i) 45 cm, 20 cm   (ii) 900 cm²
   (iii) 30 cm   (iv) 12:13

Test yourself 1

1. (a) (i) 24   (ii) 6

   (b) (i)

      (ii) $\frac{9}{10}, \frac{4}{5}, \frac{3}{4}, \frac{7}{10}, \frac{13}{20}, \frac{3}{5}$

   (c) €5508

2. (a) $\frac{4}{5}$, 80%, 0.8; $\frac{3}{4}$, 75%, 0.75; $\frac{2}{5}$, 40%, $\frac{4}{10}$

   (b) (i) T   (ii) T   (iii) F(32)

   (c) ALBANIA

3. (a) (i) 6 ℓ (ii) 36

   (b) (i) $\frac{1}{4}, \frac{3}{10}, \frac{2}{5}, \frac{1}{2}, \frac{3}{5}$

      (ii) $\frac{1}{2}$, 60%, 0.65, $\frac{2}{3}, \frac{3}{4}, \frac{4}{5}$

   (c) (i) J   (ii) H   (iii) D

      (iv) I   (v) C

4. (a) $7\frac{1}{2}$ cups of flour, 5 tsp baking powder, $\frac{5}{8}$ litre of milk

   (b) (i) 8%   (ii) 7.5%   (c) 8400 ppl

5. (a) Same (both 24)

   (b) (i) $22\frac{1}{2}$ km

      (ii) 28 veggie sausages, 1050 g rice, 7 ℓ water

   (c) (i) (a) correct

      (ii) (a) correct

      (iii) (b) correct

   (d) 3:11

Chapter 2: Algebra 1

Exercise 2.1

1. $10x$

2. $7a$

3. $5a + 8b$

4. $6x + 2y$, i.e. $2(3x + y)$

5. $15a + 6b$, i.e. $3(5a + 2b)$

6. $7x + 5y + 4$

7. $7x + 4$

8. $4x + 3$

9. $8a + 3b + 2$

10. $6x + 1$

11. $5a + 4b$

12. $5ab + 2$

13. $3p - q + r$

14. $2k + 5$

15. $7ab - 3c$

16. $4xy + 11z$

17. $5ab + 5cd$

18. $11x - 8xy$

19. $8a + 10$

20. $10x^2 + x$

21. $-t - 4w$

22. $-6h - 9$

23. $3m^2 + 2m + 3$

24. $11a^2 - a - 1$

25. $14a^2 - 11a$

26. $7ab - bc$

27. (i) $4x + 11$ (ii) $8a - 1$ (iii) $8x + 6$

28. $a:x + 2y + z$, $b:4x + 2y$, $c:2y + 3z$, $d:4x + 4y + 3z$, $e:3x - 2y$, $f:5x - 2y$, $g:8x - 4y$

29. (i) $4p + 2$ (ii) 3   (iii) $2x$ (iv) $5x + 4$

30. (i) $\boxed{3x + 1}$, $\boxed{x + 3}$

    (ii) $\boxed{3x + 1}$, $\boxed{4 - 2x}$

    (iii) $\boxed{2x}$, $\boxed{4 - 2x}$

    (iv) $\boxed{7 - x}$, $\boxed{x + 3}$

    (v) $\boxed{7 - x}$, $\boxed{3x + 1}$, $\boxed{4 - 2x}$

    (vi) $\boxed{7 - x}$, $\boxed{3x + 1}$, $\boxed{x + 3}$

    (vii) $4x + 10$

31. (i) $3b$ (ii) $5w$

    (iii) $4j$ (iv) $3j, 4, 3k$

32. $2 - 5d$

33. $a:x + y$, $b:3x - 2y$, $c:7x - y$

34. (i) x, y (ii) -4 (iii) two

    (iv) $+3xy$ (v) $+6$

Exercise 2.2

1. (i) $12a$ (ii) $21x$ (iii) $16m$

   (iv) $48a$ (v) $6mn$ (vi) $6pq$

   (vii) $6k^2$ (viii) $6ab$

2. (i) a^2b (ii) $2ab^2$ (iii) $6a^2b^2$

   (iv) $10cd^2e$ (v) $6ab$ (vi) $18abc$

   (vii) abc (viii) $12x^2y$

3. (i) $-15x$ (ii) $-14m$ (iii) $12a$

   (iv) $-27m$ (v) $30k$ (vi) $14a$

   (vii) $-2ab$ (viii) pq (ix) $-10mn$

   (x) $6tw$ (xi) $-56xy$ (xii) $-30m^2$

4. $11x + 7$ **5.** $8x + 7$

6. $13x - 8$ **7.** $x + 2$

8. $18x - 20$ **9.** $3x - 14$

10. $a - 1$ **11.** $a - 5$

12. $4x^2 - 4x - 6$ **13.** $x^2 + x - 24$

14. $2x^2 + 7x + 3$ **15.** $2x^2 + 11x + 12$

16. $2x^2 + 11x + 5$ **17.** $3x^2 - 10x - 8$

18. $2x^2 + 3x - 9$ **19.** $2x^2 + 6x - 8$

20. $2x^2 - x - 3$ **21.** $x^2 - 5x + 6$

22. $2x^2 - 7x + 6$ **23.** $4x^2 + 7x - 15$

24. $2x^2 - 11x - 6$ **25.** $3x^2 - 13x - 10$

26. $2x^2 - 13x + 15$ **27.** $10x^2 + 11x - 6$

28. $2x^2 + 7x - 4$ **29.** $2x^2 - 8xy + 6y^2$

30. $12x^2 + 5xy - 3y^2$ **31.** $4x^2 - xy - 5y^2$

32. $x^2 + 8x + 16$ **33.** $4x^2 + 12x + 9$

34. $4x^2 - 4x + 1$

35. (i) $8x + 2$ (ii) $3x^2 + 5x - 2$

Exercise 2.3

1. (i) 15   (ii) 9   (iii) 7   (iv) 4

2. (i) 10   (ii) 8   (iii) -10 (iv) 8

3. (i) 8   (ii) 5   (iii) 3   (iv) 3

4. (i) 5   (ii) -18 (iii) 10   (iv) -14

5. (i) 9   (ii) 5   (iii) 0   (iv) 6

6. (i) 5   (ii) 16   (iii) 35
   (iv) 1   (v) 2   (vi) 21
   (vii) 14   (viii) 19
7. (i) 29   (ii) 4
   (iii) 2   (iv) 3
8. (i) COW   (ii) MOUSE   (iii) OTTER
9. (i) 9   (ii) 6   (iii) 6
   (iv) 9   (v) 12   (vi) 7
   (vii) 5   (viii) 7

Exercise 2.4

1. (i) 6   (ii) 14   (iii) 7
   (iv) 9   (v) 5   (vi) 8
   (vii) 33   (viii) 15
2. (i) 7   (ii) 4   (iii) 10
   (iv) 4   (v) 3   (vi) 6
3. (i) $x = 4$ (ii) $x = 9$ (iii) $x = 7$
   (iv) $x = 7$ (v) $x = 7$
4. $x = 7$ **5.** $x = 16$ **6.** $x = 7$
7. $x = 4$ **8.** $x = 3$ **9.** $x = 7$
10. $x = 6$ **11.** $x = 4$ **12.** $x = 5$
13. $x = 3$ **14.** $x = 4$ **15.** $x = 1$
16. $x = 6$ **17.** $x = -4$ **18.** $x = 4$
19. $x = 6$ **20.** $x = 5$ **21.** $x = 2$
22. $x = 6$ **23.** $x = 6$ **24.** $x = 14$
25. $x = -9$ **26.** $x = 10$ **27.** $x = 2$
28. $x = 3$ **29.** $x = 14$ **30.** $x = 3$
31. $x = 1$ **32.** $x = 10$ **33.** $x = 2$
34. $x = 3$
35. (i) $x = 5$ (ii) $x = 5$
36. (i) $x = 2$ (ii) $x = 2$
37. $x = 7$
38. (i) $a = 2$ (ii) $m = 3$
   (iii) $n = 2$ (iv) $a = 2$

Exercise 2.5

1. (i) $3x + 2 = 17; 5$ (ii) $4x + 1 = 13; 3$
   (iii) $3x - 4 = 2x; 4$ (iv) $4(x + 2) = 20; 3$
2. $4x + 3 = 3x + 8; 5$
3. 2   **4.** 4   **5.** 9
6. 15   **7.** $(x + 4); 4, 8$ **8.** 6, 11
9. (i) $6x + 1$ (ii) 9
10. 7
11. (i) $(6x + 2)$ cm   (ii) $6x + 2 = 44; x = 7$
12. (i) $(4x + 20)°$
   (ii) $4x + 20 = 180°; x = 40°$
13. Chair – €50, stool – €40
14. $x = 7$
15. $x + 5 = 3x - 7; x = 6$; 11 cm
16. 10 years old
17. 48
18. (i) 15   (ii) 9.5   (iii) 10

Exercise 2.6

1. $x + 2$ **2.** $x + 3$ **3.** $x + 7$
4. $2x + 1$ **5.** $3x + 1$ **6.** $x - 2$
7. $2x - 4$ **8.** $2x + 1$ **9.** $x - 7$
10. $3x - 5$ **11.** $5x + 4$ **12.** $3x - 4$

Test yourself 2

1. (a) (i) $2x + 3$ (ii) $4y + 18$ (iii) $2k + 22$
   (b) (i) 4   (ii) -6
    (iii) -3 (iv) 22
   (c) (i) $x = 3$ (ii) 7
2. (a) (i) $8x + 3$ (ii) $6x - 5$
   (b) A
   (c) (i) -3 (ii) 4
3. (a) (i) 12   (ii) 4
    (iii) 12   (iv) 2
   (b) (i) $g + 15$ (ii) $12 - t$
   (c) $4(x + 3) = 48; 9$
4. (a) (i) $8x - 22$ (ii) $x^2 + 18x$
   (b) (i) A – 52, B – 66, C – 18, D – 32, E – 15, F – 9
    (ii) D   (iii) F
    (iv) A and B
5. (a) (i) $4a + 4b$ (ii) $2p + q + 2$
   (b) (i) $7 - x$ (ii) $6 - 4k$
   (c) $x = 3; 21$
6. (a) All = 21
   (b) $2 - 4x^2; 10(x + 3)$
   (c) (i) €150   (ii) $T = a + 6b$
   "He had no room left for the milk after drinking his bath".

Chapter 3: Sets

Exercise 3.1

1. A Venn diagram; $A = \{1, 3, 4, 6, 8\}$; $\#A = 5$
2. (i) T (ii) F (iii) T (iv) F
3. Is an element of; is not an element of;
   (i) $\in$ (ii) $\notin$ (iii) $\in$ (iv) $\notin$ (v) $\in$
4. A and C; both contain exactly the same elements
5. (i) $\{1, 3, 4, 5, 6, 7\}$ (ii) $\{1, 7, 8, 9, 10, 11\}$
   (iii) $\{1, 7\}$
   (iv) $\{1, 3, 4, 5, 6, 7, 8, 9, 10, 11\}$
6. (i) $\{4, 5, 6\}$ (ii) $\{4, 5, 6, 7, 8, 9, 10\}$
   (iii) $\{7, 8\}$ (iv) $\{\} (\varnothing)$
7. (i) 7   (ii) 6   (iii) 3   (iv) 10
8. U

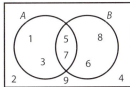

9. (i) {*a, e, i, o, t, u*}　　(ii) {*o, p, q, r, s, t, u*}
　　(iii) {*o, t, u*}
　　(iv) {*a, e, i, o, p, q, r, s, t, u*}
10. (i) {1, 2, 3, 5, 6, 7, 8, 9}
　　(ii) {1, 5, 6, 8, 9}　　(iii) {2, 3, 7}
11. (i) {3, 4, 5, 6}　　(ii) {3, 4, 8, 9}
　　(iii) {2, 7, 8, 9, 10}　　(iv) {2, 5, 6, 7, 10}
　　(v) {3, 4, 5, 6, 8, 9}　　(vi) {2, 7, 10}
12. (i) 7　　(ii) 7　　(iii) 14
　　(iv) 11　　(v) 3　　(vi) 3
13. (i) {2, 4, 6, 8, 9, 10}　　(ii) {1, 2, 7, 8, 9, 10}
　　(iii) {1, 3, 4, 5, 6, 7}　　(iv) {2, 8, 9, 10}
14.

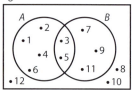

15. (i) *T*　　(ii) *T*　　(iii) *T*
　　(iv) *T*　　(v) *T*　　(vi) *F*
16. (ii) {*e, f, g*}　　(iii) 1
17. Is a subset of; is not a subset of;
　　(i) ⊂　　(ii) ⊂　　(iii) ⊄　　(iv) ⊄

Exercise 3.2

1. (i) {1, 2, 4, 5, 7, 8}　　(ii) {3, 9, 10}
　　(iii) {1, 3, 5, 7}　　(iv) { }
2. (i) {*a, c, e*}　　(ii) {*f, g, h*}
　　(iii) {*f, g, h, i, j*}　　(iv) {*a, c, e, f, g, h, i, j*}
3. (i) *T*　　(ii) *F*　　(iii) *T*　　(iv) *F*
　　(v) *T*　　(vi) *T*　　(vii) *T*　　(viii) *F*
4. (i) {2, 4, 8, 10}
　　(ii) {3, 9, 15}; no; set difference is not
　　　commutative
5. (i) {5, 6, 8, 12}　　(ii) {1, 2, 3, 4, 6}
　　(iii) {0, 15}　　(iv) {5, 6, 8, 10, 12}
　　(v) {1, 3, 6}　　(vi) {1, 2, 3, 8, 10, 12}
6.

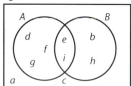

; (i) 3
　(ii) 4
　(iii) 2
　(iv) 7

8. (i) *T*　(ii) *T*　(iii) *T*　(iv) *F*　(v) *T*　(vi) *T*

Exercise 3.3

1. (i) 5　　(ii) 30　　(iii) 11　　(iv) 7
2. (i) 12　　(ii) 11　　(iii) 2　　(iv) 7
3. (i) 40　　(ii) 33　　(iii) 28　　(iv) 14

4.

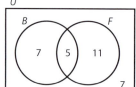

; (i) 7
　(ii) 7
　(iii) 18

5.

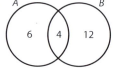

6. (i) 23　　(ii) 17　　(iii) 9　　(iv) 31
7.

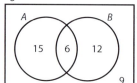

; (i) 33
　(ii) 24
　(iii) 9

8.

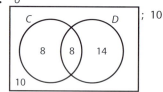

; 10

9. (i) 33　　(ii) 12　　(iii) 16
10.

; (i) 4
　(ii) 10

11. (i) 6　　(ii) 10　　(iii) 22
12. 32
13.

; (i) 7
　(ii) 9
　(iii) 13

Test yourself 3

1. (a) (i) {2, 3, 4, 5, 7}　　(ii) {3, 5, 7}
　　　(iii) {1, 6, 9, 10, 11}　　(iv) {1, 9}
　　(b) (i) 7　　(ii) 9　　(iii) 12　　(iv) 8
2. (a) (i) {2, 3, 5, 6, 7, 8, 9}
　　　(ii) {1, 4, 8, 9, 12}
　　　(iii) {1, 2, 3, 4, 5, 6, 7, 8, 9, 12}
　　　(iv) {2, 3, 5, 6, 7}

(b) (i) 30   (ii) 17   (iii) 7
     (iv) 8   (v) 15

3. (a) (i) {4}   (ii) {2, 3}
     (iii) {1, 2, 3, 4, 8}   (iv) {1, 2, 3, 8}
     (b) (iv) is true

4. (a) (i) {a, b, c, d, e}   (ii) {c, d, g, h}
     (iii) {a, b, c, d, e, g, h, k, l, m}
     (iv) {c, d}
     (v) {g, h, k, l, m}
     (vi) {k, l, m}
     (b) 6

5. (a) (i) {2, 4, 5, 6, 8}
     (ii) {2, 3, 4, 5, 6, 7, 8}
     (iii) {3, 7}
     (iv) {2, 5, 8, 9}
     (b) (i) 28   (ii) 12   (iii) 12

6. (a) 12, 18
     (b)

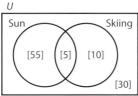

Chapter 4: Factors

Exercise 4.1

1. (i) 3   (ii) 6
     (iii) 7   (iv) 7

2. (i) $4x$ (ii) $3n$ (iii) $5x$
     (iv) $3a$ (v) $3x$ (vi) $2ab$

3. $4(x + 2)$ **4.** $6(a + 2b)$
5. $7(x + 2y)$ **6.** $11(2a + 3b)$
7. $12(x - 2y)$ **8.** $b(a + c)$
9. $2a(x + 2y)$ **10.** $x(x + 1)$
11. $5x(x - 2)$ **12.** $3a(a + 2)$
13. $4x(x - 3)$ **14.** $6b(a - 2c)$
15. $7xy(x - 2)$ **16.** $3x^2(2y - 5)$
17. $4(x + 4)$ **18.** $6(x + 3y)$
19. $10(a - 4b)$ **20.** $a(b + y)$
21. $3b(a + c)$ **22.** $2x(y - z)$
23. $7x(y + 2z)$ **24.** $5b(a - 3c)$
25. $6a(x - 2y)$ **26.** $x(x + 4)$
27. $3x(x + 3)$ **28.** $5x(x + 2)$
29. $6a(a - 2)$ **30.** $7a(a - 3)$
31. $10x(x + 4)$ **32.** $5x(5x - 3)$
33. $7x(x - 4)$ **34.** $6x(2x + 3)$
35. $5x(3x + 5y)$ **36.** $3x^2(1 - 2y)$
37. $x(x^2 + x + 1)$ **38.** $3ab(b - 2)$
39. $12xy(1 - 2x)$ **40.** $5x^2(3x - 7)$
41. (i) PARROT   (ii) THRUSH
     (iii) GROUSE   (iv) STARLING

Exercise 4.2

1. $(x + 4)(a + b)$ **2.** $(2a + 3)(x + 4)$
3. $(y + z)(x + y)$ **4.** $(b + 2c)(a + 3)$
5. $(x - 6)(a + 3)$ **6.** $(x + y)(2a - 3b)$
7. $(2x - 3)(3x + 1)$ **8.** $(3b - c)(2a - 1)$
9. $(a + b)(x + y)$ **10.** $(b + d)(a + c)$
11. $(c + 3)(a + b)$ **12.** $(p + q)(m + n)$
13. $(2b + 3d)(a + c)$ **14.** $(7x + 3)(a - b)$
15. $(c + 2)(a - b)$ **16.** $(c + 2d)(a - b)$
17. $(a + b)(2x + 3y)$ **18.** $(4 + a)(x - y)$
19. $(3 + x)(a - b)$ **20.** $(a + 4)(x - 2)$
21. $(b + d)(2a - c)$ **22.** $(a + b)(2x - y)$
23. $(x + b)(x + a)$ **24.** $(a + c)(a - 2b)$
25. $(y - z)(4a + x)$ **26.** $(m + n)(3x - a)$
27. $(x + z)(x - y)$ **28.** $(2 - c)(x - y)$
29. $(3 - b)(x + y)$ **30.** $(5 - c)(a + b)$
31. $(x + y)(x - 2)$ **32.** $(a + b)(a - 3)$
33. $(a - b)(x - 1)$ **34.** $(y - z)(a - 2b)$
35. $(x + 1)(2a - 3b)$ **36.** $(a - 1)(x + 2y)$
37. $(a - b)(b + c)$ **38.** $(b + 2d)(a - c)$
39. $(a - 3)(b + 3)$ **40.** $(3a + 2b)(x - 2y)$

Exercise 4.3

1. $(x + 2)(x - 2)$ **2.** $(x + 4)(x - 4)$
3. $(y + 6)(y - 6)$ **4.** $(y + 10)(y - 10)$
5. $(x + y)(x - y)$ **6.** $(x + 4y)(x - 4y)$
7. $(a + 3b)(a - 3b)$ **8.** $(2x + y)(2x - y)$
9. $(3a + 1)(3a - 1)$ **10.** $(2x + 3)(2x - 3)$
11. $(3x + 10)(3x - 10)$ **12.** $(10x + 1)(10x - 1)$
13. $(2a + 5b)(2a - 5b)$ **14.** $(6x + 7y)(6x - 7y)$
15. $(1 + 6x)(1 - 6x)$ **16.** $(1 + 10a)(1 - 10a)$
17. $(7 + 9x)(7 - 9x)$ **18.** $(8 + 9y)(8 - 9y)$
19. $(8x + 5y)(8x - 5y)$ **20.** $(xy + 1)(xy - 1)$
21. (ii) $5(c + d)(c - d)$ (iii) $3(a + 3b)(a - 3b)$
     (iv) $3(x + 5y)(x - 5y)$ (v) $3(2a + 3)(2a - 3)$
22. 720   **23.** 160
24. 400   **25.** 109
26. 1140   **27.** 5200
28. 36 000   **29.** 85 800

Exercise 4.4

1. $(x + 2)(x + 1)$ **2.** $(x + 2)(x + 2)$
3. $(x + 7)(x + 1)$ **4.** $(x + 3)(x + 2)$
5. $(x + 6)(x + 2)$ **6.** $(x + 7)(x + 2)$
7. $(a + 4)(a + 3)$ **8.** $(x + 3)(x + 1)$
9. $(a + 4)(a + 2)$ **10.** $(a + 6)(a + 3)$
11. $(a + 8)(a + 2)$ **12.** $(a + 6)(a + 4)$
13. $(x + 8)(x + 3)$ **14.** $(x + 10)(x + 2)$
15. $(x + 9)(x + 3)$ **16.** $(x + 11)(x + 2)$
17. $(x + 10)(x + 3)$ **18.** $(x + 6)(x + 5)$
19. $(x + 11)(x + 3)$ **20.** $(x + 12)(x + 3)$

21. $(x + 11)(x + 4)$ **22.** $(x + 5)(x + 4)$
23. $(x + 17)(x + 1)$ **24.** $(x + 16)(x + 2)$
25. $(x - 3)(x - 1)$ **26.** $(x - 3)(x - 2)$
27. $(x - 4)(x - 2)$ **28.** $(x - 4)(x - 1)$
29. $(x - 4)(x - 3)$ **30.** $(x - 5)(x - 2)$
31. $(x - 7)(x - 2)$ **32.** $(x - 8)(x - 3)$
33. $(x - 5)(x - 3)$ **34.** $(x - 6)(x - 3)$
35. $(x - 5)(x - 4)$ **36.** $(x - 10)(x - 2)$
37. $(x - 7)(x - 5)$ **38.** $(x - 6)(x - 4)$
39. $(x - 12)(x - 2)$ **40.** $(x - 9)(x - 3)$
41. $(x - 6)(x - 5)$ **42.** $(x - 10)(x - 3)$
43. $(x - 15)(x - 2)$ **44.** $(x - 9)(x - 4)$
45. $(x - 12)(x - 3)$ **46.** $(x - 9)(x - 5)$
47. $(x - 10)(x - 4)$ **48.** $(x - 8)(x - 5)$

Exercise 4.5

1. $(x - 2)(x + 1)$ **2.** $(x - 3)(x + 1)$
3. $(x - 4)(x + 1)$ **4.** $(x - 1)(x + 3)$
5. $(x - 4)(x + 3)$ **6.** $(x - 3)(x + 4)$
7. $(x - 6)(x + 2)$ **8.** $(x - 5)(x + 2)$
9. $(x - 10)(x + 1)$ **10.** $(x - 7)(x + 2)$
11. $(x - 5)(x + 3)$ **12.** $(x - 2)(x + 9)$
13. $(x - 3)(x + 6)$ **14.** $(x - 3)(x + 7)$
15. $(x - 6)(x + 4)$ **16.** $(x - 3)(x + 8)$
17. $(x - 12)(x + 2)$ **18.** $(x - 6)(x + 5)$
19. $(x - 3)(x + 10)$ **20.** $(x - 15)(x + 2)$
21. $(x - 4)(x + 7)$ **22.** $(x - 14)(x + 2)$
23. $(x - 4)(x + 9)$ **24.** $(x + 3)(x - 12)$
25. $(x - 4)(x + 10)$ **26.** $(x - 8)(x + 5)$
27. $(x - 20)(x + 2)$ **28.** $(x - 9)(x + 5)$
29. $(x - 2)(x + 8)$ **30.** $(x + 4)(x - 12)$
31. $(x + 7)(x + 2)$ **32.** $(x - 9)(x - 3)$
33. $(x - 4)(x + 6)$ **34.** $(x - 7)(x - 1)$
35. $(x - 7)(x - 2)$ **36.** $(x - 8)(x + 4)$
37. $(x + 12)(x + 2)$ **38.** $(x - 6)(x + 7)$
39. $(x - 5)(x + 10)$ **40.** $(x - 7)(x - 4)$
41. $(x - 10)(x + 6)$ **42.** $(x - 12)(x - 5)$

Test yourself 4

1. (a) (i) $9x(x + 4)$ (ii) $5b(a + 3c)$
       (iii) $6a(x - 2y)$ (iv) $6x(x^2 - 3y)$
   (b) (i) $(a + b)(7 + x)$ (ii) $(a - 5b)(a + c)$
   (c) (i) $(x - 5)(x - 11)$ (ii) $(4x + 11)(4x - 11)$
2. (a) (i) $(p - 2)$ (ii) $(4n + 1)$
       (iii) $(3x - 1)$ (iv) $(d - 3)$
   (b) (i) $(n + 1)$ (ii) $(n + 4)$
       (iii) $(n + 6)$ (iv) $(n - 8)$
   (c) (i) $(12 + 3b)(12 - 3b)$
       (ii) 600
3. (a) (i) $(x - 3z)$ (ii) $(x - 3z)$
   (b) (i) $(2a - b)(3x + y)$ (ii) $(x - 6)(x - 9)$
   (c) (i) $(6x + 1)(6x - 1)$ (ii) 1080

4. (a) (i) $4(2a + 3b - 4c)$ (ii) $6x(x - 3)$
   (b) (i) $(5 + y)(x + y)$ (ii) $(x - 2)(x - 11)$
   (c) (i) $(4 + ab)(4 - ab)$ (ii) $(x - 5)$

Chapter 5:
Bills – Interest – Income Tax

Exercise 5.1

1. €594.90   **2.** €282.12
3. €381.26   **4.** €1264.32
5. (i) 671   (ii) €140.91
6. €347.25   **7.** 480
8. €407.33
9. D. Maher – €143.35; G. O. Gorman – €198.85
10. €65.70
11. €205.52
12. €94.34
13. (i) €25.20   (ii) €39.20   (iii) €17.60
   (iv) €25.20; total cost = €107.20
14. €900
15. (i) 8   (ii) €640   (iii) 5
16. (i) €12.60   (ii) €31.52
17. (i) 30c   (ii) 75c   (iii) €1.20
18. €15.90
19. (i) €2780   (ii) €4320
   (iii) €2280   (iv) €5880
20. (i) €1152   (ii) €1275.90
   (iii) €926.80   (iv) €848; €260 000

Exercise 5.2

1. (i) 0.06   (ii) 0.08   (iii) 0.075   (iv) 0.095
   (v) 0.1   (vi) 0.13   (vii) 0.125   (viii) 1.06
   (ix) 1.12   (x) 0.84
2. (i) 220   (ii) 144   (iii) 260   (iv) 102
3. (i) 320   (ii) 18   (iii) 1110   (iv) 15
4. (i) €799.50   (ii) €145.20
   (iii) €340.50   (iv) €1380
5. €119.90   **6.** €200
7. €800   **8.** €120
9. A: €184.80, B: €368, C: €2.43, D: €30 000,
   E: €37.80, F: €10 560, G: €1120
10. 25%
11. (i) €60   (ii) 10%
12. 25%   **13.** €1380
14. (i) €600 each   (ii) 15%
   (iii) 5%
15. €60; €18   **16.** 30%
17. (i) €245   (ii) €240
18. (i) €920   (ii) €1104
19. 20%   **20.** $21\frac{1}{3}$%
21. (i) €320   (ii) 17%

Exercise 5.3

1. (i) €6 (ii) €8 (iii) €8
   (iv) €21 (v) €18 (vi) €84
2. (i) €24 (ii) €52.50 (iii) €85.50
   (iv) €132 (v) €68 (vi) €812.50
3. (i) €27 (ii) €127.50 (iii) €103.50
   (iv) €300 (v) €203 (vi) €29.40
4. (i) €324 (ii) €954 (iii) €1664
   (iv) €1960 (v) €1207.50 (vi) €748
5. €48, €96
6. (i) €9 (ii) €42 (iii) €96
   (iv) €63 (v) €15 (vi) €130
7. (i) €16 (ii) €60
   (iii) €135 (iv) €147
8. (i) €112 (ii) €30
   (iii) €144 (iv) €135
9. (i) €684 (ii) €1755
   (iii) €1625 (iv) €2250
10. (i) €300 (ii) 2

Exercise 5.4

1. €49.44   2. €133.12
3. €92.25   4. €188.10
5. €57.12   6. €178.50
7. €126.10   8. €305.28
9. €162.47   10. €224.76
11. €122   12. €1505.28
13. €1736.44   14. €1663.20
15. €15 540.35

Exercise 5.5

1. €730   2. €29 729
3. €120, €120, €78   4. €120.50
5. €424   6. €136.80
7. €5640
8. (i) €174 (ii) €876
9. (i) €520 (ii) €67.20 (iii) €452.80
10. (i) €3240 (ii) €8660 (iii) €42 100

Exercise 5.6

1. (i) $435 (ii) 86 250 yen
2. (i) $585 (ii) €615.38
3. (i) 108 000 yen (ii) €75
4. (i) £960 (ii) €750
5. €400
6. (i) 4900 Canadian dollars (ii) €4000
7. (i) €250 (ii) €423.53
8. (i) 6900 kr (ii) €163.04
9. (i) €2868
10. (i) €6737 (ii) 7980 rand

Test yourself 5

1. (a) (i) €60 (ii) €7.50
   (b) 30%
2. (a) (i) €495 (ii) €512
   (iii) €481.75
   (b) €329.69
3. (a) (i) €731.50 (ii) €936
   (b) 641
4. (a) (i) €24.60 (ii) €8.85
   (b) €102.40
5. (a) €208
   (b) €111.24
6. (a) (i) A – €1190, B – €1210
   (ii) €20
   (b) (i) 72 000 baht (ii) €55
7. (a) €255.49
   (b) €651.60
8. (a) (i) 14% (ii) 7%
   (b) (i) €6880 (ii) €35 120
9. (a) Ⓐ, $\times 1.76$; Ⓑ, $\times 0.76$; Ⓒ, $\times 1.24$;
   Ⓓ, $\times 0.24$; Ⓔ, $\times 1.2$; Ⓕ, $\times 0.8$
   (b) (i) €991.20
   (ii) 2250 km
   (c) A(€0)

Chapter 6:
Perimeter – Area – Volume

Exercise 6.1

1. (i) 46 cm (ii) 42 cm (iii) 56 cm
2. (i) 126 cm^2 (ii) 104 cm^2 (iii) 187 cm^2
3. (i) 30 cm (ii) 36 cm^2
4. (i) 36 m^2 (ii) 27 m^2
5. (i) 20 cm^2 (ii) 15 cm^2 (iii) 30 cm^2
6. (i) 56 cm^2 (ii) 120 cm^2 (iii) 120 cm^2
   (iv) $31\frac{1}{2}$ cm^2 (v) 60 cm^2 (vi) 240 cm^2
7. 100 cm^2, 182 cm^2, 270 cm^2
8. (i) 220 cm^2 (ii) 165 m^2 (iii) 24 cm^2
9. (i) 312 cm^2 (ii) 126 cm^2
10. (i) 7 cm (ii) 16 cm (iii) 22 cm
11. (i) 5 cm (ii) 12 m (iii) 25 cm
12. (i) 6 cm (ii) 7 cm (iii) 9 cm
13. (i) 10 cm (ii) 14 cm (iii) 12 cm
14. (i) 58 cm (ii) 54 cm (iii) 58 cm
15. (i) 12 cm^2 (ii) 24 cm^2 (iii) $x = 8$ cm
16. 20 m^2; 25 m^2
17. (i) 21 cm^2 (ii) 55 cm^2 (iii) 165 cm^2
18. (i) 3600 cm^2 (ii) 2520 cm^2
   (iii) 4.5 cm (across); 4 cm (top-to-bottom)

Exercise 6.2

1. (i) 240 cm²   (ii) 63 cm²   (iii) 165 cm²
2. (i) 60 cm²   (ii) 52.5 cm²   (iii) 30 cm²
3. (i) 6 cm   (ii) 7 cm   (iii) 4.5 cm
4. (i) 126 cm²   (ii) 154 cm²   (iii) 120 cm²
5. (i) 5 cm   (ii) 6.5 cm   (iii) 12 cm
6. 322 cm²; 154 cm²
7. (i) a : 6 cm², b : 4.8 cm², c : 7.2 cm²
   (ii) a : 1.5 cm, b : 1.6 cm, c : 4 cm

Exercise 6.3

1. (i) 12 cm³   (ii) 30 cm³   (iii) 63 cm³
2. (i) 32 cm²   (ii) 62 cm²   (iii) 102 cm²
3. (i) (a) 2304 cm³   (b) 1120 cm²
   (ii) (a) 7680 cm³   (b) 2368 cm²
   (iii) (a) 360 cm³   (b) 372 cm²
4. (i) 248 cm²   (ii) 474 cm²   (iii) 750 cm²
5. 84 more cubes
6. (i) 900 cm³   (ii) 368 cm³   (iii) 532 cm³
7. (iv) 88 cm²
8. (i) 125 cm³   (ii) 150 cm²
9. (i) 5 cm   (ii) 7 m   (iii) 20 cm
10. (i) 4 cm   (ii) 96 cm²
11. (i) 5 cm   (ii) 125 cm³
12. (i) 15   (ii) 405 cm³
13. (i) 6   (ii) 24
    (iii) 7   (iv) 168
14. (i) 3840 cm³   (ii) 60
15. 60
16. (i) 6ℓ   (ii) 1.6ℓ   (iii) 6.75ℓ
17. (i) open   (ii) 1936 cm³   (iii) 836 cm²
18. (i) 9 cm × 4 cm   (ii) 2 cm
    (iii) 72 cm³   (iv) 124 cm²
19. (i) 64 cm³   (ii) 96 cm²
20. (i) 7 cm   (ii) closed
    (iii) 672 cm³   (iv) 472 cm²
21. (i) C   (ii) F   (iii) B
22. (i) C   (ii) B   (iii) F
23. (i) 126 cm³   (ii) 162 cm²
24.

25.

Exercise 6.4

1. (i) 1.5 m   (ii) 3.5 m   (iii) 9 m
   (iv) 3.25 m   (v) 6.4 m
2. (i) 80 km   (ii) 6 cm
3. (i) 6 m   (ii) 24 m   (iii) 40 m
   (iv) 7.5 m
4. (i) 120 cm   (ii) 3.6 m   (iii) 1.35 m
5. 6.2 m; 2.7 m
6. (i) (a) 400 m   (b) 1 km
      (c) 1.7 km   (d) 2.5 km
   (ii) (a) 50 cm   (b) 20 cm
      (c) 2 m   (d) 135 cm
7. (i) 17 km   (ii) 4.4 cm
8. (i) 7.52 m   (ii) 2.16 m
9. (i) (a) 12 cm   (b) 8.5 km
   (ii)

```
          D  ◄─── 9 cm ───►  C
           ┌───────────────┐
  7.5 cm  /                 │ 8.5 cm
         /                  │
        A └───────────────── B
          ◄──── 12 cm ────►
```

10. 1 : 40 000; 75 cm
11. (i) 1 : 200   (ii) 6 m   (iii) 30 m²
12. (i) 50 cm   (ii) 1 : 25

Test yourself 6

1. (a) 44 cm²
   (b) (i) 576 m³   (ii) 432 cm²
2. (a) 105 cm²   (b) 4.5 cm   (c) 7 cm
3. (a) 105 cm
   (b) (i) 330 000 cm³   (ii) 330ℓ
   (c) face 3
4. (a) 99 m²   (b) 66 cm³
   (c) 126 cm² (9 cm × 14 cm)
5. (a) (i) 18 cm²   (ii) 72 cm²   (iii) 54 cm²
   (b) (i) 4 cm   (ii) 252 cm³   (iii) 254 cm²
6. (a) (i) 12 m²   (ii) 8 m²
      (iii) €960   (iv) €112
   (b) (i) 1 km   (ii) 14 cm
7. (a) (i) 27 cm³   (ii) 3 cm
   (b) (ii) 5.5 m   (iii) 1 : 50

Chapter 7:
Statistics 1 – Collecting Data

Exercise 7.1

1. (i) N   (ii) C   (iii) C   (iv) N
   (v) N   (vi) C   (vii) C   (viii) N
2. (i) D   (ii) C   (iii) D   (iv) C
   (v) D   (vi) C

3. (i) Categorical   (ii) Continuous
    (iii) 4 legs – D; 4 years old – C; 4 *munchies* – D
4. (i) N   (ii) O   (iii) O   (iv) N
    (v) N   (vi) O   (vii) O
5. Eight candidates – Numerical data (discrete)
    Order from 1 to 8 – Categorical data (ordinal)

Exercise 7.2

1. (i) P   (ii) P   (iii) S   (iv) S
3. (i) Overlap between 'not very often' and
    'sometimes'; Not specific enough; no time-
    frame provided
4. Q(i) is the one to use as Q(ii) is a leading question
5. (i) Too personal
    (ii) May cause embarrassment
    (iii) Biased
    (iv) Leading question
    (v) Too personal/embarrassing/shaming
    (vi) Too personal
    (vii) Leading question
6. (i) Too personal, first name would suffice
    (ii) 'Often' and 'sometimes' are too vague
7. (i) Question is too personal and response boxes
    aren't specific enough/are too subjective
9. QA – Too subjective/potentially embarrassing
    QB – Biased question which encourages a
    positive response

Exercise 7.3

1. (i) 820   (ii) 40
2. (i) • People already at a cinema are much more
       likely to be regular "cinema-goers"
      • No men surveyed
3. These people are likely to be "sporty", i.e. not
    representative
4. B
5. B; this sample best represents the community
    at large.
6. Method 2

Test yourself 7

1. (i) C   (ii) N   (iii) N   (iv) C   (v) C   (vi) N
2. (i) D   (ii) C   (iii) C   (iv) C   (v) D   (vi) C
3. (i) No   (ii) Yes   (iii) Yes   (iv) No   (v) Yes
4. (i) Primary   (ii) Secondary
    (iii) Secondary   (iv) Secondary
5. (a) (ii) is better
    (b) Inherently biased sample as they are
       clearly 'pro-libraries' people
6. (a) (i) Potentially embarrassing
      (ii) Too personal and assumes car
        ownership
      (iii) Too personal
    (b) Far too restricted, 'rush-hour' not included

7. (a) (i) Patently absurd as you can only phone
       someone if they own a phone!
      (ii) Reliable sample for those who shop
        at *Zacs Discount* but definitley not
        adequately representative of the
        general public
      (iii) Far too small a sample; results likely to
        be unreliable
      (iv) Number of issues here; First, the question
        assumes that you were insulting your
        neighbours. Second, it is a rude/offensive
        question. Third, it is the sort of question
        which may receive a dishonest answer
        as someone is unlikely to admit to
        continuing to insult his/her neighbour
    (b) (i) No, but it might be
      (ii) Up the number of trials to 100 or more
      (iii) Increasing the number of trials in an
        experiment and increasing the size of
        a sample in a survey both yield more
        reliable and accurate conclusions/
        observations.

Chapter 8: Probability

Exercise 8.1

1. 12
2. HH, HT, TH, TT
3. (i) 18   (ii) 6   (iii) 3
4. 36   **5.** 24   **6.** 27
7. (i) 36   (ii) 12
8. 12
9. (i) four   (ii) 128

Exercise 8.2

1. (i) even chance   (ii) certain
    (iii) impossible   (iv) unlikely
    (v) likely   (vi) even chance
    (vii) likely   (viii) unlikely
    (ix) even chance   (x) likely/certain
2. (i) event 1 : unlikely
      event 2 : even chance
      event 3 : even chance
      event 4 : impossible
      event 5 : certain
    (ii) event 1 : likely
      event 2 : certain
      event 3 : impossible
      event 4 : unlikely
      event 5 : likely
3. (i) B   (ii) C   (iii) C   (iv) A   (v) B   (vi) C
4. (i) (b), (a), (c)   (ii) (b), (a), (c)

5. (a) & green, (b) & red, (c) & blue
6. (i) 6   (ii) 8   (iii) 2

Exercise 8.3

1. (i) (a) red, blue
       (b) red, green, yellow, blue
       (c) red, blue
   (ii) (a) $\frac{1}{2}$ (b) $\frac{1}{4}$ (c) $\frac{1}{2}$

2. (i) $\frac{1}{4}$ (ii) $\frac{1}{2}$ (iii) $\frac{1}{4}, \frac{3}{4}$

3. (i) $\frac{1}{6}$ (ii) $\frac{1}{3}$ (iii) $\frac{1}{2}$
   (iv) $\frac{1}{2}$ (v) $\frac{1}{3}$ (vi) $\frac{1}{2}$

4. (i) $\frac{3}{10}$ (ii) $\frac{2}{5}$ (iii) $\frac{7}{10}$
   (iv) $\frac{3}{5}$ (v) $\frac{3}{10}$ (vi) $\frac{3}{10}$

5. (i) $\frac{1}{11}$ (ii) $\frac{2}{11}$ (iii) $\frac{2}{11}$
   (iv) $\frac{4}{11}$ (v) $\frac{4}{11}$

6. (i) $\frac{1}{6}$ (ii) $\frac{3}{8}$ (iii) $\frac{2}{5}$

7. (i) $\frac{1}{4}$ (ii) $\frac{1}{9}$ (iii) $\frac{4}{9}$
   (iv) $\frac{1}{36}$ (v) $\frac{1}{18}$ (vi) $\frac{1}{6}$

8. (i) $\frac{1}{13}$ (ii) $\frac{1}{13}$ (iii) $\frac{3}{13}$
   (iv) $1\left(\frac{13}{13}\right)$ (v) $0\left(\frac{0}{13}\right)$ (vi) $\frac{2}{13}$

9. (i) $\frac{1}{4}$ (ii) $\frac{1}{2}$ (iii) $\frac{1}{2}$
   (iv) $\frac{1}{13}$ (v) $\frac{3}{13}$ (vi) $\frac{2}{13}$

10. (i) $\frac{10}{13}$ (ii) $\frac{7}{13}$ (iii) $\frac{7}{13}$
    (iv) 0

11. (i) Red and any other colour which is not red or black
    (ii) Red and any other colour which is not red or blue

12. (i) $\frac{1}{6}$ (ii) $\frac{3}{8}$ (iii) $\frac{1}{6}$ (iv) $\frac{1}{12}$

14. (i) $\frac{1}{7}$ (ii) $\frac{2}{7}$ (iii) $\frac{1}{6}$ (iv) $\frac{1}{3}$

15. (i) $\frac{5}{12}$ (ii) $\frac{1}{6}$ (iii) $\frac{1}{12}$ (iv) $\frac{1}{12}$
    (v) $\frac{5}{12}$ (vi) $\frac{7}{12}$
    ; As every disc has either an odd or an even number on it

16. (i) $\frac{3}{10}$ (ii) $\frac{7}{20}$ (iii) $\frac{13}{20}$ (iv) $\frac{7}{20}$

17. (i) $\frac{2}{5}$ (ii) $\frac{3}{10}$ (iii) $\frac{11}{25}, \frac{1}{6}$

18. (i) $\frac{1}{100}$ (ii) $\frac{1}{10}$ (iii) $\frac{1}{20}$
    (iv) $\frac{21}{25}$ (v) 30   (vi) 20
    (vii) 25   (viii) all 100

19. $\frac{3}{7}$

20. (i) $\frac{4}{13}$ (ii) $\frac{4}{13}$ (iii) $\frac{5}{13}$ (iv) $\frac{9}{13}$

Exercise 8.4

1. (i) $\frac{1}{4}$ (ii) $\frac{1}{4}$ (iii) $\frac{1}{2}$

2. (i) $\frac{3}{16}$ (ii) $\frac{1}{2}$ (iii) $\frac{3}{16}$ (iv) $\frac{3}{16}$

3. (i) $\frac{1}{18}$ (ii) $\frac{1}{9}$ (iii) $\frac{1}{6}$
   (iv) $\frac{1}{3}$ (v) $\frac{2}{9}$ (vi) $\frac{5}{18}$

4. (ii) (a) $\frac{3}{16}$ (b) $\frac{9}{16}$ (c) $\frac{5}{8}$

5. (i) $\frac{1}{16}$ (ii) 1   (iii) $\frac{3}{8}$
   (iv) $\frac{1}{4}$ (v) $\frac{7}{16}$ (vi) $\frac{9}{16}$

6. HHH, HHT, HTH, HTT, TTT, TTH, THH, THT
   ; (i) $\frac{1}{8}$ (ii) $\frac{3}{8}$ (iii) $\frac{1}{8}$ (iv) $\frac{7}{8}$

7. (i) $\frac{1}{9}$ (ii) $\frac{1}{12}$ (iii) $\frac{1}{12}$ (iv) $\frac{5}{36}$

8. (i)

Consonants	R	AR	ER	IR
	L	AL	EL	IL
	D	AD	ED	ID
		A	E	I

Vowels

   (ii) $\frac{1}{9}$ (iii) $\frac{1}{9}$ (iv) $\frac{2}{9}$

9. (i) $\frac{2}{9}$ (ii) $\frac{4}{9}$ (iii) $\frac{5}{9}$

10. (i) RBG, RGB, BRG, BGR, GRB, GBR   (ii) $\frac{1}{3}$

Exercise 8.5

1. As the two sets of six throws are completely independent. Thus the probability of him getting four heads again is not 1, but $\frac{15}{64}$; roughly fifty

2. (i) $\frac{1}{6}$ (iv) Closer in (iii)

3. (i) $\frac{1}{2}$ (ii) $\frac{3}{4}$
   (iii) Nicky's result; greater number of trials conducted

4. $\frac{3}{10}$

5. 0.6

6. $\frac{3}{8}$

7. (ii) 0.6

8. (i) $\frac{7}{36}$ (ii) $\frac{1}{3}$ (iii) 3

9. 0.35

10. (i) $\frac{9}{20}$ (ii) $\frac{1}{4}$ (iii) $\frac{21}{40}$
    (iv) $\frac{9}{40}$; yes, because there are more games being considered

11. (i) 0.24 $\left(\frac{24}{100}\right)$ (ii) 0.1 $\left(\frac{10}{100}\right)$ (iii) 0.8 $\left(\frac{80}{100}\right)$

12. $\frac{3}{10}$

13. (i) $\frac{1}{6}$ (ii) $\frac{1}{2}$ (iii) $\frac{1}{2}$

14. (i) 0.5   (ii) 0.55   (iii) 0.6
    (iv) yes   (v) the council's

15. (i) $\frac{7}{20}$ (ii) c. 420

16. Barry's dice was fair; unlike Rachel's and Leanore's, there is a relatively even spread of outcomes which is what one would expect from a fair dice

17. (i) $\frac{2}{5}$ (ii) around 32

18. (i) 0.3   (ii) 24

Test yourself 8

1. (a) (i) $\frac{2}{5}$ (ii) $\frac{6}{25}$ (iii) $\frac{16}{25}$

    (b) (i) $\frac{7}{10}$ (ii) $\frac{1}{10}$ (iii) $\frac{1}{20}$

       (iv) $\frac{3}{10}$ (v) $\frac{3}{20}$

    (c) Both equally likely to have the winning number $\left(\frac{1}{60}\text{ chance}\right)$

2. (a) A & (iii), B & (i), C & (ii)

    (b) (i) 24 times   (ii) 4   (iii) $\frac{1}{8}$

    (c) Almost definitley unfair; the '2 face' showed way above $\left(\frac{11}{25}\right)$ what the expected frequency of a fair four-sided dice would be $\left(\text{around }\frac{1}{4}\right)$. Also, 100 throws was a fairly large number of trials to conduct and so the results ought to be reliable

3. (a) (i) $\frac{1}{4}$ (ii) $\frac{3}{8}$ (iii) $\frac{3}{8}$

       (iv) $\frac{5}{8}, \frac{8}{8}$ (i.e. 1); there were only three different colour counters in the bag and accordingly the probability has to be 1.

    (b) (i) $\frac{1}{2}$ (ii) $\frac{1}{52}$ (iii) $\frac{5}{13}$

       (iv) $\frac{3}{26}$ (v) $\frac{1}{13}$ (vi) $\frac{7}{13}$

    (c) (i) 160   (ii) 240

4. (a) 90% chance $\left(\frac{9}{10}\right)$

    (b) (i) 12   (ii) $\frac{1}{12}$ (iii) $\frac{1}{4}$ (iv) $\frac{1}{6}$

    (c) 80

Chapter 9: Statistics 2 – Measures of Average and Spread

Exercise 9.1

1. (i) 7   (ii) 12   (iii) 5.7   (iv) bus

2. (i) 10   (ii) sun   (iii) $\frac{1}{4}$

3. 5

4. (i) 8   (ii) 2

5. Each number appears twice

6. (i) 32   (ii) 6   (iii) no   (iv) no

7. 171 cm

8. (i) 6   (ii) 14   (iii) 3.6

9. (i) 7   (ii) 24   (iii) 3.7

10. 10.5

11. (i) 7.5   (ii) 21   (iii) 6.75

12. (i) 9   (ii) 9

13. (i) 9   (ii) 9

14. (i) 7   (ii) 17   (iii) median = 8

Exercise 9.2

1. (i) 5   (ii) 9   (iii) 14   (iv) 7

2. 61

3. 26

4. €6.30

5. 9; 7.5

6. 36

7. (i) 24   (ii) 11

8. (i) 36   (ii) 5

9. 11

10. 13 cm

11. 12

12. 25

13. 8

14. (i) 18   (ii) 12   (iii) 0

15. €1.73

16. 6; 10; increased by 4

17. 30

18. 156; 12

19. 4, 4, 6, 10, 11 or 4, 4, 6, 7, 14, . . . etc.

20. (i) 61   (ii) 60   (iii) 59

     (iv) Barry   (v) 5

Exercise 9.3

1. (i) 11   (ii) 24   (iii) €16

2. (i) 82   (ii) 17

3. (i) has the greater range

4. (i) 1.8   (ii) 9

5. (i) Ann : 44; John : 20; John is more consistent

    (ii) Ann

6. (i) Emer : 82; Anna : 83

    (ii) Emer : 20; Anna : 12

    (iii) Anna

7. (i) 45 mins   (ii) 50 mins   (iii) 20 mins

    (iv) 60 mins

8. (i) Leinster : $25\frac{1}{3}$; Munster : 25

    (ii) Leinster : 21; Munster : 12

9. 9 and 5

10. 70 or 1

11. (i) True   (ii) Possible   (iii) False

12. (i) Possible   (ii) False   (iii) Possible

13. (i) Yes, 8   (ii) Yes, 8

    (iii) No; 8 + 8 or 7 + 9, . . . etc.; 14 + 2

Exercise 9.4

1. (i) 2 (ii) 1
   (iii) 6 of the 8 numbers < mean – not representative
2. (i) Range
   (ii) (a) 6 (b) 5 (c) 5
   (iii) Mean, median or mode
3. Mean = 17; median = 3; median
4. Mode (black)
5. (i) 30.57°C
   (ii) Data closely bunched
6. (i) 26.55 (ii) Mode
7. (i) Denim
   (ii) It is the only average we can get
8. (i) (a) 7 (b) 5
   (ii) Mode, though in this instance the mode and median may be one and the same!
9. (i) (a) 94 kg (b) 53 kg (c) 87.44 kg
   (ii) Median

Exercise 9.5

1. (i) 4 (ii) 3 (iii) 2; 6
2. (i) 7 (ii) 8 (iii) 3
   (iv) 36 (v) 33.33%
3. (i) 1 (ii) 4 (iii) 2
   (iv) 150 (v) 3
4. (i) 8 (ii) 2 (iii) 180
   (iv) 3 (v) 32
5. Mean = 3; mode = 1 and 2
6. (i) 60 (ii) 30
   (iii) 50% (iv) 2 year olds
   (v) 3 year olds
7. (ii) 2 (iii) 10%
8. 3
9. (i) 3 (ii) 1 (iii) 25% (iv) 26
10. (i) 19 (ii) (41-60) (iii) (61-80)
    (iv) one cannot get an exact mean
11. (i) 50 (ii) (11-20) and (21-30)
    (iii) (1-10) (iv) 29
    (v) Not necessarily as the sample is restrictive (only takes students into account)

Test yourself 9

1. (a) (i) 14 (ii) 29
   (iii) 17 (iv) 14
   (b) 86
2. (a) (i) 47 (ii) 6
   (b) 2
3. (a) Mean = 7, median = 3, mode = 3; median or mode as all but one of the values are below the mean and so the mean is misleading

(b) (i) 1, 3, 9 or 1, 4, 9 or 3, 5, 9 or 4, 5, 9
   (ii) 1, 3, 4 (iii) 1, 5, 9 or 1, 3, 5
4. (a) 60 (b) 165 (c) 2.75
   (d) The mean would increase very slightly (by 0.02)
5. (a) (i) Ordinary
   (ii) Not dealing in numbers; so only average we can get
   (b) (i) 5, 8, 11 (ii) 4, 4, 7 (iii) 20, 27, 28
6. (a) Mean – 5.1, mode – 0, median – 2; median
   (b) (i) 318 (ii) $35\frac{1}{3}$ (iii) 32
7. (a) (i) 5 (ii) 4 (iii) 5
   (b) (i) 1280 km (ii) 516 km
   (iii) $224\frac{1}{2}$ km
8. (a) 3.6
   (b) (i) Tim, largest range (58) (ii) Derek
9. (a) (i) €376.67
   (ii) €245; no two values the same; Median
   (b) 45, 2

Chapter 10: Geometry 1 – Triangles and Quadrilaterals

Exercise 10.1

1. (i) The line segment [AB]
   (ii) The line AB
   (iii) The ray [BA
2. $A = 117°, B = 85°, C = 45°, D = 140°, E = 70°, F = 23°$
3. $A = 70°, B = 110°, C = 150°, D = 30°, E = 140°, F = 40°, G = 62°, H = 118°, I = 62°, J = 128°, K = 52°, L = 128°, P = 147°, Q = 33°, R = 147°$
4. (i) 4 (ii) 7 (iii) 4
5. (i) 7 (ii) 6 (iii) 4
6. $a = 110°, b = 70°, c = 46°, d = 134°, e = 60°, f = 120°$
7. $a = 48°, b = 132°, c = 132°, d = 132°, e = 160°, f = 20°, g = 20°, x = 131°, y = 131°, z = 131°$
8. $a = 61$ (alternate angle), $b = 119$
   ($a° + b° = 180°$, i.e. straight angle), $c = 110$
   (corresponding angle), $d = 70$ ($c° + d° = 180°$),
   $e = 65°$ (interior angles sum to 180°), $f = 65°$
   (vertically opposite angles)
9. $a = 96°, b = 96°, c = 84°, d = 72°, e = 68°, f = 112°, g = 68°$
10. $p = 80°, q = 80°, r = 75°, s = 105°$

Exercise 10.2

1. (i) (a) $d°$ (b) $t°$ (c) $w°$
   (ii) (a) $a°$ and $b°$ (b) $q°$ and $p°$ (c) $x°$ and $z°$
2. $a = 104°, b = 26°, c = 85°, d = 95°, e = 141°, f = 118°, g = 66°$

3. $a = 70°, b = 30°, c = 40°, d = 109°$
4. $a = 70°, b = 70°, c = 72°, d = 72°, e = 62°,$
   $f = 56°$
5. $a = 65°, b = 40°, c = 52.5°, d = 60°, e = 30°$
6. $p = 106°, q = 37°, r = 37°, d = 25°, e = 130°,$
   $f = 50°, v = 59°, w = 31°, x = 59°, y = 121°$
7. $a = 73°, b = 73°$
8. $x = 54°, y = 80°, z = 60°$
9. (i) $x = 65°, y = 50°$
   (ii) $x = 70°, y = 70°$
   (iii) $x = 50°, y = 65°$

Exercise 10.3

1. (i) $A \& C, B \& D$ (ii) 180°
2. $A = 80°, B = 115°, C = 65°, D = 105°, E = 75°$
3. $A = 120°, B = 60°, C = 80°, D = 45°, E = 75°,$
   $F = 55°, G = 55°$
4. $x = 66°, y = 72°$
5. $A = 30°, B = 70°, C = 35°, D = 65°, E = 28°,$
   $F = 112°, G = 52°$
6. (i) 68° (ii) 50° (iii) 100°
7. $A = 41°, B = 100°, C = 46°, D = 69°, E = 31°,$
   $F = 37°, G = 63°$
8. (i) 8 (ii) 11 (iii) 10 (iv) 7
9. (i) 6 (ii) 4 (iii) 9
   (iv) 6 (v) $\angle BOC$ (vi) $\angle BCD$
   (vii) $\angle ABD$ (viii) $\angle ACD$
10. (i) $x = 70°, y = 40°, z = 40°, r = 70°$
11.
12. $a = 121°, b = 89°, c = 129°, d = 51°$
13. $x = 55°, y = 55°, z = 70°$
14. (i) 1, 2 (ii) 1, 2, 3, 4 (iii) 1, 4
    (iv) 1, 2, 3, 4 (v) 1, 2, 3, 4 (vi) 1, 2
    (vii) 1, 2, 3, 4 (viii) 1, 4
15. (i) 80° (ii) 77° (iii) 55°

Exercise 10.4

1. (i) 5 (ii) 10 (iii) 8.6
2. $P = 44\,cm^2, Q = 46\,cm^2, R = 50\,cm^2$
3. $x = 5, y = 13, z = 10$
4. $a = \sqrt{41}, b = \sqrt{45}, c = \sqrt{89}, d = \sqrt{28}, e = \sqrt{24},$
   $f = \sqrt{57}$
5. $\sqrt{32}, \sqrt{50}, \sqrt{98}$ 6. 20 cm
7. 5 m 8. 80 m
9. 47.3 cm 10. 24 m
11. 28 km 12. Yes (both 50π sq. units)
13. $a = 5, b = \sqrt{50}$ 14. 637 m

15. (i) Yes (ii) No (iii) Yes (iv) No
16. (i) 6, 17.5, 18.5 (ii) $\sqrt{5}$, 2, 3
    (iii) 7, 24, 25 (iv) 4, 7.5, 8.5

Test yourself 10

1. (a) $a = 110°, b = 70°, c = 140°, d = 55°,$
      $e = 125°$
   (b) $A = 50°, B = 70°, C = 68°$
2. (a) $a = 40°, b = 80°, c = 48°$
   (b) $a = 63°, b = 30°$
3. (a) $A = 35°, B = 67°, C = 40°, D = 65°, E = 33°,$
      $F = 107°, G = 45°$
   (b) $a = 55°, b = 50°$
4. (a) $x = 10, y = 25, z = 8$
   (b) $a = 74°, b = 53°, c = 142°, d = 68°, e = 38°,$
      $f = 74°$
5. (a) $x = 105°, y = 25°, z = 50°$
   (b) $x = 56$; isosceles $\triangle$
6. (a) (i) $a = 115°, b = 115°$
      (ii) $a = 56°, b = 68°$
      (iii) $a = 48°, b = 66°$
   (b) $A = 125°, B = 44°$
   (c) $x = 105°$

Puzzle 'TAKE OUT THE R'

Chapter 11: Time and Speed

Exercise 11.1

1. (i) 30 (ii) 15 (iii) 24
   (iv) 105 (v) 42
2. (i) 7 hr 58 min (ii) 8 hr 24 min
   (iii) 5 hr 22 min
3. 40; 7 hr 40 min; 8 hr 20 min
4. (i) 3 hr 15 min (ii) 6 hr 30 min
   (iii) 7 hr 50 min (iv) 8 hr 30 min
   (v) 7 hr 5 min (vi) 7 hr 55 min
5. (i) 2 hr 36 min (ii) 1 hr 26 min
   (iii) 1 hr 41 min
6. (i) 06.00 (ii) 10.45 (iii) 16.00
   (iv) 17.20 (v) 19.30 (vi) 08.45
   (vii) 12.00 (viii) 23.40 (ix) 03.15
   (x) 15.15
7. (i) 11.40 am (ii) 3.35 pm
   (iii) 12.20 pm (iv) 12.30 am
   (v) 10.15 pm (vi) 4.20 am
   (vii) 10.35 am (viii) 2.30 pm
   (ix) 6.45 pm (x) 11.12 pm
8. (i) 01.25 (ii) 22.30
   (iii) 06.50 (iv) 16.45
9. (i) 4 hr 10 min (ii) 3 hr 32 min
   (iii) 8 hr 9 min (iv) 2 hr 37 min
   (v) 15 hr 30 min (vi) 3 hr 28 min

10. A and (i), C and (ii), D and (iii), B and (iv)

11. $36\frac{1}{4}$ hr (36 hr 15 min)

12. 10.55 pm

13. 3 hr 48 min

14. 14.26

15. (i) 3 hr 35 min (ii) 19 min
(iii) 1 hr 53 min (iv) Train 2
(v) 2 hr 55 min (vi) 2 min
(vii) 38 min (viii) Train 2 (by 7 min)

16. A – 2 hr 11 min, B – 09.37, C – 17.24,
D – 6 hr 1 min, E – 10.35, F – 09.21

17. (i) 2 hr 45 min (ii) €27

Exercise 11.2

1. (i) 240 km (ii) 260 km
(iii) 198 km (iv) 72 km

2. (i) 3 hr (ii) $2\frac{1}{2}$ hr
(iii) 20 min (iv) 45 min

3. (i) 50 km/hr (ii) 60 km/hr
(iii) 60 km/hr (iv) 70 km/hr
(v) 50 km/hr (vi) 135 km/hr

4. 180 km/hr   **5.** 2 hr 30 min

6. 189 km   **7.** 72 km/hr

8. 104 km/hr   **9.** 70 km/hr

10. $4\frac{1}{2}$ hours   **11.** 72 km/hr

12. 5 hr 12 min   **13.** $53\frac{1}{3}$ km/hr

14. 12 m/sec   **15.** 42 km/hr

16. 72 km/hr   **17.** 20 m/sec

18. 24 km/hr   **19.** 54 km/hr

20. (i) 86 km/hr (ii) 67ℓ (iii) €113.90

21. Cheetah (100 km/hr), Antelope (80 km/hr),
Racehorse $\left(67\frac{1}{2}\ \text{km/hr}\right)$, Deer (45.7 km/hr)

22. 8 km/hr

Test yourself 11

1. (a) (i) 02.40 (ii) 22.50
(b) 1 hr 15 min (c) 40 min each

2. (a) (i) 3 hr 15 min (ii) 8 hr 35 min
(b) (i) $2\frac{1}{2}$ hr (ii) 88 km/hr
(c) 6000 m

3. (a) 12.50 am
(b) (i) 240 km (ii) 3 hours (iii) 80 km/hr
(c) 2160 km

4. (a) (i) 06.15 (ii) 13.45
(iii) 21.52 (iv) 00.15
(b) 9 litres
(c) (i) 40 min (ii) $19\frac{1}{2}$ km/hr

5. (i) 3 hr 12 min (ii) $62\frac{1}{2}$ km/hr
(iii) €44

6. (a) 6 km/hr (b) 12.24 pm
(c) 16.25 (d) 25.2 m

Chapter 12:
Simultaneous Equations

Exercise 12.1

1. Correct   **2.** Correct   **3.** Correct

4. Incorrect   **5.** Incorrect   **6.** Correct

7. Incorrect   **8.** Correct   **9.** Incorrect

Exercise 12.2

1. $x = 6, y = 3$ **2.** $x = 2, y = 4$ **3.** $x = 3, y = 2$

4. 1, 4   **5.** 3, 5   **6.** 2, 1

7. 3, 2   **8.** 2, 1   **9.** 3, −1

10. −2, 4   **11.** 3, 2   **12.** −2, 1

13. 2, 3   **14.** −3, 4   **15.** 4, −2

16. 3, −1   **17.** 1, 2   **18.** 5, −2

19. 2, 1   **20.** 3, −2   **21.** 7, −3

22. 1, 5   **23.** 3, 1   **24.** 1, −2

25. 7, 3   **26.** 2, 8   **27.** 4, 1

28. 10, 4   **29.** −2, −4   **30.** 6, −2

Exercise 12.3

1. 18, 23   **2.** 5, 7

3. $x = 18, y = 32$ **4.** 10, 7

5. 12, −3   **6.** 10, 3

7. 5, 3

8. $2x − 3y = 4, 3x + y = 17; x = 5, y = 2$

9. nut – 4 g, bolt – 10 g

10. (i) 5 g (ii) 160 g

11. (i) C (ii) b – 55 g, e – 75 g

12. (i) (a) Every horse and every turkey has one
head
(b) Every horse has four legs and every
turkey has two legs
(ii) 17 horses, 15 turkeys

13. (i) (2, 1) (ii) $x = 2, y = 1$

14. (1, 4)

15. (i) $2x + 3y = 33$ (ii) $4x + 2y = 46$
(iii) $x = 9, y = 5$ (iv) 39 cm

Test yourself 12

1. (a) $x = 3, y = 4$ (b) €1.90

2. (a) $x = 5, y = 1$
(b) (i) $2a + b = 8, 4a − 3b = 1$
(ii) $a = 2.5, b = 3$

3. (a) $x = 2, y = −1$
(b) (i) $4b + 3r = 58, 5b + 6r = 86$
(ii) blue brick – 10 g, red brick – 6 g
(iii) 66 g

4. (a) $x = 6, y = 5$
(b) $2x − 3y = 3, 2x + y = 7; x = 3, y = 1$

Chapter 13: Quadratic Equations

Exercise 13.1

1. $x = 2$ or $x = 3$ 2. $x = 2$ or $x = 5$
3. $x = 2$ or $x = -3$
4. $4, -5$ 5. $-2, -6$ 6. $0, 4$
7. $0, -5$ 8. $3, -3$ 9. $-7, 7$
10. $-2, -1$ 11. $-3, -2$ 12. $-4, -2$
13. $-5, -2$ 14. $-4, -3$ 15. $-9, -3$
16. $-7, -4$ 17. $-7, -5$ 18. $-8, -6$
19. $2, 3$ 20. $3, 5$ 21. $2, 8$
22. $2, 7$ 23. $3, 7$ 24. $4, 6$
25. $3, 9$ 26. $4, 8$ 27. $4, 12$
28. $-3, 4$ 29. $-2, 5$ 30. $-7, 4$
31. $-3, 8$ 32. $-9, 4$ 33. $-8, 9$
34. $-6, 9$ 35. $-11, -4$ 36. $-5, 12$
37. $-4, 4$ 38. $-5, 5$ 39. $-8, 8$
40. $-1, 1$ 41. $-11, 11$ 42. $-9, 9$
43. $0, 3$ 44. $-4, 0$ 45. $0, 8$
46. $-9, 0$ 47. $0, 14$ 48. $-7, 0$
49. $-10, 3$ 50. $-2, 12$ 51. $-6, 2$
52. $-2, 8$ 53. $4, 7$ 54. $-10, 10$
55. $0, 11$ 56. $1, 9$ 57. $-4, 13$

Exercise 13.2

1. 6 2. 7 3. $5, 9$
4. 6 5. $5, 8$ 6. 10
7. $x^2 + x - 72 = 0; +8, -9$
8. $x^2 + 4x - 77 = 0; x = 7; l = 11$ cm, $b = 7$ cm
9. 7 cm by 4 cm
10. (i) $x^2 + 3x$ (ii) $x = 5$
11. $x = 5$ 12. $-1, 5$
13. $x(x - 6) = 16; x = 8$ 14. Alan is 5 years old
15. $x = -3, 1$ 16. Ⓑ

Test yourself 13

1. (a) (i) $x = -3, 4$ (ii) $x = 5, 7$
   (b) (ii) 7 cm by 1 cm
2. (a) (i) $x = -5, 0$ (ii) $x = 1, 8$
   (b) $x^2 + 2x - 120 = 0; -12, 10$
3. (a) (i) $x = -8, 5$ (ii) $x = -12, 12$
   (b) Ⓒ
4. (a) (i) $x = -8, 3$ (ii) $x = -2, 7$
   (b) $x^2 - 5x - 36 = 0; x = 9$
   (c) The third graph

Chapter 14: Coordinate Geometry – The Line

Exercise 14.1

1. $A(2, 3)$, $B(4, 2)$, $C(2, 1)$, $D(-3, 3)$, $E(-2, 2)$, $F(-4, 1)$, $G(-3, 0)$, $H(-4, -2)$, $I(-2, -3)$, $J(0, -3)$, $K(2, -3)$, $L(3, -2)$, $M(5, -3)$

3. (i) 1st   (ii) 3rd   (iii) 4th
   (iv) 2nd   (v) 4th   (vi) 3rd
4. (i) x-axis   (ii) y-axis   (iii) y-axis
   (iv) x-axis   (v) x-axis
5. $A(1, 1)$, $B(5, 1)$, $D(1, 3)$, $C(5, 3)$
6. (ii) $(2, 4)$
7. (iii) $D(-1, 2)$
8. (ii) rectangle   (iii) 4 units, 2 units
   (iv) 12 units   (v) 8 square units
9. (i) 4 units   (ii) 3 units
   (iii) 6 square units

Exercise 14.2

1. (i) $(5, 5)$ (ii) $(6, 3)$ (iii) $(3, 4)$
2. $(3, 2)$ 3. $(3, 3)$ 4. $(2, 4)$
5. $(5, 2)$ 6. $(3, 3)$ 7. $(3, 1)$
8. $(2, 1)$ 9. $(-1, 1)$ 10. $(2, 5)$
11. $(2, 1)$ 12. $(-1, 3)$ 13. $(3, -3)$
14. (i) $M\left(3, \frac{5}{2}\right)$
15. $(1, 0)$; x-axis   16. $B(7, 5)$ 18. $O\left(6\frac{1}{2}, 4\frac{1}{2}\right)$
19. (i) $\left(\frac{3}{2}, \frac{5}{2}\right)$

Exercise 14.3

1. $\sqrt{18}$ 2. $\sqrt{29}$ 3. $\sqrt{17}$
4. $\sqrt{5}$ 5. $\sqrt{37}$ 6. $\sqrt{40}$
7. $\sqrt{20}$ 8. $\sqrt{18}$ 9. $\sqrt{61}$
10. $\sqrt{74}$ 11. $\sqrt{20}$ 12. $\sqrt{13}$
15. $A(5, 2)$, $B(3, -2)$, $C(-3, -2)$, $D(-1, 2)$
    (i) 6   (iii) Yes, both $(1, 0)$
16. $\sqrt{2}, \sqrt{5}, \sqrt{5}$; $[BC]$ and $[AC]$; isosceles $\triangle$
17. $\sqrt{58}$
18. No $(\sqrt{13} < 3.7)$

Exercise 14.4

1. a – positive, b – positive, c – negative, d – positive, e – negative, f – negative
2. (i) b & c (ii) a & d
3. (i) $\frac{2}{3}$ (ii) $\frac{3}{2}$ (iii) $2\left(\frac{4}{2}\right)$
4. (i) 3   (ii) 2   (iii) 1
5. Because the line is falling (from left to right); $-\frac{3}{2}$
6. $a = -3, b = -2, c = -1$
7. (i) Slope $[AB] = -\frac{3}{5}$
   (ii) Slope $[CD] = \frac{4}{7}$
   (iii) Slope $[EF] = -\frac{1}{7}$
8. (i) 1   (ii) 4   (iii) $\frac{5}{3}$ (iv) $\frac{1}{2}$
   (v) -3 (vi) $-\frac{3}{2}$ (vii) $\frac{8}{3}$ (viii) $-\frac{7}{3}$
   (ix) 3
11. They are parallel as they have the same slope (3)

12. a & $\frac{1}{2}$, b & 1, c & 2

13. (i) $\frac{1}{20}$ (ii) 6 m

14. 60 m

Exercise 14.5

1. (i) 2   (ii) 3   (iii) 2
   (iv) 5   (v) -1 (vi) -3

2. (i) $(0, 3)$ (ii) $(0, 6)$ (iii) $(0, -1)$
   (iv) $(0, 2)$ (v) $(0, 4)$ (vi) $(0, -2)$

3. (a) (i) 3   (ii) $(0, 1)$
   (b) (i) 2   (ii) $(0, -4)$
   (c) (i) -3 (ii) $(0, 5)$

4. (i) $y = x + 1$ (ii) $y = \frac{1}{4}x + 2$
   (iii) $y = 2x - 2$

5. (i) 1   (ii) $(0, -2)$ (iii) $y = x - 2$

6. $a : y = 2x + 3, b : y = -2x + 2, c : y = -x + 2$

7. $y = \frac{1}{2}x + 1$ $(x - 2y + 2 = 0)$

8. (i) a & f (ii) b (iii) d
   (iv) $(0, -3)$ (v) 1

Exercise 14.6

1. $y = 2x + 1$ **2.** $y = 3x - 13$

3. $y = 4x$ **4.** $y = -2x + 11$

5. $y = 3x + 11$ **6.** $y = 4x + 16$

7. $y = -2x + 1$ **8.** $y = 3x$

9. $y = -4x - 2$ **10.** $y = 2x + 4$

11. $y = \frac{2}{3}x + \frac{4}{3}$ **12.** $y = \frac{1}{3}x + 3$

13. $y = \frac{5}{2}x - \frac{9}{2}$ **14.** $y = -\frac{3}{4}x + 3$

15. $3; y = 3x - 1$

16. (i) 3   (ii) $y = 3x - 7$

17. (i) $y = 2x + 5$ (ii) $y = 5x - 7$
   (iii) $y = -4x - 7$ (iv) $y = \frac{5}{3}x - \frac{19}{3}$

18. (i) $m = -\frac{2}{3}$ (ii) $y = -\frac{2}{3}x + \frac{7}{3}$

19. $y = x + 5$

20. $y = -2x$

21. $(2, 4); y = 4x - 4$

Exercise 14.7

1. $a : y = 3, b : y = 1, c : y = -1, d : y = -3$

2. $e : x = -4, f : x = -2, g : x = 1, h : x = 4$

4. (A): $x = 2$, (B): $x = 4$, (C): $y = 4$, (D): $y = 2$,
   (E): $y = -2$, (F): $x = -3$

5. (i) $y = 0$ (ii) $x = 0$

6. (i) $-4; (0, -4)$ (ii) $2; (2, 0)$

7. (i) $(-2, 0)$ (ii) $(2, 0)$ (iii) $(-6, 0)$

8. (i) $(0, -3)$ (ii) $(0, 5)$ (iii) $(0, -4)$

9. $\left(\frac{5}{2}, 0\right), (0, -5)$

10. (i) $(-3, 0), (0, 3)$ (ii) $\left(-\frac{1}{2}, 0\right), (0, 2)$
   (iii) $(1, 0), (0, -6)$

11. $(2, 0), (0, -3)$

12. (i) $K(4, 0)$ (ii) $P(0, -2)$
   (iii) $\frac{1}{2}$ (iv) $\sqrt{20}$

13. (i) C (ii) B

14. (i) & (C), (ii) & (A), (iii) & (B)

Exercise 14.8

1. $(1, 3)$

2. (i) $(1, 2)$ (ii) $(3, 0)$ (iii) $(-1, -2)$

3. $(4, 1)$

4. $(2, 1)$

5. $(3, 2)$

9. Not on the line

11. $k = -6$

12. $k = 3$

13. (i) $k = 2$ (ii) $t = 5$

Test yourself 14

1. (a) (i) $\frac{1}{3}$ (ii) $x - 3y + 14 = 0$
   (b) (i) $P(2, 0), Q(0, -4)$ (ii) $\sqrt{20}$

2. (a) (i) $M(2, 0)$; x-axis
   (b) (i) $\frac{2}{3}$ (ii) $y = \frac{2x}{3} + 1$

3. (a) (i) k (ii) n
   (iii) ℓ (iv) m
   (b) $3; 3x - y - 7 = 0$

4. (i) $\frac{1}{2}$ (ii) $x - 2y + 3 = 0$
   (iii) $(-3, 0)$

5. (a) (i) ℓ_1 (ii) $-\frac{1}{2}$
   (iii) $x - y + 2 = 0$
   (b) $A : y = 3x - 4, B : y = 2x + 5, C : y = 2x + 3$;
     (i) A (ii) B & C (iii) B (iv) B

6. (a) $y = 2x - 2$
   (b) (i) F   (ii) T   (iii) T   (iv) F

Chapter 15: Statistics 3 – Presenting Data

Exercise 15.1

1. (i) 15   (ii) 1
   (iii) 0 to 5 (i.e. 5)   (iv) 20%

2. (i) 18°C   (ii) 28°C   (iii) 3
   (iv) $53\frac{1}{3}$%   (v) $\frac{4}{15}$

3. (i) 42   (ii) 3   (iii) 10
   (iv) 29.2%   (v) $\frac{1}{13}$

4. (i) 25   (ii) 10   (iii) 3
   (iv) 5–10 (i.e. 5)   (v) 9

5. (i) 7 (ii) 12 (iii) 13 (iv) 4

(v) 30 (vi) $16\frac{2}{3}$% (vii) $\frac{1}{10}$

6. (i) 6 (ii) 3 (iii) 4 (iv) $\frac{1}{5}$

7. (i) 6 (ii) 16 (iii) 8 (iv) 5

8. (i) 60 (ii) 115 (iii) 1.9

9. (iii) 3 (iv) $22\frac{1}{2}$% (v) 70%

10. (i) 4 (ii) 5 (iii) 3 (iv) 0.225

Exercise 15.2

1. (i) 25% (ii) $\frac{1}{4}$ (iii) 75%

(iv) $\frac{3}{4}$ (v) 3 (vi) 9

2. (i) 25% (ii) $\frac{1}{2}$ (iii) 30 (iv) 15

3. (i) 300 (ii) 150 (iii) 100 (iv) 30°

4. (i) 105° (ii) 120° (iii) 125°

5. (i) 45° (ii) 40 (iii) Spain

(iv) France

(v) Spain and Portugal

6. (i) 60 (ii) 20 (iii) 30

(iv) 50° (v) 25

7. (i) 90° (ii) 45° (iii) 165°

8. (i) Bus – 120°; Car – 90°; Train – 72°; Walk – 48°; Bicycle – 30°

9. (i) $\frac{1}{3}$ (ii) 90 (iii) 40 (iv) 5

10. (i) 75° (ii) 120 (iii) 45

11. (i) $\frac{1}{3}$ (ii) 25% (iii) 120

12. A – 225°; B – 15°; C – 75°; D – 45°

13. (i), (iii) and (v)

14. (i) 150

Exercise 15.3

1. (i) 4 (ii) 27 years (iii) 8

(iv) 36 years (v) 16%

2. (i) 26 sec (ii) 8 (iii) 24

(iv) 39 sec (v) 68 sec (vi) 45 sec

(vii) 12

3. (i) 26 (ii) 49 (iii) 8

(iv) 20%

4. (i) 20 (ii) 5 (iii) 43

(iv) 76 (v) 35%

5. (i) 34 cm (ii) 6 (iii) 7

(iv) 163 cm (v) 3 : 2

6. (i) 50 (ii) $75\frac{1}{2}$ (iii) 9 (iv) 40%

7. (ii) 8 (iii) $33\frac{1}{3}$% (iv) 16 (v) 15

8. (i) 22 to 84 (i.e. range of 62)

(ii) 7 (iii) 25% (iv) $58\frac{1}{2}$ marks

(v) 57.7 marks

Exercise 15.4

1. (i) 3 (ii) 3

(iii) 17 (iv) 07.40-07.50

(v) 23

2. (i) 40 (ii) 40

(iii) (60-70) kg

3. (i) 20 (ii) 16

(iii) (6-9) km (iv) 62

4. (ii) 28 (iii) 12

5. (i) 7 : 30am (ii) 45

(iii) Breakfast (iv) 10.30 am-11.30 am

(v) 'Elevenses'

6. (ii) 16 (iii) (20-40) km

(iv) 2

7. (i) 16 (ii) 64

(iii) (30-40) sec (iv) 22

8. (i) 12 (ii) 60

(iii) (50-60) years (iv) $\frac{1}{10}$

(v) 21

Exercise 15.5

1. (i) 2 (ii) 4 (iii) 8

(iv) 3 (v) 9 (vi) 27

2. Graph only shows part of the scale

3. (i) Area of column for 'fish 2' increased dramatically by larger width

(ii) Increased width and depth (and by extension, volume) of carton B creates illusion of greater production despite the actual productions being the same

(iii) Scale doesn't start at 0

(iv) 'Creative' cubes (area and volume) mislead

4. Vertical axis unlabelled; cylinders of varying radii used

5. (i) Graph shows only part of the vertical scale

Test yourself 15

1. (a) (i) 36 (ii) Friday

(iii) Mon, Tues

(iv) The small sample size of 36

(b) (ii) 26 years (iii) 24 years

(iv) 15%

2. (a) (i) 42 (ii) 3

(iii) 10

(b) (i) 36 (emails) (ii) 28 (emails)

(iii) 14 (iv) 47

3. (a) (i) 15 (ii) 90°

(iii) 30 (iv) $33\frac{1}{3}$%

(b) (i) As the continuous data is grouped

(ii) 7 (iii) 8

(iv) 16

4. (a) (i) 48 – highest, 30 – lowest
     (ii) 4   (iii) 88%
  (b) (i) Red – 120°, Blue – 90°, Green – 75°,
     Purple – 45°, Others – 30°
    (iii) A bar chart
5. (a) (i) €1200   (ii) (a) 120°   (b) €400
  (b) (ii) 15
    (iii) Number of department heads – discrete,
    number of hours – continuous
    (iv) (40-45) hour interval

Chapter 16: Indices – Scientific Notation – Reciprocals

Exercise 16.1

1. (i) 2^3 (ii) 5^4 (iii) 6^5 (iv) a^3
  (v) k^4 (vi) $(-2)^3$
2. (i) 9   (ii) 8   (iii) 64   (iv) 1000
  (v) 16
3. (i) 3^2 (ii) 6^3 (iii) 3^5 (iv) 5^6
  (v) 5^3 (vi) 3^7 (vii) 5^6 (viii) 2^8
4. (i) 3   (ii) 3   (iii) 4   (iv) 2
  (v) 2   (vi) 3   (vii) 3   (viii) 5
5. (i) 12   (ii) 18   (iii) 32   (iv) 50
  (v) 36   (vi) 72   (vii) 8   (viii) 16
6. (i) 4   (ii) -27 (iii) -18 (iv) -32
7. (i) $2^2 \times 3^2$ (ii) $3^2 \times 4^3$ (iii) $5^3 \times 3^2$
  (iv) $4^2 \times a^2$ (v) $3^3 \times a^3$ (vi) $5^3 \times a^3$
8. (i) 3^2 (ii) 5^2 (iii) 3^3
  (iv) 10^3 (v) 9^2 (or 3^4)   (vi) 8^2 (or 4^3)
9. (i) 5^2 (ii) 3^4 (iii) 7^2
  (iv) 3^4 (v) 5^7 (vi) 7^2
10. (i) 800   (ii) 150   (iii) 7600
  (iv) 300   (v) 7
11. (i) 8   (ii) 16   (iii) 9   (iv) 343
12. (i) 16   (ii) 64   (iii) 81   (iv) 64
  (v) 10 000
13. (i) F (ii) T (iii) F (iv) F
14. (i) 36   (ii) 64   (iii) 100   (iv) 9
  (v) 64
15. (i) 3   (ii) 6   (iii) 9   (iv) 16
  (v) 18   (vi) 12   (vii) 3   (viii) 4
  (ix) 6   (x) 3
16. (i) 9   (ii) 114   (iii) 34   (iv) 16
17. (i) 2   (ii) 3   (iii) 10   (iv) 4
  (v) 3
18. (i) 24   (ii) 3   (iii) 36   (iv) 24
  (v) 52   (vi) 14
19. (i) 2   (ii) 3   (iii) 3   (iv) 6
  (v) 3   (vi) 3   (vii) 3   (viii) 2
20. (i) 8, 7   (ii) 6, 5   (iii) 8, 8   (iv) 3, 1

21. C is false
22. (i) 22   (ii) 11   (iii) 17
  (iv) 5   (v) 35   (vi) 24
  (vii) 42   (viii) 2

Exercise 16.2

1. (i), (iv)
2. (i) 200   (ii) 340   (iii) 5700
  (iv) 28 400   (v) 581   (vi) 2940
  (vii) 18 370   (viii) 9843
3. As the 'a part' (in this case 30) is not a number
  between 1 and 10. 3×10^4 is the same number
  (30 000) written in standard form
4. (i) 2.8×10^1 (ii) 6.4×10 (iii) 8×10
  (iv) 1.5×10^2 (v) 4.67×10^2
5. (i) 4×10^2 (ii) 6.5×10^2 (iii) 2×10^3
  (iv) 2.7×10^3 (v) 6.92×10^3
6. (i) 7.8×10^3 (ii) 9.46×10^2
  (iii) 1.54×10^4 (iv) 3.89×10^4
7. (i) 2.4×10^3 (ii) 1.28×10^4
  (iii) 8×10^3 (iv) 1.29×10^4
8. (i) 7.21×10^2 (ii) 2.56×10^2
9. (i) 580   (ii) 510
  (iii) 15 000   (iv) 13 000
10. 6.28×10^3 **11.** 1.39×10^3
12. 8.79×10^2 **13.** 3.98×10^3
14. 9.564×10^3 **15.** 8.76×10^3
16. 8.6×10^2 **17.** 9.64×10^4
18. 7.834×10^3 **19.** 12 000
20. 7000   **21.** 152 000
22. 106 000   **23.** 2.4×10^5
24. 1.5×10^6 **25.** 5.6×10^7
26. 7.5×10^5 **27.** 3.29×10^6
28. 7.65×10^8 **29.** 2.28×10^7
30. 3.84×10^7 **31.** 2.5×10
32. 2×10^3 **33.** 1.2×10^2
34. 1.9×10^3
35. (i) Earth
  (ii) 5.9×10^3 km (or 5900 km)
  (iii) 1.95×10^4 km
36. (i) Yangtze – 6300 km; Congo – 4700 km;
    Danube – 2840 km; Seine – 780 km
  (ii) 4.7×10^3 km
  (iii) 7.8×10^2 km
  (iv) six times

Exercise 16.3

1. (i) $\frac{1}{4}$ (ii) $\frac{1}{12}$ (iii) 3
  (iv) $\frac{5}{2}$ (v) $\frac{4}{5}$
2. (i) 0.11   (ii) 0.08   (iii) 0.04
  (iv) 0.08   (v) 0.34

3. 225
4. 1156
5. 39.69
6. 153.76
7. 1024
8. 681.21
9. 3.24
10. 0.81
11. 84.64
12. 0.2916
13. 3.5
14. 7.3
15. 12.6
16. 30.4
17. 7.6
18. 9.9
19. 40.0
20. 48.5
21. 0.9
22. 0.8
23. 20.78
24. 51.23
25. 972
26. 529.92
27. 58.91
28. 21.95
29. 18.17
30. 46.23
32. (i) 7.9   (ii) 9.1   (iii) 12.5
33. (i) 0.16   (ii) 1.27   (iii) 4.22
    (iv) 44.28   (v) 2.50

Exercise 16.4

1. (i) 80   (ii) 100   (iii) 30
    (iv) 130   (v) 430
2. (i) 300   (ii) 100   (iii) 700
    (iv) 1900   (v) 7400
3. (i) 1000   (ii) 2000   (iii) 9000
    (iv) 18 000   (v) 28 000   (vi) 33 000
4. (i) 1.4   (ii) 12.3   (iii) 0.5
    (iv) 12.1   (v) 0.7
5. (i) one   (ii) two   (iii) one
    (iv) two   (v) three
6. (i) 70   (ii) 40   (iii) 300
    (iv) 600   (v) 3000
7. (i) 580   (ii) 990   (iii) 2900
    (iv) 5900   (v) 25 000
8. (i) Roughly 5000 disgruntled farmers descend
    on *The Dail*
    (ii) 40 000 filled the *R.D.S.* for sell-out concert
9. (i) 0.47   (ii) 0.063   (iii) 2.4
    (iv) 0.67   (v) 55.0
10. 72 700;   (i) 73 000   (ii) 70 000
11. (i) 40   (ii) 2   (iii) 125
12. (i) 3   (ii) 3   (iii) $2\frac{2}{3}$
13. 40, 60, 300
14. (i) 5   (ii) 360   (iii) 9

Test yourself 16

1. (a) (i) 46 400   (ii) 46 000
      (iii) 50 000
    (b) (i) 48   (ii) 32
      (iii) 72
    (c) (i) 7.4×10^3 (ii) 6880
2. (a) $\sqrt{144}$, 4^2, 2^5, 3^4 (12, 16, 32, 81)

(b) (i) 2   (ii) 2
    (iii) 3   (iv) 2
    (c) (i) 400   (ii) 7300; 7.7×10^3
3. (a) (i)88   (ii) 92
    (b) (i) 2830   (ii) 7.93×10^3
    (c) (i), (iii) (ie 16)
4. (a) 2   (b) 5
    (c) 680, 9000; 9.68×10^3
5. (a) (i) 3   (ii) 9
    (b) (i) x^3 (ii) $8a^5$
      (iii) $6a^5$
    (c) 314.56
6. (a) 106
    (b) (i) 3740   (ii) 5.82×10^3 (c) 19.61
    (d) *A & F, B & G, C & D, E & H*

Chapter 17: Circles and Cylinders

Exercise 17.1

1. (i) Radius   (ii) Chord   (iii) Diameter
    (iv) Arc   (v) Semicircle   (vi) Sector
    (vii) Segment   (viii) Tangent
2. (i) 62.8 cm   (ii) 25.12 cm
    (iii) 75.36 cm   (iv) 56.52 mm
3. (i) 88 cm   (ii) 132 cm
    (iii) 220 cm   (iv) 44 cm
4. (i) 50.3 cm   (ii) 131.9 cm
    (iii) 69.1 cm   (iv) 56.5 m
5. (i) 81.64 cm   (ii) 94.2 cm
    (iii) 251.2 cm
6. (i) 33 cm   (ii) 11 cm
    (iii) $58\frac{2}{3}$ cm
7. (i) 72 cm   (ii) $42\frac{2}{3}$ cm
    (iii) 47 cm
8. (i) 31 cm   (ii) 45 cm
    (iii) 75 cm
9. 91 cm
10. Each is the same distance (4π m)
11. 189 m of tape
12. (i) 0.75 m   (ii) 80 m

Exercise 17.2

1. (i) 314 cm^2 (ii) 50.24 cm^2
    (iii) 452.16 mm^2 (iv) 254.34 cm^2
2. (i) 616 cm^2 (ii) 1386 cm^2
    (iii) 3850 m^2 (iv) 154 cm^2
3. (i) 201.1 cm^2 (ii) 1385.4 cm^2
    (iii) 380.1 cm^2 (iv) 254.5 mm^2
4. (i) $\frac{1}{4}$ (ii) $\frac{1}{3}$ (iii) $\frac{1}{6}$ (iv) $\frac{1}{8}$
5. (i) 1386 cm^2 (ii) 77 cm^2 (iii) $821\frac{1}{3}$ cm^2
6. (i) 189.97 cm^2 (ii) 150.72 cm^2 (iii) 244.48 cm^2
7. (i) $r = 5$ cm   (ii) $r = 11$ m   (iii) $r = 13$ cm

8. (i) $r = 7$ cm   (ii) 44 cm
9. (i) 14 cm   (ii) 616 cm^2
10. (i) 14 cm   (ii) 42 cm^2
11. (i) $r = 35$ cm   (ii) 3850 cm^2
12. (i) 89 cm^2 (ii) 74 cm^2 (iii) 164 cm^2
13. 65.98 cm^2
14. (i) 6 cm   (ii) 7.74 cm^2

Exercise 17.3

1. (i) 1848 cm^3 (ii) 2816.4 cm^3
    (iii) 18 480 mm^3
2. (i) 836 cm^2 (ii) 1106 cm^2
    (iii) 3872 mm^2
3. (i) 54 259 cm^3 (ii) 402 m^3
    (iii) 1413 cm^3
4. 24 640 cm^3; 25 l
5. 706.5 cm^3
6. (i) $V = \pi r^2 h$ (ii) $350\pi = 14\pi r^2$
    (iii) $r = 5$ cm
7. 16 cm
8. 6 cm
9. 10 cm
10. C.S.A. $= 2\pi rh$; 3.5 cm
11. 7 cm
12. 4938 cm^3
13. (i) 1570 cm^3 (ii) 14.13 kg
14. 176 cm^3; 1792 cm^3
15. $h = 16$ cm

Test yourself 17

1. (a) (i) 44 cm   (ii) 154 cm^2
    (b) (i) 9043 cm^3 (ii) 1507 cm^2
2. (a) 812 cm^2
    (b) 56 cm^2
3. (a) (i) 139.3 cm^2 (ii) 45.7 cm
    (b) 6250 cm^3
4. (a) 235.5 cm^2
    (b) (i) 20 000π cm^3 (ii) 160π cm^3
      (iii) 125
5. (a) $\frac{5}{6}$; 94.2 cm^2 (b) 9119 cm^3; 9ℓ
6. (a) (i) 78   (ii) 3099 cm^2
    (b) 14 cm

Chapter 18:
Geometry 2 – Triangles and Circles

Exercise 18.1

1. A & D, B & C **2.** B, E, G, H, I, J
3. (i) [DE]   (ii) [BC]   (iii) [DF]   (iv) [AB]
4. (i) [MN]   (ii) [YZ]   (iii) $\angle MLN$ (iv) $\angle YXZ$
5. (i) [XG]   (ii) [LN]   (iii) [AX]

6. *SAS*
7. (i) *SSS*   (ii) *SAS*   (iii) *SAS*
    (iv) *ASA*   (v) *RHS*   (vi) *ASA*
8. A & D
9. Yes (*RHS*)
10. *SSS*
11. Yes; *SSS* ([BD] is a common side)
12. *SAS* ($|\angle AOB| = |\angle COD| \ldots$ vertically opposite
    each other)
13. *ASA*; (i) [EF]   (ii) [AB]   (iii) 35°
14. $x = 70°$, $y = 10$ cm
15. *SSS*; ($|\angle ABC| = |\angle ADC|$ as they are opposite
    angles in parallelogram)

Exercise 18.2

1. (i) [SR]   (ii) [LM]   (iii) 8
    (iv) 16.4   (v) 7.5
2. (i) $1 : 2$ (ii) 14.4   (iii) 4
3. $x = 13.5$, $y = 18$
4. (i) $2 : 4$ (ii) $2 : 3$ (iii) 12 cm
    (iv) 9 cm   (v) $\sqrt{72}$ cm (or 8.5 cm)
5. (i) $p = 6$, $q = 13.5$
    (ii) $x = 9$, $y = 1$
6. (i) 1.5   (ii) $x = 6$, $y = 4.5$
7. Same shape (i.e. same angles) but different
    sizes; $x = 21$, $y = 15$
8. (i) [RQ]   (ii) [RP]   (iii) [QP]; 9
9. (i) [KL]   (ii) [EF]   (iii) 15
10. (ii) [DF]   (iii) $x = 13\frac{5}{7}$ cm; $y = 9\frac{1}{7}$ cm
11. (i), (ii), (iv), (v)   **12.** 2 m

Exercise 18.3

1. (i) 10 cm   (ii) 10 cm
    (iii) 5 cm   (iv) 5 cm; isosceles
2. (i) The angle in a semicircle is always 90°
    (ii) 45°   (iii) Right-angled and isosceles
3. (i) 90°   (ii) 30°   (iii) 40°
4. $A = 90°$, $B = 90°$, $C = 30°$, $D = 90°$, $E = 40°$,
    $F = 35°$
5. (i) $x = 55°$, $y = 50°$ (ii) $x = 90°$, $y = 38°$
    (iii) $x = 45°$, $y = 53°$
6. (i) both radii   (ii) 90°   (iii) 35°
    (iv) 55°   (v) $|OB| = |OC| = $ radius
7. (i) 60°   (ii) 60°
8. (i) $x = 90°$, $y = 50°$
    (ii) $x = 32°$, $y = 58°$
    (iii) $x = 15°$, $y = 60°$
9. (i) $x = 70°$ (ii) $x = 57°$ (iii) $x = 35°$
10. Right-angled; 10; 5
11. (i) 20 cm   (ii) 30°   (iii) 90°   (iv) 60°
12. 8 cm

Test yourself 18

1. (a) $x = 90°, y = 25°, z = 52°$
    (b) (i) & (iv); *SAS*
2. (a) $x = 55°, y = 43°$ (b) *A* & *B* (*SAS*)
3. (a) *SSS*   (b) $a = 90°, b = 34°$
4. (a) (i) $\angle ADC$ & $\angle ABC$ (ii) $45°$
      (iii) $70°$
    (b) (i) equiangular triangles
      (ii) $x = 9, y = 10.5$
5. (a) (i) $x = 60°, y = 45°$
      (ii) $x = 90°, y = 32°$
      (iii) $x = 45°, y = 55°$
    (b) *SAS*; (i) [*BC*]   (ii) [*EA*]
      (iii) $\angle BCD$

Chapter 19:
Patterns and Sequences

Exercise 19.1

1. (i) 13, 15, 17, 19   (ii) 17, 20, 23, 26
    (iii) 24, 28, 32, 36   (iv) 12, 10, 8, 6
    (v) 30, 25, 20, 15   (vi) $0, -4, -8, -12$
2. (i) 16, 32, 64   (ii) 54, 162, 486
    (iii) 81, 243, 729   (iv) 25, 36, 49
    (v) 9, 27, 81   (vi) $\frac{4}{5}, \frac{5}{6}, \frac{6}{7}$
3. 16, 19, 22
4. (i) 2, 6, 10, 14   (ii) 5, 8, 11, 14
    (iii) 3, 8, 13, 18   (iv) 30, 26, 22, 18
    (v) $-10, -7, -4, -1$
5. (i) 'Add 3 to the previous term'
    (ii) 'Add 4 to the previous term'
    (iii) 'Add 5 to the previous term'
    (iv) 'Subtract 2 from the previous term'
    (v) 'Add 3 to the previous term'
    (vi) 'Add $1\frac{1}{2}$ to the previous term'
6. (i) 10, 12, 14   (ii) 16, 26, 42
    (iii) 32, 64, 128   (iv) 82, 244, 730
7. 18
8. (ii) 11   (iii) **29**
9.

1st term	Term-to-term rule	2nd, 3rd, 4th and 5th terms
8	$+5$	13, 18, 23, 28
5	$+4$	9, 13, 17, 21
9	$+3$	12, 15, 18, 21
0	-3	$-3, -6, -9, -12$
-12	$+5$	$-7, -2, 3, 8$

10. (i) 14   (ii) 26
11. (i) 7   (ii) 1, 5   (iii) 1, 4
12. (i) 34, 55   (ii) 3

13. 80, 242
14. Pattern:

    Position: 4, 5
    Term: 11, 14, 17
15. 1, 2, 4, 8, 16, 32
16. (i) 7   (ii) 127
17. (i) 8, 10, 12   (ii) 22, 16
    (iii) 6, 16, 26   (iv) 7, 13, 16, 22
18. (i) $11111 \times 9 + 2 = 100001$
    (ii) $33333 \times 11 = 366663$
    (iii) $9 \times 12345 = 111105$

Exercise 19.2

1. (i) Square, circle
    (ii) 2, 6, 10; Yes, the circle is the second shape
      in each block of four shapes
    (iii) Triangle   (iv) Square
    (v) Square   (vi) Circle
2. (i) Green   (ii) Blue
    (iii) Red   (iv) Blue
    (v) 5, 10, 15, 20   (vi) 30th
3. (i) 8, 4   (ii) 4
    (iii) 6   (iv) 23rd
4. (i) Circle   (ii) 5, 10, 15; 20
    (iii) Circle   (iv) Semicircle
    (v) Semicircle
5. 8, 16, 24, 32, 40, 48, 56, 64, 72, 80;
    (i) |8, 6, 4, 2, 0| , |8, 6, 4, 2, 0|
    (ii) 5   (iii) 0

Exercise 19.3

1. (i) 2, 4, 6, 8   (ii) 4, 7, 10, 13
    (iii) 1, 5, 9, 13   (iv) 7, 9, 11, 13
    (v) 1, 6, 11, 16   (vi) $5, 3, 1, -1$
2. As the difference between the terms is a
    constant in each sequence
3. (i) 5, 7, 9, 11, 13   (ii) $T_{20} = 43, T_{100} = 203$
    (iii) Constant difference is $+2$
5. 2, 5, 10, 17; No, differences between the terms
    vary
6. (i) 5, 8, 11, 14, 17, 20   (ii) $T_{100} = 302$
7. (i) 3, 6, 9, 12 etc.
8. 7, 9, 11; Difference between terms is a constant (2)

Exercise 19.4

1. (i) $+4$ (ii) 4
    (iii) $Tn = 4n + 1$ (iv) 81
2. (i) 3   (ii) 4   (iii) 6   (iv) 5
3. (i) 3   (ii) 3   (iii) 5
    (iv) 5, 2   (v) 2, 5   (vi) 4, 1

4. (i) $T_n = 2n + 3$
   (ii) $T_n = 3n + 2$
   (iii) $T_n = 4n + 2$
5. $T_n = 4n + 3$; $T_{10} = 43$, $T_{20} = 83$
6. $T_n = 4n + 4$;
   (i) $T_{10} = 44$ (ii) $T_{30} = 124$; T_{19}
7. (i) 'Subtract 2 from the previous term'
   (ii) -2 (iii) $T_n = -2n + 14$
   (iv) -6 (v) 14th term
8. (i) $T_n = 3n - 6$ (ii) $T_n = -5n + 25$

Exercise 19.5

1. (i)

   (ii) 6, 11, 16, 21, 26, 31
   (iv) 101   (v) 10th
2. (i)

   (ii) 15

   (iii) $T_n = 2n + 1$ (iv) Diagram 16
3. 10, 13, 16;
   (i) 19   (ii) $T_n = 3n + 1$
   (iii) 151
4. (i) 13   (ii) $T_n = 2n + 3$
   (iii) Pattern 24
5. (i) 21   (ii) 'Add 5' matchsticks
   (iii) $T_n = 5n + 1$ (iii) Pattern 13
   (v) No

Exercise 19.6

1. 4, 7, 12, 19, 28; As the 2nd difference is a constant (2)
2. (i) 2, 5, 10, 17   (ii) $-1, 2, 7, 14$
   (iii) 1, 7, 17, 31
3. (i) First differences : 1, 2, 3, 4; Yes, quadratic
      Second differences : 1, 1, 1
   (ii) First differences : 3, 5, 7, 9; Yes, quadratic
      Second differences : 2, 2, 2
   (iii) First differences : 5, 7, 9, 11;
      Second differences : 2, 2, 2; Yes, quadratic
4. (i) 36, 48   (ii) 39, 52
5. (i) 24   (ii) 35
   (iii) The second difference between the terms (2) is a constant
6. (i) 81, 243, 729   (ii) Not a constant
7. 2, 4, 8, 16, 32, 64; exponential sequence
8. 6, 12, 24, 48

Exercise 19.7

1. (i) €24   (ii) 6.4 km
   (iii) 8 km   (iv) €2 difference
3. 3, 5, 7, 9, 11; a linear graph

4.

Day	Height (cm)
4	10
5	12
6	14
7	16

   (ii) 14 days   (iii) 29 days
5. (i) €30   (ii) €105
   (iii) 5 hours   (iv) €200
6. (i) €100   (ii) Week 8
7. 3 hr 20 min
8. (i) The term-to-term rule involves adding a constant (i.e. 4)
   (ii) $T_n = 4n + 2$ (iv) Straight line

Test yourself 19

1. (a) (i) 15   (ii) -2 (iii) 108
   (b) 44, 120
   (c) (i) 15, 21, 27   (ii) 17, 27, 39
      (iii) 27, 81, 243
2. (a) (i) Yellow, green   (ii) 3, 8, 13, 18, . . .
      (iii) 48th position   (iv) blue
   (b) Quadratic sequence; constant 2nd difference
3. (i) €25
   (iii) The previous week's savings plus €5
   (iv) 16 weeks
   (v) €7
   (vi) Yes; he will have €101 saved after 13 weeks with the extra savings, enough to buy the €100 phone
4. (a) (i) -2 (ii) 4
      (iii) 9   (iv) 15
   (b) (i) 13, 17, 21   (ii) 29
      (iii) $T_n = 4n + 1$ (iv) Shape 25
5. (a) (iii)
   (b) (i) 6, 5, $4\frac{1}{2}$ (ii) No; No
   (c) (i)

   (ii) 15   (iii) $T_n = 3n$
   (iv) 21st pattern

Chapter 20: Algebra 2: Inequalities – Algebraic Fractions

Exercise 20.1

1. (i) T   (ii) T   (iii) F   (iv) T
   (v) F   (vi) F   (vii) T   (viii) T

2. (i) $>$ (ii) $<$ (iii) $>$ (iv) $<$

3. (i) $x < 4$ (ii) $2 > -3$ (iii) $S \leqslant 40$
    (iv) $b \leqslant -5$ (v) $A \geqslant 18$ (vi) $A \leqslant 60$

4. (i) 1, 2, 3   (ii) 1, 2, 3, 4, 5
    (iii) 1, 2, 3, 4, 5, 6   (iv) 3, 4, 5, 6
    (v) 1, 2, 3, 4   (vi) 2, 3, 4, 5, 6, 7

5. (i) $-2, -1, 0, 1$ (ii) 0, 1, 2, 3, 4
    (iii) $-3, -2, -1, 0$ (iv) $-4, -3, -2, -1, 0$
    (v) $-4, -3, -2, -1, 0, 1$
    (vi) $-2, -1, 0, 1, 2, 3$

7. (i) $x > 3$ (ii) $x < 3$
    (iii) $x = 3$ (iv) $x \leqslant 3$

8. (i) $x \geqslant 1$ (ii) $x \leqslant -1$
    (iii) $x < 4$ (iv) $x > -6$
    (v) $x > 6$ (vi) $x < 2$
        ($x \in R$ in each case)

10. (i) $n \geqslant 6$ (ii) $n \leqslant 5$ (iii) $n \leqslant 10$ (iv) $n > 5$

Exercise 20.2

1. Ⓐ,Ⓑ,Ⓓ,Ⓔ   **2.** Ⓐ,Ⓒ,Ⓓ,Ⓔ
3. $x \leqslant 5$ **4.** $x \leqslant 4$
5. $x \leqslant 4$ **6.** $x \leqslant 3$
7. $x \leqslant -2$ **8.** $x \leqslant 4$
9. $x < -3$ **10.** $x \leqslant 2$
11. $x \leqslant 5$ **12.** $x \leqslant 3$
13. $x < 2$ **14.** $x \geqslant -1$
15. $x \leqslant 6$ **16.** $x < 3$
17. $x \geqslant 1$ **18.** $x \leqslant 3$
19. $x \leqslant 4$ **20.** $x < 3$
21. $x \geqslant 3$ **22.** $x < -2$
23. $x \geqslant -2$ **24.** $x \leqslant -3$
25. (i) $1, \frac{2}{5}, -20$ (ii) $\sqrt{10}, \frac{13}{4}$
26. (i) Sometimes   (ii) Sometimes
    (iii) Sometimes   (iv) Never
    (v) Always   (vi) Sometimes
    (vii) Sometimes   (viii) Always

Exercise 20.3

1. $\frac{7}{6}$ **2.** $\frac{27}{20}$
3. $\frac{2}{3}$ **4.** $\frac{1}{8}$
5. $\frac{5x}{6}$ **6.** $\frac{8x}{15}$
7. $\frac{13x}{4}$ **8.** $\frac{19x}{15}$
9. $\frac{x}{12}$ **10.** $\frac{3x}{10}$
11. $\frac{9x}{10}$ **12.** $\frac{7x}{20}$
13. $\frac{2x+1}{2}$ **14.** $\frac{2x+5}{2}$
15. $\frac{3x+5}{3}$ **16.** $\frac{8x-6}{3}$

17. $2x + 1$ **18.** $\frac{4x-2}{3}$
19. $\frac{7x+14}{6}$ **20.** $\frac{11x+2}{12}$
21. $\frac{7x-11}{12}$ **22.** $\frac{5x-2}{10}$
23. $\frac{3x-16}{6}$ **24.** $\frac{7x-13}{12}$
25. $\frac{2x+7}{12}$ **26.** $\frac{13x+1}{14}$
27. $\frac{-4x+7}{12}$ **28.** $\frac{19x-17}{10}$
29. $\frac{5x+9}{12}$ **30.** $\frac{6x-7y}{20}$
31. $\frac{15x-31}{12}$ **32.** $\frac{-14x+9}{12}$

Exercise 20.4

1. $x = 6$ **2.** $x = 20$ **3.** $x = 9$ **4.** 5
5. 7   **6.** 3   **7.** 3   **8.** 3
9. 6   **10.** 6   **11.** 4   **12.** 11
13. 3   **14.** 2   **15.** 6   **16.** 11
17. 3   **18.** 6   **19.** 6   **20.** 4
21. 7   **22.** 6   **23.** 4   **24.** 5
25. 10   **26.** 1   **27.** 2   **28.** 12
29. 1   **30.** 4   **31.** 3   **32.** 6
33. 6   **34.** 9   **35.** 5   **36.** $2\frac{1}{2}$
37. 8   **38.** 6   **39.** 2   **40.** 2
41. 8   **42.** 30
43. (i) $x - 4 = \frac{x+2}{3}$ (ii) 3 units

Exercise 20.5

1. 8   **2.** 18   **3.** 16   **4.** 20
5. 9   **6.** 7   **7.** 6   **8.** 24
9. 16   **10.** 15, 18

Exercise 20.6

1. (i) $5a$ (ii) $2y$ (iii) $3c$
    (iv) $3b$ (v) $2x$ (vi) $8b^2$
    (vii) $7x$ (viii) $4b$
2. (i) $\frac{4}{3}$ (ii) $\frac{k}{2}$ (iii) $2b^2$
    (iv) $4ab$ (v) 2   (vi) $\frac{9}{2}$
    (vii) $9b$ (viii) $2a$
3. (i) APPLE   (ii) LEMON/MELON
4. $2(a + b)$ **5.** $x + y$ **6.** 4
7. $\frac{1}{2}$ **8.** $\frac{4}{3}$ **9.** $\frac{3}{x}$
10. $\frac{1}{3}$ **11.** $x + y$ **12.** $\frac{x}{3}$
13. $\frac{2}{x}$ **14.** $\frac{1}{x+y}$ **15.** $\frac{x-y}{2}$
16. $\frac{1}{x+3}$ **17.** $x + 4$ **18.** $\frac{x+1}{2}$

19. $\dfrac{1}{x-2}$ **20.** $x+6$ **21.** x

22. $\dfrac{x+3}{x+2}$ **23.** $\dfrac{x+5}{x+2}$ **24.** $x+5$

25. $\dfrac{x-2y}{3}$ **26.** $\dfrac{x-5}{4}$ **27.** $\dfrac{x+7}{x+5}$

Test Yourself 20

1. (a) (i) $x \leqslant 5$ (ii) $\dfrac{11x+9}{12}$

  (b) (i) $\dfrac{a^2}{2}$ (ii) $x=10$

  (c) (i) 1, 2, 3, 4, 5, 6 (ii) 2, 3, 4, 5, 6, 7, 8
   (iii) 1, 2, 3, 4, 5

2. (a) (i) $x \geqslant 2$
   (ii) $-4, -3, -2, -1, 0, 1, 2, 3, 4$

  (b) $\dfrac{7x+3}{6}$

  (c) $x-3$

3. (a) (i) $2x$ (i) $4y$

  (b) $x \geqslant 2$

  (c) $x=3$

4. (a) (i) $x \leqslant 2$ (ii) $x \geqslant -3$
  (b) (i) $x=10$ (ii) $x=11$

  (c) (i) $\dfrac{a}{3b}$ (ii) $x-3$

5. (a) $x \leqslant -3$ (b) $\dfrac{5x+34}{12}$

  (c) 4, 9

6. (a) (i) $-3, -2, -1, 0, 1, 2$
   (ii) 1, 2, 3, 4

  (b) $x+5$

  (c) $2x-6 = \dfrac{x}{2} + 3$; $x=6$; 6 units

Chapter 21: Functions

Exercise 21.1

1. (i) 2 (ii) 16 (iii) 11
  (iv) 5 (v) 6 (vi) 15
2. (i) 'Subtract 6'
  (ii) 'Multiply by 4'
  (iii) 'Multiply by 2, then add 1'
  (iv) 'Multiply by 3, then subtract 4'
  (v) 'Divide by 2, then add 3'
  (vi) 'Subtract 5, then multiply by 3'
3. (i) 2, 10, 12 (ii) 12, 10, 8
4. 9, 12, 15, 18, 21
5. (i) $y=2x+6$ (ii) $y=8x-9$
  (iii) $y=\dfrac{x}{4}-3$ (iv) $y=4(x+3)$
6. (i) $x \to 3x+2$ (ii) $x \to 5x-2$
  (iii) $x \to \dfrac{x}{3}-6$ (iv) $x \to 2x+7$
7. (i) 'Multiply by 5' (ii) 'Add 4'
  (iii) 'Divide by 4'

8. (i) 'Subtract 1' (ii) 'Add 1'
  (iii) 'Subtract 2' (iv) 'Add 2'
9. (i) 3, 5, 7 (ii) 10, 16, 13
  (iii) 5, 8, 20 (iv) 4, 8, 10

Exercise 21.2

1. (i) {1, 2, 4, 5, 7} (ii) {3, 6, 4, 7, 9}
  (iii) {(1, 3), (2, 4), (4, 6), (5, 7), (7, 9)}
  (iv) (i) 'Add 2'
2. (i) Domain – {1, 2, 3, 4}
   Range – {6, 7, 8, 9}
  (ii) Domain – {2, 4, 6, 8, 10}
   Range – {5, 9, 13, 17, 21}
3. (i) Yes
  (ii) No (the element c is paired with two
   elements in the range)
  (iii) No (iv) Yes
4. As no two couples have the same input
5. As the input 2 has two different outputs,
  i.e. 5 and 10
6. (i) Yes
  (ii) No (each element of the domain does not
   map on to only one element of the range)
  (iii) Yes
7. $y = 2(x+3)$; 8, 10, 12, 14, 16
8. (a) (i) {0, 1, 3, 5} (ii) {3, 4, 5, 8}
   (iii) {3, 4, 5, 6, 8}
  (b) (i) {−2, 2, 3, 7} (ii) {−4, 6, 9}
   (iii) {−4, 2, 6, −3, 4, 9}
9. (i) {3, 5, 9, 13}
  (ii) {(0, 3), (1, 5), (3, 9), (5, 13)}
10. {2, 5, 11, 17}
11. (i) {−13, −5, 3, 11}
  (ii) {(−2, −13), (0, −5), (2, 3), (4, 11)}
12. 9, 11, 13, 15, 17; $y = 2x+7$
13. $f(x) = 4x+10$; 30; 3
14. 10, 0, 5, −6

Exercise 21.3

1. (i) 3 (ii) 9 (iii) 12
  (iv) 18 (v) −6
2. (i) 7 (ii) 9 (iii) 13
  (iv) 3 (v) −3
3. (i) 2 (ii) 5 (iii) 11
  (iv) 14 (v) −4
4. (i) −3 (ii) −2 (iii) 1
  (iv) 1 (v) 13
5. (i) 5 (ii) 1 (iii) 11
  (iv) 6 (v) $5-2k$
6. (i) $x=2$ (ii) $x=1$ (iii) $k=-2$
7. (i) 1 (ii) −5 (iii) 0
  (iv) −22 (v) −10

8. (i) $x = 2$ (ii) $x = 3$ (iii) $x = -2$
9. $\{(1, 3), (2, 8), (3, 13), (4, 18)\}$
10. (i) 2 (ii) 8 (iii) 16
    (iv) -2 (v) -4
11. $\{-4, 1, 6, 11, 16\}$
12. (i) 16 (ii) $x = 2$ (iii) $k = -2$
13. (iii) $(2, -1)$
14. (i) $\{(-2, 14), (-1, 8), (0, 4), (1, 2), (2, 2)\}$
    (ii) $\{14, 8, 4, 2\}$

Test Yourself 21

1. (a) (i) 4 (ii) -2
      (iii) -8 (iv) -7
    (b) (i) $\{2, 3, 4, 5\}$ (ii) $\{3, 6, 8, 13\}$
    (c) (i) -11 (ii) $x = 3$
      (iii) $k = -1$
2. (a) 9, 11, 13, 15, 17
    (b) (i) Yes (ii) No
    (c) (i) 7, 35 (ii) $k = 5$
3. (a) $\{-1, 4, 9, 14\}$
    (b) As the input 1 has two different outputs
    (c) $a = 2$
4. (a) 'Add 3'
    (b) $\{-13, -10, -7, -4\}$
    (c) (i) €43 (ii) 4 km
5. (a) (i) 10, 4, -5, 25 (ii) 10, 2, -8, -14
    (b) $a = 18, b = -14, c = 4$
    (c) (i) $x = 5$ (ii) $x = 2$
      (iii) $x = 10\frac{1}{2}$
6. (a) $(1, 2), (3, 12), (0, -3)$
    (b) 5, 8, 12
    (c) $k = -5$

Chapter 22: Graphing Functions

Exercise 22.1

1.

x	$2x - 3$	y
-1	$-2 - 3$	-5
0	$0 - 3$	-3
1	$2 - 3$	-1
2	$4 - 3$	1
3	$6 - 3$	3
4	$8 - 3$	5

2.

x	$3x - 4$	y
-1	$-3 - 4$	-7
0	$0 - 4$	-4
3	$9 - 4$	5

3. $f(1) = 1, f(2) = 3, f(3) = 5; (1, 1), (2, 3), (3, 5)$

4. $f(0) = -2, f(1) = 1, f(2) = 4$
5. $f(1) = -1, f(2) = 2, f(3) = 5; (1, -1), (2, 2), (3, 5)$
8.

x	$4 - 2x$	y
0	$4 - 0$	4
1	$4 - 2$	2
2	$4 - 4$	0
3	$4 - 6$	-2

11. $(4, 0), (0, 4)$ **12.** $(6, 0), (0, -6)$
13. $(-2, 0), (0, 4)$ **14.** $(-2, 0), (0, 1)$
15. (i) 4 (ii) 1 (iii) -3
    (iv) -3 (v) 5
16. $(3, 2)$

Exercise 22.2

1.

x	$x^2 - 4$	y
-3	$9 - 4$	5
-2	$4 - 4$	0
-1	$1 - 4$	-3
0	$0 - 4$	-4
1	$1 - 4$	-3
2	$4 - 4$	0
3	$9 - 4$	5

6. $\left(-\frac{1}{2}, 0\right), (3, 0); (0, -3)$

8. $(-1, 0), (3, 0)$ **9.** $x = -1, \frac{3}{2}$

10. (i) $\left(\frac{1}{2}, 0\right), (3, 0)$ (ii) $(0, -3)$

Exercise 22.3

1. (i) $(1, 0), (3, 0)$ (ii) -1
    (iii) $-1, 5$ (iv) $x = 2$
2. (i) $-1, 1$ (ii) $-2, 2$
    (iii) 3 (iv) -1
3. (i) $-1.4, 3.4$ (ii) $-2.4, 4.4$
    (iii) 10 (iv) -6
4. (i) $-1, 3$ (ii) 0, 2
    (iii) $-1.5, 3.5$ (iv) 3
    (v) $-2\frac{1}{4}$ (vi) $x = 1$
5. (i) $-1, \frac{3}{2}$ (ii) $-1.9, 2.4$
    (iii) -3 (iv) 3
6. (i) $(-1, 1), (3, 9)$
    (ii) $x = -1$ or $x = 3$
    (iii) x-values the same
    (iv) The x-values of the points where the line
      and curve meet
7. (i) 0, 2 (ii) $-1, 3$ (iii) 1
    (iv) 3.5 (v) 0.4, 2.6 (vi) $x = 1$

8. (i) -4 (ii) 6   (iii) $-3, 2$
(iv) $-3.7, 2.7$ (v) 1
(vi) $-1, 3; x = -1$ or $x = 3$
9. (i) $-3.8, 0.8$ (ii) $-3.3, 0.3$ (iii) $-2.4, 0.4$
10. (i) 12   (ii) 12.30 pm, 3.30 pm
(iii) 10.00 am, 6.00 pm
(iv) 5 hours

Test Yourself 22

1. (a) (i) -5.5 (ii) 1.5
(b)

x	$2x^2 + 3x - 6$	y
-4	$32 - 12 - 6$	14
-3	$18 - 9 - 6$	3
-2	$8 - 6 - 6$	-4
-1	$2 - 3 - 6$	-7
0	$0 + 0 - 6$	-6
1	$2 + 3 - 6$	-1
2	$8 + 6 - 6$	8
3	$18 + 9 - 6$	21

(i) $-2.6, 1.1$ (ii) $-2.2, 0.7$ (iii) 3
2. (b) (i) $x = 0, 2$ (ii) $x = -1, 3; x = 1$
3. (a) $-3; 6; (0, -3), (6, 0)$
(b) (i) -2.7 (ii) $-3.2, 1.2$
(iii) $-3.8, 1.8$
4. (a) (i) 5   (ii) 7
(iii) 3   (iv) -1
(v) 0
(b) A & $y = x^2 - 2$, B & $y = 2 - x^2$,
C & $y = 2x$ (coefficient of x^2 is positive,
coefficient of x^2 is negative, linear function)
5. (a)

x	$3 - 2x$	y
-1	$3 + 2$	5
0	$3 - 0$	3
3	$3 - 6$	-3

(b) $(0, 0), (1, 5), (2, 8), (3, 9), (4, 8), (5, 5), (6, 0)$;
(i) 45 m   (ii) 34 m
(iii) 0.4 sec, 5.6 sec   (iv) 3 sec

Chapter 23: Trigonometry

Exercise 23.1

1. $A = 56\,cm^2$, $B = 36\,cm^2$, $C = 28\,cm^2$,
$D = 50\,cm^2$, $E = 34\,cm^2$, $F = 25\,cm^2$
2. $a = 5$, $b = 13$, $c = 15$
3. $x = \sqrt{52}, y = \sqrt{32}, z = \sqrt{44}$
4. $a = 8.1$, $b = 6.7$, $c = 7.9$

5. $a = 11.1\,cm$, $b = 6.2\,cm$, $c = 8.8\,mm$
6. (i) Yes   (ii) No   (iii) Yes
(iv) No   (v) Yes
7. $[AC]$; 9 cm   **8.** 21 m
9. 68 cm   **10.** 15.9 m

Exercise 23.2

1. (i) 10   (ii) 5   (iii) 13
2. (i) 8   (ii) 4   (iii) 12
3. (i) 6   (ii) 3   (iii) 5
4. (i) 6.4   (ii) 2.5   (iii) 9
5. (i) 5   (ii) 1   (iii) 7
6. (i) 4   (ii) 2.3   (iii) $\sqrt{32}$
7. (i) $\frac{9}{15}\left(\frac{3}{5}\right)$ (ii) $\frac{12}{15}\left(\frac{4}{5}\right)$
8. (i) $\frac{12}{5}$ (ii) $\frac{12}{13}$

Exercise 23.3

1. (i) $\frac{5}{13}$ (ii) $\frac{6}{10}$ (iii) $\frac{20}{29}$
2. (i) $\frac{12}{13}$ (ii) $\frac{8}{10}$ (iii) $\frac{21}{29}$
3. (i) $\frac{5}{12}$ (ii) $\frac{6}{8}$ (iii) $\frac{20}{21}$
4. (i) $\frac{8}{17}$ (ii) $\frac{7}{25}$ (iii) $\frac{4}{5}$
5. (i) $\frac{15}{17}$ (ii) $\frac{24}{25}$ (iii) $\frac{3}{5}$
6. (i) $\frac{8}{15}$ (ii) $\frac{7}{24}$ (iii) $\frac{4}{3}$
7. (i) $\frac{1}{2}$ (ii) $\frac{1}{2}$
(iii) $\frac{1}{\sqrt{3}}$ (iv) $\frac{\sqrt{3}}{2}$
(v) $\frac{\sqrt{3}}{1}(\sqrt{3})$ (vi) $\frac{\sqrt{3}}{2}$
8. 9; (i) $\frac{9}{15}$ (ii) $\frac{12}{15}$ (iii) $\frac{9}{12}$

Exercise 23.4

1. 0.5592   **2.** 0.9613   **3.** 0.2079
4. 0.8829   **5.** 1.4826   **6.** 3.4874
7. 0.3249   **8.** 0.9205   **9.** 0.1736
10. 0.3443   **11.** 0.8090   **12.** 0.5299
13. 2.4751   **14.** 0.6249   **15.** 0.3090
16. 0.4540
17. (i) 48°   (ii) 12°   (iii) 57°
(iv) 31°   (v) 10°   (vi) 66°
18. (i) 63°   (ii) 42°   (iii) 78°
19. (i) 28°   (ii) 55°   (iii) 67°
20. (i) 64°   (ii) 48°   (iii) 65°
22. (i) 2.43   (ii) 4.85   (iii) 6.76   (iv) 6.55
23. Sine; 0.6, 37°

Exercise 23.5

1. Sine, cosine, tangent, cosine (from left to right)

2. (i) 6.0   (ii) 10.4   (iii) 13.1
3. $x = 5.4, y = 37.1, z = 21.1$
4. (i) 28   (ii) 47   (iii) 14
5. (i) 7.4   (ii) 46.2   (iii) 21.4
6. 32 m   **7.** 4 m
8. 6.7 m   **9.** 58 m
10. (i) 6.6   (ii) 7.5
11. Cosine; 51°
12. $P = 37°, Q = 52°, R = 37°$
13. 44°   **14.** 13°

Exercise 23.6

1. 6.1 m   **2.** 320 m
3. 28 m   **4.** 13 m
5. (i) 21 m   (ii) 34 m
6. 9 m   **7.** 53°
8. Alternate angles (with the horizontal ∥ sea level); 172 m

Test Yourself 23

1. (a) (i) 10   (ii) 8
     (iii) 0.6   (iv) 0.75
   (b) (i) $\frac{1}{2}$ (ii) $\frac{1}{2}$
     (iii) $\sqrt{3}$
2. (a) 13;
     (i) $\frac{5}{13}$ (ii) $\frac{12}{13}$
     (iii) $\frac{12}{5}$ (iv) 33 m
3. (a) 10.2   (b) 4.7 m
4. (a) (i) 56°   (ii) 34°
   (b) 15.6 m
5. (a) 1 metre
   (b) (i) 7.6 m   (ii) 23°
6. (i) 13.1 m   (ii) 9.9 m; 3.2 m

Chapter 24: Drawing and Interpreting Real-life Graphs

Exercise 24.1

1. (i) 30 km   (ii) 1 hour
   (iii) 45 km   (iv) 75 km
2. (i) 140 km   (ii) 70 km/hr
   (iii) $2\frac{1}{2}$ hr   (iv) $2\frac{1}{2}$ hr   (v) 56 km/hr
3. (i) 9.00 am; 3.00 pm   (ii) 30 km
   (iii) 9.45 am, 2.00 pm
   (iv) 10.00 am-10.30 am, 12.00 pm-1.00 pm
   (v) 9.00 am-10.00 am (20 km/hr)
4. (i) 20 km   (ii) 20 km
   (iii) 1.00 pm
   (iv) Increase (the line gets steeper)
   (v) 40 km

5. (i) 90 min   (ii) 20 min
   (iii) 10 km   (iv) 20 km/hr
6. Ⓐ & (i), Ⓑ & (iii), Ⓒ & (ii)
7. (i) 7.00 am   (ii) 150 km
   (iii) 50 km/hr   (iv) 50 km
   (v) 2 hours   (vi) 50 km/hr
8. (i) Adam   (ii) Twice
   (iii) 1.00 pm   (iv) 150 km
   (v) Adam – 200 km; Conor – 350 km
9. Jill departed at 10.00 am and reached her destination at 2.00 pm. She stopped to rest once for one hour and she did so 40 km from home on the outbound leg of her journey. She was driving for a total of $5\frac{1}{2}$ hours and her average speed during this time was 43.6 km/hr. Her average speed for the return part of the journey was faster (48 km/hr).
10. (i) 75 km
   (ii) 10.45 am and 12.15 pm
   (iii) 1.30 pm   (iv) 75 km
   (v) Darren; 30 min

Exercise 24.2

1. (iv)
2. (i) $37\frac{1}{2}$ miles   (ii) 50 miles
   (iii) 48 km   (iv) 24 km; Yes
3. No; the graph is linear (i.e. a straight line) but it does not pass through the origin and therefore it is not a directly proportional graph
   (i) 95°F   (ii) 59°F
   (iii) 10°C   (iv) 38°C; 13°C to 32°C
4. (i) €70   (ii) €55
   (iii) 80 min   (iv) 40 min
   (v) €40
5. (i) 65 kg   (ii) 75 kg
   (iii) 178 cm; between 60 kg and 70 kg
6. (i) 158 pints   (ii) 45 litres
   (iii) 170 pints   (iv) 6000 litres
7. (i) 10 m   (ii) $4s - 5h = 0$
   (iii) $18\frac{3}{4}$ m
8. (i) €12   (ii) €24
   (iii) 8 km
   (iv) There is a minimum charge of €3
9. (i) 8ℓ   (ii) 60 km
   (iii) 3ℓ   (iv) Yes
   (v) $y = \left(\frac{3}{20}\right)x$ or $\ell = \left(\frac{3}{20}\right)k$; 45ℓ

Exercise 24.3

1. (iii)
2. Ⓐ
3. (i) (a) & A, (b) & C, (c) & B
   (ii) Ⓐ & B, Ⓑ & C, Ⓒ & A

4. Route *A* & (iii), Route *B* & (i), Route *C* & (ii)
5. (i) 7.00 am
   (ii) From 10.00 am to midday
   (iii) From midday to 2.00 pm
   (iv) (a) Noon   (b) 3.00 p.m.
   (v) 26°C
   (vi) 11°C
6. (i) & ⒟, (ii) & ⒞ (iii) & ⒝, (iv) & ⒜
7. (i) & (c), (ii) & (b), (iii) & (a)
8. (i) 80 m   (ii) 60 m   (iii) 52.5 km/hr

Chapter 25: Geometry 3: Transformations – Constructions

Exercise 25.1

1. (i) 5 units to the right
   (ii) 4 units to the right
   (iii) 1 unit up and 4 units right
   (iv) 1 unit right and 3 units up
   (v) 2 units right and 3 units up
   (vi) 1 unit left and 4 units up
2. (i) 5 units right and 3 units up
   (ii) 11 units right and 1 unit down
   (iii) 4 units right and 5 units up
   (iv) 7 units right and 6 units down
   (v) 4 units left and 5 units down
6. (i) B   (ii) [DC]   (iii) O   (iv) [AB]
7. (i) B   (ii) [BC]   (iii) △BCE   (iv) [BE]
8. (i) [EC]   (ii) E   (iii) △BEC
   (iv) D   (v) [AD]   (vi) △BEC
9. (i) A(2, 4), B(3, −2), C(−2, −3), D(−5, 1)
   (ii) A′(7, 6), B′(8, 0), C′(3, −1), D′(0, 3)

Exercise 25.2

3. (i) The point F   (ii) [EF]
   (iii) [DF]   (iv) △DCF
   (v) △EFD   (vi) [CF]
4. (i) & (iii)
5. M, O, D, A, Y
7. (i) B   (ii) A
   (iii) [DA]   (iv) △COD
   (v) [CO]   (vi) △CBD
   (vii) [OA]   (viii) CDAB
8. *C*
9. (i) D   (ii) A
10. (i) Axial symmetry in *y*-axis
   (ii) Axial symmetry in *x*-axis
   (iii) Central symmetry in origin
11. Central symmetry in *C* and axial symmetry in *AB*
12. *D*
13. (i) A′(4, 5), B′(1, 4), C′(5, 2)
   (ii) A′′(−4, −5), B′′(−1, −4), C′′(−5, −2)
14. (i) 2   (ii) 2   (iii) 5   (iv) 0
15. (i), (ii), (iv)
16. (i) A.S.   (ii) Tr.   (iii) A.S.   (iv) A.S.   (v) C.S.

Exercise 25.4

4. |AC| = 4.6 cm, |DE| = 3.1 cm, |XZ| = 7.7 cm
5. (i) |AC| = 3.1 cm   (ii) |AB| = 5.4 cm
6. |AC| = 5.9 cm, |DF| = 5.2 cm, |XZ| = 9.2 cm
9. |AC| = 10.8 cm
11. 8.3 cm
13. (ii) 111 m